ANOTHER WAY OF LIVING

Books by John Bainbridge

LIKE A HOMESICK ANGEL

THE SUPER-AMERICANS

GARBO

THE WONDERFUL WORLD OF TOOTS SHOR

LITTLE WONDER, OR *The Reader's Digest* AND HOW IT GREW

Another Way of Living

A GALLERY OF AMERICANS WHO CHOOSE TO LIVE IN EUROPE

By John Bainbridge

HOLT, RINEHART AND WINSTON

NEW YORK CHICAGO SAN FRANCISCO

Published simultaneously in Canada by Holt, Rinehart and Winston of Canada, Limited.

Library of Congress Catalog Card Number: 68-12696

First Edition

SBN: 03-068660-1

Printed in the United States of America

FOR BETTY SICRE

For other Americans, there had been the grand discovery of European culture, another way of living, a promise of some enlargement of inner freedom

—Morley Callaghan
That Summer in Paris

ANOTHER WAY OF LIVING

GALLERY NOTES

"If life had a second edition," the English poet, John Clare, once wrote in a letter to a friend, "how I would correct the proofs!" To this plaintive remark anyone over twenty is apt to respond, "Who wouldn't?" For everybody knows that one of the big troubles with life is that it rarely offers a second chance. We're handed a part, and, with no rehearsal, we go ahead and play it as best we can. The part may not suit us in the least, but to change it—there's the rub. Thus, most of us know the man who has done well in business but is restless and unhappy because all along he wanted to be a teacher; the doctor who has always thought he was cut out to be a painter; the banker who would rather be an architect; the advertising man who dreams of being a writer; and so on and on. It is a long and melancholy roster, and to everybody on it—hail and farewell. This book is not about them.

The subjects of this book are a happier breed. They are Americans who have been blessed with a second chance, and have chosen to use it to make a new life in Europe. These lucky men and women, for whom life does indeed have a second edition, have been called "the new expatriates." It is a term they resent, and with reason. In our immaculate society, to call a person an expatriate is roughly the equivalent of passing the word that he may be a bit short on patriotism, a bit long on tax-dodging, and have a proclivity to loose living besides. He may be guilty on all counts, or on none. It doesn't matter. If he has chosen to live outside the United States, he is generally regarded by his fellow citizens as a rather dubious character.

"What most Americans can't seem to get through their heads is how anybody in his right mind could possibly want to live anywhere except in the States," Mrs. Pedro Gandarias, a native of Atlantic City who is married to a Spanish banker and industrialist, told me with a mixture of amusement and exasperation. "If you try to explain why you like living in Europe, they think you're un-American." Her experience is not unique. "I remember when I told a man who had been a client of our firm that my wife and I had decided to go live in Portugal," Philip Carter, a former New York advertising executive has recalled. "He looked at me in a most peculiar way, and then he said, 'Phil, I can't understand how an old-line American like you could do a thing like that.' He emphasized the 'old-line American' bit to make sure I got the point." Henry Ketcham, the creator of "Dennis the Menace," who has lived for many years in Switzerland, told me that friends he sees on visits to America still often make him feel that he has somehow let our side down. "It's perplexing when you go back, and well-meaning but rather innocent friends ask why you wanted to give up your American passport," he said. "Of course, you tell them that you haven't given up your passport, and would never think of doing such a thing. Then they say, 'Well, what are you living over there for, anyway? Why don't you come home and pay your taxes the way we do? What's the matter with the U.S.A.?' You'd think, for God's sake, you were a traitor."

All of this is really quite strange. Here we are, a nation wholly descended (the Indians included) from expatriates, and yet we look askance automatically at anybody who does today what we venerate our forebears for having done, as time goes, only yesterday. Probably the best clue to this riddle is our robust chauvinism, which, ironically, has prevented us from recognizing that expatriation, in this century, is simply an expression of the old American pioneering spirit. This elemental fact is obvious to Europeans, who take a reasonable attitude toward expatriation, it having long been for them a commonplace of existence. "In a sense, modern America (except for a few daring men at Cape Kennedy) is a country with an exploring spirit and nowhere to explore," John Fowles, the British novelist, has written. "The lure of expatriation is surely a form of the lure of driving back the frontier. The true expatriate has directed his wagon train toward other frontiers, other trails, other improvisations in new territory, other red Indians to beat off, other desperate settlings in unknown lands. America, for real Americans, is always just over the next range of mountains; but now these mountains must be ungeological ones."

In every age, of course, some Americans have preferred not to cross the mountains. They have also been among the first to say it's not worth doing. "The argument for traveling abroad is not all on one side," observed Walt Whitman, who never traveled abroad. "There are pulses of irresistible ardour, with due reason why they cannot be gainsaid. But a calm man of deep vision will find in this strenuous modern spectacle of America as great sights as anything the foreign world, or the antique, or the relics of the antique, afford him." What the poet was saying, back there in the nineteenth century, was See

America First—hardly a novel idea, even then. Noah Webster had promoted that notion as early as 1785, twenty years before Lewis and Clark had hacked their way across the continent to discover what was out there for Americans to see first. Webster, writing (appropriately) in the *American Magazine*, not only admonished his countrymen to confine their pleasure jaunts to the domestic scene but declared rather crossly that foreign travel should "be discountenanced, if not prohibited." Not long afterward, he sailed for England. Consistency has never been a major handicap of America-Firsters.

Down through the years, the spiritual heirs of Noah Webster have concentrated their collective intellect on thinking up one pretext after another to discourage Americans from traveling abroad, not to mention living there. So far, the results of the recurring stay-at-home campaigns have always been the same: Americans have gone abroad in ever-increasing numbers. This is hardly surprising, since it is against the American grain to cotton to the idea of being fenced in. Nor is it unexpected that the majority of Americans who journey (fifteen million last year) go to Europe. The lure of Europe, for Americans, is a deep-seated, often ambivalent, but singularly potent urge that has remained undiminished for centuries. The feeling is natural enough, since Europe is where most of us, sooner or later, came from, and we are drawn back to it to satisfy a vague but persistent longing to trace our origins beyond the budding civilization into which we were born. In the process, we hope, we will be able to discover our own identity.

Never before has the opportunity—or the need—to acquire self-knowledge through foreign exposure been as great as it is today. And never before has the quest been undertaken by so many Americans, not only by the tourists on their twenty-one-day excursions but also by the men and women who pack up their belongings and go abroad to live. Even allowing for the fact that Americans are probably the most migratory people on earth (we change our residence, on the average, every seventh year), the size of the second group is impressive. It has now reached the point where some two and a half million Americans—more than 1 per cent of the population—reside outside the country. "No nation, not even Britain at the height of her imperial power," James Reston has remarked, "ever had such a vast company scattered across the world."

To a great extent, the reason for this unprecedented outward-bound migration can be traced to Britain's decline as an imperial power. With the fading of the Empire, we took over from the British the lonely and tricky task of minding the world, or trying to, and that undertaking, as we have found, demands the services abroad of a multitude to carry out our military commitments and also to handle our expanded diplomatic activities, foreign aid programs, and a variety of other global ventures and misadventures. Members of the armed forces together with civilians employed by government agencies, and their families, account for well over half of the Americans living overseas. Because of the immense postwar expansion abroad of American commercial and financial interests as well as extended activity in the religious and cultural areas, the second largest category of Americans overseas is made up of businessmen, technical experts, missionaries, teachers, doctors, journalists, and assorted other employees of private organizations.

There is a third category of overseas Americans. It is the smallest and most interesting. It consists of the Americans who live abroad not because they have to on account of their job or duty, but simply because they want to. They are there purely out of choice. This book is about them.

While it is convenient to separate Americans living overseas into these three tidy categories, it doesn't work out that neatly in so-called real life. For one thing, it could be maintained that just about all Americans living abroad, with the exception of the military, are there, in a sense, by choice. A person isn't apt to join the Foreign Service unless he wants to live in a foreign country. Nor is he likely to apply for a job in the foreign department of a bank or of any other private or public organization if he doesn't want to leave home. Almost always, the people who fill these jobs are volunteers, and many come to like the life abroad so much that they keep on volunteering until they retire. For example, I know several Americans who have spent almost their entire professional careers working in the Paris branches of New York banks or of other American concerns and who, rather than accept being recalled to the home office, would resign on the spot and look for other jobs in Paris. Their counterparts can be found all over Europe.

At the same time, there are a great many more Americans working overseas not because they have actually chosen to live abroad but rather because they have been *willing* to do so in the hope that a tour of foreign duty will improve their chances for future advancement back at headquarters. This motive has become increasingly prevalent among American businessmen abroad, particularly in the higher echelons, which have come to be considered a kind of seedbed for the production of future corporation presidents. So, the distinction between the Americans who live abroad by choice and those who live there by design cannot always be drawn on the basis of being on the payroll of an American concern. Nevertheless, except in a few instances and mainly by way of illustration, Americans working abroad for public or private organizations do not figure in this book. It seemed to me that this ground rule was necessary because of the virtual impossibility of determining whether the decision of these Americans to live overseas was made solely out of choice.

I also decided fairly early on to limit the subject matter to the overseas Americans who choose to live in Europe. That is where most of them are anyway, though some, to be sure, do live elsewhere. There are, for example, the three bachelors from San Francisco—a lawyer, a stockbroker, and a manufacturer's representative—who got away from it all by pooling their assets and cutting out to Tahiti, where they bought and rejuvenated a rundown hotel, which has become so popular with tourists that the owners now have to take time from their skin-diving and other pleasures to supervise the building of more bungalows to accommodate more guests. There is also the former New York architect and amateur painter, who, tiring of the Manhattan routine, took off for Thailand, where he has developed a silk weaving and exporting business that employs some two thousand weavers and grosses over a million dollars a year. Then there is the young engineer from Ohio who earned his degree attending night school and now has a multimillion-dollar construction company in Australia. There are others as interesting, but all of these so-called new expatriates belong in another book.

Even if "expatriate" had not become, in our lexicon, a rather soiled word, it would still not be properly applied to the Americans we are considering—those who live in Europe by choice—because "expatriate" literally means "to withdraw from one's native country; to renounce the rights and liabilities of citizenship where one is born and become a citizen of another country." The Americans who go to live in Europe do, of course, withdraw from their native country, but the number who have become citizens of another country is infinitesimal. To judge from our history, the American temper does not favor the taking of foreign citizenship. On the contrary, one of the distinguishing characteristics of the Americans living in Europe is the tenacity with which they hold onto their American passports. This is true even of the American women who are (and intend to remain) married to Europeans, and hence will probably never again return to live in the United States. It seems that the greater the distance in space or time that an American finds himself from the United States, the more highly he values his passport.

Along with their determination to remain American citizens, the

Americans living in Europe also share the expectation of returning eventually to live in the United States. This does not apply, of course, to the American women who have married Europeans, and there are certain other Americans in Europe who may never return, but they are the exceptions that prove the rule. The return may not be planned for next year or ten years from now or at any determined time in the future, but it is rare to encounter an American living by choice in Europe who doesn't have tucked away in the back of his mind the thought of eventually going back where he came from. "Apparently, there is a time in life when these foreign shores and this apparently easy living look damned good to a lot of Americans," I was told by an American named Benn Reyes, who has worked abroad in various branches of show business for over a quarter of a century, "but after a while the luster wears off, and they go back to Dayton or Steamingshorts. It isn't Mom's apple pie, necessarily, that lures them back, but no matter how great the foreign attraction was in the beginning, eventually—maybe even as long as twenty or thirty years—practically all the cats go home to die."

In the meantime, the Americans who have chosen to live in Europe take a very close interest in American affairs, primarily through reading but also through correspondence and in conversations with other Americans visiting Europe. More often than not, the Americans in Europe that I talked to said that they felt they were better informed about their country than when they were living there. They not only want to keep abreast of American affairs but also to identify with them and even to participate in them. Thus, they have staged civil rights marches in European cities, and, in the 1964 presidential election, enthusiastically organized Johnson-for-President and Goldwater-for-President committees all over the Continent. The latter activity was little more than an exercise to let off their collective steamy frustration, since, for all practical purposes, they are unable to vote. They are nevertheless obliged to comply with the United States income tax laws. This combination creates what the Americans who have chosen to make their residence in Europe consider an intolerable case of taxation without representation. It was partly to rally support to change this situation that a pair of American residents of Paris recently formed a non-profit organization called the League of Americans Residing Abroad, known to its members as LARA, which now has an office in Paris and another in Washington, D.C., where it is registered as a lobby. The fact that Americans living abroad now have that sine qua non of American life—their own lobby in Washington—is further evidence that no matter where they live they still feel close to the mother country.

No, Americans with these persuasions can hardly be called expatriates. The old terminology doesn't apply. Like Henry James, the contemporary Americans who choose to live in Europe are fascinated by what James called "Europe's lighted and decorated stage." Unlike him, they are not prepared to become permanent players on it. Their heart is in America. Their home is in Europe. They embrace both. They have become a part of both, and they will remain a part of both, whether or not they ever go home to live. In many respects, these Americans in Europe are a new class, and as such, in need of a new term to describe them. Perhaps it would be appropriate to call them Ameropeans.

The Ameropeans have no real historical precedent. The closest approximation no doubt would be the Americans who flocked to Europe after the First World War—the group that came to be known as the "Lost Generation." Primarily writers and artists, they thought of themselves as real expatriates, and they were, in the sense that they expected to make their permanent residence abroad. They were fed up with America—in their view, a dull, materialistic, money-grubbing society, completely barren of culture. Their disenchantment with the America of that era—Harding, Prohibition, the glorification of captains of industry, the scorning of writers and artists and intellectuals—was total, and they chose exile in Europe. Unlike practically every American who had preceded them, these angry pilgrims departed with the full conviction that they were turning their backs on America forever.

The participants in this artistic emigration, the largest ever made from the New World, included Ernest Hemingway, F. Scott Fitzgerald, John Dos Passos, E. E. Cummings, Louis Bromfield, T. S. Eliot, Stephen Vincent Benét, John Peale Bishop, Malcolm Cowley, Ezra Pound, Matthew Josephson, Archibald MacLeish, Glenway Wescott—in fact, every important writer of the time except William Faulkner and Robert Frost. (Frost had earlier lived three years in England, where his first two books of poems, in which no publishing firm in America had shown the slightest interest, were at last brought out by an English publisher. Faulkner spent the summer of 1925 on a walking tour of Europe, but never settled there.) Nearly all of the writers converged on Paris, and so did the painters, such as Thomas Hart Benton, Grant Wood, and John Steuart Curry, and also the composers, such as Virgil Thomson, George Antheil, and George Gershwin. The American colony was further brightened by the presence of the brilliant journalist, Janet Flanner, the pioneering photographer, Man Ray, and the founders and publishers of *transition*, Eugene and Maria Jolas. Presiding over this impressive array of transplanted talent was Gertrude Stein, a native of Pennsylvania, who had studied medicine before turning to literary pursuits, and who had settled in Paris in 1903. The influence she exerted through her famous salon and through the criticism of the work of the other American expatriates in Paris, particularly the writers, is generally considered to have been of more consequence than her own writing, which tended to be obscure. However, her explanation of why Paris had become the mecca of so many gifted Americans was curiously lucid. "Paris," she said, "was where the twentieth century was."

In addition to the creative people, many other Americans who had found life at home unbearably arid and who possessed the means or ingenuity to get away from it also made their way to Paris in the twenties. "The 1920's were a period of nomadization for thousands of Americans," Janet Flanner later wrote. "They came in droves to France to graze on herbage more succulent than their senses or stomachs had known at home." Among the grazers were well-to-do lawyers, bankers, brokers, and a few doctors and dentists, including Dr. D. Hally-Smith, who left his native Illinois at age twenty-six to practice in Paris and still lives there. Other figures in the American colony included Sylvia Beach, who opened her famous bookstore, Shakespeare & Company, and was the first to publish the complete *Ulysses;* Natalie Clifford Barney, who made her Friday Afternoons a literary institution, and Mr. and Mrs. Gerald Murphy (his father owned Mark Cross, a Fifth Avenue specialty shop), a singularly attractive couple upon whom Fitzgerald patterned the characters of Dick and Nicole Diver in *Tender Is the Night.* "It wasn't parties that made it such a gay time," Mrs. Murphy once recalled. "There was such affection between everybody. You loved your friends and wanted to see them every day, and usually you did see them every day. It was like a great fair, and everybody was so young."

But everybody grew older, and, as the twenties came to a close, the festive atmosphere was clouded by the repercussions of the stock market crash and the ensuing depression, which forced many expatriates to go home. They were joined by others who felt that they had absorbed the European experience to the limit, or had decided that it wasn't worth the effort of trying to. Some of the pilgrims, who had approached the culture of the Old World figuratively jerking the forelock, left it sporting a chip on their shoulder. "America is just as goddamned good as Europe," said Malcolm Cowley, the writer, expressing a judgment seconded by many of his contemporaries who had joined the homeward trek.

As the thirties wore on, the return of the natives was hastened not only by cultural ennui but by practical considerations, in particular the increasingly ominous signs of the Second World War. When hostilities broke out, the ranks of the American expatriates had dwindled to a mere handful. Gertrude Stein remained in Paris; T. S. Eliot, the poet from Missouri, who had become a British subject, stayed on in his adopted country; Ezra Pound, the poet from Idaho, continued to make his residence in Italy, where he had lived for a quarter of a century; and Bernard Berenson, the noted art historian, elected to stay on in his famous villa, I Tatti, near Florence, which had been his home for more than forty years. A few other expatriates who had lived so long abroad that they had become French, English, or Italian in everything but nationality also refused to leave. With these few exceptions, the Americans, by 1940, had departed from Europe's no longer lighted stage.

They soon returned. During the Second World War, they came by the hundreds of thousands as soldiers, and, in the peaceful invasion that got under way soon after the shooting stopped, they have come by the millions as tourists, and to a lesser extent but still in record numbers, as residents. One person who is well qualified to remark on the difference in the composition and complexion of the Americans who lived in Europe before the Second World War and those who make their residence there now is Marc Slonim, the distinguished author and educator, who has been a member of both groups, with an intervening long interval in America. "I have the feeling that there are no longer any expatriates from America, either theoretically or practically," Mr. Slonim, who now lives in Switzerland, told me a while ago. "At least, they are not expatriates in the sense that we used the word in the twenties and thirties. What struck me about the American writers, artists, musicians, and intellectuals whom I knew in Paris between the wars was their complete rejection of America. They considered themselves genuine expatriates. They talked about the impossibility of writing in America, about the puritanism, the narrow-mindedness, the Babbittry. They had nothing good whatsoever to say about the country. Now, if you examine the same group in Europe today, you'll see that the change is tremendous. Formerly, the members of this group, who were the predominant part of the American colony, came here to live. Today, they by no means consider their life here to be permanent. They set a limit, more or less, on how long they will stay before they have even left home. The experience, therefore, has an entirely different intonation. Nowadays, they come for a while to absorb the European atmosphere, to look for inspiration, and to make some contact with classical roots. Then they go home. William Styron lived in

France for a couple of years. John Cheever spent a year or so in Italy. Tennessee Williams comes over from time to time, and so does James Baldwin, and no doubt there are others. But, as a rule, they don't stay. There are, however, a few who do. For example, Irwin Shaw has lived in Switzerland for many years, and James Jones has lived in Paris for quite a while. These two also illustrate another change in the writers now living in Europe—many have already been successful before coming here. Those in earlier generations came here to get their start. No, it is quite different today. No longer is there a colony of expatriates who consider Montparnasse more important than Greenwich Village."

I asked Mr. Slonim what he considered the principal reason for this change.

"One reason is that Americans now have a stronger feeling for their country," he replied. "They are no longer ashamed of it. Furthermore, they have less illusions about Europe. But the main reason is the great cultural leap that America has performed. It is no longer just a money-grubbing society, though money has remained an important barometer in American life. The establishment of a thriving publishing industry is one indication of the cultural improvement. The expansion of education is another. The development of New York as the art center of the world is still another. And yet another is the change in the terms of literature from a hobby to a respected and respectful business. One could go on in this vein at some length. In short, it's a different America. One can imagine a writer in the twenties looking around and saying, 'The hell with it.' One cannot conceive of a writer saying such a silly thing today."

If the Americans who choose Europe as their residence nowadays aren't motivated by rejection of their own country, what does impel them to live abroad? To give a quick answer—there is no longer, as a rule, any one single reason, though there are exceptions, such as the American women who live in Europe because they are married to Europeans, and also the blacklisted Hollywood screen writers and directors who moved to Europe during the McCarthy era simply because they had a chance to find work there. Generally, however, the decision to live abroad stems from a cluster of reasons, which would include some combination, among others, of the search for adventure, the prospect of cheaper living, the urge to pioneer, the opportunity to move up the social scale, the desire to escape from racial discrimination as practiced in the United States, the chance to make money, the attractions of a civilization not dominated by the Puritan ethic, the wish to broaden the education of children, the longing for a simpler existence, and the quest for culture, novelty, and inspiration.

A much better way of answering the question of why many contemporary Americans prefer to live in Europe—as well as how they live—is to let some of them speak for themselves. In the pages that follow, they do. Some are gifted with expertness of expression; others, possessing no verbal flair, are nevertheless often, because of wider experience, equally informative. Some prefer to talk mainly about the ideas involved in living abroad; others, about the mechanics of foreign living. Some take a serious view; others, a light one. All have something useful, entertaining, critical, instructive, contrary, or insightful to say about living abroad. The cumulative effect of their collective thoughts will, I hope, contribute to an understanding of the Ameropean way of life, for I have long believed, as a British critic once observed, that "social history is most illuminating when it approaches the big through the small and when it deals with real people and not with categories."

Before introducing the Ameropeans, a word about how I became acquainted with them. I met nearly all of them during a period of two years that I recently spent with my wife traveling in Europe. We started out in Finland, having flown from New York to Helsinki, moved on by ship to Sweden, where we bought a car, and drove from there for some twenty-seven thousand miles, traveling as far south as Tangier and taking up residence for fairly long periods of time in Paris, Geneva, Rome, London, Madrid, Marbella (one of the less à Go-Go settlements on the Costa del Sol), and finally in an English village called Nettlebed, about an hour's drive from London.

I found very few Ameropeans in Scandinavia. Apparently the climate, the high cost of living (a fifth of Scotch costs the equivalent of twelve dollars in Helsinki), the shortage of housing, and the general sense of isolation combine to keep Americans from taking up residence there. Everywhere else, I discovered, Ameropeans abound. There were so many more than I had expected that it seemed I could have gone on interviewing them forever. (At one point, in fact, my publisher cabled to ask if that was my intention.) Since it wasn't, regrettably, a lifetime project, I had to keep moving from country to country; invariably, it was necessary to leave before talking to all of the Ameropeans I had hoped to interview.

The only rule I followed in selecting those I did interview was to look for men and women who were interesting—not just because they happened to live abroad but because they had qualities that would make them interesting anywhere—and who were as varied as possible in background and occupation. Most of them I encountered after getting to Europe, although I arrived there with a long list of possibilities. Among these, naturally, were many well-known Ameropeans, including William Holden, Irwin Shaw, Her Serene Highness Princess Grace, John Huston, Douglas Fairbanks, Jr., and so on. While these and many other celebrated Ameropeans appear in this book, many others do not. Three of them—Ava Gardner, J. P. Donleavy, the novelist, and T. S. Matthews, the former managing editor of *Time*—are not included because they said they didn't want to be. (They are, by the way, the only three Ameropeans who declined to be interviewed.) There are a few others, including Orson Welles and Jean Seberg, whom I wanted to see and who were willing to be interviewed, but had to be left out because our respective schedules could never be fixed to make a meeting possible. Finally, a few other well-known Ameropeans, including John Paul Getty, the close-fisted billionaire and contributor to *Playboy*, are not included because, for one reason or another, they have never interested me, and I didn't bother to look them up. Furthermore, as I learned once again, celebrity is no guarantee of brilliance, and it was generally among the uncelebrated, though not necessarily unprominent, that I found the Ameropeans who were the most perceptive and articulate.

With one exception, all of the interviews were tape-recorded. The exception was Princess Grace, who informed me in advance that she preferred that the interview not be taped, so in that case I took notes. However, it was with reluctance that I bowed to the royal prerogative, because use of a tape recorder not only provides a degree of accuracy that cannot be achieved even by a reporter able to do shorthand (I have met only one in my life who could), but has the additional advantage of relieving the interviewer of the necessity of taking notes and thus improves the chance of turning the atmosphere of an interview into that of a conversation. The tape recorder that I used was a small, lightweight, battery-powered machine that I carried in an attaché case. Since the recorder didn't have to be plugged into an electric outlet, the machine could be set in motion unobtrusively, and interviews could be conducted wherever circumstances were most favorable. I think that most of the people I talked with were quite unaware of its presence.

In any event, I had no trouble getting Ameropeans to talk. This would scarcely come as a surprise to any experienced journalist, for, as the late A. J. Liebling, one of the most experienced and gifted of them all, once observed, "There is almost no circumstance under which an American doesn't want to be interviewed. We are an articulate people, pleased by attention, covetous of being singled out." The Ameropeans, if anything, are even more so. At least, that is true of the ones I encountered, and I think one reason (beyond the natural one of being pleased to see somebody from home) is that they have very little opportunity to talk to anyone about what it's like to be an Ameropean. Their fellow Ameropeans obviously are not much interested in talking about the subject among themselves, and when they make trips back to the United States, they discover, as do all travelers, that nobody really cares to hear all about the experience. In me, the Ameropeans found a kind of captive audience, and generally made the most of the opportunity—always to my pleasure. As a consequence, and also because I have always agreed with Liebling that "the worst thing an interviewer can do is talk a lot himself," my part of the conversation usually consisted of not a great deal more than rather infrequent questions. For the most part, the editing of the interviews has been confined to eliminating repetitions and unfruitful digressions, excising questions of mine that were not essential (though not so many, I trust, as to make the interviewees seem like egocentric monologuists), and rearranging some sequences for clarity. Otherwise, the interviews are printed as spoken.

Admittedly, my freehand system of selecting the Ameropeans who appear in this gallery is rather far removed from the rigid methodology favored by the social scientists when undertaking the study of a group. This book was not intended to be the definitive sociological work on the Ameropeans, complete with charts, tables, and conclusions. Rather, the intention was to treat the subject in such a way that a reader could, in effect, sit down and talk informally with a sampling of Ameropeans, and, after hearing what they have to say about their way of life, form his own conclusions about it, if he cares to.

As one listens to the people assembled in this gallery, he is apt to be impressed by the variety of reasons they give for choosing to live in a foreign land. Underneath them all, however, runs a force that Willa Cather memorably described after she had herself lived abroad: "One cannot divine nor forecast the conditions that will make happiness; one only stumbles upon them by chance, in a lucky hour, at the world's end somewhere, and holds fast to the days, as to fortune or fame."

GALLERY NOTES

If we begin, as seems proper, with a retrospective exhibit of Americans who have chosen to live in Europe, the first portraits on view will be of members of the Lost Generation who still make their residence abroad. This collection is, of necessity, a small one. As noted earlier, most of the intended expatriates of that period eventually came home, among them Malcolm Cowley, who remarked years later, "The whole European adventure was sort of a fairy story with the son running away from the cruel stepmother and wanting to look for treasure and coming home to dig for it, and possibly finding it, in his own father's backyard." However, a few American exiles of that era—in many ways, the precursors of the Ameropeans—found the treasure they were looking for in Europe, and remained there.

> "I wanted beauty, with a capital 'B.'
> I hadn't had any in Indiana."

Janet Flanner, who has been described as the most gifted and versatile of the great foreign correspondents, has been contributing, under the pen name "Genet," her famous "Letter from Paris" to *The New Yorker* since 1925. When a collection of these celebrated letters, titled *Paris Journal*, was published, in 1965, the London *Sunday Times* said of its author: "She has every virtue, every grace, needed for her job—a style remarkable for clarity, concision and wit, a deep understanding of every class in France, political clairvoyance, and an instructed love for literature and all the other arts." Although best known for the work signed "Genet," Miss Flanner has also written some of *The New Yorker*'s most distinguished "Profiles," contributed to other periodicals, and translated books from the French. Like her prose, she is stylish, wise, witty, crisp, and elegant. She is in what she terms her "not quite middle seventies," but, as her friend, Mary McCarthy, recently remarked, "she could be sixty or a hundred and sixty, for she gives a sense of enormous durability and toughness; also, with her white hair, she resembles a portrait of the *Directoire* period." She favors gray suits (the red ribbon of the Legion of Honor gracing the left lapel); speaks in a voice of velvety huskiness; and projects not only in conversation but in laughter and even in repose an attractive histrionic quality. When she is interested in a topic, which seems to be about 99 per cent of the time, she tends to discourse, and with a kind of mesmeric effect. Throughout our interview, it seemed that she was not answering questions but instead using them as the framework on which to compose a number of impromptu, polished oral essays.

My meeting with Miss Flanner was held late one morning in the Paris hotel room where she has lived since 1949. Her room, on the top floor of the Hotel Continental, is small and crowded but with a basic orderliness. There is a fine Augsburg ivory inlaid seventeenth-century table on which she works and a Buhl cabinet which figured in the suite of the Empress Eugenie, widow of the Napoleon of the Second Empire, who lived in the hotel after his death. Otherwise the furnishings are unpretentious. The view from the French window and the little balcony are magnificent, taking in the Gardens of the Tuileries, a corner of the Louvre, the dome of the Invalides, and the Eiffel Tower.

I knew Miss Flanner's essential biographical facts: born in Indianapolis of Quaker parents; attended private school until seventeen; spent a year and a half in Europe with parents; returned to study at the University of Chicago for two years, when requested to leave ("They did object to my coming in so often at three in the morning. I was mad on dancing."); reviewed movies for the Indianapolis *Star;* did free-lance writing in New York; moved to Paris in 1922. As I told her, what I was interested in, to begin with, was why she had come to live in Europe.

MISS FLANNER: I should think that I came from pure aesthetic selfishness. If I had been born in a prettier part of the country than I was born in, which was flat and cornland, I probably wouldn't have been so eager to appreciate the beauties of Europe. I moved to Paris, I should think, because I'd never been in France before. When I lived abroad with my parents, we had done only northern Europe. My elder sister was studying piano with Ossip Gabrilovitch, Mark Twain's son-in-law, in Berlin, which was the center for piano at the time, and we went there to visit her. We spent a winter in Berlin, living in a musical pension, and then a summer in Munich, followed by a tour of England

and Scotland. After that, we were to have spent a year in France, but my father's money—what little he had—ran out, and so we were obliged to return to America. Money is almost always the reason either for moving back where you came from or for moving some place new, with hope.

Certainly one could live more cheaply in Europe at that time than in Greenwich Village, which is where I had been living. There was also the question of certain creature comforts. One thought one had better food, and one did have cheap red wine here. That was, I should think, healthier than bathtub gin, which is a foolish thing to bring up now, but there was already a sense among Americans that they liked better things to eat than they were getting, no matter how good the apple pie was. Americans were already, I think, being either pushed or led by some sort of yearning for what was not statelier mansions or the stately homes of England but for some greater amount of civilizing social elegance than we had yet developed. Certainly, it was not the be-all and end-all, but many so-called intellectual Americans were moving out. They were sprouting out of their own corn seed or wheat seed. That, as one looks back, was a most definite impulsion.

We're made up of immigrants, and some of us were going to emigrate. That was our choice then. Leaving home was part of our sense of liberty. That's why we were able to begin anew. That's why all the writers and painters who came here in the early 1920s began afresh. In that sense, we *were* emigrés. Most of us were not necessarily the brightest boys and girls in the class, but we were the most restless. We wanted something we weren't getting. One of the things we certainly wanted, if we had had any particular education in aesthetics, was something more beautiful than we were getting. Not only landscape. I mean, buildings, architecture. Landscape is in the lap of God, you know.

I certainly came abroad to satisfy a passionate yearning, a kind of emotional necessity, for aesthetics, for beauty. It was the selfishness of the joy of the eye. My eyes—I wanted to see with both of them. I wanted to see more beauty than I had seen in Germany, which I had never particularly liked. I should think that, innately, I was a wine-drinker rather than a beer-drinker. Still am. I wanted beauty, with a capital "B." I hadn't had any in Indiana. That's where I come from. I do not wish to go back. Nor do I wish to renounce my appetite for aesthetics. It's moved me enormously all the years I've lived here. I was consumed by my own appetite to consume—in a very limited way, of course—the beauties of Europe, the long accretions of architecture and poetry and civilization and education, the beautiful gardens, the beautiful palaces, the towns made with what they call promenades so people can promenade about. I was consumed by this necessity, a kind of magnificent malady, a fever to take part, if only as an onlooker, in the fantastic creations of gifted men, of architects, of painters, of genius. Of architects, in the first place, because architecture is what you look at mostly at first—the outsides.

As one with a semi-Quaker education, I certainly wasn't suited, or fitted, I suppose, for what I took as my first architectural aid. I took Henry Adams's *Mont St. Michel and Chartres*, because it was a story of the two main church growths in France, Romanesque and Gothic. Henry Adams gave me a complete guidebook in most excellent nineteenth-century English, and I used it. I visited these principal Romanesque and Gothic churches that Adams described, and, beginning with my excited appreciation, I came after years to know them individually and well—better, I daresay, than some of the French. I traveled by rail, usually third-class, especially for short journeys of only five or six hours, and often lived in second-class hotels. Usually, though, I stayed at the little provincial third-class hotels—quite nice, almost always clean—and ate with gusto what was put in front of me. We used to get the most wonderful buckwheat cakes in Normandy, where they used to eat a lot of buckwheat. They would flip them over onto a soft poached egg or a soft butter-fried egg. One of the best luncheons I've ever eaten.

Yes, I've always been an egotist. I think that's one of the things that moves you when you are young. I had been greatly influenced by Walter Pater. I cared about *Marius the Epicurean.* I didn't fancy myself with a title that high—as an epicurean—but I was determined to find out what the content had been of the emotional life of people who are only secondary like me. We only came to look. We were not the great creators. We were the constant gazers at the beauty other people had made. I was probably a born serious tourist. I loved then to travel. I loved to move about. I love to look. I'm very simian-minded. My eyes are very important to me. I remember so much through my eyes—far more, I should think, than through the ears.

Did you feel that the search on which you had embarked—the quest for a sense of beauty—had ended when you first sighted Paris? Did you feel that this was it?

MISS FLANNER: Oh yes. I thought Paris was quite *it.* The color of the gray stone, the carvings, and the fancifulness of many of the buildings—they still retained their epochal trademarks of history. History has trademarks—a style. Architectural history has trademarks. It's composed of the various kinds of styles, and, of course, there they are, on the façade of a building. The way the roof was made. The way the windows are put in. Mansard. Almost all Americans know about a mansard window. Well, there it is—up on front of the garret. And a pity they don't have more at home. The garret would have been a place to dwell. The beef-eye windows—I was quite fascinated when I first saw them. Those round windows, specifically for looking out. Rather good spying, I should think.

I don't think that the aesthetics problem has been of such acute importance to Americans generally and lately as it was to a few of us then and as it is generally to native Europeans, especially in their youth. Possibly I carried it to excess. I was hypersensitive to that, because I cared so passionately about it. To me, ugliness had become synonymous with aesthetic ignorance.

Before I came to Paris, I had been in Greece for about three months. The Parthenon affected me more than anything I had ever yet seen. I had arrived by day on a ship, and I wouldn't look up at the Acropolis all day. It was in the month of July, I think, and it was the first night of the full moon. At that time, under full moon, travelers could go up at night and visit it. All day I reserved my eyes from looking at it. I prevented myself from seeing it. I wanted the great excitement of seeing it at first glance, in the marble white moonlight. This was rather theatrical, but I think well-chosen on my part. I wanted the best that I could obtain, with the greatest accumulation of both nature and creation. That night, my friend and I hired a cab and drove up in style, though I suppose that was the only way we could get there, in any case. I was so overcome by what I saw that I wasn't able to climb the steps and go into the temple. I simply sat outside. What is the poem—you know Shelley's "Indian Serenade," which describes the weakness that beauty can inflict? "O, lift me from the grass/ I sigh, I faint, I fail/ Let thy love in kisses rain/ On my cheeks and eyelids pale." I could get no further than looking. I was in reality in a temporary paralysis of the overextension of my aesthetic senses. Next morning, in the bright hot sunshine, I went up again, and this time I moved slowly inside into the precinct.

As time and youth passed, I learned backgrounds of thought by reading, but I learned more about the emotion of the imagination—the movement of the imagination of man—by looking at architecture than I did by pursuing history itself. This has meant a great deal in my life. This is what I came to Europe to obtain, what I've pursued since I've lived here—what has fed me, what has rewarded me, in my own imagination.

In order to carry on this pursuit, was it necessary for you to work, to make an income?

MISS FLANNER: Oh, at first I could have stayed here without working. I had a very small income inherited from my father. At that time, you could live, without any frill or fanciness, very cheaply in Paris. You could have a glass of red wine at noon and a couple of glasses at dinner and well-flavored, ordinary food, and live in a cheap, modest hotel, where you had hot and cold running water (no private bath, of course)—you could live on about sixteen hundred, seventeen hundred dollars a year, if you could rely on your mother to send you that extra two hundred and fifty dollars for Christmas, which she always did, bless her. Oh yes, you could make ends meet. As Ernest said, Ernest Hemingway said, in the early days—he came a little later than I—"You can live on less than less." A wonderful aphorism. Which was very true. Ernest and his first wife lived on less than less. There was something magnificent about Ernest's hospitality. They usually had an egg at lunch. So, if you were invited to lunch, you had an egg, too. There was always a glass of wine, usually some boiled potatoes. Ernest cared far less than I about aesthetics. What he cared about was the action and the emotional body of the traveler. He was a born traveler as he was a born novelist. I was not.

Do you think that you could have developed as a writer if you had remained in the United States?

MISS FLANNER: Not at all. Well, not the same kind of writer. I learned more by being in France about writing the English language than I could possibly have learned in America. I learned a great deal more about writing English by writing for Ross, the founder of *The New Yorker*, and by reading the French newspapers, which have an excellent style, than I could have learned with such economy of mind anywhere else. There are only one or two newspapers anywhere that have high style today. In Paris, we still get it at night from *Le Monde*, which is practically oratorical. Oh yes, even in those early days I read the French newspapers, from Right to Left. That was the way I learned. I was excited by the news. I was excited by the exactitude of the French language. To this day, a taxi driver will say, "I don't think you mean quite that word, Madame. Now, let's see, the more exact word, if I may say so, Madame, would be. . . ." And then we get into a long talk about linguistic accuracies while he is dangerously talking to me over his shoulder and continuing to drive.

Paris is very different now. Of course, it has to be. Every place is very different now. From the time the original thirteen states became forty-eight and now fifty, America has itself become a kind of universal development. From the end of World War One, the young French were eager to have something of our American aesthetic. For we have one. It was not architectural. It came mostly from the musical talent of our Negroes and of our Jewish composers. Clearly it did not spring up from our Anglican puritanism. We now supply to others everywhere our most peculiar indigenous aesthetic richness, our jazz, to which others have added their own melodic richness, as in South America or Mexico, for instance. Europeans have an ever-increasing passion for our music. The Russians can't stop their young people from admiring and having jazz. This was our creation, our art. It was created by the two races, which had the least immediate social chances. The Negroes, especially, found themselves as master creators, as singers, as jazz players. Jazz was our great invasion of Europe. Jazz is our great return emigration.

Paris has become Americanized. All France, through its big cities, has become Americanized. Oddly enough, we Americans were at first very popular because of what the French wanted from us—our twentieth century. Now they are taking our language, our slang and business jargon and have inserted it into their own language. The mixture is called Franglais. Which began with the French saying, "*Très bien*, O.K." They have since taken over everything they can fasten their ears on to. Now they're even talking about "*finalise*"—"to finalize." And all the new office structures here are "buildings," of "grand standing," which in Franglais means absolutely up to date. Then there are the "selfs"—the cafeterias. These *selfs*, by the way, provide a good quick lunch for the secretaries and young fellows who used to go home on the bus to lunch and waste those two hours. Now, they have a good sandwich at what they call a snack bar or maybe a hot dog. They are very fond of these. They serve them on little soft French rolls or on baguette bread. And grill them. Delicious. The hot dog has been our contribution to gastronomy, I suppose.

Well, the Roosevelts thought enough of it to serve it to the King and Queen of England, at Hyde Park.

MISS FLANNER: Yes, that was true. And I believe they said the King ate quite a lot.

Getting back to Europe, the beauty that you found here and the precision of the language were the two things that gave you the most satisfaction?

Miss Flanner: Those were the things I desired. Those were highly educational for me. One other thing was highly instructive. That was the development of one's critical judgment. Taste, as it is called. That the French have got by experienced instinct. Their basis is what they call *le mesure*—the proportion. But even proportion and moderation are really a question of the critical faculty. It is not a question of whether this is so much better than that, it is a question of *why*, and what makes it so.

Certainly, a dominant part of the aesthetic civilization of France is based upon the creative faculty of choice. Choosing is a form of creation. It is a preference—the exercise of aesthetic or logical reasons based upon values, for consciously preferring this to that. This is a form of civilization—choice. Not because a thing is advertised, and you've got to have it because the Joneses have it, but because it is appropriate to your taste and preference. That is the great civilization of France—choice. Taste, based upon nothing else. In America, buying just what is advertised—that is not taste. That's opportunity.

The French are always talking of their logic. Well, you'll not always find it in their actions, but it does exist in their language. I care about language. I care about writing. I knew as a very young child—five or six years old—that I wanted to write. I was then a very good little speller. Now I can't spell at all, the result of being very bad at typing. But I am still on the pursuit of the perfect and the correct and the appropriate word. I care about that with almost an engineer's passion. The engineer finds the particular little piece that makes the thing tick or gives it perfect balance. That I still love. I have a sense of almost rapture when I think I have found that perfect little piece which is a word. Often, I have to labor to find it; it might take half an hour or an afternoon of trial and error. That adjective is not right; this adverb does not suit. Then, one of two things happens. Either I find what I want or I come to the second conclusion, which is equally important for a writer: I take it all out and throw it away. Either you get a small flower that is worth saving or you dig up that corner of the garden, and start planting again. Writing is very fascinating and can eventually be highly rewarding. Ross knew what he wanted and very precisely. When he offered me the chance to do a Paris letter for *The New Yorker*—that was in 1925, the magazine's initial year—he said, "I'm not paying you"—and maybe he should have stopped right there, pretty nearly—"I'm not paying you to tell me what you think. I'm paying you to tell me what the French think." Well, this was perfect advice and often not easy to follow. The French are complicated thinkers. But Ross's rule has made my life work, till now.

What did Ross pay you, at the beginning?

MISS FLANNER: He started me at thirty-five dollars a letter, and I paid my own expenses. When I went to the opera in order to write about it, I had to buy my own ticket—and for everything else I attended as well. I knew more about the seats at the top of the Paris Opera than anybody else in town, I daresay. There were exactly two excellent gallery seats—way to one side, between two pillars. If you leaned against a pillar, you had comfort and a wonderful view of the stage, far away. I think those seats cost about eighteen cents apiece. I did two letters a month, each of about fifteen hundred words. I was living in a modest hotel over in the St. Germain des-prés district. With the seventy dollars from the letters and the small income from my family, it felt like clover. Three years later, I persuaded Ross to give me a raise. I asked for fifty dollars a letter. He gave me forty-eight! On that I didn't move into fancier lodgings. I did eat better, and drank somewhat better wine, and I was able to travel more.

The important thing was that Ross left me perfectly free to work out the form of the Paris letter. It seemed to me that it had to contain a certain amount of reporting on what was going on in books and theaters, on what was happening in the countrysides in the way of wheat and wine crops and peasants' reactions. About 1930, I also started writing slightly about politics but Ross seemed not to notice it, so I wrote more and more. And always I gave my information in terms of the French reaction to it, like giving the climate of French minds toward things French. This worked out as so logical a formula for use by *The New Yorker* that it was judged to be a good formula for any kind of foreign letter. When other magazines began using foreign correspondence, it became a regular term. An editor would say to a writer going abroad, "Send us a Paris Letter from Rome." Or Cannes or Salzburg. That was a great compliment to Ross.

And to you.

MISS FLANNER: Maybe. Well, probably. I supplied the verbiage and did the reporting, but Ross created the idea. He was the one who had the sense to see that foreign news, in limited quantities, and of a special selected sort, was of great interest to a metropolitan city like New York. Letters, of course, are the most intimate form of printed correspondence. But I have never used the first-person pronoun. I never say "I." When I feel the necessity of identification for some special reason, I say, "Your correspondent." The thing is to report what you have seen, or read, or want to communicate in a temperate manner in which your style of thinking or of writing develops its own news value. But you leave your ego out. There's no sense in writing, "I was utterly surprised" at thus and so. Write explicitly what it was that surprised you. It ought to surprise everyone, if it's that odd and if you have written it well enough.

I wanted to ask what things surprise or impress you when you go back to the United States. I believe you once said that you think it is very difficult to feel romantically about America and that one of the appeals of Europe is that one can develop what you called "a legitimate romanticism" about it.

MISS FLANNER: That is utterly true. Yes. We are not a romantic people. So we are not inclined to feel romantically about our country. We feel loyally, instead. We may feel even more loyal when we are here than when we are there. I think it's quite true about "Home Sweet Home," you know. I think it's a song you're more likely to sing very, very far away than on the front porch.

No, we are not a romantic people. We are sexually a very acute and very active people. We are *now*, that is. When you think that practically the only literature we had before *Peyton Place* was based on nobody's having any noticeable sex, one sees how far we've come. Too far, it might seem. I reread *The Scarlet Letter* four or five years ago, and I became so indignant I could hardly finish it. Of course, I'm a straight, old-line feminist and suffragette. I became so indignant with that cowardly preacher. Simply because nature has arranged it so that only the woman has the baby, he was able to avoid all social guilt. I mean, having the baby was not a single act on her part. Parthenogenesis, after all, has not yet been perfected. There's always a gentleman at the bottom of the woodpile. But the poverty of the imagination of our Puritans! And the cruelty of our childhood Sundays. And the lack of imagination among our grandparents except on the subject of hellfire for sinners. There seemed to be desperately little social utility in the early churches in America—Puritan churches. Our civilization was too largely founded upon "No!" European civilizations have largely been founded upon "Yes"—with restrictions. In my generation we were really robbed of a lot of the best part of our early years by the inherited Puritanism of our country. And that's why quite a lot of my generation came over here. We thought we could fall in love with life with more pleasure. And we did, too.

Which reminds me that John Levee, a young painter from California who now lives in Paris, has said that the difference between life in the United States and in Europe is that in America, a parent puts food in front of a child and says, "Eat it. It's good for you." In Europe, the parent says, "Eat it. It's good."

MISS FLANNER: It is so true. Pleasure. There again, one comes back to what I sought here. Hedonism in its proper sense—that's what I was after, I suppose. That is a word which is certainly not enrolled in our Constitution. But we must not forget that our Constitution was a very remarkable, curious document. "Life, liberty, and the pursuit of happiness." At the time the French were absolutely scandalized by it. The French clergy said, "Happiness? This is not a political matter. This belongs only in the province of the Virgin, by devotion." Oh, happiness was considered a great political impropriety. We were the first people who ever invoked it. And it's a glorious heritage. The pursuit of happiness is our great sublime political invention. I don't think we really need much beyond that. At any rate, we're still pursuing it.

You know, there's no education like discovering who you are, whatever you are. Walden Pond was, for Thoreau, a very fine place for him to understand who he was. I am glad that I was able to understand who I was, within my limited self-knowledge, and that it came to me in this beautiful foreign city.

Can you imagine yourself living happily anywhere except in Paris?

MISS FLANNER: Not so happily, no. Oh, I love living in New York. And I think San Francisco is the most charming, daintiest, most fanciful city America ever founded. Up and down those little roller-coaster hills. So pretty. That cool fog. New York is stunning, really stunning. Stunning in the sense that it falls on one's eyesight. One is crushed by its extraordinary invention, the invention of itself on those granite rocks. Most Europeans never recover from their view of New York. They're permanently astounded. There's nothing like it. Oh, New York is a very great city.

But your view is still that it is a very great city to visit?

MISS FLANNER: Oh, no. I would enjoy living in New York. When I go back and stay two or three months and get used to it again, I love living in New York. Habit, you know, in the end, is the thing that shapes us all. I'm habituated to living here, in Paris. This is my voluntary habit of life. I've spent the years since 1922 to 1967 here, with four years of the war out in New York—forty-one years. In fact, I've spent more than half my entire human existence in this city. That's a long habit—a long and delicious and increasingly costly habit.

"Why do they remember us if we're 'lost'?"

Man Ray, painter, photographer, and one of the founding fathers of Dadaism, is, like Janet Flanner, in his middle (or not quite middle) seventies, a charter member of the Lost Generation, and a very lively personality. When I telephoned to make an appointment, he said that because of rheumatism he generally stayed in bed until one o'clock in the afternoon and spent only an hour or two at his studio but that he would arrange to see me there for half an hour. Arriving at the studio, a large, high-ceilinged affair on Rue Ferou, I was greeted by Mr. Ray, a rather slight man, who looked very chipper in a blue blazer, gray slacks, black horn-rimmed glasses, brown beret, and a white shirt with an unusual-looking necktie, about which I made some comment. "That's not a necktie," he said. "It's a shoelace. I haven't worn a tie in twenty-five years. I use anything instead—shoelace, piece of thread. It goes with my not liking to pack or to travel." On shelves near the entrance were some of his favorite "objects," which he was assembling for an exhibition to be held in Milan and in New York and called "Objects of My Affection." He told me the titles of some of them. One, made of plaster and shaped like a loaf of French bread, was called "*Pain Peint*." Another, a cluster of feathers balanced on a scale, was titled "Featherweight." A third, consisting of a shiny black toilet seat framing a large photograph of an egg bore the title "*Trompe l'Oeuf*." Then I followed Mr. Ray into his studio, where he bade me be seated on a venerable couch. He said he preferred to stand. For the next hour and forty-five minutes, never sitting down and showing no signs of fatigue, he delivered himself of a cascade of observations on art and life, with special emphasis on his own.

RAY: If you had read my book, *Self Portrait*, which is sort of an autobiography—I'm the only one in it who is sharp; everyone else is out of focus—you would know why I first came here. I was born in Philadelphia, and we moved to New York when I was a kid. I know every square inch of New York. I lived there until I was thirty years old. I went to school and then to art schools. I began to paint seriously and exhibit, but it was a tough struggle.

As I say in my book, my first thirty years were unhappy, miserable. I was a modern painter, and I wasn't understood. I was considered a joker, a fake. The things I did then are in museums and in collections now. At the time, though, I was criticized, attacked, rejected, even refused exhibitions. They didn't think I was serious enough. It is only the man who is not sure of himself who is serious always. They questioned my "profundity." "Seriousness," "profundity"—those words ought to be eliminated from the dictionary. Just as I would like to eliminate the "Lost Generation"—that haphazard phrase invented by Gertrude Stein, out of spite, I think. Why do they remember us if we're "lost"? They keep talking about us all the time.

I came over here, in 1921, only for a visit, to look around the museums and meet some other people who were doing advanced work. I was a novelty for the French. They received me very gracefully. They didn't question my sincerity. They even organized an exhibition for me, and since I had been so unhappy in New York with dealers and collectors, I decided to stay here.

I'd had the illusion that I might be able to sell my paintings here, but I found I couldn't. The French were buying even less than the Americans, so I figured, "I know how to make photographs. Maybe that will bring in bread and butter." So, during the first twenty years I was in Paris, I had a photographic studio. That's how I made my living. I continued painting, but I refused to sell my pictures. If somebody liked one, I'd give it away. My friends, who were writers, would say, "How I like that picture. If I had the money, I'd buy it." I'd say, "You really like it? Take it." I gave away all the paintings I brought over. Some of them are in museums now. The poor writers who couldn't make a living out of their poetry sold them for good prices. More power to them. Maybe they helped make my reputation as a painter. That's how they make reputations here. That's another reason I stayed in Paris. There was communication between the different artistic creative activities. The writers are aware of what the painters are doing. The painters are often poets and writers themselves. We always hobnob together. The writers write prefaces for us when we have exhibitions. We illustrate their books. The collaboration here is marvelous. In America, everything is compartmentalized, pigeonholed.

As a photographer, I was in demand. I was like a doctor. Everybody needed me. It was like selling bread and meat. I led a double life. The photographic life, which got to be very social, smart, dressing for dinner and all that. The other life, sort of bohemian, with the avant-garde writers and painters in Montparnasse and Montmartre. I managed to keep the two separate, knowing that the one and the other could not get together.

Oh, I worked hard, but I didn't feel I was working at the time, any more than a man playing football for fun would feel he is working. You know, there's excitement, and that takes out the drudgery. I've made a habit of that since childhood. When I quit the art schools and decided to paint freely, I decided that anything approved of by the Academy was not anything I was going to do. After one or two rejections for exhibitions, I made my other decision: never to submit a picture to a jury or in competition for a prize. Dealers said, "You're wrong there. That's the only way to get on." I said, "I'm not trying to get on. I just want to be able to live long enough to do my work and have fun." Liberty and the pursuit of pleasure—that's my goal. I believe in absolute individualism and the one-man job.

Back in the earlier days, did you spend your time mainly with the other Americans living here or with the French painters and writers?

RAY: With both. I knew them all. I knew Gertrude Stein very well. If Hemingway had some gripes about her, I have some, too. Other people, like Picasso and Duchamps, I saw a great deal more of and got to know. They accepted me. To Gertrude Stein, I was a photographer who was going to help her with her publicity. That's all. She was always asking for photographs. She never paid a penny for one of them. She had lots of money, but always pretended to be hard up.

You stayed on in Paris, then, until the Second World War?

RAY: I stay in a place until I'm kicked out. I hate to move, and I hate to travel. When the Germans came here, I couldn't stand it any longer. We weren't in the war yet, but it was impossible. The Germans tried to put me to work. They said, "We've got lots of work for you to do. Lots of work, and more money than the French paid you." I said, "But not as much as the Americans will pay me. That's why I'm going back." That they understood.

I went back to the States. I looked around New York, got my old depressions back again. I decided my life was finished. I'd left twenty years of work here. I decided I'd go to Hawaii or Tahiti and disappear, like Gauguin. That's all. On my way, I drove out to California with a friend. First time I'd driven across the continent. I got to Hollywood. There were palm trees, sunlight, the Pacific Ocean, lots of space. No skyscrapers. Made me feel taller. So I said, "Why go any further? I'll stay here a while." And instead of staying two weeks, as I'd planned, I stayed eleven years.

In Hollywood, I painted mostly. Gave some lessons. Once in a while I did a photograph, but mostly I painted. I paint because I think that's the most important work a man can do.

Why did you leave California and come back here?

RAY: It got depressing after eleven years. Some of my best friends had left. Most of them had died, you know. I knew lots of people in the movie industry, and you see divorces and homes breaking up. Finally, my landlord doubled my rent, and I figured, "Well, with the money I'm going to spend next year on rent I can go somewhere else. Where can I go? Back to Paris, where I know the ropes." That's all there was to it. I might have gone to Tokyo or Constantinople, if I had known my way around those places. I knew that I didn't want to go back to New York, under any circumstances, to settle permanently.

I like New York when I go over for a visit. I have a wonderful time. I was there last year for the coming-out of my book, and I had two big exhibitions—all of my old things that I had left in America that were condemned in the early days. I go over every two years for an exhibition.

Do you think you might ever return again to life in the United States?

RAY: If there's another catastrophe here, I'll probably go back again. Find some nice quiet place, if possible—not New York or Hollywood. I have relatives in Princeton, who will put me up or even build a house for me, if I want it. I'd be just as happy. I've spent half of my life in America and half in France, and there is no preference. None whatever. I live within my own four walls. I have nothing to do with my surroundings. The world that concerns me are a few people who are in the know. I love Paris, and I love America, too. I love lots of things in America as I love lots of things in Paris, and there are lots of things here that I detest, too. If I don't like something here, it's my fault. I can't change the French manners or psychology any more than I can change what I don't like in America. I run into a lot of morons in America, and I run into a lot of hypocrites here. I say, "France is the least polite country in the world. Their politeness is irony." But I like that. Even when they're polite with me about my work, they're ironical, I feel. I prefer that.

"I don't live in France at all because I think that there is anything superior about life over here."

Maria Jolas, a tall, majestic-looking woman with an expansive, affable manner and a voice of extraordinary richness, has been described as "the leading lady of the literati" of the twenties and thirties. A native of Louisville, Mrs. Jolas was co-editor, with her late husband, of *transition,* the famous review that was something of a Bible for the Lost Generation. She also founded and directed a bilingual school in France, and she is well known as a distinguished translator. Mrs. Jolas lives in an apartment on the Rue de Rennes, and it was there that I called upon her. We talked for a while about the trip she had made the year before to the United States, her first visit there in eighteen years, and then she told me how she happened to come to Paris in the first place.

MRS. JOLAS: I was very much interested in music when I was a girl. In November, 1913, I went to Berlin to study singing with Lilli Lehmann, the great, great soprano, and I stayed there until the following June. Then I went back to Louisville to spend the summer, but, owing to the outbreak of the war, I was unable to return to resume my studies. To make a long story short, somebody recommended a teacher who had come from France to New York, so I went to New York and studied with her during the years of the war. When it was over, she decided to return to France, and I followed her there. It was as simple as that. There was no romanticism. No chestnut trees in bloom. No April in Paris. In fact, the lights were still out in France when I arrived. That was in 1919.

In 1925, I met Eugene Jolas, and we went to America, and were married there, in 1926. He was born in America, brought back to Lorraine when he was two, and stayed there until he was sixteen, when he returned to America. So he was an American citizen. In fact, he served in the American Army in both wars. His culture was European, and, shall we say, his heart was American. He used to often say to me, "You know nothing about America. You've never suffered and longed for America as I did when I was a young man."

After we were married, we went to New Orleans, and were more or less planning to live there. I was not rooted anywhere in particular, and he, being a newspaperman, wasn't either. He was very anxious to start a magazine. He thought for a moment of doing it in New Orleans, but realized that that was rather far from the movement, literary and otherwise, that he was interested in. We realized that very interesting things were happening in Paris, where we had met and where we had lived, and so we came back here. We didn't leave again until the lights were off once more, in '39.

It was an exciting moment in Paris, in 1926, when we arrived here. There was the Dadaist group. Joyce was living here. The Russian Ballet had already livened things up. Cubism had been very exciting. Then came Surrealism. Stravinsky was here. Picasso was here. The American writers and painters and composers were here. There was something almost indescribably magnetic about Paris at the time—a kind of extraordinary rendezvous that everybody seemed to have come to almost without realizing why. I think we ought to be quite honest about one thing: that life was extremely inexpensive for Americans in Paris at that time. It was not the least bit difficult. You had a choice of places to live. You could get a small room, a small studio, a small apartment. You could get a big apartment. You could get a house. And any one of them for practically a song. In 1927, we rented the house that is now General de Gaulle's home at Columbey-les-Deux-Eglises, for the equivalent of a hundred and twenty dollars a year. It was a charming old place, covered with vines. And the rent—just think of it—ten dollars a month.

Do you think this "sordid economic facility," as you once called it, was the most important factor in drawing people to Paris at that time?

MRS. JOLAS: I think it was *an* important factor but not the principal one. There were many other reasons. In 1932, we published an article in *transition* titled "Why Do Americans Live in Europe?" which consisted of answers to that question by a number of Americans. Let me get that issue.

The first answer is from Gertrude Stein. She says, being very sparing, of course, of punctuation, "America is now early Victorian very early Victorian, she is a rich and well nourished home but not a place to work. Your parents' home is never a place to work it is a nice place to be brought up in. Later on there will be place enough to get away from home in the United States, it is beginning, then there will be creators who live at home." In other words, it is not possible to work in one's parents' house, but the time will come when America will change, and then the artist can work there, you see. And she was right in that respect.

Hilaire Hiler, the painter, was the next to answer. He says, "When Albrecht Dürer was asked by letter why he remained so long in Venice, he replied, 'Because here I am considered a gentleman; at home, a loafer.'" He proceeds to charge that in America "there are no facilities for the enjoyment of leisure or apparatuses for reflection." Then we come to Robert McAlmon, the novelist, who speaks of himself as one of "the deracinated ones." There was some pretty fancy talk in those days. And he goes on: "I prefer Europe, if you mean France, to America because there is less interference with private life here. There is interference, but to a foreigner, there is a fanciful freedom and grace of life not obtainable elsewhere."

They said that—that they found "grace of life" here—in many ways. Here is Leigh Hoffman, another artist: "My principal reason for living abroad is that I prefer to live, insofar as such a thing is possible, with the maximum of pleasure and the minimum of friction. The struggle for existence in America, into which I early plunged, reached such an intensity that it finally became intolerable, hence I fled. Call it an evasion or what you will, but I, for one, can see little reason for remaining in a land where the people are dominated by a single and basic idea—that of making a living. Art can never flourish in such an environment."

George Antheil, the composer, wrote: "Musically, it is absolutely impossible to live in America. A young composer has absolutely no future in America, because, even if he attains the very peak of eminence, he cannot hope to make a livelihood, whereas in Europe he stands a chance of making anywhere from a decent livelihood to even the accumulation of a fortune." The principal reason for this, he said, is that there are hundreds of first-class operas in Europe and only two in America. Another expatriate, Emily Holmes Coleman, the novelist, said, "America is the enemy of the artist, of the man who cannot produce something tangible when the whistle blows. I am afraid that will always be so—America's prosperity will be the death of her artistic impulses."

So, you see, there were a great many reasons besides the financial one that brought Americans to Paris at that time.

To return to your own life here, you and your husband stayed on until the Second World War?

MRS. JOLAS: Yes, and our two daughters who had been born here. We lived through the traumatizing experiences of the defeat. I had moved my school to a chateau near Vichy, and we stayed on until October of 1940. The children were ten and thirteen when we went back to America. Having been born here and having gone to school here, they were really rather miserable away from France. American life was so different. They had but one idea when the war was over, which was to come back. My husband had already gone over with the Psychological Warfare Division of the Army, and by 1946, we were all back in France. The girls picked up their lives, finished school, met Frenchmen, and married them. Now I have five French grandchildren.

Your daughters are obviously going to remain here, but I wonder if you have ever thought of going back to the United States to live.

MRS. JOLAS: Well, you know, you can't uproot old trees. The fact is that this particular tree has been growing here now for nearly forty-five years, with a five-year interval during the war. My children are here, and my grandchildren are here. I even have a little plot of ground in the Seine-et-Oise, where I plant my radishes every spring. So, as much as one can become part of another country, I suppose I am part of this. I feel quite as much at home with French people as I do with Americans. I think Americans are simpler and easier to get along with. But I don't live in France at all because I think that there is anything superior about life over here. It just happened that my life has been made here. I am always indignant when I am called an exile. I am *not* an exile. I am just an American who lives in France. That's all. And all my French friends realize that. "*Madame est Americaine*"—they always say that. I've never tried to be French.

Several people have spoken of the anti-American sentiment they sometimes encounter here. Does that happen to you, or have you been here so long and become so much a part of the scene that French people would not speak in that way to you?

MRS. JOLAS: Oh, I am obliged to say that I have lived through at least two extremely virulent periods of anti-Americanism. One was around 1926 and '27. That had to do with war debts, and it was almost impossible to speak English on a cafe terrace without being glowered at. The most virulent period was shortly after the Second War, particularly among the intellectuals and Leftist groups. The attitude toward Americans was extremely disagreeable. The present situation, I think, is more a governmental one than anything else. I don't think one would find it in just ordinary relationships.

I must say, however, that I have occasionally been forced to say in no uncertain terms to certain French people that it was America that made possible the liberation of France. And I think if they are inclined to forget it, they must be reminded. I have done it several times. I once even took my pen in hand in reply to week after week of very disagreeable allusions to the United States in François Mauriac's articles in, I believe, the *Figaro*. I don't remember the exact wording of what I said, but it was to the effect that I would like to remind him that but for the American strength and the American intervention, this beloved country would be a Nazi country today. I never had an answer from him, nor did I expect one. But I'm glad I did it. So, you see, scratch the skin of an American, and you'll find an American underneath, no matter how long he may have stayed abroad.

GALLERY NOTES

Unlike the expatriates of the twenties, who belonged to the same school in the sense that all chose exile in order to search for beauty and artistic freedom, the Ameropeans are distinguished, in the first place, by the diversity of their motives for living abroad. These are so various that generalizations about them are extremely risky. Many were nevertheless attempted by Ameropeans whom I interviewed, including Richard Condon, a former movie press agent who has made a new life as a novelist (*The Manchurian Candidate* is one of his most popular books) during the fifteen years he has lived abroad. "I think it's possible," he said, "that the reason everyone moves, except gypsies, is that we love to leave our failures and disappointments behind us and in effect to start anew—to start anew with more experience and more maturity, perhaps, but in any event to start anew. Years ago, in a book called *Finnley Wren*, Philip Wylie told an anecdote about a despondent Russian artist who decided to kill himself. He turned on the gas and sat down in front of the stove with a pad and pencil. Somebody smelled the gas in time. The police put him under a pulmotor, and the first thing he said when he came to was 'Bring me that pad.' They did, and written on it were four words: 'Think in other categories.' That's not only the greatest sermon I've ever heard, but for me, it embodies the whole concept of living abroad. It seems to me that the aspiration, or at least the end result, of living abroad is just that—to learn to think in other categories."

Since most Ameropeans, like the rest of us, prefer to believe that they order their lives on the basis of hard-headed reason, they are not apt to ascribe their decision to live abroad to the pursuit of anything as amorphous as learning to think in different ways. Instead, they are inclined to attribute their move to very sensible-sounding economic factors. For example, they may explain that their money goes farther in Europe; or that, for them, the business or professional opportunities are greater there; or they may suggest a variety of other similarly respectable, down-to-earth reasons. And it is true, as we shall see, that economic considerations do indeed play a very important part in the decision of many Americans to live abroad. More often than not, however, the economic aspect is the rationalization rather than the reason. Not surprisingly, the true motives for taking up residence abroad, as for most other things that people do, usually turn out to be emotional ones—and none the less interesting for that.

"In my opinion," I was told by James Nolan, a gregarious and candid native of Pennsylvania, who has lived abroad for some twenty years and has an unusually large acquaintance among Ameropeans, "an awful lot of people come over here because they think it would be an adventure. I know I did. I had always dreamed of coming to Europe. I suppose I felt that, being a stranger over here, I'd be freer to do whatever I wanted. Perhaps I was influenced by Hemingway. In any case, I guess I have a strong bohemian tendency, and this seemed to be the ideal place to indulge it. I suppose another reason I came to Europe was the social aspect. In America, if you've made your fortune in Minneapolis and you move to Philadelphia, you'll have a rough time joining the Philadelphia Club, getting invited to dinner by the Biddles, and so on. Those hurdles are lower over here. I know any number of Americans who are seeing people of a social stature in Europe they would never see at home. It is also true in my case. Europe gives me the opportunity to transcend social barriers that I couldn't transcend in America. I am terribly pleased to be invited by the Duchess of Rutland to come and stay at her pony farm in Gloucestershire. If I had remained in Reading, Pennsylvania, I don't think the Duchess of Rutland would have invited me to her function. That excites my imagination and gives me a sense of well-being, which, intellectually, I know is absolute nonsense. But there it is. I can't run away from myself."

The emotional satisfaction that comes from being a big frog in a small pond, not only socially but professionally, is another reason that Americans go to live in Europe. A fairly typical example of this group of Ameropeans is Edward Kreisler, who owns one of the largest and most successful gift shops in Madrid. "From 1944 to 1953," he said, "I lived and worked in New York, where I was just a piece of dust, in my opinion, along with millions of others who were struggling and just managing to exist." In Madrid, Mr. Kreisler never has to feel like a struggling piece of dust, for he not only operates a prosperous business but is also President of the American Club, one of the founders of the American School, a member of the committee that administers the British-American Hospital, Chairman of the Board of Directors of the American Chamber of Commerce, and a prominent figure in many

Spanish charitable undertakings. "I have been able to fulfill myself here in a lot of ways that I never had the opportunity to do in the United States," he said. "It makes a much richer life."

Another Ameropean who has found fulfillment abroad, though on a somewhat more relaxed scale, is Jay Haselwood, the proprietor of the Bar Parade, the most popular bar in Tangier. "I had been a schoolteacher in the States, at the University of Kentucky, where I taught commercial law, salesmanship, advertising, and economics," he said. "I taught there for three years, and then went into the Army. After the war, I stayed on to work for the Red Cross, in France. Then I moved on to Morocco, and eventually set up this place. The work isn't too hard. I come in at seven-thirty or eight in the evening and stay until one. I have a French woman bartender, who takes care of things during the day. My life is spent mostly on the beach and fishing. My idea of a good day is a bottle of beer, a couple of sandwiches, and fishing from the beach. It's not bad here. No taxes to speak of. A foolproof climate. An extremely nice mixture of foreign people—Arabs, Jews, French, Belgians, Americans, English—and that is refreshing. It used to be incredibly inexpensive, and it's still inexpensive, if you stay away from luxury things. And I guess, for the first time in my life, when I got here, I did what I wanted to do. I mean, I had never planned on teaching school. That was my father's idea."

Then there are the Americans who settle abroad more or less by chance. Not infrequently, they go for a vacation, find the life there congenial, and decide to stay. According to Jay Haselwood, that is what happened to Eugenia Bankhead, the sister of Tallulah. "She came to Tangier the way so many people do," Mr. Haselwood said. "She and a friend of hers were on a cruise, and they came ashore to spend the afternoon. They went right back to the boat, packed their clothes, and settled down here. The same thing happened to an American couple, who came from California. He was in real estate. They were taking a trip around the world, got off the boat, liked it, and bought a house. He was thinking of retiring, but, like so many Americans, he didn't. Instead, he opened a potato chip factory here. Now he sells potato chips to all the American bases in Spain. He's cleaned up."

So has an actor named Eddie Constantine, who went to Europe in the first place because he didn't have anything much better to do. In 1947, Mr. Constantine, who had had a singular lack of success in his effort to become a Hollywood actor, and had afterward landed and lost a job singing in the Radio City Music Hall Chorus, was making a living of sorts in New York, doing singing commercials. His wife, a dancer, got an offer of a job in Paris. "I came along," Mr. Constantine said recently in Paris. "Since I found work here and couldn't find it at home, I stayed." After appearing in an Edith Piaf musical, he made his film debut in a tough-guy role in a picture called *The Poison Ivy Kid*, and he has been a tremendous success ever since. So far, he has starred in about five dozen movies in the same genre, and although still virtually unknown in the United States, ranks as one of the three or four best-known film actors in Europe. He now owns three companies that produce films and publish music, a racing stable, a half-interest in a Paris restaurant, and lives with his wife and children in comfort on a 110-acre farm in what he has described as the Bucks County of France.

The reasons behind the transplantation of Eric Estorick, a Brooklyn-born art dealer who is now the proprietor of the Grosvenor Gallery, a large and handsome establishment in London, are more complex. A stout, voluble man who wears a full black beard and clothes designed primarily for comfort, he had made two extended visits to England before settling there shortly after the end of the Second World War. When I asked what had kept bringing him back, he said, "To begin with, Europe was kind of a ball for me. I think I came here under very good auspices. That is, I came to visit family, and it was a family that, within the, I would say bourgeois, Jewish community has a position of respect and some eminence. I think in this country you're accepted for what your closest associates are—at least, in the beginning. And I think it is a country, too, being a class society—and very much a class society—into which I was rather accepted, if I may use the euphemism, as somewhat of a gentleman. That gave me a kind of inner strength and security that I didn't particularly have in New York.

"Furthermore, on my two previous visits here, I had found this a very congenial atmosphere. It was a live-and-let-live society. By that, I mean that privacy, almost to the point of neglect, prevailed here, and I welcomed that facet of life at that particular time. I think, too, that in a curious way the character structure of this country better suited my kind of personal character. I was an only child and a fat boy, and I started wearing glasses when I was only three. I had fallen arches, so I had to wear high shoes. What I'm really saying is that while I could have survived in New York, I don't know where I could have gone—whether there are too many people like me there. My parents still live in New York. My father, unlike practically anyone else I have ever known, has been able to live up to his standards as a human being. And I never could, if you know what I mean. That was too perfect for me. I love my parents—we have a very close and emotional connection—but if I could tell you why, as an only child, I live three thousand miles from New York, I could answer lots of other questions."

Robert Ardrey, an affable, enthusiastic man in his middle fifties, had had a very successful career as a playwright and as one of the highest-paid screenwriters in Hollywood before deciding, in 1955, "to shake things up," as he puts it, by going to Africa to write a number of articles about that continent for *The Reporter*. "Getting out into the world created some kind of excitement in me that I hadn't known for a good many years," he told me. "I wanted to preserve it. That is why I decided to live abroad." In 1956, he moved to Europe with his wife and two sons. As a result of further travels in Africa, he developed a consuming interest in human evolution, and embarked on writing a series of books on the subject, the first two of which, *African Genesis* and *The Territorial Imperative*, have been published. They have been very successful, and Mr. Ardrey has now established himself in a new career as an amateur scientist. Since moving to Europe, he has been divorced and remarried; he and his second wife, an attractive South African actress, now live in Rome. There he plans to stay.

"There are things in Mediterranean life that I would not give up," he said. "For example, the siesta. The way to die ten years sooner is to go back to the United States and give up the siesta. They used to try to figure out why the Italians never had heart attacks. After you've lived here a while, you find out. Here, you don't live a heart-attack way of life. Seriously, if I had to consider moving back to the United States, I would have to ask myself, 'Exactly how much is this decision going to shorten my life?' I might think it was worth it. I know it would have to be an important factor in the deliberations. Fortunately, I don't have to ponder such depressing matters. I love the United States—let's understand that—but I never think about going back there to live. I have no nostalgia whatsoever. I must say I regard this as my home. In a way, I suppose we all come here looking for roots. I feel that I have found mine."

However diverse their separate reasons for choosing to live abroad, there is one that all Ameropeans have in common. That is the determination to start anew, to make a second life—the result of learning to think in other categories. Some of the transformations have been more complete than others. Some have been more successful than others. And a second life has problems, too. But one satisfaction the Ameropeans have: they will not be haunted all the days of their years by rankling thoughts of how it might have been.

"At least 90 per cent of us are of
European descent, and I don't see why we
can't come back to explore our origins."

Before becoming an Ameropean, Joseph Jay Deiss, a handsome, rangy, soft-spoken Texan in his early fifties, was a very successful New York business executive, specializing in public relations. Now he is referred to by *Time* as "Archeologist Deiss." This was in the course of reviewing the book that he recently wrote about Herculaneum, the city that suffered much the same fate as Pompeii. Mr. Deiss has also become a novelist whose work has been well received by critics in the United States and in Europe. (In addition, since my interview, he has been named vice-director of the American Academy in Rome.) The new life for Mr. Deiss began in 1954, when he retired from business to spend his entire time writing, and went to Europe with his wife, Catherine, and their two children, Susanna and Casey. They have been there most of the time since, living for the longest period in Positano, a sensationally picturesque village on the west coast of Italy, about twenty-five miles north of Salerno.

For hundreds of years, Positano was an isolated fishing village, virtually inaccessible by land. The first road into the settlement was opened around the middle of the nineteenth century, and there is still just the one artery connecting the village with the outside world. The road, a two-lane affair that barely permits vehicles going in opposite directions to pass, snakes along the mountainside over a tortuously winding course hundreds of feet above the sea. Arriving at last in Positano, one is confronted with the breathtaking sight of a village clinging precariously to a cliffside that appears to be almost perpendicular. Below is the sea. Behind are the mountains. The combination creates in some people a sense of being trapped, in others, a feeling of security. So many visitors find it congenial that during the season, traffic in and out of town is often backed up bumper-to-bumper for a very impressive distance, and it is almost impossible to find a place to sit on the beach. Out of season—or at least in April, when I was there—the village gives the impression of being delightfully deserted.

The Deisses' villa is a fifteenth-century structure that has been completely modernized, and is situated "on the top," as the locals call the residential section of the village farthest up the mountain. Mr. Deiss, casually attired in corduroy slacks, sports shirt, ascot, and soft, suede-like shoes, met me at the door of his villa. Since it was a fine spring day, we lingered outside for a while, taking in the picture-postcard view. Mr. Deiss pointed out a group of buildings far down the mountain, which, he said, had recently been bought and were being remodeled by Americans, English, and other foreigners. The structures had belonged to a group of local people, who some years ago had moved together in a kind of mass migration to the United States. They prospered there, and, feeling sentimental about their old hometown, took up a rather sizable collection, which they sent back to rehabilitate the largest of Positano's three functioning churches. "The local contractor did a very thorough job," Mr. Deiss said. "Hardly a trace of the marvelous original architecture remains."

Moving inside, we sat down in the sunny, tile-floored living room, and Mr. Deiss recalled the events that had led him to Positano.

DEISS: Coming over on the boat, we met some people, who learned that we were on our way to Sorrento, which is not very far from here, and asked us to deliver a message to a friend of theirs who lives here. So, one evening, we drove over from Sorrento, cast an eye around, and I looked at Catherine, and she looked at me, and we said, "This is it." We went back, packed up, and checked out, and came back here with the intention of staying three days. We stayed for six weeks, went off to Rome for a while, and then came back again. That was during the winter of 1955–56, the coldest winter around here since 1453, or thereabouts, but we enjoyed ourselves nevertheless.

On one of those winter nights, we were invited to a friend's house here, and among the guests were a handsome young man and his beautiful French wife. They had just come back from Castel del Monte, and he was talking about what an architectural wonder it was. I asked, "Castel del what?" He patiently told me. I asked who had built it, and he said, "Frederick the Second." In my American naïveté, I said I hadn't realized that Frederick of Prussia had ever had dominions as far south as this.

The young man gave me a really withering look, and said, "Frederick of Prussia was one of my relatives of whom I am least proud. Frederick the Second of Sicily is one of my relatives of whom I am most proud. He was a great king."

I said, "Who are you?" He said, "I am an unemployed king." He turned out to be Prince Henry of Bavaria. He took me aside, and for about two hours gave me a brief on Frederico Secondo. He sounded like a fascinating figure. A homeless boy who became King of Sicily and Holy Roman Emperor. Married three times, first at age fourteen. Had fifteen children. Spoke nine languages. Excommunicated three times, yet led the most successful of all Crusades. Kept a Saracen harem. Founded the University of Naples. Wrote the first modern biological treatise. And on and on. A Renaissance man two hundred years before the Renaissance. I sat there with my mouth open, and finally said, "This is something I have to write."

We had to go back to America, but I couldn't get Frederick out of my system. We came back for the precise purpose of writing a book about him. To get the material, we followed his trail from birth to death. We visited all the castles, scenes, and settings connected with his life, starting at the tip of Sicily and gradually working our way north into Austria, Switzerland, Germany, France, and England. That was, to me, one of the most interesting and exciting things I have ever done.

Altogether, I put in about four-and-a-half years' work, doing the research and writing that book. It was called *The Great Infidel. Time* gave it a good review, and so did Maxwell Geismar and Professor Bergen, at Yale, but nobody is really very much interested in an obscure figure of the thirteenth century.

Is this interest of yours in antiquity something that has developed since you have lived in Europe?

DEISS: I've always had a big historical sense. It has sharpened and expanded as a result of living here. After you've been here long enough, you get the feel and sense of the past so that the past can re-create itself. If you go into a ruin or walk into a castle or a Greek temple at the right time of day or the right time of night, and just sit there for a while, it's astonishing what you feel. It's an almost telepathic thing. I think it may be in part just the business of coming back to Europe. At least 90 per cent of us are of European descent, and I don't know why we can't come back to explore our origins. It seems to me that in America we have cut off our past too sharply, with the result that we don't understand ourselves as much as we should. Viewing America from Europe is a very important experience. After having lived here for a while—we have a house on Cape Cod, and we go back and forth—it seems to me that every member of Congress should be required to live in Europe for at least six months. And every psychiatrist and psychoanalyst should be required to live in Italy for a minimum of two years. If they did, they would learn that people can behave in ways that they—the analysts and psychiatrists—might not necessarily approve of but that can make those who follow that line of behavior happy.

What would you have the congressmen do?

DEISS: The first thing for them to do is not live in the Excelsior Hotel, in Rome, or in the Hilton. They might learn to appreciate some of the things about Italy that we enjoy, such as the fact that superpatriotism does not exist here. An Un-Italian Activities Committee would be unthinkable. Generally, the atmosphere is much more relaxed. The people are more relaxed. Intellectually, there's a lot more excitement. There are more points of view. More opinions. You are entitled to hold a minority opinion, and present it without being crucified. You can be a professor in a university, and hold a very unpopular point of view, but you won't get fired for it.

There are a lot of bad things about Italy. I could talk for hours about the difficulties of life here, the complications, the inadequacies, the problems you have in dealing with people because of the huge illiteracy and the education of the Church. These people are taught the lives of the saints but not, for example, that mosquitoes come out of larvae, which is something of an omission in a country that was once racked by malaria. Our maid doesn't have the faintest idea of bacteria. She thinks they are insects. If you are upper class, you get a fine education. If you are lower class, you get practically none.

I have heard Americans say—and I have said—that one of the reasons for living in Italy is that life here is simpler, less complex. And, in a way, it is. In fact, I have the feeling that we are looking for a kind of earlier simplicity and innocence, which have vanished from our industrial civilization. One of the things that first impressed us about Rome —this great city of almost two million people—was that when we woke up in the morning in our hotel on the Via Sistina, we could hear roosters crowing. People were keeping chickens on the roofs. There is a sense of security in waking up in the morning and hearing a rooster crow, which only people who have lived close to the land or in small towns can understand.

You get the same feeling here from the fresh fruit and other things that come to you directly from the land. And there is also a feeling of the apparent ease of life. People say Italians are lazy. Nothing could be further from the truth. They work like dogs, though it all seems very slow and simple. Of course, you never get anywhere on time. And nobody ever gets to you on time. If you say anything about being late, they say, "What's the hurry? Are you going to catch a train?"

To get some things done here, even the simplest things, is absolutely maddening. For example, not long after we bought this house, it was obvious that my stairway—actually, it's a communal stairway, used like a sidewalk—going down the mountain was going to be washed away, because so many of the stones were loose. So, I wrote a letter to the mayor, pointing this out. Nothing happened. Two months later, I wrote him a special-delivery letter. This time, they sent two workmen.

They took a look, said, "Yes, the stairway is going to wash out," removed a few stones so it *would* wash out, and went away. Six months later, after heavy rains, I wrote another special-delivery letter, pointing out that the stairway had become very dangerous. The two men came back again, put up barriers so nobody could use the stairway, and departed. Within twelve hours, the barriers were gone. Someone had taken them off to use for firewood. At the end of the second year, when some of the boards gave way, I got off another special-delivery letter, with the usual result. Last Christmas, there was a big rain, and three-quarters of the stairway went. This time, I sent a telegram to the mayor. Nothing happened. Not even a barrier was put up. Finally, about the middle of February, there was another big rain, and the stairs went completely. I sent another telegram, waited a month, and then drew up a legal document, which I sent to the Prefect, in Salerno, who has control over this area. Three days later, a crew of workmen arrived, and started putting in a new stairway. They did a first-class job. I guess the moral is, you just have to have a certain amount of patience.

(*Mrs. Deiss came into the room, and I was introduced. An attractive, friendly woman, she had brought tea for all of us, along with cheese and some wonderful bread. I asked where it came from.*)

DEISS: It's made locally. There are two bakeries in town, and they make bread as they always have, baking it over charcoal. It is exactly like the bread that was made in Pompeii as far as the shapes are concerned, and it probably tastes very similar.

MRS. DEISS: We shop locally for a lot of things besides bread. Usually, we go to Naples once a week to load up with cheeses and staples. In the summer, there are always plenty of fruits and vegetables here, but in winter, it's very limited, and we have to go to Naples more often. We usually have some other reason to make the trip. Jay usually goes to the library there a couple of times a week.

DEISS: The library is an experience in itself. It's in an old converted palace. A large part of the staff are Neapolitan female intellectuals. On the off chance that you've never met a Neapolitan female intellectual, I can tell you that they are quite good-looking, not at all like the dowdy American library types. The place is full of incredible stuff. I found, for example, an eyewitness account of an early fifteenth-century execution in Venice, in Latin, which was tucked away there. It's not in any of the bibliographies in Rome.

One of the interesting things that I discovered when I was working on *The Great Infidel* is that there still exists in almost every small town in Italy a group of intellectuals whose chief interest in life is in what would seem to us to be most obscure historical matter. For example, in the Arno Valley there is a village called San Mineato al Tedesco, and in the village is a tower, which was built by Frederico's grandfather. This was the key to the resolution of the crisis in Frederico's life, because his closest friend and chancellor was blinded and imprisoned there. In the course of my research, I went to San Mineato al Tedesco to see the tower. It was a fantastic experience.

First of all, the local *conte* organized a luncheon for me with the village intellectuals. One of them was a schoolteacher. Another was a small bureaucrat in the regional government administration. The others included the librarian and the young assistant to the old priest, and, of course, the *conte*. The luncheon conversation began with the Holy Roman Emperor Otto IV and ranged to Dante. That was the time span. They got very excited, and carried on violent arguments with one another. It was marvelous.

In the afternoon, they took me into the archives, and began pulling out medieval documents and books, blowing the dust off them, and translating an enormous amount of material about the tower and the people involved. They seemed to be having the time of their lives. At the end of the afternoon, they were exhausted, but one or another of them helped me for many days after that. This experience is a fair example of what you can do here in the way of research, and also I think it illustrates a very engaging facet of the Italian character.

Another sidelight on the Italian character was revealed in the course of that visit. This tower was of no military value whatever during the war, but as the Germans retreated, they destroyed it. They had previously done some unpleasant things there. They had rounded up a group of about ninety townspeople—men, women, and children—herded them into a section of the cathedral, and hand-grenaded them. There is a plaque outside the cathedral, telling what the German barbarians did there. Anyway, at the end of the war, the village had some reparations money from the government to do with as they wished. So they had a vote in the town. Should they build a new hospital? Should they build a new hotel in the hope of attracting tourists? Should they improve the road? Should they put in a new draining system? Well, instead of doing any of these things, they voted to rebuild the tower. They sorted through the rubble, picked out the stones that were usable, and hand-carved others so expertly that they are practically indistinguishable from the original pieces.

This respect for the continuity of culture still exists, but is under very heavy assault from the *nouveau riche*—the fast-buck boys, who are tearing down the old and putting up some pretty shoddy new stuff. Positano is a national monument. It's not supposed to be changed. If buildings are modernized, they are supposed to conform to a certain architectural style. There has been one hell of a fight after another, because people either don't get the proper permits, or they go ahead and build whatever they damn please, and pay a fine for contravening the regulations.

When we first came here, we had very much the same *feeling* about this place that we had about Cape Cod, though, of course, the physical appearance is entirely different. Our house on the Cape is on Winds Pond, right in the middle of the seven lakes. It was described by Thoreau. People come from all over America to see the house, because it has such beautiful lines, such proportion. It's buried deep in the woods, a wonderful spot. Oh, it's heaven there, especially if you like Thoreau. But there were just as many difficulties with the local administration there as here. All of a sudden, the real estate operators started cutting the trees, putting down asphalt roads, and laying out nasty little get-rich-quick developments. Luckily, the government stopped them. The National Park Service saved it, so now there is again a semblance of what was there before. But the woods are full of little houses here and there and there and there, so the feeling is no longer what it used to be. As I say, the same thing is now happening here, so sometimes you wonder if it wouldn't be better just to go back to New York and get a flat on Second Avenue, and not worry about what's happening on Cape Cod or in Positano. By the way, are there any flats left on Second Avenue?

It would probably be easier to find space in a brand-new office building.

DEISS: I suppose. Coming back to New York after having lived in Italy, I find the architecture has a coldness about it that is quite formidable. There is something a little repellent after having lived with, for example, Renaissance architecture, which is so much a part of this landscape, and has such grace of form and such livability, such warmth. The new Italian forms, compared with that, are in general grotesque, but at least they have color. They don't have this awful sense of grayness that you get from the new buildings in New York. Once you have become accustomed to being surrounded with architecture that has a certain grace and proportion, you never cease wondering where and how that original purity was lost.

MRS. DEISS: I guess we're remnants of another century.

DEISS: We're antediluvian. We don't belong in this world. (*Picking up a small metal sculpture and handing it to me*) Here is another reason why we enjoy living in Italy.

It's beautiful. Is it Etruscan?

DEISS: Well, we got it from what we like to think of as the last Etruscan. One day, driving through Tuscany, we took a wrong turn, and missed the main road. Catherine said, "Since we've taken a wrong turn, let's just go on until we come to a town." We continued on until we came to one of those hill towns about a mile or so from the highway, and started poking around to see if we could find a place to spend the night. As we were walking down the main street, we came to a big archway, leading into a courtyard, and walked in. On one side was a green door, with a great old padlock on it, just like the padlocks at Pompeii, and behind it we heard tapping. I knocked on the door, and finally it was opened. There stood a little man, wearing a blue beret, his hands covered with glue. I looked in, and saw that he was making one of the most beautiful eighteenth-century inlaid tables you ever saw in your life. An exquisite piece—beautiful geometric design. Really high-powered stuff. I thought to myself, "This man is a genius."

Well, it turned out that he was a genius. He took us up into his house, and we found out that he not only made this beautiful inlaid furniture, but he also wrote poetry. Incidentally, poetry is still a big thing in Italy. They have a half hour of it on the radio every day. All sorts—thirteenth-century, modern, religious. Anyway, our friend in the blue beret wrote poetry, and he read some of it for us, and we complimented him, and he was very pleased and excited. Then he said he also did sculpture, and took from a drawer a bronze, which, he said, he had made. It was Etruscan bronze—an Etruscan warrior about nine or ten inches tall.

MRS. DEISS: He also had a number of smaller ones.

DEISS: He showed us the smaller ones later. They were in various processes of being cured. We asked how he did it. He said that he used Etruscan bronze, and he knew just how to bury the pieces for certain lengths of time in various types of soil to make them look real. When they were finished, he put them on display in his shop, and sold them, though not as originals. This beautiful one of the warrior, however, was not for sale. He wouldn't let anyone have anything to do with it. He said he considered that his finest work, and it was so good, in fact, that a committee of six experts had come to examine it. Five thought it was original, and the sixth thought it was a fake. I said, "Well, it would be easy to tell from the bronze." He said, "I told you it was Etruscan bronze." I said, "Where do you get Etruscan bronze?" And then he said, "I get it from the coins we take out of Lake Trasimeno." Now, it's true that Etruscan coins have been recovered from Lake Trasimeno, which is near Umbria, part of ancient Etruria, so I began to think that this was a kind of lady-or-the-tiger story. He showed us some other things he'd done—the smaller ones Catherine mentioned—but none of it was up to the quality of the warrior. When we left, he had us completely convinced that he had done it. And then we got to thinking and thinking that, on the contrary, it was real. He had found it, you see. And if it is real, he can't have it. By law, it must go to the government, or he would have to sell it on the blackmarket. Since he was a poet and an artist, and a Renaissance man and a true Etruscan, he could not part with it. And the only way he could keep it was by telling people he had done it himself. A true artist.

And a clever one.

DEISS: You can see why Italy is interesting. You never can tell when something like that will happen. And you often find people of considerable interest much nearer at hand. On this peninsula there are several people of very variegated personalities and background, ranging from writers and artists and retired businessmen to people in Ravello, who live in huge villas and give parties like the kind they gave in West Egg in *The Great Gatsby*. You know, a dinner for eighty-five people, and half the guests wind up in the swimming pool. Here in Positano, we have a man who used to be a top executive in an important company in Pennsylvania. I suppose he's fifty-five. Retired. He has taken up the study of antiquity, and it's really astonishing how completely he has immersed himself in this new life. He and his wife bought a house that used to be a bakery a thousand years ago, a fact they discovered when they started restoring the walls.

MRS. DEISS: They came here, as we did, thinking they were going to stay a day or so, and they never left. Positano got them. Something odd happens to people who come here.

DEISS: It's strange, but it does happen again and again. There was a man named Sam—well, we'll just call him Sam. He was a naval architect. He had a big firm of his own. Then he had a heart attack. They told him he might not live more than a year or two, so he decided to take a trip around the world. And alone, since he had been unhappy most of his life with his wife and two daughters.

He came here for two days. He spent some time on the beach. Then he walked up the hill. It was a very severe exertion at first. He discovered that if he did it slowly, he could make it up these steps. He was about fifty. He sat around and had some drinks at the Buca—that's a hotel down on the beach, and in those days, it was patronized mostly by fishermen—and he enjoyed just listening to them. He decided to stay a few more days. Then he fell in with a very good friend of ours—a contessa who is very experienced in the world, very amusing and delightful and highly educated. He started seeing her often, and they began having discussions about Plato and all sorts of things. So, he stayed a few more days and then a few more. Six months later, he was still here. A year passed, and he was still here. He was living every minute of it, looking at the bikinis, relaxing at the Buca, dining with the contessa. Finally, his wife found out where he was, and came over and took him back.

That's one of the saddest stories I've ever heard. Did you ever learn what happened to him after that?

DEISS: The contessa got a couple of letters. He said he had been restored to the old routine, but he hoped to come back for a visit. He never has. I remember one thing he used to talk about a lot—of course, it's hardly a novel observation, but it's true—you don't think much about time here. The newspapers are supposed to arrive here one day late, but if the road is washed out or there's some other trouble, they may get here quite a bit later. It's relaxing to read the news when it's several days old. You don't feel so agitated about it.

Have your children enjoyed living here?

DEISS: Yes, I think they have. One of the reasons we decided to give them an exposure to European experience is that we wanted them to realize that you don't have to behave in a certain prescribed way to be a regular guy or a regular girl. Our daughter went to school in Switzerland and then to the Sorbonne. She's now trying to decide whether to go back to school in Geneva or to go to a college in America. Incidentally, she speaks Italian without accent. Casey dropped out of college, worked for a while in a factory in New York, and decided to become an artist. He has some pictures in a gallery in Rome and also in a gallery in New York. Next thing, he may get a break.

It's a very interesting experience to walk around the University of Naples and mingle with the students and see what they look like and what they talk about. It's very different from an American university. You have bad things here, but you don't have drag races and the narcotic problem and all those other things. These kids reflect a different background, a different culture. They can still, if they wish, concentrate on intellectual interests.

You've traveled a great deal in Europe, but apparently you've found nowhere else that you would rather live than here.

DEISS: Yes, and that rather surprises me, because my background is all northern European. On my mother's side, my family came to America in 1658, from England. On my father's side, they came from Switzerland, in 1884. I've gone back to the places where they came from, and when I was in those villages, I got a very peculiar feeling of being two people. In England, I would think, "If old great-great-grandfather John had stayed put, I would be living on this street, in that house, and how would I feel, and what would I think?" And then in Switzerland: "If they'd stayed here, I would be living in this village, full of rich peasants and bourgeoisie, and I'd have gone on like the rest of them, and wound up in the chemical industry or something of the kind." But then I wouldn't have the feeling of Texas and of the frontier and all these other American feelings. It creates a curious sense of I-am-an-American-but-I-am-also-this.

I have tried very hard to find some Italian connection in my background, but there is none whatsoever. Yet I feel more at home in Italy than in any other country in Europe. And, in a certain cultural sense, more comfortable than in America, because I like the landscape in Italy. I like the architecture. I like the pace of my life. So, the only conclusion I can come to is that, at some point, there must have been a wandering Roman soldier.

But I get very homesick. We all do. Then we go back. When we go back to Cape Cod, we play Italian music, eat spaghetti, and drink Italian wine. There is a kind of double homesickness. Homesick—but for what? Positano? Texas? Cape Cod? New York? Which is home? I don't know.

"If you don't see them today, you can see them tomorrow, or ten years from now. There's no rush here."

Mrs. Arnaldo Ferroni, a native of Dedham, Massachusetts, is an attractive, relaxed, dark-haired woman, whose husband represents both Swissair and American Export Lines Isbrandtsen in Florence. The Ferronis live with their two young children in a picturesque villa—it was originally the granary on a great estate—that is about ten minutes by car from the center of Florence, and is situated on a hill overlooking the city. Among other attractions on the property are two magnificent cypress trees, the oldest ones in Florence. I was invited to the villa for lunch, and drove there from town with Mr. Ferroni, an amiable, shrewd, witty man with a considerable fund of humor, who bears a rather striking resemblance to Pierre Salinger, and is almost always referred to by his nickname, which is Pussy. A gourmet and an accomplished cook, he personally does all of the family's food shopping. He has his bread baked in the country by a peasant family and delivered fresh daily to his office; he brings the supply home at lunchtime. On the day of my visit, he had supervised the preparation of a memorable meal—the *pièce de résistance* was a succulent fish of impressive dimensions that had been flavored with herbs, wrapped in grape leaves, and leisurely broiled over a charcoal fire—which was expertly served by a white-gloved butler named Dante. (The other servants comprise a cook, a nursemaid, and a gardener.) Mr. Ferroni, who describes himself as a monarchist and a medievalist, delights in argument, so the conversation at lunch, when he wasn't viewing the changing Italian social scene with deliberately exaggerated alarm (he said he was depressed by the fact that when he goes hunting nowadays, the gamekeeper tips his hat only three times, in contrast to former days, when he tipped his hat no less than five times, and he fears the black day is coming when he will not tip his hat at all), consisted largely of a wide-ranging casting of doubt on the wisdom of certain aspects of democracy as practiced in the United States. Mrs. Ferroni and I dutifully rose to the bait. After lunch, her husband returned to his office, and I talked for a while with Mrs. Ferroni separately. Recalling the kind of mock-serious discussion at lunch, I asked if she very often tries in earnest to explain the United States to her Italian friends.

MRS. FERRONI: Not any more. I used to try. We don't have many American friends any more, and I am always outnumbered. When something unusual occurs in the United States, Italian friends still look at me and say, "How could that happen?" I can't explain all those things. I'm not a political expert. And if you're not there, you know even less, because all you have to go on is what the Italian papers feed you.

In the beginning, though, I was worse than any missionary. I still feel obliged to defend and explain, in a way, but I get the feeling that it's hopeless. They give you a blank look, you know, and you have the uneasy feeling they're thinking, "Oh, this is just more American talk." The difficulty is that one doesn't have enough information to refute everyone he encounters who's hostile, and so the tendency is to sort of sidestep. This annoys me, too. But I can't convert everyone in Florence, not to mention Italy.

How long have you lived in Italy? How long have you been married?

MRS. FERRONI: The answer to both questions is the same—eleven years. I met Pussy here. I was on vacation. I used to work for TWA in New York, in the ticket office on the corner of Fifth and Fiftieth. I came here on vacation, and I went into the local TWA office, which Pussy used to run. I knew a boy in the office, and when I stopped in to see him, he introduced me to Pussy. He already knew something about me through a friend of his named Freddy, who used to be manager of the Excelsior Hotel, where I was staying. He and Pussy used to be quite a lively pair. You see, Freddy, being manager of the hotel, used to have first look at the girls who stayed there, because he would check their passports to see how old they were, and where they came from, and all that. He and Pussy used to take turns. Oh, it was terrible. Terrible. It was Freddy's turn that time, actually. Well, anyway, that's the way I met Pussy.

I didn't know Italian when I came here, but, of course, Pussy spoke perfect English. I learned Italian from a maid I had, who came in in the morning. She wasn't actually a maid, but someone Pussy's family had known for twenty years and someone you could call on if you needed help, which I certainly did. I learned Italian from doing shopping with her. I don't like the Italian I speak, actually. I'd prefer to speak radio-announcer Italian—you know, without accent. When I speak Italian in Rome, everybody laughs at me.

But I know at least one Roman friend of yours who says that you surprise everyone because the Italian you speak is so pure.

MRS. FERRONI: I fool people because I can speak so rapidly. I don't hesitate, because I think in Italian. But it's not good Italian I think in. It's very ungrammatical.

When were you last in the United States?

MRS. FERRONI: Six months ago. That was the first time I'd been back in almost five years.

That would seem to suggest that it wasn't hard for you to divorce yourself from the United States.

MRS. FERRONI: That's true. It's much harder for me to divorce myself from here. I guess that's a terrible thing to say. I was perfectly happy to leave, and I was very unhappy to return. I couldn't wait to get back here. I only go back because I have family there and children to show off to them.

Of course, the day-to-day living here is different, but it's not difficult. The only thing you miss are people. Exclusively. It still frustrates me very much that I'm not able to vote in the United States, but I suppose I'll get around to accepting that. I have never missed any *thing*. You don't miss things like sour cream and the corner drugstore. You really don't. That's why I don't go along with people who say, "Oh my, isn't it wonderful how you've adapted." It's not wonderful at all. The real test of adaptability would come if somebody now offered Pussy a very good job in New York, and by some miracle, which would never happen, he would consider going to live there. That would be very tough for me. Very, very hard.

Have you ever lived in Florence? It's a matter of slowing down, an ease of living. It's not only servants and things like that. It's a way of living that's—what do you say?—that's more comfortable. That's all. You have more time. I lived in New York for so long, and I *never* did everything I was supposed to do. Not only supposed to do, but *wanted* to do. You would read about things, and you would say, "Oh, I must see that exhibit. I must go to that concert. And he's only going to be here for two days, so I must try to get tickets now." And so on and on. You never did it all, and you got left feeling frustrated. Here, one finds there is little to pick and choose among. If Oistrakh comes and plays his violin, my goodness, you know about it three months in advance, and that's *it*. You look forward to that event, and when it comes, you savor it. It's not just something to squeeze into the schedule. Of course, you can always go around and see the Florentine artists. But you don't have to hurry. If you don't see them today, you can see them tomorrow, or ten years from now. There's no rush here.

I have a lot more time than the Italian women, because they spend their days playing canasta and being fitted for dresses and going to the hairdresser, none of which I spend much time at. I go to the hairdresser's about as often as Pussy goes to the barber. If you don't live the way a Florentine woman lives, you have an awful lot of time. There's nothing in America that compares with Florence. It's not a small town. It's an important city. I keep trying to hold that thought.

How do you get along with Italian women? You see more of them, I suppose, than American women.

MRS. FERRONI: Yes, I do. There have been so many Americans here who have married Italian women, or the other way around, and there couldn't be more than 1 per cent of them who celebrated a twenty-fifth anniversary or anything approaching that. It's just been a history of disasters, so, at the outset, when I came here, they all sort of shrugged and conveyed the idea, "Maybe. Who knows?" It's not that they look at you in a nasty way. They take you shopping, and they take you to their dressmakers and all that. And they expect you to have children—more than one. Their attitude is one of sort of hoping for the best, but without too much faith. It's sort of depressing, in a way. You know, you get married, and they make you think, "Oh my, maybe it's a bad mistake." I didn't, although I had every reason to think so. My mother sent me off with a pat on the head, and the kind of if-you're-happy-I'm-happy thought. Not my father. He didn't say to Pussy, "Can you support my daughter, young man?" Or anything of the kind. No. He said, "You don't know what you're getting into, young man. You don't know how spoiled this girl is. You better wait a year and think it over." He really put Pussy through it.

One thing my father couldn't have realized is that the style of living I am accustomed to as an American—the kind of friendly, open way that Americans have—would be a great asset to Pussy in his business. There is no Florentine woman who, for any reason whatsoever, would open her house and entertain, for example, a whole gang of Seventh Avenue dress manufacturers. Not because she wouldn't want to help her husband. Not because she's a snob. But because she's too shy and too uncertain of whether her service is up to snuff, whether her tablecloth is ironed properly, and so on. Believe me, this is true. It's the reason why Americans are very rarely invited to people's homes here. It's not because of this talk about a closed society. It's part of the whole formal way of living. In America, you say, "The So-and-So's are in town for two days, and I know the curtains are being cleaned, and the children have a cold, and so on, but I want to see them." And you do. Not here. It is true that other Italians do criticize your home and your service and all that, and a Florentine woman just won't let herself in for it if she can avoid it.

Some American women who have married Italians have told me that they have found it almost impossible to make friends with Italian women.

MRS. FERRONI: I have only two intimate Italian women friends. I wish I had more. But I'm not wild about women, anyway. I never had a lot of girl friends. There are a lot of American women here I could be friendly with, but Pussy would prefer to spend his time socially with Italians. And so I would say that our circle of friends is 99 per cent Italians. With Italian women, you see, one doesn't have a meeting of minds about much of anything—about tastes, background, history, or whatever. Also, we are in an age group that grew up in the war. It was quite different here, of course, and that also sets one apart. For instance, your friend may be having a lot of dental work done, and she's not yet thirty. Well, that's an effect of the war. There are lots of things like that. You can't help feeling—well, not guilty, but there is a sense of separateness. It's a different world.

> "A great many of my friends in the United States have made an awful lot more money than I have, but I don't know any who have had as much fun as I have."

Wallace Beene, an alert, amiable, experienced journalist, is head of the Madrid bureau of *Stars and Stripes*, the newspaper published for American servicemen overseas. A man of medium height, he has gained some twenty pounds since moving to Spain. "It's mainly the fault of the almonds," he told me. "When you go into a bar in Spain, instead of being served popcorn and peanuts, you're served a plate of almonds and probably some olives. It's tough on the waistline. But worth it." The almond problem has not affected his wife, who is trim, dark-haired, and attractive. I called on them late one afternoon in their apartment, which is in a very pleasant section of Madrid, a couple of blocks from the Castellana Hilton, and over drinks and almonds, they talked about some of the pleasures and problems of living in Europe.

BEENE: In 1959, my wife and I decided if we were going to get to Europe before we were forty years old, we'd better pack up and leave, so we came over with the idea that we would stay a few months, and if I found a job, we would send for the children, who had been left with the grandparents. If not, we'd take the Grand Tour, spend our few dollars, and return. We made a wonderful drive through Scandinavia and then through East Germany—at that time, you could come down from Sweden to Berlin—and had a lot of memorable experiences along the way. We had sort of forgotten about being permanently in Europe, but then, driving through Frankfurt, I saw a sign that read *Stars and Stripes*, and I said, "Well, let's go see these people." As I learned later, they hadn't hired anybody in the previous eight months. I walked in, and the managing editor said, "Yeah. Take the desk over there." It was that sort of thing—just a sheer fluke.

We spent two years in Germany, and then I was offered the bureau here. We had come to Spain on a vacation while still living in Germany, and we'd decided right then and there that Madrid was for us. We've been here for four years now. I prefer to live in Europe, because, among other things, I have found out that where my salary in the United States was about equivalent on the social-economic scale to that of an apprentice bricklayer, over here I can live as economic royalty on the same amount of money. It's made a big difference in our life. We've been able to do everything we wanted to do. I have been able to travel all through Europe, to the Middle East, Africa, Russia, and to all kinds of odd countries. Also, my job in itself is fascinating. I get to pick my own assignments. I'm a thousand miles from my headquarters, which are in Frankfurt. It's a very pleasant arrangement. I can pretty much set my own pace.

Is the fact that money goes farther here the primary reason for your decision to stay on?

BEENE: No. I would say that the primary reason is that I find it a richer life in the variety of cultures and people. Even the Americans I meet over here seem to be much more interesting than those I meet back home.

MRS. BEENE: Also, we come from the South, where we've always heard about the marvelous air of gracious living from our grandparents, but we never had been fortunate enough to enjoy it. Here, I can write back to my grandmother and say, "Now I know exactly what you meant."

BEENE: I suppose we ought to call ourselves the last of the carpetbaggers. Actually, it's been delightful as far as living is concerned. My wife and I have both adapted to it, and our children have done remarkably well. We live essentially in an American community because of my work. The children go to American schools and have American friends, so they are not deprived of their American heritage and culture. My son was six, and my daughter was two when we came over. When the children get a little older, we'll probably return to the United States. We don't want them to have the rootless, stateless background that you see in the overseas military society. That gives the children no identity. We also have a certain amount of guilt, because both my wife and I are only children, and since our parents are getting elderly, we feel that we are depriving them of a lot of pleasure by keeping their only grandchildren over here. The children themselves are always anxious to get back to the States, because, of course, their grandparents show them a wonderful time.

MRS. BEENE: I don't think that living abroad does children any harm if they are living in a very warm, secure, affectionate family. Because help is so easily available, too many mothers here, I think, just take off, and have what really amounts to nothing more than an audience with their children for five minutes a day. This I would object to, but in our case, I don't think our children have been deprived of anything. On the contrary, they have had the best of two cultures.

BEENE: Speaking of help, I think it's amusing the way some Americans really take to the servants here. We knew one couple, middle-class Americans, who, at home, might be able to afford a cleaning woman half a day a week, if they were lucky. They came over here and really branched out. Started living on the grand scale. They had two chauffeurs—one to drive his car and another to drive hers, taking her shopping and the child to school. Something happened one day, and one of the chauffeurs didn't show up, at which point the woman exploded, "How can anyone be expected to get along with only *one* chauffeur?"

They can never go home again.

BEENE: The fact is that they went back to New York, lived there for about six months, and came back. They're living in France. You can be sure they don't have two chauffeurs there.

A lot of the older American residents say that prices have become high here. They would consider the rent on this apartment, for example, to be rather high. We pay a hundred and sixty dollars a month, plus utilities. But for a world capital, and for this location—this is a quiet neighborhood, which is rare in Madrid—and for the facilities we have here, including a garden for the children to play in, it doesn't seem high to me. It's certainly a long way below what we'd pay in the States.

We have made some very good friends here—almost all of them Americans. We tried the establishing of rapport with Spanish people, and we met some very nice ones, but it never quite worked. I think that Americans make them uncomfortable for various reasons. One is that very few Spaniards have a home in which they can entertain you. Almost nobody lives in an individual dwelling in Madrid, except the aristocrats and the very, very wealthy. So, when you entertain Spanish friends, you meet them in a hotel lobby, and you go out to dinner. Then there is always the one-upmanship. You've got to be very careful not to take them to a restaurant that's a little too expensive, because then they won't be able to take you to a less expensive restaurant—one they can afford—without losing face. It's a very delicate matter.

However, we have met some fascinating Spanish people, including the Duke and Duchess of Valencia—the so-called "Red Duchess." She was a big buddy of Franco's at one time, and then he grabbed one of her estates. She fought back, and wound up in jail for a spell, and has been his outspoken enemy ever since. Her husband is a world-renowned horseman and one of the most colorful people I've ever known. We spent a marvelous weekend with them. Drinking champagne at eleven in the morning. The fact that you have the opportunity to meet people like that—and we've met many other fascinating figures elsewhere in Europe—is one of the reasons I like living here. A great many of my friends in the United States have made an awful lot more money than I have, but I don't know any who have had as much fun as I have. Here, too, I collect antiques, which is something I couldn't afford to do at home.

I should think, considering all that you've said, that you would approach the idea of returning to the United States with considerable misgiving.

BEENE: This is the big question: What do you do for an encore? What can you do that is going to be similarly interesting, stimulating, and exciting?

You have obviously found much to like about life in Europe. I wonder what you have found to be some of the less attractive aspects of living abroad.

BEENE: I think the main thing is that you're always playing in someone else's backyard, where you have no control. You feel as if you are always walking a tightrope, and if things get out of hand, you are inevitably going to be the loser. For example, you may be driving down the street, and if, even through no fault of your own, you happen to hit a boy on a bicycle, or something like that, you're apt to find yourself surrounded by a mob, beating your car in. It can happen just that fast. The people are emotionally volatile, and it makes no difference how well you speak the language. You are always the foreigner, always the intruder.

A story they tell here is about an American who was driving up in northern Spain, and, in passing a gypsy band on the highway, hit a child. Being a law-abiding citizen, he stopped and tried to help, but the child had been killed. The gypsies whipped out their knives, and cut him to ribbons. Killed him on the spot. Somebody else drove up and, seeing that there had been an accident, was ready to offer help, and the gypsies had at him, too. He got cut on the arm, but managed to get back in his car and drive away. He went to the next town and told the Guardia Civil about it. The Guardia Civil loaded up, went out where the gypsy band was, took every male member of the band, lined them up against the wall, and let them have it. Case closed.

Whatever the truth of that story, I have nothing but the highest regard for the Guardia Civil. This is probably the most crime-free city of its size in the world. A woman can walk from one end of Madrid to the other at three o'clock in the morning, and never have a worry. It's the same way in the provinces. I would feel perfectly safe in any remote area of Spain, unlike Mexico and Italy, for example. Most tourists confuse the Guardia Civil with the Gestapo or something of the kind, but to me, they mean protection, and I'm very glad to see them there.

Does the fact that you are living here under a dictatorship affect your life very much?

BEENE: Well, let me say that I've changed my opinion to a certain extent about this regime since living here. The Spanish press is, of course, still a joke. The absolute iron grasp of the Catholic Church is, I think, a hideous thing. There are many other aspects of this setup that I don't like at all. But as for the feeling of any kind of repression or being nervous or worried about a knock on the door in the middle of the night or anything like that, nothing could be further from my mind. A lot of people have the idea that Spaniards would be afraid to say boo about Franco, but you can go to any bar and sit around, and you'll hear plenty of criticism. A lot of people will tell you what they think about Franco. They're not living in fear. Their attitude has been explained to me by the aphorism that the devil they know is better than the one they don't know.

Speaking of the Catholic Church, you will notice that it has not been naïve enough here, as we were in the United States, to assume that you could legislate gambling, sex, and liquor out of existence. These things are always available in good Catholic countries. In this country, prostitution is more like the old courtesan days than as we know it in our part of the world. In the first place, the girls have no pimps. There is no payoff to the police. They suffer no social handicaps. They frequent the best places. They are in the Palace Hotel and Hilton Hotel bars at lunchtime and in the evening. Nobody is in the least inclined to be short with them as long as they behave themselves. They have complete freedom. They're rather a jolly sort, and apparently they enjoy their work. At least, there's no downtrodden look about them.

As for liquor, why, in this very poor country, haven't they put tremendous taxes on liquor, as all the big, prosperous nations have? This is probably the cheapest country in the world to drink in. The bartenders here have a very heavy wrist.

The liquor prices are almost incredible, especially if you come here, as I did, from England. Maybe it was because I had been living in England that I was struck by what seemed to be a lack of public manners here. There seems to be a great deal of pushing and shoving in public.

BEENE: That results from the fact that what you have here is a situation where everything is inadequate. The bus system is hopelessly overloaded. The subway is hopelessly overloaded. There has been a tremendous influx of people into the cities. They built Torremolinos, which is now a city of two hundred thousand during the height of the season, and they suddenly discovered there wasn't a gas station in town. They had one down the road a few miles, but none in town. Little things like that happen all the time. Actually, in all the time I've been here, I've never had anyone be deliberately rude to me, whereas that will happen to me in France fifteen minutes after I cross the border.

MRS. BEENE: I'm convinced that Spaniards are more polite to foreigners than they are to their own countrymen. I go into shops, and I'm invariably treated with consideration, but if a Spanish woman comes in and her dress or whatever is not ready, they will have a terrible exchange. Yet, neither one seems really offended. The customer will wind up saying, "Well, I'll be back tomorrow. Please have it ready for me then." You would have thought they were never going to speak to each other again.

BEENE: It's the same when you see two Spanish men arguing face to face. You'd swear they were coming to blows, but they never hit each other. If you hit somebody here, you're in trouble. If you land in jail, you land awfully hard. People here have a profound respect for Spanish jails.

Really, I suppose, what seems like a lack of public manners is just an expression of the anarchy in the Spanish character, which helps to make it an attractive one.

BEENE: Very much so. It gives them a wonderful freedom of spirit. The Countess of Quintanilla said in her book that it is this aspect of the Spanish character that makes everybody feel that he is somebody. I think this is good. The Spaniards may not have a hell of a lot else, but they do have pride.

> "One of the great virtues of living abroad is that you *are* a foreigner. That's the *main* thing you are. I find it a very helpful tag to wear."

Robert Cabot, of the Boston Cabots, is a former State Department official, who now devotes his time to writing, and lives with his wife and two daughters in the tiny village of Impruneta, which is about twenty minutes by car from Florence. A slender, scholarly-looking man whose manner is cordial but somewhat reserved, he was wearing rough country clothes when he greeted me late one rainy spring morning in the courtyard of Villa Guidorelli, his comfortable but unpretentious residence, situated in gently rolling countryside. He said he had just come from his writing cottage, and when I expressed an interest in seeing it, he kindly supplied me with a pair of sturdy boots and a raincoat, and we walked and slid a considerable distance into a wooded ravine, at length arriving at a secluded, one-room, austerely furnished structure, which, Mr. Cabot said, he had built mostly by himself. Returning to the villa, Mr. Cabot asked the maid to brew a pot of tea, and, after we had settled into some well-used chairs in the living room, I said that I had been told by friends of his that, unlike some Americans living in Europe, he had decided to settle there because he likes it without any qualification.

CABOT: Well, who knows? Who knows? It's a complicated mixture of reasons why I'm here, I'm sure. The simplest one is that, having suddenly decided to spend full time writing, I felt that I couldn't stay in the community where I was, which was Washington, D.C. That is a community that simply doesn't support writers. To have dropped out of government—for ten years, I had been in various parts of foreign aid, which had taken us to Rome for three years and to Thailand and then back to Washington—to have left that and taken up writing full time would have been considered pretty eccentric in Washington. And Washington—for that matter, America—does not encourage eccentricity. So, we came here. One reason we came to Florence is that we thought we'd find good schools here for our children. They are now thirteen and eleven. We've been here for four years, which is longer than we've lived anywhere else.

You said that you had "suddenly" decided to give full time to writing. Did something in particular precipitate the decision?

CABOT: It probably appeared more sudden than it actually was. I had decided to leave the government perhaps a year before I actually did so. One reason that I drew it out was that I didn't want to appear to be leaving in a fit of temper or protest, which has always struck me as an idiotic way to cancel off part of one's career. Who gives a damn, after all, if you do retire or leave in a huff? I wanted to leave gracefully, finish the job I was doing, not hurt anybody, and not make any splash. I think I succeeded in doing that.

Did you have a novel in mind that you wanted to write when you came here?

CABOT: No, I didn't have anything useful to work on when I came here. It was several months before I got started on anything. It was a kind of personal psychoanalysis, shall we say. Even when I got through with that, the book I began working on—and spent almost two years on—got discarded. Some bits of it I may be able to use in my second novel, which is about two-thirds done now. No one has read it. In fact, no one has read anything I've written, except myself. Not a soul. Maybe when I come to write the next novel, I will let others read it, but right now, I really haven't the courage.

I started this novel two years ago. It's going very slowly—on a good day, I may write perhaps four hundred and fifty words—and I get dreadful interruptions that cut out many, many days. It may be because of a trip I have to make, or the comings and goings of members of the family, or a house guest that comes for three or four days.

How do you manage this common problem of guests who drop in?

CABOT: One way is living outside of the city. We aren't even in the Florence phone book. And we're kind of rude now and then, I guess. The first year we were here, we had no telephone, and no one at all called on us. Then we decided to somewhat rejoin the human race, and put in a telephone, and then my wife went to work part-time as a librarian at I Tatti, the Berenson villa, which, as you know, Harvard is running as a center for Italian Renaissance studies. Through that, we began to expand, so I guess now we know a couple of hundred people in the Florence area, and that's enough.

What kind of social life do you have with these people?

CABOT: Florence is a very interesting town in that respect. You can select from a very broad spectrum. There is the American diplomatic community, which is not a hard-driving group but contains some interesting people. Then there is a lot of aristocracy in the Italian community that we see, partly because they're intermarried and because they speak more English. There's very little of the *dolce vita* aristocracy that you find in Rome, because most of that was created by Mussolini and the Pope and so forth. Here, you have a much older and truer, if you will, aristocracy. A good many of them are lawyers or in other professions. Beyond the aristocracy are other interesting people, such as professors at the University of Siena, some artists, and one or two writers, although the Italian writing colony here, I gather, is awfully small. They are more or less holdovers from the thirties, when Florence was a very lively literary town. We also see a lot of the peasants around here. Some of them are our best friends. I would say that the peasants in this part of Italy are the kindest and most understanding people of any social class that I have found anywhere in the world.

What kind of social relationship do you have with them?

CABOT: Well, of course, it isn't the same as if we were also peasants. The relationship would be different if for no other reason than that we are foreigners. In fact, one of the great virtues of living abroad is that you *are* a foreigner. That's the *main* thing you are. I find it a very helpful tag to wear. Anyway, because we are foreigners, the peasants find us a novelty, and we find them a novelty, too. They often invite us to a meal or to some special occasion, such as the harvest festival banquet. We try to reciprocate. For example, we usually put on a little Christmas show with our daughters and some of the peasant children around here, and we invite a group of them in. It's been very rewarding.

I used to be a very strong believer that Americans living abroad should spend more time seeing foreigners and not be so damned provincial, but I'm much more relaxed on the subject now. Hell, let's have friends wherever we can find them. Don't be too concerned about their nationalities. In our case, I think it has wound up that about half of our friends here are Italians and half are Americans and other non-Italians. I think there are something like four hundred Americans in Florence, other than students, people passing through, and Italo-Americans. There are probably several thousand of the last—Italians who hold American passports, and have come back here to retire or for some other reason. Of the four hundred resident Americans, I suppose we know maybe a hundred or a hundred and fifty. But the social life does not encroach. Life here is more regulatable than any other place I've lived. I have now stabilized my existence so that I go into town only one morning a week—on Tuesdays. Here, you can run at your own speed.

How did you happen to pick Florence rather than, say, Rome or Paris or London?

CABOT: Well, Rome we deliberately didn't pick, because we'd lived there before. I didn't want to go back and relive the same life, move into the same ruts. A lot of people do that, especially diplomats who have retired there, because they liked it so much, and perhaps have found other jobs. It is a somewhat pathetic existence, I think. Also, Rome, even four years ago, was becoming an almost impossible place to live, as far as I'm concerned. It's just too damned crowded. Too much traffic. Too much noise. Too unmanageably big.

When you decided to leave America, had you made up your mind to live somewhere in Italy?

CABOT: Oh, we had thought about the Pacific islands and Japan and England and France and all of the other places that cross one's mind when he leaves his own country. But having lived in Italy and having loved it simply as a country, knowing Italian, and thinking quite seriously about the school problem—all of these things made us settle in Italy. And within Italy, having decided against Rome, Florence seemed the most likely alternative. Milan is a pretty dreadful place, Venice is a bit too special, I've always thought—a bit too isolated, too ivory tower. Verona might have been a good place. It is a lovely city, interesting, and quite active. If one doesn't want to hide away in a little fishing town or something like that but requires a city that gives you a certain amount of life, I think that Florence is a fairly logical choice. And I think other people are beginning to realize this, too. Of course, Florence has traditionally provided a romantic background for artists and writers, particularly in the nineteenth century, although, actually, Florence isn't particularly romantic. It's a very austere, almost dreary town, as you find when you wander the streets and look at it closely. I think people came to realize that by the beginning of this century, and that may have accounted for the very sharp drop in the foreign colony. However, just recently, there seems to be developing a new nucleus of Left Bankism in Florence. I can see why. Florence is not as much of a tumult as Paris or Rome. It's more containable, more understandable, less stereotyped.

You said earlier that one of the reasons you came here was the promise of good schools for the children. How has that worked out?

CABOT: Well, the situation is not entirely happy. They are both in Italian schools. They are certainly learning more than they would have in the schools they would have been attending in Washington, and they are probably enjoying the learning process more than they would have in the States. On the other hand, they're not enjoying friendships in anywhere near the number they would have in Washington. I think that is partly because life in Italy is based more firmly on the family than it is in America, and connections outside of the family are generally not very close or important. Here, children always go back into their family when they get out of school rather than racing around to the homes of school friends, as they do in the States, and this makes friendships harder to start. I would like our children to have a lot of friends, but on the other hand, that can be very distracting, and the friends that one has at that age don't last very long.

Have you considered sending the children to boarding schools where they would probably have a better chance of making friends?

CABOT: Well, yes. When we came to Florence, we put them both into a so-called *collegio*, which means a state-run boarding school. They were day students, however. They were there for a couple of years, and then we took one of them out, because the class she was in was below par. The students were bad, and the teacher was impertinent. Furthermore, the boarding school, for which you pay tuition, attracts almost exclusively children of the Florentine *nouveau riche.* Some aristocracy, but not very much. The parents of these boarding school children became so damned boring. They all go to the same parties, the same place to ski, the same place for summer, and they all have the same tastes. That became awfully annoying, and was another reason to take that daughter out and put her in an ordinary public school. There, unfortunately, she has the same problem of being in a rather monotonous, mono-color group. This time, her classmates are the children of artisans and small shopkeepers. But the children are really nicer, and they're politer, too, and harder-working.

Do your daughters talk much about wishing they were back in Washington?

CABOT: Some. They still think of themselves as Americans, and their closest friends, they *think*, are the ones they knew four years ago. They would realize that isn't true if they were to see those friends. There's a considerable amount of nostalgia still in their lives, which is pretty sad, but I think it is probably more than offset by other things.

Is there any nostalgia still in your life and in your wife's?

CABOT: Oh, sure. Sure, there's nostalgia. In fact, we're going back to the States this summer, mostly for the children, but I guess also for ourselves, to some extent. We'll be there for two months, seeing family and old friends. Most of the time we'll be in Martha's Vineyard, which is where most of our Washington friends go for the summer.

That will be the first trip back in four years?

CABOT: The first for me. My wife and children went back two years ago for part of the summer. I'm not sure that living abroad is desirable, living away from one's home community, breaking one's roots, *if* one had a home community, a genuine one, and had genuine roots. But I don't think most of us do.

I have always been under the impression that you and your family had roots in Boston.

CABOT: Well, sure, there's a family there, but I made that decision twenty years ago—not to be in that community. Having broken from the original family community—and it was against my will in a certain sense, although perhaps I was a little more deliberate and cold-blooded in making the break than most people—it didn't seem to me to make much difference whether one lived in Washington or Tokyo or Florence or any other place.

When you decided not to be in the family community, did you move away? Or how did you break the ties?

CABOT: I don't think it's necessarily physical. I think it's more of a psychological break. I think it's an expression of dissatisfaction—this overworked word, "alienation"—that compels one to break. Additionally, when you consider what a writer has to do, it seems to me that a break is essential. A writer can't be part of his community. He has to be a refugee, has to be a displaced person, psychologically if not geographically.

That is another reason for living abroad. When you live outside of your own country, you are, first of all, accepted or rejected as a foreigner. Everything else about you is subordinated. This business of nationality is a shield in a sense—something that you can hide behind.

Being a foreigner also immediately gives you an individuality that you don't have to fight for. Of course, you miss a lot, and I'm not sure that in an ideal world one should move away. You miss the tradition. You miss the community. You miss the family. You may miss inspiration. But I don't think that one in my particular situation can live at home. In a psychological sense, I don't think I have any home. I can't think of any alternative, for me, to living right here.

And yet you have some doubt about the desirability of living abroad.

CABOT: I meant that in a sociological and historical sense rather than applying it to my own personal case or to this particular moment in history. Van Wyck Brooks wrote a very good book, *Dream of Arcadia,* about the American artists and writers who came to live in Italy in the nineteenth century. I think, as he points out, that they found a kind of romance and permanency in Italy that they didn't find in America. I am sure that this was also an element in our own decision to leave the States and come here. I mean, there is no question but what there was a certain romantic aspect involved. Although I knew Italy pretty well and realized that it was going to hell awfully fast, even before we came here, I still had the hope that it had much further to go than America before it went completely to hell. One could borrow on its romantic past for at least a few more years. Also, one might live—what shall we say?—more pleasantly, more romantically, perhaps more comfortably, perhaps more cheaply. And all of this has proved true. Very much so.

Did you buy this property, or do you rent it?

CABOT: We rent. We would kind of like to buy it, but the owner, who is a professor of optical engineering at the University of Florence, won't sell. It's bigger than we need. We have closed off two rooms as well as a chapel. When we moved in, the rent was sixty dollars a month. We now pay about eighty. But it has no central heating, it had only rudimentary lighting, so we had to modernize that, and the furnishings were terrible. We had to begin to accumulate our own furniture. We found the chairs in the dining room in a little mountain community up in the Apennines. They were all handmade by an eighty-year-old man, and they cost a dollar and ten cents apiece. We went to an antique factory for a good many of the other things, and that is a lot of fun. It isn't quite as phony as it sounds, because the pieces may be real antiques, but a leg may be missing or a panel rotted away. These parts are replaced in the factory. For example, the side-piece in the dining room is a real antique, except that the base is new. In New York, you'd probably pay fifteen hundred dollars for that, whereas we paid about a hundred and twenty. That was four years ago. These factories are being discovered now. In fact, the last time we were at the one we generally go to, we saw a New York buyer there. Disconcerting.

Now that you have the place furnished and quite modernized, do you plan to stay on more or less indefinitely?

CABOT: I guess so. We still own a house in Washington. Ironically, it's the most secure and probably the most beautiful place we have ever found, and yet there it is, in Washington. We lived in it for four months after we built it. In fact, before we broke ground, we knew we were coming here. We did it anyhow. Why? I don't know. Maybe it was just lack of courage. I stayed on leave of absence from the government for more than a year, and I suppose the house in Washington is a kind of leave of absence, too. It's an anchor back there, if I want to pull in on it. It's on the Potomac—an area called Bull's Neck. There are eight of us in a group that owns one side of the river—some sixty acres. The property is twenty minutes from the heart of Washington, and yet it has every aspect of real wilderness. It still has deer on it. You can look down on the river and expect to see Daniel Boone paddling up in his canoe. Behind it are some of the worst aspects of America—thousands of acres of housing developments, highways, airfields, shopping centers—chewing up that north Virginia countryside in a most appalling way. In ten years, it will be an almost unbelievable contrast to go through all of that and come onto our little enclave. Of course, it should be a national park or a national monument or something. It's just too good to be in private hands. In fact, I don't believe in property ownership at all. This is just too unfair, too undemocratic.

When you came to Italy, you said you had decided to settle in Florence. How did you find this particular villa?

CABOT: By driving around and asking the peasants if they knew of any place that was empty. It was a considerable task. I suppose that one common problem about choosing to live in a foreign country is that you have to count on a tremendous loss of time and energy in finding a place to live. It really took at least six or eight months before I felt that domestic problems were making no more than a normal demand on my time.

When I wasn't involved with those problems, I worked on the writing, but the first year was generally unsatisfactory. I got very little done—only about thirty or forty pages—that whole winter. It's only been this last year that I've been able to see the end of the book I'm working on. It's a pretty strange book, really. I don't have any proper names in the novel at all, either people or places. In fact, there is no *stated* locale. I have characters, but they appear and disappear without one's being quite sure where or how. It's a fantasy, too. I'm afraid it's going to be almost unpublishable.

Can you keep on writing if you don't publish?

CABOT: Yes. Theoretically, I could. Puts me in a really unique situation.

This summer, as you've mentioned, you'll be spending in the United States. Normally, do you spend the summers here, or do you travel?

CABOT: Normally, we spend our summers on an island called Giglio, in the Mediterranean. It's a small, rather primitive island south of Elba, and is only just being discovered by tourism. We are, fortunately, on the non-touristic side, so, for the time being, it's all right. There's a daily ferry to the island, and after that we take a bus to the other side, and then walk about ten minutes. What we have there is a tiny, two-room hut with an attic, where our daughters sleep, and it sits on a cliff, high above the sea. Beautiful place. The tourists have come in now, and prices all over the island have gone way up, but we never wanted to buy, in any case. We have a very friendly permanent renting relationship with the peasants who own the little place. In fact, we are the godparents of one of their children.

Really, I can spend one day on that little island, and go out to our little orchard and pick a bunch of grapes and enjoy that magnificent view, and find justification for all kinds of hardships and all kinds of dislocation. It really is an extraordinarily complete pleasure. You have to work for it. It's a terrible battle to achieve it.

Work for it in what sense?

CABOT: Just to find it. It isn't there for the asking. Not everyone can do it. The obvious example of one who can't is the poor bastard of a tourist who comes over here on a bus tour, and is shuttled from one cockroach den to another, and never sees anything in a foreign language or has any relationship to the country, really. Of course, it has become increasingly difficult for anyone to find Italy under its veneer of Americanization. Fifty years ago, it could have been found with ease and pleasure. Perhaps that's why the dream of Arcadia was a fairly realistic and fruitful dream then, and probably isn't now, unless you're ready to really work for it. As for ourselves, I think we've been able to realize the dream, even if only temporarily and in a rather abbreviated and, shall we say, somewhat embittered form.

GALLERY NOTES

One of the major attractions of the Ameropean way of life, I was told again and again by those who have chosen it, is that an American can live better on the same amount of money in most places in Europe than he can in the United States. Of course, tourists and commercial travelers do not find this to be so, nor do the Ameropeans who insist on trying to duplicate all the conveniences of American life. Even those who accommodate to European standards do not enjoy the "celestial cheapness" that Henry James ascribed to life in Italy during an earlier day. However, despite the fact that prices have gone up steeply everywhere in Europe during the past decade, and are still going up, the relative cheapness of living there vis-à-vis the United States is still a fact.

While the economic factor means little or nothing to a few wealthy Ameropeans, it was a compelling reason that many others, particularly those in creative fields, decided to live abroad. Among the latter is James Metcalf, an artist and sculptor who was born in New York, and served during the Second World War in Italy, where he was wounded, losing several fingers on his left hand. "I have an 85 percent disability, and actually, that is one of the reasons I could be an artist," he told me. "The pension gave me the freedom to study and continue my development. After the war, I decided to go live in Majorca. My pension was then about a hundred and fifty dollars a month, and in Majorca, back in those years, you could live like a king on that. Also, Robert Graves, the British poet and classicist, lived there, and I wanted to do some work with him." (Incidentally, economics had been one of the two most important reasons that Graves himself had settled in Majorca. "I chose Majorca as my home, a quarter of a century ago," he wrote in 1958, "because its climate had the reputation of being better than any other in Europe. And because I was assured, correctly it proved, that I should be able to live there on a quarter of the income needed in England.") After some three years in Majorca, Metcalf moved to

Paris. I met him there, and we talked about a number of things, including the cost of living abroad. I mentioned that I had recently read the results of a United Nations survey, which showed that it costs slightly more to live in Paris than in New York. "What that doesn't take into account," Mr. Metcalf said, "is that here one can live according to a lower standard of living and be satisfied with it. The area we live in is anything but fashionable, and our apartment is comfortable but very plain. If you lived in its counterpart nearly anywhere in America, you would be regarded as a very strange character. But those things don't matter here. It isn't necessary to maintain a high standard of living for status reasons."

The same situation exists in Italy, according to Robert Schneider, a former professor of romance languages at City College in New York, who left that post to move with his wife and family to Rome, where he is the proprietor of a prosperous art gallery. "When you compare the cost of living here with the cost of living in New York," Mr. Schneider said, "the important thing to remember is that here you may live on a lower scale, with a modest apartment and so on, and yet be in a high enough social category. In the States, I think, if you don't keep up with the Joneses, you almost have to fall below. As a college professor and with growing children whom I wanted to educate properly, I did not earn a salary that permitted me to rise to the level that I was able to reach here on the same income. And that is to say nothing of the domestic service that we are able to have here and that allows my wife so much more freedom than she ever had before."

The unimportance of keeping up with the Joneses as far as housing is concerned was also remarked by Henry Ketcham, the popular and affable cartoonist, who has lived in Geneva for almost a decade. "People who are going to be here for a long time usually try to find something to buy," he said. "We tried, but anything we looked at that had any charm started at well over a hundred thousand dollars, and that would be for a place that you would pay about forty thousand dollars for in the United States. Most people probably wind up doing what we have done, which is to rent an apartment that is very pleasant but not as large or fancy as one that we would rent in the States. I think it is generally true that the Americans living here live comfortably but not at all extravagantly, and they are somewhat relieved that they can simplify their living. No one is expected to have much of a lavish setup, so there are very few showcases here. You're just supposed to have something that's comfortable and reflects your taste. You see, you don't have the stigma of status here. I wouldn't say that it is non-existent. I don't think that status is non-existent whenever you have three people in a room. I think the status symbols here are different. I would say that one of them would be freedom of time. Also freedom to travel. To know the most interesting people in the area—not the most chic but the most interesting. Perhaps to have a chalet in Gstaad or San Moritz or Chamonix. Occasional shooting trips into Austria or Spain. Golfing in Scotland. You can do these things with ease by spending the same amount of time and covering the same distance as you would, say, in going from New York to Miami."

Furthermore, you can probably do them more cheaply, I was told by James Nolan, an Ameropean who has private means but generally holds down a job, usually in some branch of public relations. "Europe is a great deal more expensive than when I came here, in 1948," he said, "but, assuming that you declare your income and pay your taxes, what you have left still seems to go further in Europe than in America, and it seems to me that there's more comfort in Europe. Here, you are nearer the amenities of life. It may not necessarily be true, but it seems to me that it's easier to charter a yacht out of Nice or the Italian Riviera than it is in Florida or California. Besides, you can probably get your yacht a little bit cheaper here. When you live here, it's certainly easier to go skiing. And golf is much more available. Your chances of getting on an uncrowded golf course are better in Europe than in most places in the States, though there are far fewer golf courses here. England, of course, is a golfing paradise. I am now a member of the Royal Berkshire Course, which is a marvelous one. I pay twelve dollars a year in dues as an out-of-the-country member. Even if I lived in England, I'd pay only a hundred dollars a year. In America, a golf course that could be compared with it would cost a thousand dollars a year, at the very least."

While shelter, along with golf club dues and other items that make up the cost of living, is generally cheaper in Europe than in America, it can present quite as many problems, as I learned from Guy Murchie, a former airline navigator and author of *Song of the Sky* and other books. He and his wife moved to Europe in 1955, and embarked on a house-hunting tour that took them through Denmark, Holland, Germany, Switzerland, France, Italy, Portugal, and Spain. "Finding a place to live is quite a nuisance over here," he said, "mainly because there are no real estate agents as we know them at home. There, of course, they take you out to lunch and show you all kinds of places, and they usually have pretty good information about what they show. In Austria or Germany or Switzerland or just about anywhere else on the Continent, you find people who call themselves agents, but about all they know about a place is a brief description that the owner has given them over the telephone or by letter. The agents never seem to go around themselves to see the house. I think their commission is only about 2 per cent, so they don't work too hard, and they'll send you out on one wild goose chase after another. It may take you half a day to find a place that the agent can't direct you to because he's never been there, and when you locate it, you find it was rented or sold four months earlier. The agent hasn't heard the news. After that happens three or four times, it gets discouraging. There are a few other wrinkles. In northern Austria, we found a house we both liked—a kind of chalet that looked very comfortable. Just about the time we were ready to close the deal, the owner said, "I don't know whether we told you that there's a grandmother's clause that goes with this house." Looking into that, we discovered that it's quite common in Austria for a family that has a grandmother or some other elderly relative whom they need to take care of to build a house with the provision that one or two rooms, usually the best ones, belong to her as long as she lives. She buys her own food and takes care of her quarters, but they are hers for life. It's their system of Social Security, I guess. We backed out of that deal. We didn't have anything against the old lady, but we figured maybe the family did, since they were getting rid of her."

At length, Mr. Murchie and his wife decided to settle in Spain, their choice being influenced mainly by the climate and the cheapness of living, and in Malaga, on the southern coast, they found an apartment to their liking. The rent was twenty dollars a month. "It had three very large rooms in addition to a kitchen and a bathroom," Mr. Murchie said. "Of course, it was all pretty primitive—no bathtub, no hot water system. The kitchen had city gas, but not much else. No refrigerator and only a tiny sink. However, we got an ice box, put screens on the windows, and generally fixed the place up. It wasn't bad at all. We stayed there for four years." After that, they bought a house of their own in Malaga, for which they paid five thousand dollars. They have since spent an additional ten thousand dollars on improving and enlarging it. The real estate tax on this property comes to about twenty dollars a year.

Another writer, Richard Condon, has also made a rather thorough investigation of the housing situation in Europe, though on a higher financial level. When I talked with him, he was living with his wife (their two daughters are married) in a ten-room furnished house, about three miles from Geneva, which rents for just under five hundred dollars a month. "We've been looking for the past five years for the ideal place, and there is no such thing," Mr. Condon said. "If the climate is good, there is something wrong with the food, and if the food is good, there is something wrong with the people. We've looked in France, England, Spain, Greece, Italy, and Portugal, not to mention Switzerland. The climate in Portugal is wonderful, and we went a considerable distance toward settling there. In fact, we had put down twenty-four hundred dollars on a piece of property, and hired lawyers and architects, but we had to cancel it. We had intended to build a Portuguese country-style house, as required by law of foreigners, but then we discovered that the natives are allowed to build their version of hot-dog stands and other freakish commercial structures among these lovely houses. It seemed silly to put your life savings into a house under those circumstances, so we came back and started looking here again.

"Within two weeks after our return, we saw an ad in the Geneva newspaper for a piece of property almost an acre in size and located forty miles from Geneva and twenty from Lausanne. We went to look at the property, which is in the Commune of Yens—it sounds like something named by Sigmund Freud—and found it was a piece of high land situated in rolling farm country. It has a marvelous, forty-five-mile, panoramic view of the entire lake, with Geneva at one end and Lausanne at the other. In front are the French Alps and behind are the Jura Mountains. A man who lives in the vicinity is a geopolitician at Lausanne University, and he estimates it will be two hundred and thirty years before the population explosion begins to affect this area.

"Anyway, we bought the land, for which we paid eighteen thousand dollars—land in this area probably costs as much as it does anywhere in Europe—and engaged a local architect. This is important, because he knows where to get the labor force, and is aware of all the local regulations and conditions. In our case, he also turned out to be a marvelous architect. The plans for the house are finished. It will be built on three levels, have ten rooms, three terraces, steam room, garage, wine caves, and what the architect calls the archives—a file room where I can keep my papers. The house will cost about a hundred thousand dollars, which is more than it would cost to build in the United States. One reason is that Switzerland doesn't produce all the building materials required, so there is an import duty on a great many things used in the construction. Also, there is practically no native labor force, aside from stone masons, and so the hod-carriers and other laborers are imported and expensive. As for taxes, since this is farm land, you pay a land tax, which doesn't come to more than a hundred dollars, when you purchase it, and that's it. You don't pay that again. You do pay an annual water tax, but that is very low. All the taxes for the entire year are somewhere around fifty-five dollars. If, by any chance, we should decide that we wanted to sell the house, we could, of course, and we could sell it at a considerably appreciated rate. An old-fashioned house, situated not far from us and about the same size as ours and with the same amount of property, was sold recently for a hundred and seventy-five thousand dollars. So, our place is a fine investment. Furthermore, I'd rather look at the view from any one of our terraces than at a bunch of stock certificates."

> "That romantic nineteenth-century cliché that one can be poor but happy turns out to be quite true."

Frederick S. Wildman, Jr., a bright, ebullient, gregarious man in his late thirties with a rather boyish look despite his heavy black mustache, made his first trip to Europe at age six, when he accompanied his father, a New York wine importer, on a business trip to France. The younger Wildman subsequently made numerous other visits abroad, attended Le Rosey, an exclusive preparatory school in Switzerland, and, after finishing college (St. John's, in Annapolis) and doing his Army service, went back to Europe to live. The move was prompted not alone by the cheapness of living there, but, since he had decided to eschew the family business in favor of pursuing a writing career, the economic consideration was by no means unimportant. He now lives with his second wife, an attractive Swedish woman, in a large, comfortable villa in Churriana, a quiet Spanish village a few miles from Torremolinos, which was once a fishing village of great charm, but, as Mr. Wildman remarked when I called on him, has now been quite effectively spoiled.

WILDMAN: The whole tenor of this area has radically changed since I've lived here. It was much more amusing in the bad old days. The baroque characters who used to collect here a few years ago have moved away, and crassness and commercialism have taken over. It seems to happen to all good places. They start out as artist colonies, because artists look for the best, the cheapest, and the warmest, and they also have a good eye. They are followed by millionaires with good taste, who like that sort of semi-eccentric life. They, in turn, are followed by millionaires with bad taste. The millionaires with bad taste are followed by the bourgeoisie, who want to rub shoulders with the millionaires and princelings. And they're followed by everybody. It's extraordinary, because this whole coast has gone through that pattern in two years. It's like looking at a kaleidoscope—things are being shaken up so quickly and changing so much.

All of this is progress, as they say. It's true that the post office works better, but this part of the country is becoming sort of the Atlantic City of Spain. However, if you live back from the sea, as we do, you can get away from it. Move back a few kilometers into the country, and you can have the world of the twentieth century and the world of the sixteenth century at the same time. And I must say I do love Spain. I think the lower classes of Spain are the most elegant, the most noble, the most polite, the most gracious people that I've run across in my life. Of course, they also have a tremendous inner dignity.

The first thing that ever happened to me in Spain was so shocking that it taught me an immediate lesson. I came to Spain for the first time in 1950, during a summer vacation from college. I was making a little tour around in a car. At that time, Spain was like a concentration camp. First, there had been their Civil War. After that came what amounted to a blockade imposed by the United Nations, which was pyramided on top of an extremely impoverished country, pyramided on top of a terrible drought. Conditions were inconceivable compared with what they are now. Nothing but dirt roads, broken up by gulleys and full of potholes. There were no gasoline stations as such. You were given a card that told in what towns you could find gasoline, and you had to look around for the places where they ladled it out—usually, right out of a fifty-gallon drum.

It took me eighteen hours to cross the border, because in those days xenophobia was running rampant here, and if you were a foreigner, they were going to reciprocate, no matter who you were. When I finally got across the border, I wanted to get something to eat before starting the drive. There was a restaurant in town that was supposed to be more or less for tourists, so I parked the car and asked a man on the street if he knew where this restaurant was located. He said that he did and, moreover, that he would take me there. Off we trotted. It turned out to be a long walk—about a kilometer. I was extremely embarrassed. This man was really emaciated, and he had no shoes. Practically nobody had shoes then. He was, as a matter of fact, in tatters. Well, when we reached the restaurant, I said, "Here, let me give you something for your kindness," and reached in my pocket. He looked at me for a second with complete contempt. Not exactly contempt, but with that look you see in Goya, where they stiffen the shoulders, and he asked me if I would like to have a drink. I said I would very much, so we went into a bar. He asked me what I wanted. I said, "*Vino blanco.*"

And he had *vino blanco*. Then he put down—in those days, a glass of wine was something like twenty-five centimos—he put down what must have been his last half peseta, we drank the wine, he wished me luck, and left. That doesn't happen in many countries.

Four years later, I came back again. At that time, there was an old American admiral whom I had known in Annapolis living in Madrid, and he asked me to come there and help him on a project. So, I went and lived for about six months in Madrid, which I loved. Madrid is a very easy city to live in. I loved the whole aspect, and after I got back to America again, I always wanted to come back here.

The urge to return became stronger during those years of the good, amiable Dwight D. Eisenhower, when there was a kind of ossification of every kind of process that adds vitality or thought to a country. Really, that kind of sanctimonious smog that spread over the whole countryside was pretty unbearable. It was smugness raised almost to a religion. I simply couldn't stand it after a while. There was, I suppose, a faint element of rebellion, but I think, by and large, people leave their environment because they get fed up with being judged by it. If one doesn't want to put up with a lot of petty criticism or have to think about doing things in a certain accepted way, one simply leaves that environment for another in which he can concentrate on what he wants to do.

In any event, I have been living here, in this environment, since 1960. Before that, I had been in England, where I worked in the British Museum on a book I was preparing about the Spanish Armada. Then I went to France and did some research there. I was married to an English girl at that point, and since the English and the French don't get along at all, she couldn't stand it. She went home for Christmas to see mother, and that was that. I went back to England, thinking that she would trot along behind me back to France, but lo and behold, she stayed. Well, that left me psychologically pretty well shaken up. I returned to France, and stayed there for about three months, and then I just had to get out. Bayard Osborn, who is a sculptor and an old friend, has a house down here, and he invited me to come for a visit. As many people do, I came intending to stay three or four weeks, and here I am.

I think one reason that people come here—and stay on—is simply that Spain is so incredibly cheap. I lived here for three years on what, by American standards, would be a poverty income. One year, it amounted to only fifteen hundred dollars, which the two of us lived on in a little town here. Of course, we didn't live like this, but we didn't suffer, either. The extraordinary emphasis that is put on physical comfort in America seems to me to be almost completely superfluous. One doesn't need central heating, really, except in the northern part of America. One thing that annoys me in a minor way is that time, light, heat, and season have been erased almost entirely in every twentieth-century country. The strawberries are there all year round. Winter and summer can hardly be differentiated unless you go outside. There's electric light, so night becomes as clear as day. I enjoyed living in a house that didn't have electricity, and so we had pools of light that could change the tone entirely. I learned that one can live happily on very, very little. It's curious, but that romantic nineteenth-century cliché that one can be poor but happy turns out to be quite true.

You're obviously not living on a poverty income now. Do you have to earn all the money it takes you to live?

WILDMAN: I have had to, but not as of now. I now have an outside income of three thousand dollars a year, which isn't enormous, but it keeps things going. On top of that is the income I earn from writing, mainly about wine. Last year, my income was eleven thousand dollars, which, in Spain, is the equivalent of thirty thousand. Actually, we can live comfortably on six. We rent this house furnished, and we have two maids. A lovely little patio. The sea is a kilometer and a half away, and there's a little swimming pool, too.

It might be difficult for some people to find anything wrong with this picture.

WILDMAN: Boredom. To a very large extent, of course, boredom is inner, but finally one has to be triggered off. I think that almost all of the things that people create are essentially reactions to situations which are presented to them. When the situations get to be the same, one begins to stultify, unless one has a Kafka-like mind, which I don't. I need something in which I can create a response, both formally and informally. You get it through the theater and movies, and you get it through conversations in bars and that sort of thing. Here, the situations tend to become repetitive. You form your own tight little incestuous knot—maybe fifteen or twenty people to whom you talk. Everybody knows what the other person is going to say well ahead of time, because everyone knows what everyone else's reactions are going to be. The group gets too inbred, and as a result, the whole social fabric gets weaker.

It's true that people do work here, but I think it's much easier to work in a city, because, in the first place, the city imposes its own sense of discipline upon you. A city does certain things at certain hours and certain things at other hours, and you're left alone during those times. Here, everybody operates on his own time. Almost everybody visits when he damn well pleases, and that's a disaster. I have a kind of desire, I guess, to be liked, which causes me to exude bonhomie, and also, any excuse will get me away from what I'm doing. I enjoy it, but I think to myself as it happens, "Oh God, I'm going to be involved in this for a week before I get back on the track again." That's rather menacing. This place isn't isolated enough. I think the best arrangement would be to spend six months in a place like this and six months in a major city over here.

It's no mistake that Athens, with forty thousand people, had all the action. It wasn't going on in Thebes, and it wasn't going on in Corinth. And it's no mistake that in Elizabethan England that just about everybody was in London instead of being in Norwich or Exeter. There is something to be gained by being where things are going on. There is that reciprocal triggering effect. In cities, there are electrical moments that you can feel in the atmosphere. When one goes out of the city, the atmosphere becomes bosky and bovine, and one becomes provincial. As you can see, I'm garrulous, and I like the sort of thing you find only in cities.

That's one of the reasons I'm looking forward to going back to New York in a few months for a visit. I haven't been back for five years, but I never think of myself as being permanently away, although I'm not sure what "permanently away" is. When I'm over there, I think about coming back here. I feel just as much at home here as I do in America. Mass communications have so moved everybody together, and so many things now run right across national boundaries and attitudes, that the experience of living in Europe is no longer the same sort of thing by any means as it was for somebody who came over in 1910, for example. I rather regret it, because I think one thing that makes Europe so agreeable is its variousness, which is rather lacking in America. The foreignness is certainly wearing off here, but it's not all gone yet, thank God.

"The way we live in Madrid would cost
me about a hundred thousand dollars
a year to duplicate in New York."

Anthony T. Paget, Jr., a tall, robust, black-haired, well-tailored man in his early forties, with an outgoing nature and unalloyed Irish ancestry, received his primary education at parochial schools in New York City, and then attended Duke University on a basketball scholarship. During the Second World War, he served for four and a half years in the Army, and was wounded three times, most seriously when his left arm was pierced by shrapnel in southern France. "I was very happy about the whole thing, because I knew this was the good one that was going to get me home," he told me. "Instead, I wound up a prisoner in a German hospital. At first, I had been turned over to the French and put in a hospital for tubercular women. I was out most of the time. When I did wake up, the two male attendants in the hospital were always carrying me up and down the stairs and from one room to another because the Germans were looking for me. I'd be lying there, and all these women patients would run over and give me a great big kiss. Of course, when you're young, you don't know how to take advantage of those things. Then I developed gangrene, and since they had no doctors there, they decided to turn me over to the Germans. I'll always remember the nurse who arranged it—a great big Alsace-Lorraine woman by the name of Koch. She was tremendous. They put me in a donkey cart, and she started walking down between the French lines and the German lines, holding the donkey by the bridle with one hand and with the other, waving a white flag with a Red Cross on it. The shelling is going on, and I'm going out of my mind. It's like a bit out of a World War I movie. She led the donkey down the side of the hill into the town, where the Germans were. They took me in and operated right away—amputated my arm, and saved my life."

After the war, Mr. Paget settled in New York City, started working as an advertising space salesman, married a girl he had grown up with, and began raising a family. The story of how he happened to leave New York and start a new life with his family in Europe he recounted one afternoon in his apartment in Madrid.

PAGET: Everybody knows the life of a space salesman in New York. You might be making a lot of money, but you never wound up with any. You wound up borrowing money. I was drinking more than I was supposed to, like everybody else, and being very funny around P. J. Clarke's and other saloons. I was working for Ziff-Davis, and I had a contract, but we agreed to disagree. That was only about three months after the contract had been signed, so I had to be paid off for nine months. For the first time in my life, I ended up with a lot of money in my hand. I said to my wife, Therese, "We'll just pick up and take a good, long vacation in Europe." We had five kids. The oldest was five and a half. The youngest was seven months. My wife thought I was crazy. We're both from the same town on Long Island

—Douglaston. Her father was a very famous composer—James Hanley. He wrote "Back Home in Indiana," "Rose of Washington Square," "Zing Go the Strings of My Heart," and a lot of Ziegfeld. Therese said, "You're out of your mind." I said, "Well, *I'm* going for a year." That helped to settle the matter. We got out of the States within three weeks.

I had decided to come to Spain. The reason for picking Spain was that it was the cheapest place to live. Also, they had nice beaches and a temperate climate. We both like the beach, and we thought it would be great for the kids. We didn't come direct, though, because I thought I'd make a better deal by coming over on a Holland-American line one-class ship and then taking the train down from Holland. You see, the kids wouldn't pay any fare on the train. That's the way we did it.

The ship took nine days to Rotterdam. Had a wonderful time coming over. Then, the day before we landed, four of the kids came down with chicken pox. Tony, the oldest, had already had it, and nothing had happened to the other children then. Now, all except Tony came down with it. There was a German woman on the ship who noticed it first. She kept saying, "Those children look funny." She kept her little kid away as far as she could. When I saw the kids blossom with the chicken pox, I looked at the back of the contract that you sign on the ship, and it said that if the ship is held in quarantine or anything else like that, you will be held responsible for any monetary expenses. I figured we couldn't possibly run the risk of having that happen, so we got them all dressed up in their winter clothes. It was the twenty-ninth of May, a very hot day, and everybody is looking at us very oddly as we go through customs. The kids have got hoods on and all that. They're all saying, "I'm hot, daddy." And we're saying, "Stop scratching. Get down that gangplank." We got them all off, and then on the dock we ran into that German woman. She took one look, and said, "I told you so."

In Rotterdam, we found a friendly cab driver, who took us to a nice small hotel, and we put the children to bed. I hadn't planned to stay in Rotterdam, so, of course, I had no guilders. In fact, except for just enough francs to see us through one night in Paris, all I had was Spanish money. The reason was that back in those days—1958—there was a tremendous gray-black market in pesetas in Spain and in Tangier and in New York. At least, that's what somebody told me in New York, and advised me to put all my money into pesetas before coming over, which I did. I brought enough money to last for three months. Once we got to Spain, we'd be living in clover. Every month, I would receive my pension check, which came to a hundred and eighty-three dollars a month then—it's about three hundred a month now, and I have it sent to my mother—and so we would have no problems for a year. Then we would go back, and I would go to work again on Madison Avenue. That was the plan.

After putting the children to bed in Rotterdam and calling a doctor, the first thing I had to do was change some pesetas into guilders. The pesetas were very soft, and the guilders were very hard, so I lost 50 per cent on that transaction. The doctor said all the children needed was rest. We decided it would be more interesting to stay in Paris while they were getting over the chicken pox, so we packed up all our gear and went down to the railroad station. For five children and ourselves we had three steamer trunks, a couple of camp trunks, and a few bags. I assumed that the baggage would go all the way on my railroad ticket. No, sir. I had to pay extra for each piece, so I had to change some more pesetas, and lose 50 per cent again.

I remember sitting on this big deluxe train that runs between Rotterdam and Paris—one of those EET trains. Individual chairs. Great food. I thought this was wonderful in comparison to the Long Island Rail Road or anything like that. Everybody sits down and puts a napkin under his chin, and he's got the bottle of wine and the big meal laid out, and all of a sudden he looks up and sees one of my children scratching like a monkey. And we're whispering in a loud voice, "Stop scratching. Stop scratching. You'll ruin their meal."

We stayed in Paris for three days, and then took the night train to Biarritz, arriving there the next morning. You have to change to a Spanish train at Biarritz, so everything gets unloaded and moved. Every time I turn around, I'm handing out money. I can't figure out the language, so I'm just holding out my hand, and they're helping themselves. I know I'm being robbed, but what can I do?

On the train coming down from Paris we had booked second class. There's no reason to go first class on a French train, because second class is impeccable. Now we get on this Spanish train with our second-class tickets, and this is my introduction to Spain. Well, no second-class seats on Spanish trains, we discover. They ask if we want first class. My back went up. The money's being spent like water, and I say, "I'll take third class." So we all pile into third class. It's something. Wooden seats, and like riding in a truck after being in a limousine. The children are over their chicken pox. That is, they've stopped scratching, but their faces look horrible. It's been pretty rugged for them, and here they are now in this Spanish train, and it was hot. Oh, my God, was it hot. However, there weren't many people when we pulled out of Biarritz, and we had all this space to ourselves. I figured, "This isn't too bad. Awfully hot, but we'll just have to bear with it."

Then the train stops at Hendaye and Irun, and a lot of people get on. At San Sebastian, a whole crowd of people get on, and this time they get on with chickens and goats and you name it. They're all crowding in, and every time the train stops, more keep pushing in, and meanwhile the heat's beating down worse and worse, and I'm thinking, "Oh, my God, what have I got myself into? And I can't even speak the language." Finally, I said to Therese, "I'll go up to first class and fix it for us to move up there. I'll pay the difference." The aisles have filled up with people standing there with their livestock and so on, and it takes me hours, it seems, to get through all the third-class coaches up to first class. I found the conductor, and with sign language and my tickets and so on, I got it across that I wanted first class for my wife and five children and myself. I got it all arranged, and started to plow my way back.

Meantime, the third-class conductor is down at the other end, trying to collect a ticket off Therese. She says, "My husband has the tickets," and he doesn't understand anything, and he's about to put her and the children off at the next stop. So, I come back and get that straightened out, and I say to Therese, "It's all fixed for first class. You stay here while I take two of the children at a time up to first class." I take off again, pushing two of the children ahead of me. The conductor had put us in a compartment with three Spanish people, who had just finished their lunch in the dining car. They're elderly women, and they're sitting back, taking their siesta. I come in and deposit the two children with these horrible faces. The ladies look a little annoyed, but they lean back again and resume their siesta. When I come back again—this time with two more children, Therese, and the baby, who's hot and crying—the ladies jump up and start yelling, "Conductor! Conductor!" We cleaned out the whole compartment. Of course, we paid for only two seats. We pulled down the shades, and everybody lay back, and took it easy the rest of the way to Madrid.

How long did you stay in Madrid?

PAGET: After looking at the hotel bill for our first week in Madrid, I decided we better get to the beach in a hurry, so I went down to have a look around Alicante, on the eastern coast. We weren't interested in the southern coast, around Torremolinos, because I didn't want to try to keep up with the international set. I found a beautiful place in Benidorm, which is about a forty-five-minute drive north of Alicante. I think the beaches there are the most beautiful in Spain. It's quite a fashionable resort these days for Spanish people. We rented a five-bedroom, three-bath apartment with a terrace on the *esplanada,* right on the sea. They were the newest apartments in town. We paid seventy-five dollars a month, and that's furnished with everything, including silverware, glassware, linens—the works. We had a couple of maids, and we paid each of them about seven dollars and a half a month. Prices were ridiculous in those days. Everything has gone up about three times since then.

All told, what did your monthly expenses come to in Benidorm?

PAGET: The pension money was enough—a hundred and eighty-three dollars. Food was very cheap in those days. I stopped drinking Scotch. I found out about Spanish brandy, and thought it was very good. It cost about thirty cents a bottle then. A glass of wine used to cost about two cents, or a little less. So, your drinking didn't cost you anything, and we smoked a brand of cigarettes that cost about eight cents a package. After New York, it was almost unbelievable.

How did you spend your time?

PAGET: I didn't do a thing. I used to get up when I felt like it, and have breakfast out on the patio. Then walk into town and get my paper—they had no American papers then, just English. Then go up to the barbershop—I'd grown a great big Pancho Villa-type mustache—and get a shave, which cost about five cents, and then have another cup of coffee in the café and read the paper. Then walk back home, get into my swimming trunks, and join Therese and the children on the beach. I would sit under a parasol, because I didn't want to get too much sun. Then I'd ask the maid to go and get me a bottle of cold beer out of the icebox. I'd lie there and think, "I wonder what the people I know in New York would say if they could see me now? Who could have a better life than this?"

Believe me, it was a wonderful change. I used to be a very fast-paced person. Like everybody else in New York, you have to keep up or you're not going to survive. The problem back in the States, I find, is that people just don't have the time to unwind. It's not that they don't want to. This is a shame. Over here, we have the time.

How did your wife adapt to this life? Did she like it as much as you did?

PAGET: Oh yes, but there were problems and hardships. We had a gypsy maid who stole us blind. When we would go to the beach, her parents would come by in a donkey cart, back it up, and load the stuff in. It was murder. There were the sicknesses of the children. Therese had to learn the language, and get used to a different way of shopping. And, of course, she missed her friends and family. We were the only Americans living in Benidorm then, and I think she felt pretty cut off.

Just before Thanksgiving of that first year, we decided to go down toward Malaga and stay there for a while, because Benidorm shut up completely. The hotels closed, and only one café stayed open. So, we packed up and took the train down south. We stopped at Granada, because we wanted to see the Alhambra. We stayed at a hotel for three days, and liked Granada so much we took a suite of rooms in a *residencia*, which is like a pension. Beautiful place.

Then, all of a sudden, I got sick with hepatitis. Boy, I was dying. That was the end of my two-fisted drinking days. I was really yellow. Even the soles of my feet turned yellow. I had had it once before, when they called it yellow jaundice. It came then from a bad blood transfusion. This time, it was infectious hepatitis. It's a common thing around this country. If you don't wash fresh food carefully, you're apt to get it. When I was lying there in bed, I remember it rained for fourteen days and fourteen nights. At one point, the power went off, and the whole town was without light for three days and nights. There I am, with a raging fever, and there's been no blood test, no urinalysis. This doctor we had used to come to see me to get out of the rain, and he'd feel my pulse, and say, "Open your mouth," and he'd smell my breath, and say, "*Grave. Grave.*" Then he'd say, "*Señora*, may I see you a minute?" Then he'd say, "Fifty pesetas." Well, that was a fortune.

Back home, of course, when the doctor comes and finds you need a shot of penicillin, he gives you a shot of penicillin. Here, if you need medicine, the doctor gives you a prescription, you go to the pharmacy and buy the medicine, and then you call a *practicante*, who is like a male nurse. He comes and gives you the injection. You pay him, too. Anyway, this doctor kept coming and saying, "*Grave. Grave.*" Whenever he didn't have anything else to do, he'd figure, "I can collect another fifty pesetas, and get out of the rain." One night, I was very depressed, which is the way you get with hepatitis. I had been running a fever of about a hundred and four for a couple of days, and it hadn't broken. So, the doctor came in, and after going through his little routine, said, "Are you people Catholic?" My wife said, "Yes." I was a Catholic going to church in those days. He said, "Well, I think we'd better call the priest." And I rose up and said, "GET RID OF HIM!" That was the end of that one. After a while, we found a good young doctor, who had just gotten a Fulbright Scholarship, and finally I got better.

It was a long process. When I was able to get out of bed, I was down to about a hundred and thirty pounds. By this time, we had an apartment—twelve rooms—that cost us forty dollars a month. We usually had four or five maids, all of them working for practically nothing—about three dollars a month—just to get out of the cold and have a place to sleep and eat. Of course, the apartment had no such thing as central heating or hot water. You kept warm by sitting around a table covered with a big, heavy tablecloth, and underneath there is a *brasero* with a fire in it made of ground-up olive pits. We'd sit around the table with the *brasero* going, and we'd eat all kinds of hot food—hot beans and hot potatoes and that sort of thing. Never a regular meal, like steak or fish. After we'd eaten all this hot stuff, I'd say, "Everybody ready for bed?" And, bang, everybody would race and jump into bed. Nobody slept alone. You had to keep warm, so probably a couple of the children would be in bed with us, or they'd jump into bed with the maids. The children ended up getting lice in their hair from the maids, and we had to shave their heads. This was horrible for the girls. It's funny, looking back. New York was never like this.

When spring came, and I was getting stronger and stronger, I used to go down to the Plaza Nueva and sit around in the sun. It was a wonderful place. That's where the men who come in from the country do all their trading. The gypsies are there, selling birds and flowers. The bullfighters and impresarios all hang out around there. I got to know a lot of these people. By that time, I was beginning to speak pretty good Spanish. In fact, it was the best Spanish I ever spoke, because Therese and I were the only people around there who spoke English. We made many very good friends there. To this day, I can go into Granada, and stop in a bar, and one of these old people I knew then will take off his hat, and say, "*Don Antonio, el Americano con el gran bigote y cinco niños.*"

I tell you, I really decided right there in Granada that I would like to stay in Spain, because the people are great people. From then on, I began to wonder if there would be a possibility of working over here.

What surprises me is that while you're living in an apartment with no heat and having no regular meals, and you've just been sick and almost died because the doctor is incompetent—this is when you decided you wanted to stay.

Paget: It was because all of a sudden I realized how great the Spanish people are and how you can figure out a way of living happily in Spain in spite of a lot of things that aren't what you're accustomed to. I also realized that I didn't want to live at the beach. That's something I guess everybody dreams about, but once you have experienced it for a long period of time, you find it isn't so great. I need the stimulation of a city. Maybe that's because I come from New York.

Therese and I both love New York. There isn't a greater town in the world, as far as I'm concerned. But I wouldn't like to live there any more. New York used to be a town for New Yorkers. It's changed a lot. I was there about a year ago. All my friends seem to live away out in the suburbs now. There's nobody to have a drink with or dinner with, unless it's business. The people I know all seem to be getting along fine. Moving ahead according to plan. Getting a bigger house with a bigger garage to hold another and bigger car. Everybody seems to be running faster and faster to keep up with the Joneses. And they all look forward to Friday night and Saturday night, when everybody gets drunk. There's nothing wrong with that. In my day, I didn't always wait until Saturday night. But they don't seem to be getting much fun out of life.

Anyway, I decided I wanted to stay in Spain, and I wanted to get a job. Actually, I wasn't strong enough yet to go to work, so in the spring, we went back to Benidorm, and I got back on my feet. We were still the only Americans there, but now they were getting a lot of English tourists on group tours. It turned out that one of the guides—or couriers, as the English referred to them—became a bit too gay, and they had to get rid of him. They had no one in Benidorm who could speak English and Spanish, so they asked me if I would fill in. I was feeling pretty good by then, so I said I would. The agency that was running these tours was Sir Henry Lunn, out of Marble Arch, London. The job consisted of my going up to Valencia in a bus, meeting the group—there were usually eighty-four people in a group—clearing them through customs, bringing them down here, assigning them their hotel rooms, and then going around to the various hotels every day and selling them tickets to the bullfights, side trips to here and there, and so on. I had to set them straight on one thing, because they had a habit of snapping their fingers at me and calling, "Courier." I'd look at anyone who did that, and I'd say, "I beg your pardon. I happen to be working for Sir Henry Lunn, but no one snaps their fingers at me. I must tell you that I retired at the age of thirty-four. I have five children and a big chalet, and I am only doing this work to help out a friend." From then on, I had nothing but respect from those people. They said,

"Well, you *are* different from the couriers we usually have." It was "Mr. Paget" all the time. Sir Henry Lunn paid me something like two thousand pesetas a month, but I got a commission every time I turned around. The guy who took pictures of the people coming off the plane was giving me money, and so was every shop, every restaurant. I wound up making about four hundred dollars a month, so I finished out the season.

In the fall, we left Benidorm, and moved up here to Madrid. We had made quite a few friends who lived here, and they found a very nice *residencia* for us—a kind of penthouse with four bedrooms, maid service, switchboard, room service, and we paid something like eighty-five bucks a month. Therese got a job first—at the Air Force base. She had worked in advertising and public relations in New York before we were married. She still works at the base, doing secretarial work in what they call the Directorate of Information, which is a big word for public relations. The reason she works is very interesting. To live like a Spanish *señora* might be a big deal for a while for some women, but we've been here long enough to know that it's a very boring life. The American colony here consists of the military and then a bunch of others who have hung on since the building of the bases. They started small businesses, and seem to stick very closely together. They travel in a set, and I don't have anything in common with them. I've gotten to the point where I don't want to become a millionaire. I'm not comparing houses or how much I make with anybody else. That is a great thing about being over here. Back in the States, you look around, and you say, "Oh, there's So-and-So. He's making more money than I am, and I've got more talent than he has. I just got a bad break." So you get upset about it, and your wife gets upset about it. Then you can't eat too good. Then you drink too much. Over here, money isn't really important as long as you have enough to live on. As long as you conduct yourself like a gentleman, nobody is concerned with how much money you make.

When did you start to work here?

PAGET: A few months after Therese. I got started because of the blocked pesetas. The U.S. had lent a great deal of money to Spain, which could not be repaid in the usual way. It had to be used to purchase Spanish goods. So, working with a Spanish partner, I started representing certain Spanish companies that made cognac, gloves, furniture, and so on. We sold these products to American installations here—PX's—and accepted pesetas in payment. We did very well. Somewhere along the line, as a result of meeting all these people, I got a call from a company in London, asking me if I could fly up there to discuss representing Carling Black Label beer in this area. I did, and took it on a commission basis. I had a good success with that, and then I took on others—National Distillers, Bacardi Rum, Liggett & Myers, Distillers Company, Ltd., Gordon's Gin, and so on. Basically, I sell to the military—to the PX's in Spain, Portugal, Morocco, the Canary Islands, the Azores, and the Balearic Islands. Everything is on a commission basis, which is the way I like to work. I am also on a kind of consulting basis to the representatives of our firms here who sell to Spanish retailers. I collect a commission on what they sell. For me, this work is a lot easier than what I did in New York, because there I was selling intangibles, and here, I'm selling tangibles. It's a breeze.

Is the business doing well enough so you can save any money?

PAGET: Maybe a couple of thousand dollars a year. But I'm living well. I'm renting a big apartment. I've got two maids. I'm running a car. There's the summer house to pay for—we still go to Benidorm every summer. And I've got five children going to private schools. Of course, by New York standards, the school cost is ridiculous. For tuition and all the extras, like uniforms, books, pencils, and the bus, the total comes to about a hundred and eighty dollars a month for the five, and they're going to the best schools in town. They're so far ahead of the American schools it isn't funny. I feel very bad when I say that, but it's the truth. I believe in a classical type of education, and that is exactly what they're getting here. When I lived in New York, I thought everything there was the greatest, but I must say that education here is superior.

What plans do you have for the boys' secondary education?

PAGET: This is something that really bothers me. They are Americans, competing with Americans. If they think like Spaniards, and have this attitude of "Get me this and get me that" and "Let's wait until tomorrow," they are going to have a hell of a tough time. It will help if they go to college in the United States, and that's what we plan to do.

Have you any idea of going back to live in the United States?

PAGET: It's a question I have asked myself an awful lot. I don't know what could make it interesting enough for me to go back. Of course, I miss a lot of things—conveniences, mostly. But I've grown used to the inconveniences over here. If I walk into an elevator, and there's a sign on it saying "*No funcione*," I don't get upset that I have to walk nine floors. Sure, I'm upset, but I'm not surprised. Or there's no heat, because the *portero* got drunk the night before and didn't get up in time to stoke the furnace. I understand these things.

You relax, and it's a good life. We belong to a country club, the Club de Campo, which is wonderful for the children. It cost a thousand dollars for a life membership, and the dues are about five dollars a month. That's for the whole family. There are two swimming pools and a wading pool for children, an Olympic-size pool for grownups, golf courses, tennis courts, skeet shooting, archery, riding, polo ponies and instruction, restaurants for children and adults, and I don't know what else. Our children take swimming, tennis, and riding lessons. They ride three times a week. The price of the lessons has gradually gone up. It used to be ten pesetas for half an hour. Now it's twenty-five pesetas—forty cents. We have a gracious life over here, which is very hard to do in New York, no matter how much money you have. There's the difference. The way we live in Madrid would cost me about a hundred thousand dollars a year to duplicate in New York.

GALLERY NOTES

The possibility of living more comfortably on a modest income in Europe than in America is based not only on the relatively lower cost of European living but also on the income tax benefit granted to Americans living abroad. Briefly, this allows Americans who spend a minimum of seventeen out of eighteen consecutive months (501 days) in another country a tax exemption of twenty thousand dollars a year on income for services performed outside the United States; after three years' uninterrupted residence abroad, the exemption increases to twenty-five thousand dollars a year. The exemption applies only to wages, salaries, and fees received for the rendering of personal services; it does not apply to income from property, such as stock dividends, royalties, or capital gains, nor does it apply to income received from the United States government or to pensions.

During one period in the recent past, the tax exemption granted to Americans living abroad provided a tax loophole almost as notorious as the oil depletion allowance. This is what happened. Until the end of the Second World War, Americans who resided permanently outside the United States had always been exempted from paying taxes on income earned abroad. After the war, there was a tremendous demand for Americans to go overseas for limited periods of time to administer foreign aid programs and to participate in the expansion of American business. To attract people to these jobs, Congress amended the law to extend the tax exemption enjoyed by Americans who lived abroad permanently to those who lived abroad for only eighteen months. The change had the intended result as well as an unintended one.

No sooner had the new exemption become effective than a flock of affluent Americans, including several movie stars, decided that Europe was the ideal place to live, at least for eighteen months, and flew off to set up housekeeping there. They acted in films and did their other work, and pocketed the proceeds intact. It was wonderful while it lasted. One actor, who had moved to France, reported 1960 earnings of

$600,000, all tax exempt. The same year, another actor, who had taken up residence in Switzerland with his wife, reported joint non-taxable earning of $2,200,000. (Had they lived in the United States, their tax would have exceeded $1,800,000.) After a while, the newspapers began printing stories about American celebrities who were exploiting the loophole; it was closed in 1963, when Congress voted to limit the exemptions to their present levels.

When the 1963 provision (which was sometimes referred to in the newspapers as the Gary Cooper Law or the William Holden Law, since it was presumably intended to affect them, among others) went into effect, the charm of European living suddenly evaporated for a number of celebrated Americans, and they returned home. They had by then succeeded in creating the picture of all Americans living abroad as artful tax dodgers, an image that persists in some quarters and is keenly resented by bona fide foreign residents, particularly businessmen, who contend that the current exemptions are now too low to enable American companies to recruit the best qualified people to work overseas. America, they point out, is the only country that requires its citizens who work abroad to pay income tax.

While Americans living abroad pay taxes to the country in which they make their residence, those taxes, with very few and unimportant exceptions, are deductible from their U. S. income tax. To ease their overseas taxation, it is common practice among American businessmen stationed abroad to have part of their salary paid in the currency of the country in which they are stationed and part in dollars in the United States. For example, Martin Sheppard, an executive of TWA, who has lived in Rome for more than twenty years, told me that he receives part of his corporate income in lire in Rome and part in dollars in New York. His taxes in Italy, from a federal standpoint, are based on the salary that he is paid there. In addition, he pays the so-called community or family tax, which, he says, is not based on one's income but on his style of living. "In order to determine that tax," Mr. Sheppard said, "they send investigators around to talk, for instance, to the *portiere*, who is not only the doorman and janitor but the spy and know-all. They find out from him how many cars you have, whether you entertain a lot, whether you have a dog, how many servants, and so on. They ask the *portiere* if you often go out in a tuxedo or if your wife goes out wearing a long gown. For that reason, some Italians I know keep their evening clothes at the office. The investigators also find out if you have a mistress, and if you do, since that involves money, your tax goes up.

"Then there are other taxes, such as the tax on a dog. If you have a

French poodle, as we do, you pay a higher tax than somebody who has a police dog, because the poodle is considered a luxury dog, and the police dog is classed as a working dog. You also have to pay a tax for your television, a tax for your radio, and a tax for your cigarette lighter. There is also, of course, a tax on cigarettes and on gasoline, which costs more than eighty cents a gallon. The tax on your automobile—the so-called road tax—ranges from fifty to three hundred dollars a year, depending on the power of your automobile. It would be even more for anyone foolish enough to own an American car here. That tax would run to about six hundred dollars a year. We have two European cars, and for both of them together, we pay slightly more than one hundred and thirty dollars a year just for the privilege of having those cars on the road.

"The government, knowing that they cannot collect all of these taxes, has a fantastic system of indirect taxation. This is a kind of federal sales tax, and it involves charging a tax of 3.3 per cent on every transaction from the sale of raw materials through every step of the production, distribution, and sale of every article produced here. The way it works out, the actual direct income tax becomes almost insignificant, while the pay-as-you-go indirect taxes mount up very high. If you were to combine the direct and indirect taxation, I think you would find that you pay more taxes altogether here than you do in the United States."

> "People always take the most venal view of your living here. They always say it's a tax-dodge sanctuary."

Irwin Shaw, the short story writer, novelist, and playwright, is an Ameropean of long standing, having made his residence in Europe since 1951. He was one of the first Americans to discover Klosters, the charming Swiss village, high in the Alps, that is now a famous ski resort, and liked it so much that he built a house there, a very comfortable and attractive place that he calls Chalet Mia. Swiss on the outside and New York-California on the inside, it is a five-minute walk from the center of the village, which is situated in the German-speaking part of Switzerland. There is no doubt that Shaw is the Number One American in Klosters. If the postmaster or anybody else wants to locate any American who is visiting Klosters, or is expected, or has been there, Shaw is the authority consulted. The menu at the Chesa Grischuna, the most fashionable hotel in town, features a dish called Trout à la Shaw, a toothsome offering remindful of Dave Chasen's. "I had to teach them how to do it," Shaw says. He works in a stone-and-wood studio, located a short distance from his house, that has a large fireplace, a bath, and other conveniences and a magnificent view of the mountains. When I visited him there one Sunday afternoon in December, he was wearing slacks, a red woolen shirt, and loafers, and he looked fit. A onetime football player at Brooklyn College, he is a burly man in his early fifties, with a friendly if somewhat forceful manner ("You've *got* to have a good time at Irwin's parties," a Hollywood agent, visiting Klosters, told me. "If you don't, Irwin will brain you."), an assured, rather breezy way of talking, and a hearty way of laughing. The interview got started without much help from me.

SHAW: Why do I live abroad? Everybody who comes to interview me here, or in Paris, or in Rome, or wherever I happen to be, makes that the first question. It is a sign of the political and cultural immaturity of the United States that the question is even asked. People have lived in countries other than their own since the beginning of civilization. Look at the way the English have lived. Who would ask an Englishman living in Florence or Hong Kong or Istanbul, "Why do you live here?" They live there because they're enjoying themselves, or it is profitable, or because they don't like the English climate, or by accident, or because they have interests in a foreign place that are better served by their living there.

In New York, I'm asked this question ten times a day. The answer is that you live where you like to live at the moment, if you can. Ask anybody why he likes to live in Paris. It's like asking him, "Why do you want to have dinner with Greta Garbo?" Paris is the most beautiful city in the world, plus the fact that it has been for so long a cultural and intellectual convention hall. Why shouldn't one want to live there?

I lived in the United States all my life until the war. During the war, all of a sudden, I was sent around the world as a soldier. I'd never been out of the country before that, except for one trip to Cuba, and two days in Montreal. I felt parochial when I was traveling all over North Africa and all over Europe. I said, "There's a whole world here I know nothing about, really, except from books, and this is something I'd like to explore." Even so, I didn't come to Europe immediately to live. I came in '51 for a holiday with my wife and son. He was then one year old. I was thirty-eight. By accident, somebody loaned me his apartment in Paris for two months, and our visit stretched on and on. Even after deciding to live in Europe, I still kept my apartment in New York, thinking, "Well, I'll go back next year." Then I began to realize that I was more interested in living here. Life is more varied. In an hour, you're in Rome or London or Madrid, and a whole new world of interests opens up for you.

But I'm no expatriate. There may be some Americans who are, but I'm not one of them. For example, this year, I think I was in the United States for five months. You go back and forth. It doesn't cost much any more. Often, somebody pays my traveling expenses for business reasons. All my publishers are in the United States. When I have to make a contract for a book, or work on a book, or have a play on, I may be there for months.

How did you happen to choose Klosters as a place to live?

SHAW: Again, by accident. People pretend that they do everything by design. I don't believe that. I mean, everybody, *everybody*, does everything by accident. I'm here because of Peter Viertel, a writer who also lives here now. He is a skier, and I did my first skiing with him, in Sun Valley, and he told me about this place. At that time, he was here for the winter, so I came for a month. I fell in love with the place, and I came back. You know, I'm an athlete, and I feel I need to exercise. And skiing turns out to be the best sport I've ever engaged in. I saw that I could live this life—that is, ski as much as I like and at the same time do my work—and so I decided to settle here. That's my program. I work in the morning and ski in the afternoon.

Is it actually possible for you to work every morning and ski every afternoon as a regular thing?

SHAW: Yeah. Absolutely. Why not? I get up early, and I have all morning to work, because the best skiing around here is around mid-day. The sun is at its height, and there are the fewest people skiing. So I skip lunch most of the time, have a bowl of soup on the mountain someplace, and ski until four or five o'clock. In the spring, you have to reverse that; because then you have to ski at seven o'clock in the morning. So I ski early in the day, have lunch, try to take a little siesta, and then work five hours before dinner. Often, if the work is going good, I don't go skiing, but four or five hours a day at the typewriter is about as much as you can do, regularly. When you're a kid, you can do more. I find if I do eight hours, I'm bushed the next day. I work a seven-day week, but I sometimes take holidays. My mother reads in the newspapers about all these things I'm supposed to be doing. She says, "You're killing yourself with overwork." And I have to keep reassuring her, "Writing is not work. It's play. You do it for fun." The only time that writing becomes work is when you deal with other people, that is, when you do a movie or a play, and you have to deal with other people's desires, ideas, criticisms, and personalities. That can become work.

When did you build the house here?

SHAW: Four or five years after we started coming here. In 1956, I think. Before that, we had been based mostly in Paris, and just came here in the wintertime. I came up here one summer, thinking I'd spend only a few days or maybe a couple of weeks. I found I liked the climate in the summertime—marvelous for work—and also the place is empty then. We decided this would be a good base. We were the first Americans to build a house here. I like to be in my own house, and we've got the conveniences—tennis courts over there, swimming pool a hundred and fifty yards away.

Do you ever have the feeling here of being cut off from the rest of the world?

SHAW: No, not at all. If I want to go to Paris, I either take the train or drive down to Landquart, which is not far, and take a sleeper from there at nine o'clock at night, and at ten minutes to eight in the morning I'm in Paris. You don't lose a working day here, and you don't lose a working day in Paris. Same thing coming back. If I want to go to America, I drive down to Zurich—a two-and-a-half-hour drive—get on a plane at one o'clock in the afternoon, and I'm in New York at four, in time for dinner. And, of course, from Zurich, you can get to just about any place in Europe in an hour or two.

Did you speak French or any other foreign language when you came over here to live?

SHAW: I spoke a kind of French. I studied French in high school and college, but didn't speak a word of it afterwards for nine or ten years. Then I went to North Africa with the Army, and naturally you had to speak French, and so I picked it up a bit. Then I campaigned in France after D-Day, and I spoke a lot more French. I didn't do anything with it after the war until I came back to Europe. Then I picked it up again, but not enough. I have no gift for languages. My accent is always American. My French is fluent but hardly beautiful. My wife learned it since being here. She speaks Italian, too. My wife speaks French to our son, and so do the French maids, but I refuse to speak anything but English to him. I think the Americans who live here or in France and speak French to their own children make a big mistake, because the kids then don't have the correct feeling for any language. My son speaks English like an American, he speaks French like a Frenchman, and he speaks Italian like an Italian. He graduated from the public school in Paris, and there, German was considered the language of the Boche, so he resented studying it, but he's learning it now. He's at Le Rosey, which I think is a very good school, but he's going to go to school in America next year.

Whose idea is that?

SHAW: Mine. Because he's American. He's visited the United States, of course, but he's never lived there. For better or worse, that's his country, and he's got to know about it.

I understand that you take your family to Gstaad from time to time to ski, and I was wondering how you would compare the social atmosphere there with Klosters.

SHAW: It's somewhat different but not as different as people say. People make a lot of foolish generalizations about places. Klosters has been called "Hollywood in the Alps" by fly-by-night newspaper people. A stupid girl from the London *Express* once came here for a few hours, and then wrote, "Every American in Klosters has imported every stick of furniture in his house from America. There's a Facel-Vega in front of every American's house." And so on. The fact is that only three American families have their permanent residence here —the Viertels, Bob Parrish, the movie director, and his family, and ourselves. None of us has a Facel-Vega, and I don't think all of us together have imported a dozen pieces of furniture from America.

People always take the most venal view of your living here. They always say it's a tax-dodge sanctuary. They say I'm just *dying* to live in America, but it's only to make money that I stay here. They don't know the facts. For example, every cent I've earned this year is taxable in the United States. People don't seem to know that writers have to pay taxes on the income from their books—on royalties—no matter where they live or where the royalties are earned. As long as you have your American passport, that's the absolute rule. And, of course, it applies to me, even though I am a resident of Switzerland, and pay taxes here. I pay taxes in Klosters, in Graubünden, and in Berne—that is, to the village, the canton, and the state.

Of course, all of those are deductible from your United States tax.

SHAW: Yeah. But anything I write, unless I write for a salary, is fully taxable by the United States. Since most of my income comes from my novels and short stories, most of it is subject to United States income tax. When I sell a book to the movies, for example, that's all taxable in the United States. I can have something published in a French magazine, something that's never been published in the United States, and I have to pay taxes on that in the United States. Look. My books have been translated into Japanese. I pay taxes on that income in America. My books are published in Polish, Hungarian, Roumanian. I pay taxes on those in the United States. I don't mind paying the taxes. What I do mind is that I'm not allowed to vote. That's real taxation without representation. If you live here, you're still a citizen of the United States, but you're not a resident of any state. All voting is by states, so no matter how much I wanted Kennedy elected, I couldn't vote for him. I can't vote for anybody. Meanwhile, the United States is taking a lot of dough away from me in taxes.

The United States is the only country that has that arrangement. If you are an Englishman and live abroad, the British government doesn't take a cent of your income. Not a cent. America is the only country that taxes your passport.

An Englishman working in America may pay no British income tax, but he does pay American income tax.

SHAW: Yeah. But if he lives in Naples or lives here, he pays a moderate tax on his residence—really not on his income. That's what they do with foreigners in Switzerland. They make an arrangement that seems fair to them. They see how you live and maybe how desirable you are—whether you're doing good for the community or not—and then they review it every couple of years. Also, they tax your real property in Switzerland—what they call your "fortune." People in America don't know any of this. The legend persists that you pay nothing.

There was a time, before 1963, when some Americans over here did have very large incomes and paid nothing in American taxes.

SHAW: Not writers. Not writers who are self-employed. Writers on salary, yes.

You do write some things on salary—a movie script, for example—and the first twenty-five thousand dollars you receive for that piece of work is exempt from United States taxes. Of course, that exemption used to be thirty-five thousand, but even so, you have that advantage.

SHAW: Yeah. But I'll tell you why that amounts to nothing. I'll tell you where the gimmick is. The amount of the Swiss tax is just about what the Americans would charge on that twenty-five thousand dollars, and I have a feeling that the Internal Revenue Service won't let you deduct the Swiss tax in that case. See what I mean? When I make non-taxable money in the United States and I pay taxes in Switzerland, the Internal Revenue Service won't let me deduct that tax. And also I can't deduct a great many of my business expenses. My secretary. I very often have two secretaries. Stuff like that. Or travel. They say, "You did that on money that wasn't taxed by the United States government."

Actually, I think a writer does get a bad deal in the United States—a very bad deal because of the fluctuation of his income. If you have a business, it's all different. A writer can spend years on a book, and even if it's highly successful, he can come out with next to nothing. Suppose at the same time a toy manufacturer comes out with some little gadget that's a big success for two years. He'll be rich for the rest of his life. Businessmen have things like depreciation of plant and machinery, depletion of resources, and all kinds of other gimmicks to cut down their taxes.

I'll tell you something. I'm criticized a great deal because I write for the movies. The reason I write for the movies is that that is the only way I can support my other work. *The Young Lions* took me two and a half years to write. Where am I going to get money for myself and my family to live on for two and a half years? You don't want to live like a dog. And you have enormous responsibilities, like everybody else. So, the only way I can finance my serious writing is by writing for the movies.

Do you think that European writers are better off, at least as far as taxes are concerned?

SHAW: Sure. You know what they do in France? France is one place where they give the writer and artist some kind of a break. The first 40 per cent of your income, no matter how big it is in any year, is not considered a question between you and the French government. The remaining 60 per cent of your income is subject to taxes. And that applies if you're a painter, a writer, sculptor, musician, poet. It's civilized, you see? What the French know is how tough a writer's life, an artist's life can be. He has one good year and then several lean ones. The idea of taxing an artist year by year is insane. Suppose you taxed

Michelangelo while he was doing the Sistine Chapel. You know? I'm laughing, but I'll tell you, I get frantic at the end of the year, figuring, "Should I write this fast and try to get the money this year, or would I be better off for taxes if I let it wait until next year?" What's that got to do with writing?

Writers and artists have no standing in the United States. They're considered freaks. If they make some money, lucky freaks. If they don't make any money, fools. It's silly to pretend it's otherwise. And the government, until Kennedy, shared that notion. He knew about writers and writing, and he tried to do something. As far as I can see, there will never be another President who will.

Well, we're talking too much about money. It's not a subject that I think about all this much. My whole idea when I began as a writer was just to have enough money so I could keep on writing. I managed that, and that's what I still care about mainly.

You've talked about the attractions of living here. What are some of the things that aren't so agreeable?

SHAW: Well, you'd have to be a Pollyanna to say everything's great wherever you go. The things that annoy you about living in Switzerland are the things that would annoy you about living in a peasant community in America—if such a thing existed. These people move slowly. They're suspicious. For example, I've offered to institute a free library here mainly for the use of the local kids and for people who come here to visit. Visitors are sometimes caught here for five days with nothing to do because of the weather. There should be some way of their getting things to read. I offered to give the books for nothing. I said, "All I want is a room, which is warm in winter—a place where people can sit down and read. It doesn't even have to be a big room." Well, it's been under discussion now for six months. I think they're saying among themselves, "Why does he want to do it?" That's what I mean by moving slowly. The peasant thing. But that's the only thing that can get on your nerves. I can say that in all the years we've lived here, we've never gotten gypped. Never.

That's what I've heard again and again from Americans in Switzerland. I've also heard that prices are high.

SHAW: This is a country with a high standard of living. Prices are low only in backward countries. The more civilized a country is, the more livable it is for the mass of its people, the higher the prices. Every time you go to a place that's cheap, you know the people are suffering. I don't like living in countries like that. Forget 'em. I visit

Spain. I wouldn't spend any real time there. I visit Yugoslavia. I wouldn't spend time there. I visit Greece. Wouldn't spend time there. Prices are very low in those three places, because the people are being ground down. In many ways, Switzerland is a much more efficient country for living than America. From the highest mountain to the deepest valley, wherever people live, there isn't a community that doesn't have electricity. You've got to pay for things like that.

This is not heaven. This is not paradise. There are problems of modern living here, like everywhere else, but for me, this is a way of escaping a lot of those problems. For instance, when I look out my window, this is what I see: the Alps, the glaciers, the sun or the stars. You don't hear any police sirens. You don't hear any buses. You don't get the stink of diesel fuel exhaust in your nostrils. At the same time, you live with great ease and efficiency. The people are eager to help you. The Swiss are among the most venturesome people I know. And there is another marvelous thing here. I don't know whether it's peculiarly Swiss or a mountaineer mentality. If you're in trouble, they risk their lives without thinking about it to get you out. I've seen that again and again. You can depend upon them. They don't let you down from the point of view of courage. It's not like in New York. People sitting in a subway car, and they see two hoods beat a soldier nearly to death, and nobody moves. That would never happen here in a million years.

"When one comes back to Switzerland, you have this quiet, this peace, this serenity, this privacy."

William Holden, the film star, moved to Europe in 1959 with his wife and two sons, then in their early teens, and purchased a villa on Lake Geneva. He remodeled the structure extensively, and by adding rooms, combining others, and installing large windows, gave it the open, spacious atmosphere typical of houses in Southern California. "Sometimes there were hot disagreements with the architect, who was Swiss, but I think the blend worked out very satisfactorily," Mr. Holden told me when I called at the villa one afternoon. "In any event, we like it, and we're happy here." I asked if, upon moving to Europe, he had considered living anywhere except in Switzerland.

HOLDEN: The common assumption in the United States is that Americans who settle in Switzerland choose this country merely for the tax advantage. That isn't true in most cases. One doesn't, of course, ignore that factor. But at the same time, you cannot ignore the fact that Switzerland has other advantages. For one thing, its geographical position, at the heart of Europe, is a great asset. It represents security and safety. And it has outstanding educational institutions. If I hadn't had a family, I would perhaps have settled in Hong Kong or in Africa, where I have some interests, but I wanted the children to become bilingual, if not trilingual. That can be done here. Because of that advantage, which is primary, really, we decided to settle here.

At the very outset, when you were making up your mind to move to Europe, to what extent did taxes influence your decision?

HOLDEN: I would say that it was a fairly important consideration. Having worked in the United States for a number of years, I found that it wasn't possible to put too much away. Here, as you know, there was an advantage. It was short-lived. We came here in 1959, and the tax advantage ended at the close of 1962. Since I didn't work in 1959, I actually had only two years of benefit under the old law. Even without the benefit, I think I still would have done it. I think my curiosity about life in Europe would have brought me here. I like living in Switzerland. I also like to travel. Over the past ten or twelve years, I have traveled about a hundred and fifty to two hundred thousand miles a year. Switzerland, I have found, is a very good base to operate from. When I'm working in Paris or Berlin or Copenhagen, I can get home for a weekend, which would be damned difficult if I were living in Los Angeles.

Another thing I love about Switzerland is the complete and absolute privacy you can have here. The most marvelous thing happened when we first moved into this house and were in the process of reconstructing it. A reporter from the Lausanne *Gazette* came out and said, "I'd like very much to have an interview." I said, "I'd love to grant the interview, but I'm terribly busy now. I have the architect here, and I really have to work with him." The reporter said, "Oh, I didn't mean to bother you now. I meant after you got settled." I told him the next few weeks were going to be quite hectic. "I didn't mean the next few weeks," he said. "I thought perhaps six or eight months from now we might get together for a cup of coffee and a chat." Now, can you imagine someone wanting an interview and being willing to wait six or eight months for it? When the interview finally did take place, there wasn't a single question that could be construed as an invasion of privacy. For one who works constantly in a kind of public relations form, which I have to do when I'm either on location or publicizing a film, you're constantly in touch with hundreds of thousands of people. When one comes back to Switzerland, you have this quiet, this peace, this serenity, this privacy. It's a terribly welcome thing.

In addition to taxes, other economic considerations have been instrumental in the making of Ameropeans. For example, the postwar decline of Hollywood as the motion picture center of the world and the resulting trend toward making movies abroad combined to propel a great many people associated with the entertainment industry to Europe. Producers were attracted by cheaper production costs as well as by government subsidies offered by many European countries, directors by a wider range of assignments, and writers by, among other things, the advantage of being near the action. While making use of these opportunities, many of those who came to work gradually developed such a liking for their new life (together with an ability to put up with what they didn't like) that they decided to stay.

Perhaps none of the Hollywood emigrants is more enthusiastic about life in Europe than Norman Krasna, a screenwriter and playwright, who lives with his wife and family near Lausanne. "Everything in Switzerland is prescribed, so it's very easy to live here if you follow the rules," he said. "Furthermore, everybody's thoughtful and polite. It's contagious. Before five minutes, I'm bowing lower than they do. You go up to a policeman to ask him something, and he's so nice you want to kiss him. And he salutes you besides. I'm crazy about that. This is a paradise. You're always at ease. It's a big country club. Incidentally, the golf course here is a botanical garden. So beautiful. I look around. Who's on the course? Nobody but me and the caddy. And she's a girl. Here, I have time to go trout fishing and do a lot of other things I've learned to enjoy. I have time to read. I don't have the telephone to bother me. If it rings, it's most likely for the children. Nobody's calling me just to pass the time. Without all those distractions, I can work better. Also, it's not like California, where you have to be nice to this one and go to lunch with that one. Here, there's a minimum of social waltzing."

As a rule, I discovered, the wives of American film people who have settled in Europe view their transplanted life with a much more critical eye than their husbands do. This is true, in fact, of the wives of practically all Americans living in Europe. The reason is simply that they have a harder time than their husbands in adjusting to life abroad. It is usually easier for the men, largely because they have what has been called "the comfortable continuity" of their profession. But they, too, have difficulties in getting used to life in a foreign setting. Everybody does. In a rather homely but touching passage, Theodore Dreiser remarked on this subject in *A Traveller at Forty*, written after a sojourn in Europe. "I felt particularly lonely at moments, being away from America," he recalled, "for the difference in standards of taste and action, the differences in modes of thought and practice, and the difference in money and the sound of human voices were growing on me. When you have lived in one country all your life and found yourself comfortable in all its ways and notions and then suddenly find yourself out of it, and trying to adjust yourself to things that are different in a hundred little ways, it is rather hard."

Dreiser was describing a mild case of what the social scientists call "culture shock," which, according to the anthropologist Kalvero Oberg, "is precipitated by the anxiety that results from losing all our familiar signs and symbols of social intercourse [such as] when to shake hands and what to say when we meet people, when and how to give tips, how to give orders to servants, how to make purchases, when to accept and when to refuse invitations," and any number of other situations of everyday life.

Usually, the first reaction of people suffering from culture shock is to reject their new environment. They complain endlessly about the people, the climate, the food, the delays in getting things done, and about a variety of other frustrations, large and small. The second phase is a kind of regression. "The home environment suddenly assumes a tremendous importance," Mr. Oberg has explained. "To an American, everything American becomes irrationally glorified. All the difficulties and problems are forgotten, and only the good things back home are remembered." Many wives never proceed beyond this phase. "Living at home," a member of this group has said, "one seldom acts like a chauvinist. It comes easily when you live abroad."

On the basis of considerable observation over the years, the Reverend Martin Sergeant, pastor of the American Church, in Paris, has concluded that while American businessmen abroad work harder than they do at home, because they not only have to handle their regular job but also entertain a stream of visiting VIP's, their wives have an even more taxing existence. "For one thing," Reverend Sergeant told me, "the businessmen are on expense accounts, so they are at the better restaurants for lunch and often at dinner. Meanwhile, the poor wife is struggling with French plumbing or with a Spanish maid, and her life is apt to be hell. The man is either working in an English-speaking office, or he has someone around to help him handle the language barrier. The women seldom have such an advantage, and this contributes to their sense of isolation. Physically, they are often stuck away some place with no other American women around, and they become more and more depressed. At the same time, the wife has the children to take care of. She has the French school to deal with as well as being concerned with the children's leisure-time activities in a strange setting. She has scores of other new situations to handle. If there is a flaw in the marriage that has been glossed over at home, when they get over here and encounter all the added emotional strain, the flaw becomes a Grand Canyon. When a family just ups and moves back to America, the reason, more often than not, is a wife who has simply not been able to adjust."

The manifold problems that confront the wives of American businessmen abroad naturally also confront the wives of Ameropeans. Generally speaking, however, they seem better able to take them in stride than the mates of the businessmen. The reason, probably, is that the Ameropeans, both wives and husbands, came to Europe out of choice, not expediency, and consequently have greater resilience and a stronger desire to cope successfully with the new environment. This doesn't mean that Ameropean wives never complain about the problems of coping. Far from it. But they do maintain a certain balance, even when they feel that, for them, the pleasures of living abroad have sharply diminished.

> "Why not have the *enjoyment* of living in
> Europe when you're young enough
> to appreciate it, and not wait until
> you're old and rich?"

Richard Fleischer, the well-known movie director (his most recent film is *Dr. Dolittle*), is a trim, amiable, discriminating man, who prepared for a career in the motion picture business by graduating from Brown University as well as from the Yale Drama School. After three years as a writer, producer, and director for Pathé News, in New York, he signed a director's contract with RKO Pictures, and moved to Hollywood. His first assignment was to make a documentary about Japan. The film won an Academy Award. On hearing the news, his father, who is cartoonist Max Fleischer, creator of "Popeye," sent his son a congratulatory telegram that said, "What took you so long?" Fifteen years and many pictures later, Fleischer moved with his wife, an attractive woman whose nickname is Mickey, and their three children to Europe. They settled first in Paris, and then moved to Rome, where they now live in a large, luxurious, completely modern apartment constructed within an ancient *palazzo* in Trastevere. "Our place is right behind the Chiesa Nuova," Mr. Fleischer explained on the phone in the course of inviting me to lunch with him and his wife. "They call it the 'New Church,' because it is only a couple of hundred years old." The terrace of the Fleischers' apartment, to which we retired after lunch, commands a magnificent view over the rooftops of Rome, and it also contains a large grill for barbecuing. This essential of existence in Southern California prompted Mr. Fleischer to begin talking about their life in Hollywood and the reasons for leaving it behind.

FLEISCHER: After directing *Compulsion*, a picture that I thought was pretty good and that got a lot of acclaim, everything looked promising. I was under contract to Twentieth Century-Fox, and I was looking forward to doing another picture that would be a challenge. But they threw a lot of projects at me that I considered inferior—it's just as hard to make a bad picture as it is to make a good one—so, as usual, I went on suspension. That's very unpleasant, because you don't get paid, and you can't work anywhere else, and you're in rustication. They offered me *Cleopatra*—that was before Elizabeth Taylor was involved—and several other big projects, none of which interested me. This went on for several months. I was bitter. After having made the most interesting and important picture of my career, I felt that I was being treated pretty shabbily.

Then Darryl Zanuck, who was in Europe as an independent producer at that time, cabled and asked me to come to Europe. He said he had a script that he thought I would like to do. So I went to see Darryl, in the south of France, and spent several days there. I read the script, and didn't like it. On the day I was to go back home, he said, "I just got another script today. I think it might interest you. Read it." It was a thing called *Crack in the Mirror*. I read it and liked it. Darryl said, "Fine. Let's make it. I'll loan you out from Fox." Of course, I was very happy.

Then I went to London, and saw the head of Fox there, who is Bob

Goldstein. Bob is really the one who turned the tide. He said, "I think you're crazy to stay in Hollywood. You could have a marvelous career in Europe. You would be able to pick and choose instead of having things thrown at you." Well, I had spent several months in Europe when we were making *The Vikings*, which we shot all over the Continent. I had my family with me, because I always bring them where I'm working on a film. They loved it, and we had a good time. I remembered that, and, after taking a lot of other things into consideration, I sat down and wrote a letter to my wife. "Pack up and come over," I said. "First of all, I want you to be here while I do this picture. Secondly, I think we should stay on and live in Europe." And my dear wife, without any comment, objection, or discussion that I knew of . . .

MRS. FLEISCHER (interrupting): I think I cried for a month. I was going to have to leave all my friends. I loved the idea of Europe, and I wanted to see it all, and the most important thing was that it was going to be stimulating and exciting for Dick. But my dear friends—leaving them. Well, I got over that, but it was a painful time.

FLEISCHER: We lived in Westwood Village. We had a beautiful house there, and we had lots of very good friends. We loved it. But when I wrote Mickey, I painted a very rosy picture. My feeling was, and still is, that I would have greater freedom—artistic freedom—living and working in Europe, that my services were more in demand and more appreciated here than they were in America, and that I could have steady employment of the kind that I wanted.

Also, I loved the idea of living in Europe. My philosophy was then, and is now: when you accumulate enough money and enough success in your life, what do you do? You usually make a trip to Europe. Here we were, young enough to enjoy it, and our children would enjoy it and get something from it. Why not have the enjoyment of living in Europe when you're young enough to appreciate it, and not wait until you're old and rich? Instead of being a tourist, why not live in the country? Be a part of it. Be able to travel anywhere you want at any time. But, of course, the main thing, for me, was the kind of work I would be able to do here.

What was the reaction of your children to the move?

MRS. FLEISCHER: Well, it's generally true, I think, that children don't like to change, but my elder son wasn't against the idea at all, because he wasn't having a very happy time in school. It took the other two—the younger boy and our little girl—who hadn't thought so well of the idea and, in fact, had been pretty upset when they first heard about it, about two months in Paris before they were absolutely delighted to be there. In the beginning, though, the little girl was anything but enthusiastic. On her first day in Paris, she said to her father, "Why didn't you leave me where I was? I was happy there." Both of us almost broke up in tears.

FLEISCHER: That's when I wanted to kill myself.

What did you say to her?

FLEISCHER: There wasn't much *to* say, except, "Just wait, and you'll see that it will turn out all right." What *can* you say? She was a little thing—between six and seven.

MRS. FLEISCHER: I had to go to Switzerland many weekends, because the boys were in school there, so this little girl and her father used to spend their Sundays together. They used to get up and make their breakfast—the help was off that day, so they had the house to themselves—and then they would go sightseeing and have lunch in a very elegant restaurant overlooking the Seine, and then go to the Louvre and all over. To this day, she cherishes those Sundays.

FLEISCHER: We used to walk through the streets, go up in the Eiffel Tower, take rides on the Métro, and have a wonderful time. Just the two of us. She soon loved Paris.

MRS. FLEISCHER: Meanwhile, I was back at the boys' school. Dick had tried to get them into the American School in Paris, which is a fine school, but their waiting list was just too long. So, he started scouring Switzerland, but it was late, and he couldn't get them into the most desirable places. Then he hit on this school—up above Lausanne—which looked very good, and there were some other Americans who were in Dick's position, and they also thought the place looked good. So, the boys registered there, and I went up to see them on weekends, and it turned out that things were just not right. There was no library. There was no lab equipment. Textbooks were missing. And they kept on saying, "Well, the library is over in the girls' school." And I would ask, "Well, when does it come over here?" And they would say, "The lab equipment is on the way from America." And, "There's a strike in the plant that's printing the textbooks." We never got anything out of them that was straight. They had a wonderful program of excuses. By Christmastime, we knew that the whole school was a fake. By then, I had explained the terrible situation the boys were in to the headmaster of the American School in Paris, and he said, "Take them out. There's a new semester in February, and if there aren't places here, I'll get them in some place." They did get into the American School in February, and I don't think they ever had a better time in school. The older one, who, as I've said, hadn't been doing well in America, found his first intellectual challenge there, both from the school and from the students.

The boys lived at home, and could take the school bus, but the headmaster insisted that Bruce, the older boy, who was fourteen then, not take the bus to school in the morning but that he go by Métro instead. It was a bit of a ride, and I was apprehensive about it at first. Later that spring, when friends from America came to visit us, they often said, "Oh, there seem to be so many tourists in Paris. So many Americans everywhere." And so on. Bruce listened to all this, and later said to me, "They don't know my Paris at seven-thirty in the morning on the Métro. There are no tourists there." You know, he really felt that he was a part of the city. The kids loved Paris, and they loved that school.

How long were you in Paris?

MRS. FLEISCHER: From September to June. Then Dick had to work in the south of France, so I loaded the children and a maid into the station wagon, and we took a leisurely trip through the Loire Valley. We caught up with Dick, where he was shooting, near Avignon, and stayed some days with him there. I think, if I were to spend the rest of my years in Europe, that that is the area—Provence—where I would like to live.

FLEISCHER: We were down there shooting part of *The Big Gamble*, which was the second of two pictures I made for Zanuck while we were living in Paris. Then I got an assignment from Dino De Laurentiis to do a picture here in Italy, so we packed up and moved to Rome. That was 1960. Again, there was a big trauma. The kids didn't want to leave Paris. They knew they would hate Rome. Everyone was very unhappy. And they were unhappy for about two weeks. Then they became mad about Rome. Now they don't ever want to leave.

Where do the children go to school here?

MRS. FLEISCHER: They go to the Overseas School, which is called an international school, but it's really an American school. It must be about 90 per cent Americans. The reason that we have kept them in this type of school, both in Paris and here, and not put them into French or Italian schools is that eventually they will go to universities in the United States. My elder son is going to Brown University now. We want their education to follow a pattern of the proper courses in the proper order to meet American university requirements. So many people who have put their children into French schools, Swiss schools,

Italian schools find that they wind up not having proper credits to get into any university in any country.

FLEISCHER: Things have been marvelous for our children in Europe. That's been the most successful part of it. Last summer, for instance—and this is probably something we wouldn't be able to do if we lived in the United States—my older boy, Bruce, left with a friend when school finished in early June, and the two of them took off on a tour of Spain. They traveled by themselves all through Spain, and on less than five dollars a day apiece. Bruce came back to Rome, spent a little time here, and then went to Exeter University, in England, for a summer course in English literature. After that, he went to the United States to college. The same summer, my younger son, who was fifteen, went to Israel, and worked on a farm. When he came back to Rome, we were in the United States, so he went to Paris with this group that had come up from Israel. Our children could now be put down in any city in the world and get along by themselves. They are completely self-sufficient.

How many languages do they speak now?

FLEISCHER: They study French in school. They speak a kind of gutter Italian. It's very ungrammatical, but it's very Romanesque. Our little girl speaks Italian rather well, because they teach it to her in school, and she speaks it all of the time to people around her.

Where did you live when you first came to Rome?

MRS. FLEISCHER: We lived in a hotel for two months while looking for the kind of house that Dick requires. Everywhere we've been in Europe, he has made a great effort to find the best living accommodations that were available. He found a place in a section of Perrioli, on a little street that has three villas and a convent on it. We had one of the villas. It was very, very quiet, and we stayed there for two years. Then we made the contract for this place, but we had to wait six months until the reconstruction was finished. That was all done by the owners—that is, at their expense. But we designed the place, using our architect. They were going to redo it anyway, so they said, "We'll redo it the way the tenant wants it." We have a two-year lease, followed by three one-year options. After that, if we want to stay longer, we will make a new deal.

You mentioned earlier that one of your first thoughts on learning of the move to Europe was reluctance to leave your friends. How has that worked out?

MRS. FLEISCHER: The friends have come here.

FLEISCHER: That's the funny part.

MRS. FLEISCHER: I've kept—I say "I" because I think a woman usually has more intimate friends than a man—them all. We see them here, and often we think that when we see them here, we enjoy one another more, because the circumstances here are so congenial. Also, other people who were very good acquaintances in the States have become dear friends, because they have come to Rome or to Klosters or someplace else, and we've become intimate over here. So, I think we have even more friends. And there's constantly someone coming through.

FLEISCHER: Our guest room is seldom empty.

Some people find that a burden.

FLEISCHER: No, it isn't a burden, because we like our friends so much, and, as Mickey says, we see them all when they come here. Since they are not at home in Europe, they hang onto us a little bit tighter than they would if we were to meet at a resort in the United States. Another thing—people who were friends of ours while we lived in Hollywood, but not terribly close friends, have become very, very dear friends here. Like Norman Krasna. We knew each other for years in California, but we had never been to each other's house. Now we meet in Klosters every year, and if he comes to Rome, he comes here to see us, and we go out every night, and we've become the best of friends.

MRS. FLEISCHER: You just have more time to be intimate.

FLEISCHER: When friends come here, we take a great delight in showing them the city. We can show them Rome in a way they wouldn't be able to see it by themselves, and, of course, they appreciate that. And when our good friends send *their* friends to look us up on their trip to Rome—people you don't even know, as a rule—we always see them and take them to dinner. If possible, we try to show them the city, depending on how good friends they are of our friends and on the amount of time we have available. These people are so appreciative that when we go back to the United States, they can't do enough for us. They do ten times more than what we did for them. We have made a lot of good friends that way. There's no place we go now, either in Europe or America, that we don't have good close personal friends.

Have you been back to see your friends in California since moving here?

FLEISCHER: We went back last summer. It was the first time we'd been back to California in four years. It looked magnificent, absolutely magnificent. I'm sure one day we'll go back and live in America. We'll stay here as long as it's comfortable. If I get a picture to do in London, we'll move to London. I'd love to live there for a while. It's my favorite city of all. We'd just sublet this, and move. Mickey, you see, is getting a little more flexible, aren't you?

MRS. FLEISCHER: For a person who is as sedentary as I am, natively, this moving around is like changing a peach into a pear. But I've really had a lot of fun, and it's done me a lot of good. If I'd stayed where I was, I would have been happy just staying in my own backyard with my barbecue and living a very limited existence. Here, for example, I'm going to coax my husband into going down to hear the Stravinsky opera tomorrow night, which I probably wouldn't have gone to the trouble of doing in Los Angeles. Instead, we would have had friends over, and that would have been it. And on Easter vacation, I'm looking forward to going to Israel, and I hope this summer to go to Sweden. California I love, but from there it's a little too far to do Israel on Easter vacation and Sweden a few weeks later.

FLEISCHER: Rome is wonderfully situated, geographically, and it's marvelous in so many other ways. It is such a beautiful place. I didn't see it that way at all the first year. Now I think it is the most beautiful city in the world. It is also one of the least stimulating. This is not the center of culture that it used to be. The theater is almost non-existent. There are practically no American films shown here. The galleries are small, not important. There is no night life to speak of. In those ways, the life here is quite barren.

MRS. FLEISCHER: Because the choice is so limited, you go to see anything that happens to come to town, whether it's good, bad, or indifferent. The flamenco dancers are here now, and we'll go to see them, although I'm not at all sure we would if we were in New York or London. One good thing—with very little in the way of television or movies, our fifteen-year-old boy goes to the opera and concerts.

What you have in Rome is good home life with very interesting people. You're not inclined to stay with your own professional group as much here as you are in the United States. Ninety-nine per cent of our friends in the United States were in the motion picture industry. Here, they are writers, artists, journalists, doctors, sculptors, diplomats, and an occasional businessman. In fact, when we invite people over or go to someone's house, we're usually the only movie people present.

The people you see here are mainly English-speaking, I suppose. What have you done about learning to speak Italian?

MRS. FLEISCHER: After we got settled, I took a crash course. For six months, I studied with a tutor practically every day. I got a good hold of the language then, but it wasn't refined. Now I've started studying again. I have reached the place where I am now doing the accent so that it won't be too vulgarly *Romano*.

FLEISCHER: I don't have the time to do that. My associates all speak English, and I have crews who speak English. I can't take the time to try to express myself in Italian on the set, and if I did, I might make a mistake, and they'd bring in the elephants at the wrong time. Mickey speaks fluent Italian, and this is important, because she has to deal with the tradespeople and the servants.

How long did it take to get the servant situation under control?

MRS. FLEISCHER: As long as we've been here we've had constant changes, constant changes. Some of it was a good deal of grief. Tears. Italians are emotional, and I'm slightly on the emotional side. Recently, I got a team together—three people who really know how to run a house—and this morning, the man told me he's leaving to go to work in a government office. That's the way it goes. And ours is not a unique situation. It is this way for everyone, because, as in every other country, as household help becomes more and more prosperous, there is less and less of it. And because the cost of living has gone up so much in Italy, men simply cannot live on the salaries paid to domestic help.

FLEISCHER: As for the cost of living here, it's exactly the same as in the United States. Our monthly "nut" is the same, to the penny, as in the United States.

MRS. FLEISCHER: There are a few things that are cheaper, such as getting your hair done, having hems put up, men's tailoring—a few services like those. But the price of meat is much more. My meat bills are tremendous. You can't get good beef here, because they don't have good grazing lands. They have to kill the animals when they are young. That's why you have so much veal, and even that is expensive.

FLEISCHER: Rent is terribly high, much higher than in the United States. If there is rent control, so much money goes under the table that the law doesn't mean much, if anything. Utilities are very high. Heating this house is outrageously expensive.

MRS. FLEISCHER: In an apartment, heating is not furnished as part of the rent. For two months, we paid a hundred and thirty-two thousand lire, which is about two hundred and thirty dollars, just for heat.

FLEISCHER: Electricity is also very high. And our phone bill, some months, is a thousand dollars. Here, you make a lot of phone calls that you wouldn't make in the United States. Servants are cheaper here than in America, but we need more of them. Then they get tremendous benefits—unemployment insurance, health insurance, and so on, all of which the employer pays.

MRS. FLEISCHER: Servants here are not as efficient, and they don't take quite the responsibility that our people do in the United States. Also, they are not accustomed to using household appliances. They break them, and the appliance companies take weeks to fix anything. The breakage by the servants is enormous. We sometimes refer to it as "smashing service." Dishes. I was going to get bone china from England and all sorts of things, and I've ended up with almost dimestore stuff. That way, it doesn't hurt so much to see the big cracks.

FLEISCHER: Things are broken almost immediately upon arrival in the house. They take the dishes and throw them in the sink. We got the new refrigerator, and the first thing—smash—the glass cover that goes over the vegetable tray is smashed to pieces. During the six months that we've been in the apartment, we've had four shelves in the refrigerator replaced. We got a washing machine and a dryer, and everybody said, "It's unheard of. It will never work." And it didn't.

Is that because of the servants or because of the water supply? Is it adequate in this building?

FLEISCHER: We're all right here, as far as water is concerned. In some places, I know, there isn't enough pressure, so there just isn't any water. My dentist is running out of water at his office. The patients can't spit. Also, his lights go out all the time. Drill stops.

What about the medical and dental services? Are they good here?

FLEISCHER: No.

MRS. FLEISCHER: If anything serious happened and it were possible, I'd be on a plane to the States in a hurry. However, we do have a doctor here that we have a good deal of faith in. The things that have happened—flu and so on—have not been serious. Knock wood.

FLEISCHER: The hardest thing to find here is a good dentist. We've had dozens of them. Now we have two that we juggle back and forth.

Mine has brand-new equipment, just like in the States. High-speed drill, supersonic device for cleaning, and a lot of other fancy stuff. He's very good indeed. Of course, this assumes that his electricity doesn't fail nor his water supply.

Getting back to the "smashing service" and other household trials, I wonder when you get to the place where amusement turns into exasperation? Most Americans seem to find the Italians very entertaining, to begin with.

FLEISCHER: That's right. It goes in cycles. Everyone we've spoken to who lives here goes through the same thing. You come here, and you love everything. You see the charm of it all. Then they get to you with the inefficiency and the breakage and the stupidity and the dishonesty. I mean, *sheer* stupidity. As a result, you enter a period when you think you cannot stand the people another minute. Really, you want to throttle every Italian with whom you come into contact. They do have an unpleasant side. I'm involved in several law suits here. They love to sue, and now we love to sue, too. That's very Italian. The time when you want to throttle them all is a sort of crisis. You pass through that, and enter a period where you say, "Oh well, this is the way it is done here, so just relax." I think we're getting into that period of the cycle now. You try to see things in the most amusing light. You laugh at everything—when it doesn't hurt too much.

> "To anybody who's lived in London
> and has had the pleasure of living among
> polite and courteous and wonderful
> people, New York is just intolerable."

Nunnally Johnson, who was born in Columbus, Georgia, in 1897, had a distinguished career as a newspaperman, mainly in New York City, before moving to Hollywood, in 1932, to become a writer and producer of motion pictures, the field in which he has since continued to work. His best-known films include *The Grapes of Wrath*, *The Man in the Gray Flannel Suit*, and *The World of Henry Orient*. The last was the American entry in the 1965 Cannes Film Festival. A tall, angular man with an extraordinarily expressive face—perhaps at its most picturesque when registering mock wide-eyed wonder—he speaks softly in a southern accent that has remained practically unimpaired. He and his wife, Doris, whom he married in 1940, live in a handsomely furnished flat—actually two flats on the same floor; he uses one as his office—at 33 Grosvenor Square, in London. I called on them there, and talked first to Mr. Johnson in his book-lined study.

JOHNSON: We hadn't intended to stay over here. I went to Rome to make a picture during the summer of 1959. It was called *The Fair Bride*. It's a thing I'd like to forget. Just a horror. Anyway, while we were in Rome, I got a call from my business manager, in California. We had put our house, in Beverly Hills, on the market at a price that we really didn't anticipate anybody paying. It really was a white elephant—a place that called for three or four servants, which we couldn't afford, even if we could have found them. The business manager said, "A guy's walked in, wants the house for the figure you set on it—no quibbling—and he'll pay all cash. He's laid down a certified check for ten thousand dollars. He wants an answer in an hour. And you'll have to be out in a month." I said, "What is this—Texas?" He was from Texas all right, but it wasn't from oil. His wife was Maxwell House Coffee.

Well, we debated the matter kind of pop-eyed. We'd lived in that house for seventeen years. I'd been in Hollywood for almost thirty years. Should I pull out? Try to settle down somewhere else at my age? Did I have the *guts* to pull out? Doris, my wife, is very loyal. Assured me I had all the guts in the world. Guts to spare. We said yes to selling the house.

So there we were, Doris and the kids and I, sitting in Rome and no real reason to go back where we lived. We'd been over about nine months, and there was some tax advantage if you stayed away for eighteen months. We didn't want to stay in Italy. I can't live in a place where I can't understand what the hell they're saying. I don't speak any foreign languages, so that narrows the choice down a little. We came here, liked it, and decided to stay.

At that time, we had three kids here, and they were pretty shaken up by being pulled up out of Beverly Hills, which is all they'd known all their lives. The young don't move about as easily as the old. They're not as flexible. We decided the only way to give them a feeling of roots would be to get a place big enough for each to have his own room. We couldn't find anything suitable with five bedrooms to rent. If they had that many bedrooms, they generally had half a bath. Well, this building was just going up. To get what we wanted, we had to take two flats, buying them the way you buy a co-operative apartment in New York, but that was the only way I could figure to let the kids live comfortably and think of this as home. They loved it. Now

I'm going to have a hell of a time uprooting them from London, if and when we ever go back.

Is that a move you are considering at present?

JOHNSON: We have no plans to leave here, but I've been collaborating on a couple of musicals—in fact, I've just come back from almost two and a half months in New York—and I imagine if these musicals go on, and we are able to get rid of these two apartments, we may go back. There's no hurry about it, mainly because we don't know where to go when we get there. I know I don't want to live in California any more. That period has passed. I hate New York. I hate Chicago. I hate the South. I hate the suburbs. And I hate the country. That narrows things down on that side. I suppose we'd live somewhere outside of New York, so it would be accessible, but you wouldn't have the horror of living in the city. I use the word "horror" after two and a half months of it. To anybody who's lived in London and has had the pleasure of living among polite and courteous and wonderful people, New York is just intolerable.

I think the greatest attraction of London is the ease with which you get along with those things and people that you just pass by casually in the course of a day. You ask a policeman something. He tells you, or he may leave his post and take you there. He thanks you and salutes. The taximen here thank you for the tip before they look at it. And I have rarely heard rudeness.

Once in a while, of course, it seems strange being here. I remember one evening a few months ago, we went out to dinner at a friend's house here. There were three couples at dinner, all from the Coast and all living here now. We had all had big houses in California and all that elaborate stuff you accumulate. And there we were at dinner, all crowded into a shabby-looking little dining room. The chairs were uncomfortable. The woman serving couldn't get between the chairs and the wall. I thought, "What the hell are we all doing here? Did sane people make this decision?"

I think I probably get more out of this place than Doris does. The problems of keeping house here are something. I said to Doris once, "When I see you smiling in your sleep, I know you're not dreaming of Marlon Brando. You're dreaming of a supermarket." She said, "That's right." To someone used to American customs in shopping, it can be pretty maddening here. No matter what you ask for, they always say, "Wednesday fortnight." And they have so goddam many holidays.

[*Mrs. Johnson, a very attractive woman, came into the study at this point, and I asked what kind of problems she encountered in running a house in London.*]

Mrs. Johnson: The mechanics of keeping house are the most discouraging aspect of living here for American housewives. We are accustomed to things that function properly, and it's wildly frustrating to have to put up with things that don't. An example. This building is new. They call it London's top luxury-type place, but actually, the bathroom fixtures have always been inadequate and malfunctioning. The other day, I asked the porter to come up, because I thought perhaps he could figure out why the toilets were working even more poorly than usual. He went into the powder room and studied the problem for a while. Then he said, "It's this water box. It will never work. You'll just have to put it up, right at the ceiling. That's the only way these things will really function. You've got to depend on gravity."

I said, "Now wait a minute. Low-flush toilets are so old that surely the mechanics have been worked out long before this. You don't mean to tell me that we still have to depend on gravity to flush a toilet."

He said, "Well, I'll tell you. Sometimes they work, but if you want a dependable one, you're just going to have to have a high-water box."

It's things like this that drive you wild. And it's the way Americans react to such things that make them unpopular. When I first came here, I would probably have blown up at the poor porter, not because he was at fault but just out of frustration. But now I try to play it very quietly, unless I'm so provoked I can't stand it any more, as I sometimes become.

It seems odd that you should find problems with mechanical things here. The English invented some pretty important machines. They didn't come late to mechanics.

Mrs. Johnson: I don't understand it, either. They are a great, scientific people. But they haven't worked out the mechanics of any of the forms that we so long ago mastered—plumbing, pressures, electricity. Take the electrical system. When you go into a shop here to buy a toaster, an electric iron, a lamp, or any other piece of electrical equipment that you would expect to find in an average household, you discover that there is no plug on the end of the cord. The wires are open. So, first of all, you take the appliance to your residence, and you decide exactly where it is going to be used. This is essential, because the electric outlets are different all over the house or flat. They require a particular kind of plug to fit into them, and they are of many different shapes and sizes. Some are flat; some are round; some have two prongs; some have three. They have never been standardized. If you want to move a lamp, say, from a hall into a living room, you would no doubt have to change the plug.

Now, you have decided where you are going to use the equipment and learned what kind of plug you need for that location. The next step is to take the equipment to your local ironmonger, as the hardware store is called, select the proper plug, and have it attached to the cord. Each piece of equipment has a fuse, and the fuses have different amps, depending on the amount of power the equipment requires. A lamp, for example, doesn't use very much power, so you would use a number five fuse in that. But if you put a number five in an electric iron, it won't work. You need a bigger fuse for irons, toasters, and so on. So, we carry a rather complete stock of fuses, ranging from two to thirteen amps.

You see, it's the intricacy. Everything is difficult. Shopping, for instance. I live within two blocks of Selfridge's. It has a fine food department: canned goods, bakery, delicatessen, greengrocer—that's fresh fruit and vegetables—wine shop. A full range. But you can't just go in, take a basket, and go around and collect all the things you have on your list. You may need a can of pineapple, a loaf of bread, a bag of potatoes, and so on. You have to buy each at a separate place, and a bill is made out in triplicate—*in triplicate*—at each place. The time consumed is maddening for a housewife who is on a time budget. What always strikes me is how much wider the profit margin could be if they just introduced some efficiency. "Efficiency"—that's a word that an American dare not say to a Britisher.

How do you go about shopping at Selfridge's? Do you have a cart?

MRS. JOHNSON: No cart. All housewives shop with a shopping bag. The thing that immediately identifies an American from a British or Continental shopper is that the American is forever without her shopping bag. She forgets it. In many shops they have no paper bags at all. They simply push the goods toward you, and you're supposed to have a way of carrying them. If you go into what they advertise as an American-type supermarket, you find that they have little carrying baskets instead of sturdy rolling carts that will hold the needs of an average family.

I have found that I get my freshest fruits and vegetables from the barrow boys—the street vendors. There is no such practice as sprinkling things with water, as we're accustomed to in America, to keep them fresh. Consequently, things wither very fast. If you buy from the barrow boys, the lettuce and celery and such things are better, because there's a certain dampness in the air, or they are rained on, and kept fresh that way. I stopped ordering greengrocer things from indoor markets, partly because their prices are not only staggering but wildly inconsistent from one place to the next. You may pay two and six for a pound of beans at one shop and at a posh one a few doors away, you may pay ten and six. That kind of range.

Once a week, I go with my housekeeper to shop in Soho, and I come home with my arms practically pulled out of their sockets with the heavy loads we carry. When I first came here, I was so disorganized about the shopping and so frantic to get fresh things that I would make the trip several times a week, and come home angry and aching and sputtering. Now I can go once a week, having learned how to preserve my meats and how to freshen my vegetables. Literally, I buy wilted things. Then I wash them, trim them, sprinkle them with water, put them in an airtight container of some kind, and then put them in the fridge. They freshen up and get crisp. The housekeeper goes with me because it takes two of us to carry the load. If I'm entertaining, I will have to make an extra trip the day before to get the things for that occasion.

That's quite a routine. Couldn't you have the stuff delivered?

MRS. JOHNSON: No. It's the same as when you buy from the barrow boys—you carry the things with you. If you buy spinach, for example, or fish, it is wrapped for you. In old newspaper. Then you put that in your carrying bag.

What has been your experience with help here? Some Americans seem to have had considerable turnover with theirs.

MRS. JOHNSON: My housekeeper has been with me ever since we've been here. She's Yugoslav-Italian. She's far from trained, but she has learned a great deal about my methods of cooking and doing things. In general, it's just about as hard to find any kind of domestic here as it is in America. The only thing is that wages have not risen here to the extent they have there. But to find a trained domestic—that's rare indeed. Most of the help now come from Spain, Portugal, and Italy. I have friends who have help who have never used a vacuum cleaner. They're used to shaking rugs out the windows. They're also used to using a feather duster to shift the dust from one place to another.

Then, there's the matter of fitted sheets. They are a very old thing in America. I've been using them in my own home for fifteen years. They cut the time-consuming task of making a bed by about two-thirds, I would say. Well, several times, I have asked in the linen departments of quite expensive places, like Harrods, "Do you have fitted sheets in these beautiful linens?" And they say "Oh no, madam. You'll find that sort of thing in one of the cheaper places."

The shopkeepers here take the position that if they don't have something, it is because it's not worth having. They can't understand why Americans embrace new things. Frozen orange juice, for example. When we first came here, frozen orange juice was almost impossible to buy. I ran from store to store, trying to find it. I remember talking to one shopkeeper about it. "Don't you think it would catch on fast—this concentrated frozen orange juice that needs only to have water added to be ready for breakfast?"

"Oh no, madam," he said. "No one would want to start a day with something cold like that on their stomach. Oh no, it would never catch on."

He's absolutely right. They think we're fools to start our day with a thing like that. They do have a good breakfast here, but it's different. They have grilled tomatoes, french fries, grilled bacon and eggs, a bowl of porridge, and their thin, dry toast.

Do you think the quality of the food you buy here is as good as you were accustomed to buying in California?

MRS. JOHNSON: Yes, I think it is very good. The good stuff is. The good stuff means Scotch beef, Dutch veal, Danish ham and bacon. There's some good English pork, but the Danish pork is the best. I find the very good Scotch beef probably the best beef I've ever had anywhere. But you have to be very selective with your butcher, and let him know your standards. My butcher happens to be in Soho. There's also a very good butcher in Sloane Street and another here in Mount Street, a block or so from us. All three of these butchers cater to the American trade.

Do you get back to the United States often enough to buy your clothes there, or do you buy them here?

MRS. JOHNSON: I haven't worked out a good system for clothes. That's my worst problem here. I won't say that there are not good clothes in this city—I am sure there are—but I've tried two couturiers, both quite expensive, and I just found the end result so disappointing that I didn't return. I have also been to three tailors that were well recommended, and I don't think I've worn the things they did for me more than once or twice. My favorite place to buy clothes is Italy.

But in other categories, there are things here that we really do appreciate. Television, for example. Groucho Marx, who is visiting here now, really popped his eyes when he looked at it. We very often look at shows like "2 Cars," which is beautifully cops-and-robbers stuff, that we could never look at in the States. British television is so superior to ours that I find when I go to the States, it's impossible to look at 75 per cent of what is put on there. Once or twice a week here, I see a play of such caliber—writing, acting, presentation—that it's a real theatrical experience. It's real quality. We don't have that. And the theater, I think, is the best I've ever seen.

JOHNSON: Oh yes. There's something going on here all the time. Big productions. And there's about one-third of the difficulty there is in going to the theater in New York. Doris and I may decide at lunch that we want to go see something that night, so I tell my secretary to get a couple of tickets, or I may do it. The ticket agent we deal with, fellow by the name of George, is right down the street here. And his commission is a couple of shillings a ticket—no more. In New York, a man has to gird himself for about a week to face the whole business of getting to the theater.

MRS. JOHNSON: He has to be in a pretty high income bracket, too. The low cost makes the theater available to so many more people here than in America. As a result, you find the people here are much more knowledgeable about it. The theater here is a constant source of pleasure and delight.

Is it enough of a delight to make up to any extent for the daily annoyances that you encounter in running this household—the inconveniences you've spoken about?

MRS. JOHNSON: I'm afraid I'll never get over the longing to make the mechanics of living function smoothly. And when you've lived in California—I'm not sure I want to live there again—but you can't get over thinking of the wonders of living in air that is not filthy all of the time. Here, as in New York, it is really very dirty. That requires laying out that extra amount of energy every day that I don't seem to have any more. There are other things. The wintertime here I find terribly depressing because of the darkness. Those short, short daylight hours and the long darkness. The gray. The cold. The dampness. The fact that vegetables run right out of season. I never knew that you could run out of carrots at some time of the year. And celery and simple things, such as apples. You find that there are things you just can't get at certain times of the year.

It was really wicked the second winter we were here. That was the dreadful winter of '63. It was a nightmare. We had thirty-seven consecutive days of snow, and since they had no facilities for cleaning it off the streets, it just piled up—snow on top of previous snow. Nothing got cleared away. Everything was frozen. The lorries couldn't get through to bring things from the ships. You couldn't get anything fresh, and we even ran out of staples. Because most of the houses here have their plumbing—the pipes—on the outside of the building, people suffered in this city like I never saw suffering. The pipes broke. You would walk about town, and it would look like one small frozen Niagara Falls after another—the whole side of a building a solid mass of ice. People had no heat. They had no water. It was almost unbelievable.

The people carried on with very little complaint. "Well, it has been a bit difficult this winter, you know," they'd say. Or, "I have felt a bit queer a few times, because we've not had heat, actually, but things will be looking up." That's admirable, of course, but at the same time, they don't set about correcting the faults, as we would. I used to say to Nunnally, "I can't stand this nation, because everything is make-do. They don't complain. They're magnificent about not complaining. And the result is that nothing improves."

You see it as a make-do nation. You understand the philosophy. But you can't subscribe to it. It continues to bother you.

MRS. JOHNSON: It continues to bother me, but at the same time, I enjoy many things here. Mainly, it's the pace. When I think of the living in New York compared to the living in London in respect to the pace, the ease, the gentleness of contact with people, the fact that you are not so rudely met on so many occasions—I don't know whether I could stand it there. One thing I do know. If I were to go back to America now, the re-entry shock would be severe.

JOHNSON: Amen.

"Unless you have a satisfying climate within yourself, you can find all kinds of excuses for not liking something, no matter where you are."

Mrs. Melvin Frank, the wife of an American movie producer, is an attractive, vivacious woman who moved with her husband and three children from California to England in 1960. After living, not too happily, in rented quarters, the Franks bought a charming, five-story house on Connaught Square, in London, and it was there, on a rainy summer afternoon, that Mrs. Frank told me, laughing frequently at some of her deliberately extravagant remarks, what she thought of England.

MRS. FRANK: Life here is like a jet flight. You're either bored to death or scared to death. You just pray that no disaster happens. If it doesn't, what the hell do you do to fill your time? If it does happen, pray harder. For instance, did you know that Charing Cross Hospital has an operating room, where they open the window for ventilation? You're lying there, cut open, and they let the coal smoke in while they're letting the steam out. I saw it on the BBC. There hasn't been a hospital built in London in two hundred years.

I've had it here. That's why I go around saying, "This is Finkville. The whole place is Finkville. A nation of finks." After a while, I calm down. But the only way to get rid of what this place does to you is to holler and scream and make jokes about it. That's the way I've coped with problems all my life—making jokes about them. You know, I have "funny" operations. I have "funny" problems with the children. And my heart's breaking all the time. I'm not so sure that you're going to want to hear what I have to say. I'm living here because my husband loves it. And there are psychological reasons for that, too. It's a man's world here. The world of men—the clubs and all—he adores that. It isn't just a matter of going to the clubs. It's the whole attitude toward women, which is much different. Much.

I do want to hear what you have to say, and, of course, one of the things I'd like to hear is why you came to England in the first place, and whether it was by choice or coercion or what.

MRS. FRANK: It was by choice, in the beginning. We got tired of Hollywood. It's a company town. You meet a lawyer once in a while, but mostly everybody there is in the same line of work. We had an acre of ground in Holmby Hills. We lived on a little island all to ourselves. We had a sixteen-room house, and the taxes were too high, and we were always understaffed. The children were fifteen, fourteen, twelve—around there. The oldest is a girl. We said, "Look, in two years or so, she'll be going to college. Why don't we take the children now, and show them what the rest of the world looks like." And as far as business was concerned, making movies in England has an attractive economic side, because the government subsidizes motion pictures here. If it weren't for this subsidy, I think you would see a mass exodus of Hollywood-American movie makers back to the States. Don't think people stay here because they like to. This is an economic thing.

How did the children react to living here?

MRS. FRANK: The two older ones loved it. They melted into the scenery. I think one reason was that they had freedom for the first time. In Los Angeles, you drive your kids everywhere. About all they ever saw of me was the back of my head. Here, they were on their own, to travel on the bus or the tube or whatever. The transportation system here is marvelous, but it took a lot of courage at first to hear them say, "Well, I think I'll take the 72 Bus. See you later." And go merrily on their way. I would quake, but it was splendid for them. The third kid had a pretty tough time of it here. The older two are sort of intellectuals, and they visited museums and things like that, but the twelve-year-old is a baseball player—a sort of Sporting Life—and it was rough on him, because it rains all the time. The two older kids would sit down with a book, but he would want to go rowing on the Serpentine, or do something like that.

Where did they go to school?

MRS. FRANK: Liz, the girl, went to the City of London School for Girls. She was the only American student in the school. She had gone to a private school in Los Angeles, and her history teacher there had come from the City of London School, so, because Liz is a good student, they made an exception and took her, although they were very suspicious. She happens to be an egghead-type child, and when she left, she led the form in everything.

It wasn't so easy for Andy and Jimmy, the two boys. They had to go to schools for American students. Well, they didn't *have* to. You can go to English schools, but the system is completely different. For example, a teen-ager, preparing for college boards, wouldn't get American history. So, to get college preparatory work, you have to go to a school for American students. There used to be two of them here. One was the Air Force School, and the other is the American School, which is privately owned. They moved the Air Force School out of London —it's now about an hour's ride out of the city—so for all practical purposes, you have no choice but the Anerican School. This was started after the Second World War, and now has an enrollment of about four or five hundred. In my opinion, it is badly staffed and badly run, but the line to get in forms at the right. I'm not going into it all, but the experience for our boys was disastrous, and we took them out. We put Andy into a tutorial school here, and then, for his last year, sent him back to Beverly Hills High School. He made Bard College, in New York. He's a music major. Liz is in Bennington, majoring in Russian. She wants to be a Ph. D. and ultimately to teach. Jimmy, the youngest, is in the International School, in Geneva, which is an awfully good school. He's going to major in girls. And here I am—no more kids. I had them all at once, and so, of course, I lost them all at once, which I expected, but I never thought it would happen here. It's a rough thing.

I'm sure it is, and yet, except for the boy in Switzerland, the children would be away at school—three thousand miles from home—if you'd stayed in California. And you probably see them as often here as you would have there, don't you think?

MRS. FRANK: No, I don't think so. I don't think the girl is going to come home this summer. That has its ironic side, since I had to force both those kids to go to college in the States. I think that children in their teens can be lured by the second-classedness of this country. The longer they stay away from America, the tougher it is to go back. I think it scares teen-agers, because America is a terribly competitive society, and everything looks as if it would be easier here. But I pushed them into going back to the States, and now that they're psychologically based there, it's very hard for them to come back here.

When they were living here, though, they liked it. After we'd been here about three months, Andy, the middle one, said, "My God, we're living in the world." So, it was marvelous then, but I never thought we'd be here this long. Yes, it was fascinating for them. My daughter went to Hyde Park Corner, and got in with the CND—you know, the ban-the-bomb group—and brought home kids who hated America, and were slurping down American coffee, and saying, "This is great coffee, but the trouble with America is . . ." you know, Vietnam, Dominican Republic, and so on. She'd bring home these long-haired guys, and we used to argue with them an awful lot. You know, I'm always defending America.

Always?

MRS. FRANK: Oh, all the time. It's interesting. I started to work with the birth control organization in North Kensington, and somehow in conversation with the ladies I work with there, the word, "high-powered," comes in very frequently. "Of course, we're not as high-powered as you Americans." Or, "Of course, we don't have the high-powered advertising that you do." That word seems to turn up all the time. It puts you on the defensive. They do it in other, funny little ways. "I'm afraid you'll have to get used to our biscuits. Ours are not quite as rich as those you have in America." That sort of thing. I say, something like, "Well, I think one biscuit is as good as another." But that doesn't seem to do much good. No matter what you say or do, you just feel out of place.

I would say, speaking of displaced Americans, that how well they adjust depends on (a) the relationship between husband and wife (b) their ages and (c) how occupied the wife is. I loved it here the first year, actually two years. I really adored it. The children were here, plus the entertainment, plus the enormous problems of running a house. It was a challenge. I had never been to Europe before, so this was all new, and I was sightseeing, and it was marvelous. But then there were the school problems, and then all the kids went away, and with one thing and another, I just didn't adore it any more. You know, I would think that any American wife, unless she has small children, will be in trouble when she goes to live abroad, whether it's in England, Japan, Spain, or wherever.

For example, one of the problems that we ran into here was housing. It was an awful problem. We rented a place in Green Street—what they call a maisonette. We overlooked a very lovely park-like area that had a little fish pond, but we weren't allowed in. Only the ground-floor people were allowed in. Now, we came from an acre of land in Los Angeles, with a fifty-two-foot swimming pool and a badminton court. My twelve-year-old would look around and say, "Can't I just touch the grass?" Well, that was rough, especially when you were paying forty-five pounds a week—like a hundred and thirty-five dollars—for a place furnished in Early Awful.

Then we rented a house in Yeoman's Row from a British woman who's married to a down-and-out Austrian count, and calls herself "Princess." The rent there was also exorbitant. Yeoman's Row is very interesting. It's just a short little street. It's what they call a cul-de-sac. The street was bombed during the war and destroyed. When they rebuilt it, they put Georgian houses on one side and London County Council Housing—what we call low-cost housing, only this is state-owned—on the other. When we first moved in there, my little boy immediately made friends with kids across the street. Lady So-and-So, who lived in the house next to ours, called me on the phone and said, "You know, those are lower-class children, and if you let them in, they'll destroy your home." That was a shock.

What did you say to her?

MRS. FRANK: I said they seemed like nice enough children to me, and I didn't plan to let them destroy anything. She said, "Well, keep them out of my garden." Which was three-by-three. I had trouble with that lady. In London, you know, the overflow drain pipe from bathtubs runs out into the street, so you can be walking down the street in your best hat, and soapy water hits you. You think it's raining soap. All it means is that someone's bathtub is overflowing. Now, just after we'd moved into Yeoman's Row, one of my kids had a bath. There's no shower to stand under all day, so the kid is taking a good long soak in the bath and running the water full force, and Lady So-and-So came out of her house—there was just a breezeway between us—with a little veil on, and it got her. She knocked on the door, and said, "Didn't anybody tell you about the water?" I said, "What water?" And then I heard this torrent. I said, "God Almighty, there's a plumbing leak." She said, "There's no plumbing leak. Your *bawth* is overflowing."

So, for one reason and another, we had an impetus to buy this house, or, strictly speaking, lease it. There are two ways of acquiring property here, you know. You buy what they call a freehold or a leasehold. A freehold you own outright, the way you buy a house in America. A leasehold you just own for a certain period of time, and then it goes back to the owner. While you own it, you do all the improving. It's a lovely racket that somebody in 1066 figured out. In Anthony Sampson's book, it tells you there are six or seven landowners in the whole of England—the Crown, the Church of England, the Duke of Westminster, the Duke of Portsmouth, and so on. They've got the land. Then people build on it, and the value of the land goes up, and then they get it back. Oh, it's beautiful.

We have an eighteen-year lease, which we bought from the Church. The Church owns most of Paddington, including buildings used as bordellos, as they call them here. They pray for them on Sunday, and go to the bank on Monday. We hope the value of this place will go up, so that when we sell it, we can at least get out what we've put into it. It is a lovely house. It's five stories high, and I'm going to die on the stairs of a heart attack and with great muscles in my legs. This house is a compromise. Have you looked at what they call flats here? Modern luxury flats? They're rabbit warrens. If you want a place with character, you have to have a house, and that means stairs. When I have to negotiate them, I just huff and puff. I'm no spring chicken. I'm fifty-two years old. I happen to have great legs. The way it works with these stairs is that if you've forgotten your lipstick, you say, "The hell with it. I'm not going up those stairs again. I'll go without it." And it costs a hundred bucks a month to heat this house. So that's a big item.

How do you think that living costs here compare generally with those in California?

MRS. FRANK: Food and housing, for value received, are very expensive, I think. We eat a lot of imported food—cake mix and things like that—and, of course, that stuff is more expensive than local products. Help is cheaper. For instance, I have two girls here—a cook and a daily. One makes eight pounds a week, and the other makes eleven. That's less than two hundred and twenty-five dollars a month for the two of them. One is Hungarian, who's been in Britain for twenty-five years. The other's from British Guiana. I've had English help. I had a British cook. She had never seen a refrigerator, so she used to put the ice cream in the vegetable crisper and the cottage cheese in the deep-freeze compartment. Steer away from British cooks. The dailies are all right.

Have you found shopping a problem?

MRS. FRANK: No. I do it all by phone. Finally, I've got it all squared away. There's one great grocery store here—Leon's, in Marylebone High Street. They're lovely people and very enterprising. They go over to America to inspect the new products. They've got Chef Milani, they've got Hershey's—everything that Harrods and Fortnum's have, without all that tailcoat stuff. You know, I still can't get used to calling a can of pineapple a tin of pineapple, so I call up and say, "Send me three tins of canned pineapple." That's your double negative in canned goods. When I first got here, the only place to buy toilet paper was in stationery stores. It was paper, so where else? It's just recently that they've put it in grocery stores. Progress.

I still catch myself saying, "Why don't they?" For instance, they holler about import-export here. They've got to export to stay alive. True? Yet, the shops in the West End all close up tight on Saturday noon, and here are these thousands of Americans, milling around and trying to buy British goods, and they can't even get in the door. I was at dinner one night at the Embassy, and I asked Mr. Callaghan, who was then Minister of Finance, about this. He said, "Mrs. Frank, nobody has been able to find an answer to this problem, because, you see, the shop assistants have always been accustomed to working a five-and-a-half-day week. So, the shopkeepers just don't see how they can work out a scheme to remain open on Saturday afternoons." So, I said, "Well, you know, somebody might just pick up the phone and call Saks Fifth Avenue in New York, and say, 'How do *you* do it?' "

Well, there you have it. They haven't been able to figure out how to stagger the hours, so a clerk doesn't come in on Tuesday morning, and works on Saturday afternoon instead. You know, after all these years, I'm as bewildered now as when I first came. I still can't get used to trying to deal with workmen who say they'll be here on Tuesday morning at ten, and never show up.

Don't you find that problem in the United States, too?

MRS. FRANK: No. Maybe in New York, but certainly not in Los Angeles. Oh no. My God, they're after the job there. Here you have total employment—total, incompetent employment. Let me tell you how it works. I wanted the drapes in this room cleaned. The people who clean the drapes won't take them down, because they're not insured against a man falling off a stepladder. So, normally, you would have to find a guy to do that, and wait for him to show up. And no one can find a handyman here. I'll tell you how I finally got the drapes down: when this room was being painted, I got the painter to take them down. Then you wait for the people to come and pick them up. Finally, they came, and then they brought them back, and they were ruined. They had pulverized the fabric or something. They looked like rags. I hollered, and they took them away to repair them. They brought them back again, and they're seven different lengths. I'm caught, because there's no insurance. I'm out six hundred dollars' worth of drapes. These sofas were recovered. Ever since, the upholstery buttons keep coming out. I've had the man back thirty times. I have this special box to store the buttons that come out. Would you believe it?

If you say so, but the British have a considerable reputation for knowing something about furniture. You know, Chippendale and all that.

MRS. FRANK: I know. This is my point: I think for the last two hundred years the English have been the world's greatest masters in blowing their own horn. They had the world bulldozed into thinking they knew what they were doing. Maybe the rest of Europe was even more incompetent. If the Germans had only known. . . . Oh, they would have lost their way here anyway. They'd never been able to find Edgeware Road. How can you figure the British? They hate to see an old building torn down and a new, functional one put up, but they're going to legalize abortions. Isn't it an amazing country? I'll never understand it.

Of course, they'll never understand us, either. Americans are kind of crazy. I have a bed upstairs that I brought from California. It's eighty-eight by eighty. It's bigger than a king. It's a king and a queen. There are special sheets that go with it. They're manufactured in the States. The sheets are a hundred and twenty-two by a hundred and eight. They cost twenty-one bucks apiece. A laundry lost four of my sheets. I was desperate, because you can't get them here. So, I'm on the phone to the governor of the laundry, and I said, "My God, you've lost my sheets!" He said, "I know, madam, but we will replace them." I said, "But you can't replace them, because the ones you have here are too small." He said, "Do you mean that the biggest sheets in England don't fit your bed?" And I said, "That is correct. They don't." He said, "Madam, how large is your bed?" I said. "It's eighty-eight by eighty." There was a long pause. Then he said, "Madam, *surely* not." Sometimes we are a little too much.

Going back to something you said earlier, I believe you said you were here not by choice but because your husband finds it agreeable here.

MRS. FRANK: That's right. I think he would stay here for the rest of his life. We do have this house, which is quite lovely, and he has an office in Grosvenor Street, and when he gets up in the morning, he doesn't have to read the Hollywood *Reporter* and *Variety*. Do you know Harry Kurnitz, the writer? Somebody asked him, "Why did you move to Switzerland?" And he said, "When I found myself getting up in the morning, picking up the *Reporter* and reading a rave review of a picture done by my best friend, and then standing up and shrieking, 'God damn it to hell!'—well, I figured it was time to get out." And this is what happens to you. It's *so* competitive. And everybody in Hollywood seems to be doing so much better than you are. Here, you're on your own. This is a dream world, as far as my husband is concerned.

I think he has got to the place where he doesn't even notice the weather very much. Of course, when I first came here and everything was marvelous, I didn't mind it so much, either. I lived through the worst winter in two hundred years. That was a beauty. Six inches of snow on the ground. Pipes all frozen and bursting. I think the English adored it. They love crises. Everybody is shaking hands with everybody else. The lower classes are smiling at the upper classes, and the upper classes are smiling at the lower classes. Everybody's in the same soup. You know, the fact that these people can put up with the weather here year after miserable year and not resort to mass suicide is a testament to human endurance, or something.

How do you cope with the weather?

MRS. FRANK: It *bugs* me. It *bugs* me. I suppose if I came from New York it would be different. But I came from Los Angeles. Sunshine. You wake up in the morning and say, "Oh God, smell the air!" Even though it's smoggy. And if you want to get away from it, you can go to the mountains. You can have a house on the desert. Here, there are no geographical rewards. When you have a cold and rainy day like this day after day after day after day, I think the barometric pressure begins to affect you. It sits on top of my shoulders, and it's all I can do to get up in the morning. You've got to work at it, if you're going to try to cope with the weather. I turn all the lights on. I wear red. It's crazy. In winter, you have to put something over you when you go out, because of coal soot snowing down. Now they have places called smokeless zones. We're in one here. That's why we can't use a fireplace in the house. You can't burn coal. I have a barbecue on this porch out here, and I thought they'd stop me from using it because of this smokeless zone, but so far they haven't. I'm out there in the middle of winter in my boots and fur coat, barbecuing steaks. I figured if an Englishman can dress for dinner in the jungle, an American can barbecue in the middle of winter.

Then comes the summer. Every time it gets up to sixty-one, the signs come out in front of the pubs on Oxford Street—"It's cooler downstairs." "Shocking weather," they're saying, and everybody's sweaty. And I've got my coat off for the first time all year. I heard someone say that there is nothing wrong with this island that towing it five hundred miles south wouldn't cure. These poor people.

Some Americans here have said that when the weather is bad, they can get their minds off of it easily, because there are so many things to do in London.

MRS. FRANK: Well, it depends on the kind of person you are. If you are the kind of woman who gets up in the morning and puts on mascara, and goes shopping, and has lunch with the girls, and that's a big day—well, you can do that here as easily as anywhere else. But that's not my idea of a big day. I was very active in the Democratic Party in Los Angeles. Here, of course, I can't get involved in political activity. Also, I organized the Women's Volunteer Service of the Los Angeles County Psychiatric Hospital. For the first time, I, as a layman, went in and worked with psychotics, and when I left, I had thirty-four other women who also came in regularly to help. It was an experiment that I alone initiated. I know exactly what I'm doing in working with psychotics. I know occupational therapy. I'm good with people. I'm good with children. There are any number of things I can do in this field.

Did you have professional training?

MRS. FRANK: None. I was analyzed, and my analyst, who held an important post at the Los Angeles County Hospital, got the idea he would experiment with lay volunteers coming in there to assist. I had finished my analysis, and because of the kind of person I am—gregarious and friendly—he moved me in there, and it worked out great. I suppose I could try to do something like that here, except that if I saw where changes ought to be made, there wouldn't be a hope in hell of getting them made. Say that I volunteered to help out in a mental hospital, all full of enthusiasm, and tried to do some simple thing, such as getting a rocking chair in the day ward for the psychotics, the first words I would hear would be, "Well, Mrs. Frank, I'm afraid that won't do. You see, we just don't have the high-powered techniques that you have in America." And immediately you're on the defensive.

Did you run into that sort of thing in working with the Planned Parenthood group here?

MRS. FRANK: No. They're a forward-looking group. They're not accepting things as they are, so an American coming in is welcomed with open arms. That's why I'm happy there. The women who come in there and volunteer their services are marvelous. They're friendly. They're not snobbish. They are gentle to the Jamaicans, the Africans, the Indians—to everyone who comes in. They're not patronizing. They are absolutely the best group of English women I've ever met.

Have you joined any other groups?

MRS. FRANK: No, this is the first one.

It has worked out very successfully, as you say. How do you know that others wouldn't as well?

MRS. FRANK: I don't, except that I have a funny peculiar hunch that if I did volunteer in a mental hospital here, it would be like going into one in Georgia. There's no use getting started. Anyway, I have a hard enough time fighting my own depression. I'm not going in and try to jazz up somebody else who's depressed. Enough is enough, you know.

One thing that many Americans here have said they find useful in taking their mind off the weather is the theater. They think it is one of the great pleasures of living here. Have you found that so?

MRS. FRANK: In the years that I've been here, I've seen four or five plays that were worth going out in the rain for.

That's your term for going out of the house?

MRS. FRANK: That's right. I've seen *Man for All Seasons*, the Zefferelli production of *Romeo and Juliet*, and maybe a couple of others that were first class. The theater is much overrated. The acting is splendid. The writing is awful. And the theaters here are uncomfortable. I was at the Old Vic the other night, and it was so frigid you needed a parka. The minute they opened the curtain, a thirty-mile-an-hour wind tore through the place. It's crazy—sitting in a theater and being cold. And at this time of the year.

It never warms up. Just yesterday, I went to the family planning group in North Kensington. They've taken over two eighteenth-century houses. It was cold in there yesterday, terribly cold. And this is June, mind you. I was working with these English ladies, and one of them came in and turned off the stove. It was too hot for her. My feet were already like lumps of ice, but I was not going to be an American. I was not going to complain. I got so chilled I had to have a hot bath when I came home. But I had made up my mind I was not going to say, "Oh, please turn on the stove, because I have no blood." I felt out of it. You see, it's very hard to get integrated.

So I suppose most of the people you see socially are Americans.

MRS. FRANK: Sure. And they're mostly show business, too, although there is the odd chance here you'll meet somebody who isn't. We've met some artists and writers and people who are in the government, but you're not apt to become friends. The Americans stay pretty much together. It's kind of sad. I have a friend who's been here ten years, and I don't think she has three English friends. We speak the same language, but they're not our kind of people. My husband has an interesting theory, which is that the English and the Japanese are quite a bit alike. For one thing, it's as difficult to become familiar with an Englishman as it is with a Japanese. There are other similarities. Both are an insular people. Both have a royal family. Both were a naval power. Both are tea-drinkers. Both are superficially polite. And so on. The politeness bit I've just about had. I call up the vegetable man over here in the mews, and I say, "I'll take two pounds of onions." He says, "Yes, madam. Thank you, madam." I say, "I'll have four pounds of tomatoes." He says, "Yes, madam. Thank you, madam." And right on down the list. I want to say to him, "Look, thank me for the whole order but not for every tomato, and we can get this over with." That bowing and scraping makes me impatient.

Have you found anything here at all that you do like?

Mrs. Frank: Yes. The bus service, the towel rails, and the water. Those three things. The water's marvelous. I think it comes from the Thames, and is purified three times, and it comes out just great. The towel rails—you know, the ones that have hot water running through them to warm the towels—I adore them. And the buses are great. So are the taxis and the drivers.

Those things are great, but they don't add up to an awful lot, do they? Oh, I don't know. This sounds very corny, but you take your climate with you wherever you go. True? You can talk around the subject, and you can do all the superficial things that make you happy momentarily, but unless you have a satisfying climate within yourself, you can find all kinds of excuses for not liking something, no matter where you are. You know, I've decided that in New York, you've got to have money. In London, you have to be in love. And wherever the hell you are, you should never be fifty-two. I guess that's about it.

GALLERY NOTES

A rather sizable number of Ameropeans took up residence in Europe in order to go into business for themselves. A number of others went into business for themselves in order to live in Europe. For whichever reason, Ameropean entrepreneurs have become familiar figures on the European commercial landscape.

A few have met the Europeans on their own ground, so to speak. For example, Remington Olmstead, a former fullback at the University of California, runs a restaurant in Rome. Mr. Olmstead arrived in Italy expecting to work in the movies, but instead, in 1959, opened a big, bold, brassy combination restaurant and nightclub called Meo Patacca. It is situated in the old city, and seats about five hundred people, mostly in candlelit caves and dungeons. The Italians find the restaurant amusing; the tourists flock to it because they feel it offers authentic Roman atmosphere. The customers are entertained by, among other things, musicians dressed up like an Italian street band, who run into the restaurant and among the tables playing typical Italian airs, like "The Bridge on the River Kwai."

A very much smaller restaurant, the Café de l'Esperance, which is situated in the town of Villers-Cotterets, on the road from Paris to Soissons, is run by another Ameropean named Irving Constant Stern. Now in his late seventies, Mr. Stern, who is a member of the family that founded the Stern Brothers department store chain, has spent a good deal of his life in France, and has a French wife. Operating the café is more or less a hobby, which he took up after retiring, in 1955. "Some of the Frenchmen call me that crazy American," Mr. Stern told a visitor not long ago. "No matter. I'm having a wonderful time." Another Ameropean, George Whitman, appears to be having a fine time running a bookshop called the Mistral, on the Left Bank in Paris. A tall man with a goatee, Mr. Whitman is a former GI who settled in Paris soon after the Second World War. In addition to selling books and prints, the Mistral has become a kind of social center for writers and poets. If they are out of funds, Mr. Whitman offers them temporary lodging without charge in a room over the shop.

Several Ameropeans have become successful art dealers, among them Robert Moses, a native of Cleveland, who owns Galleria 88, in Rome, and Sam Kaner, a Brooklyn-born, black-goateed painter, who operates the Court Gallery, in Copenhagen. Mr. Kaner studied art in New York and then in Paris, where he met and married a Danish girl. For reasons of economy, they settled in Copenhagen. Though he succeeded in selling his paintings both in Denmark and abroad, he hankered to open a gallery, because, as he has said, "I wanted to show the Danes what Americans had done since the war. I was annoyed at how mesmerized they were with French art." Eventually, with a thousand dollars borrowed from friends, he rented a small store in a working-class section of the city, and put on a show featuring works by Mark Tobey, Sam Francis, Man Ray, and Hans Hoffman. It was a great success, and so were subsequent shows. Outgrowing the store, Mr. Kaner moved into large and very posh quarters on the Stroget, Copenhagen's main thoroughfare, where he now shows pictures from America as well as Europe to a widening clientele from both continents.

Generally speaking, Ameropeans who go into business for themselves shun conventional lines and concentrate instead on businesses that have been successful in the United States but are new to Europe, such as Laundromats, telephone-answering services, drive-in car washes, while-you-wait shoe repair shops, bowling alleys, and the like. Colonel Lewis G. Wells, a former Air Force officer, moved to England in 1956 and introduced another American innovation—professional fund-raising. The Wells Organization, over which he presides, has since raised the equivalent of more than a hundred and twenty-five million dollars for British churches, schools, and universities. Eight years ago, Paul Kiernan, an Ivy League product who now lives in London, established an employment agency that specializes in recruiting executive talent for American firms operating abroad, and the firm is thriving. With capital of three thousand dollars raised from the sale of his sports car, Alan K. Jackson, a former Dartmouth track star, set up International Research Consultants, Inc. in Geneva in 1960. The organization, which performs complex technical research tasks for both American and European corporations, now has subsidiaries in France, West Germany, and Italy.

Ameropean businessmen very seldom become a part of the important industrial or banking circles of the countries in which they live, but their independent enterprises sometimes reach important financial dimensions. Samuel Cummings, a native of Philadelphia who has lived for many years in Monte Carlo, set himself up in business as a dealer in used firearms in 1952. His assets at the time consisted of savings amounting to twenty-five thousand dollars and, as he has said, "some real fine quality notepaper and a small portable typewriter." Today, Cummings is the head of a corporate maze known as International Armaments Corporation, which may be the world's largest private supplier to governments and individuals of surplus arms, ranging from rifles, swords, and uniforms to ships, tanks, and jet airplanes. The sprawling munitions combine, which Cummings directs from a sumptuous, thirteen-room apartment and office overlooking the Mediterranean, has assets of some ten million dollars.

Probably the biggest success story among Ameropean businessmen is that of Bernard Cornfeld, a graduate of Brooklyn College and a former welfare case worker, who pioneered the selling of mutual funds in Europe. Since 1956, when he set up a one-man operation in Paris and began selling mutual funds to American servicemen, Cornfeld has developed a worldwide empire, which has headquarters in Geneva and consists not only of mutual funds but also banks, insurance firms, loan companies, and an assortment of other enterprises with some fourteen thousand employees, branch offices in fifty countries, and total assets exceeding a billion dollars. The founder, who is in his early forties, has accumulated a personal fortune of more than twenty million dollars.

The typical Ameropean businessman, however, is a small operator, who has the same problems that a small businessman has in America, plus a few more. For one thing, capital is hard to acquire. Neither American nor foreign banks are apt to be interested in the kind of ventures an Ameropean usually launches; if he is able to borrow money, he is more often than not charged interest at a rate three or four times higher than what he would pay in the United States. If his business requires American-made equipment, such as would be needed for self-service laundries, it will generally cost him more, because he has to pay a steep import tax.

"When you open for business, your troubles are just beginning," I was told by James Nolan, who has worked in Europe for twenty years. "You run into local competition before long. If the idea is good, people on the spot are going to try it, too. Unless you can maintain your lead of know-how, what chance have you got? It was easier immediately after the war, when everything was chaos. It certainly isn't today. There are too many people in whatever country you want to name who want to get into these businesses, and the competition is rough. You have to remember that no matter how well you speak the language, they speak it better. No matter how good your contacts, they almost certainly have better ones and a lot more sympathetic audience from whatever authorities you have to work with. It's not an easy thing. Certainly, some Americans have succeeded very well here. But the odds are against it."

Another difficulty faced by Ameropean businessmen is that they have to contend with bureaucratic red tape and tax laws that are almost always far more frustrating than they would encounter at home. In Italy, for example, taxes are settled on the basis of negotiation. Once a year, both the taxpayer and the tax authorities declare what they consider to be their income subject to the family tax, which Martin Sheppard mentioned. It is standard practice for the taxpayer to put down a very low figure and the tax authorities to put down a very high one. (Last year, the president of the Fiat corporation calculated his taxable income at $131,200, while the tax people declared it to be $1,440,000, or more than ten times as much.) The declarations are the opening moves. Then both sides get together and bargain. Out of these negotiation sessions the actual tax that has to be paid is determined.

"It's a game you have to play," I was told by an Ameropean who runs a modest-sized business in Italy. "Two years ago, the tax people figured my family tax should be seven million lire—about eighty-five hundred dollars. Ridiculous, of course. I said it should be four hundred dollars. Also slightly ridiculous. So, as usual, I go down to the tax bureau, wearing my old clothes, no wrist watch, no ring, and I act like a real stupid American. Down there, I don't understand the Italian language good at all. Also, as usual, the tax man is adamant, so I invite him and his wife out to dinner. We go to a very good restaurant, and we do it right. Flowers for the wife. Champagne. For the tax man, you have a book. Any book will do, only you put ten-thousand-lire notes between the pages. I had one fellow call me up and say there weren't enough pages in the book. You don't win all the time. Anyway, a few days later you go back to the tax office, and the man says, "I've been reviewing your tax, and I think it is a little exaggerated." So, as it worked out two years ago, instead of paying eighty-five-hundred dollars, I wound up paying nine hundred."

Many Ameropeans have trouble getting used to the way taxes are collected in certain European countries, particularly in Italy. The haggling and the bribery and all the rest go against the grain. They find, however, that there is no alternative to accepting the system. I was told by a friend in Florence about an American who had come there from New York to set up a shoe exporting concern. He announced that he was going to operate exactly as he had in the United States; he would keep honest books and just one set; he would declare the actual valuation of his property; he would pay taxes based on that valuation; and there would be no false declarations, no bribery, no bargaining. He followed this system for three years. As often happens, the tax authorities were behind in their work. Consequently, it was three years before they got around to checking the newcomer's tax return. They saw that he had declared the value of his property to be three hundred thousand dollars, and assuming that he had put it down at one-fourth of the actual valuation, which seems to be the custom in Florence, they said his tax would be based on a valuation of one million, two hundred thousand dollars. "The poor fellow was wiped out, literally," my friend said. "They simply wouldn't believe him. After paying all his extra taxes, he had to go out of business. It's the old story. When in Italy, do as the Italians do, if you want to survive."

"New York has no hold on me any more. I don't fancy it."

Abe Aronsohn, an affable, soft-spoken, gray-haired man in his seventies, went to England in 1920 as a musician, and stayed on to become the proprietor of some of the most famous clubs in London. With his partners, who are English, he owns the Four Hundred and the Embassy, well-known night clubs, as well as a popular discotheque and the Curzon House Club, one of the city's top gambling clubs. I called on him in his office, a rather small and simply furnished room at the rear of the Curzon House Club, a handsome, three-story brick structure that was formerly a residence and was once temporarily occupied by the Queen Mother while her own house was being redecorated. When I arrived, Mr. Aronsohn was discussing some business matters with his secretary, Miss Harding, a friendly, efficient woman, who has been in his employ since 1935. At Mr. Aronsohn's suggestion, she ordered tea for the three of us, and stayed on to listen, and occasionally to comment, as he talked about his Anglo-American life and times, beginning in 1919.

ARONSOHN: I was playing at the Century Roof at the time. I played the reed instruments, including the saxophone, which was very new then. In fact, there were only three of us in New York who played it. One of the popular dance teams of that period was Maurice and Leonora Hughes. They were considered in the same category as the

Castles, though they were not as well known. They had been engaged on a six-week contract at the Savoy Hotel, in London, and Maurice wanted to take his own orchestra, because he didn't think the English musicians were good enough on jazz to play his music. He was very anxious to have a saxophone, partly because of the novelty. He had been up to the Century Roof and heard me play, and he asked the agency that I worked for to find out if I would like to go to Europe for six weeks.

Well, it was rather a difficult decision, because, in the first place, I had come to New York from St. Paul, where I was born, not to play but to go into business. I had intended to go into men's wear with my father-in-law, which we had been in in the Middle West. But business conditions, right after the war, were not good, and to have invested at that time would have been very dangerous. While waiting for things to pick up, I loafed around for a while, and then, since I'd had considerable musical experience, got a job playing in orchestras.

When this offer to go to Europe came along, I went home and told my wife and my father-in-law. My wife thought I was crazy, but my father-in-law thought it wasn't such a bad idea. Maurice had offered me three hundred dollars a week, against about seventy-five to eighty which I was earning in New York. My father-in-law said, "What better can you do? Have a holiday." So, we rented our apartment, and my wife and I came over to London. That was in 1920. I was about twenty-eight. We had no children and no ties, and could just pick up and go.

Some of the things I found here I liked. In New York, I had been used to working from seven in the evening until three, four, five in the morning. Over here, I worked from nine o'clock until a quarter to twelve. In those days, you had to play "The King" at a quarter to twelve, and finish dancing at midnight. That was the law. Playing three hours a night—we were stealing our money. I had all day long to play golf and visit and sightsee. I liked that. But we had great difficulty. The weather was horrible. It has changed considerably during the many years that we've been here. But in those days, it never stopped raining. When I came over on the *Aquitania*, the first advertisement that I saw said, "Take a Mac along and enjoy your holiday." A "Mac," you know, is a raincoat. It seemed very peculiar to me that you had to take a raincoat to enjoy your holiday. But I learned.

Well, the orchestra was very successful, and after Maurice and Leonora went back to the States, the Savoy asked us to stay on. We signed a new contract, and after completing that, signed another. We were a very successful outfit for several years. We played in many places besides London. In fact, we took a lot of jobs on the Continent, because we just couldn't stand the weather here. It was terrible, really terrible. The work was easy, and the money was good, but I hated it here.

Because of the weather?

ARONSOHN: Because of everything. For instance, there were two kinds of people in this country in those days. There were the very rich and the very poor. There were very little in between. We were accustomed to living with a medium class of people, where, if we went to a hotel, we had a bathroom. Well, there were very few hotels in this country in those days. When we first came here, we tried living in what they call "digs," which are rooming houses, but we gave that up in a hurry. After that, in the wintertime, we used to live in the Cecil Hotel, because they had central heating, though no running water in the room. In the summertime, we used to move across the street to the Strand Palace, which had running water in the room but no central heating. So, we had this constant moving, back and forth. Fortunately, I had a couple of uncles living here. They had homes in London and places at the shore, and they made life pleasanter for us.

About 1928, the man who was then the leading orchestra leader in this country, Ambrose, asked me to join his orchestra. He had just been engaged by the Embassy Club, which was considered the top place not only here but in the world. I said yes, and I played there for a couple of years. When Ambrose left to open the Mayfair Hotel, at a salary three times that of the Prime Minister—you should have seen the headlines—the managing director of the Embassy asked me to form an orchestra. Which I did, and signed a five-year contract. I also got permission to open an office and hire out orchestras to play under the Embassy name at hunt balls, debutante balls, and other big affairs around the country. The first year, we did something like sixty thousand pounds of private parties. We also had orchestras in six different hotels. Normally, the English orchestras, not knowing very much about dance music, were in the habit of playing for ten or fifteen minutes and then resting for ten or fifteen minutes. We introduced continuous music. No stopping. Which captured everybody.

In 1935, I decided to stop playing, and I opened the Four Hundred Club, in Leicester Square. It was the first nightclub here to use American ideas. It was also a place where evening dress was required. My partners never thought I could make a success of an evening-dress place in Leicester Square, but we were very successful.

MISS HARDING: It was what you might call a smart late spot for the Court circle.

I have heard it referred to as Princess Margaret's club.

ARONSOHN: Well, she was there quite a bit. So was her sister before she became Queen. And Prince Philip, too. The Queen was practically engaged there. It was *the* place. It was unique in the world.

You speak of it in the past tense, but it is still operating. Has it changed its character?

ARONSOHN: A little. In 1958, we took off the rule requiring evening dress. We had held onto it longer than any other place in town. The Savoy Hotel had taken off the rule a year and a half before we did. When we made our announcement, the newspapers headlined, "The Last of Gracious Living Disappearing from London." Oh, it's still one of the top clubs and very successful. So is the Embassy Club, which we bought in 1938, and turned into a medium-priced club. They both stayed open all through the war, except that the Four Hundred was hit early in the Battle of Britain, and was closed for about two months for repairs.

I was in America when the war broke out. My wife and I used to go back every summer for six weeks or so, and we were there in 1939. Even though the United States wasn't in the war yet, I had great difficulty in getting back. I came over alone, in December, 1939. I flew over in an airplane—it was a flying boat, actually—that was no bigger than this room. I thought it was never going to get off the water. When I got here, I went to the Piccadilly Hotel, and met with my partners, and we talked and made plans. I remember coming out of the hotel and being in the blackout for the first time. You could hear the sound of footsteps and hear noises, but you couldn't see a thing. Absolutely pitch black. It was the most frightening thing I've ever experienced—that first night.

I returned to New York, but I was able to get a visa to make two more trips back here. Each time, the traveling got harder and harder. Finally, my wife said, "If you can't get a visa for me, you're not going any more." So we went out to the Coast and I lived out there, always trying, always trying to get back. I don't know why.

MISS HARDING: You know you liked it.

ARONSOHN: Of course, we liked it. But it wasn't easy, in the beginning. I was always glad to get away until, gradually, we became friendly with some people here, and we had a home, and then when I stopped playing, we lived a more normal life. Now, I wouldn't want to live anywhere else.

MISS HARDING: How many years have you been in your flat now—thirty-eight?

ARONSOHN: Almost forty years I've been in the same apartment. In Knightsbridge, just near Harrods.

You mentioned earlier that the weather has changed considerably since you've lived here. Do you think it has improved?

ARONSOHN: Oh yes.

MISS HARDING: Oh no. You've just got used to it.

ARONSOHN: Oh no, no, no. That's not so. It's much better now. We used to have dense, dense fogs. I walked home one night, and I went right by my apartment, and I knew that area as well as I knew my hand. We don't get those dense, black, dirty fogs any more. We don't get rain *all* the time. We do see sun once in a while. Between 1920 and 1939, you never saw sun here. Never. It's much better now.

But don't you think that your view of the weather here is caused, at least in part, by having become accustomed to it?

ARONSOHN: Probably so. A little bit. Anyway, life is so much easier here. There isn't that pace you have in America. Nobody steps on you. Up until just after the last war, nobody took your business away from you if you were gone for some time. When I came back from America after the war, my businesses were all running.

Who ran them during your absence?

ARONSOHN: Miss Harding, mostly. And we had employees. They wouldn't leave you unless they had to go to war. When they came out, they came back to work. You didn't have to go to them and say, "I'll give you another ten shillings or a pound not to go to work for somebody else." There was a great sense of loyalty and a great sense of honesty in this country prior to the last war.

You're dating that also. Have those things changed, too?

ARONSOHN: Yes. Considerably. We still have some of it left. In America, they clamor for English help. They're more stable. They're a little more polite. Did you know that the English immigration quota has never been filled? Never. An English person can get a visa practically overnight to emigrate to the States.

In general, what problems confront an American who wants to go into business here?

ARONSOHN: None. There are no restrictions. None whatsoever. The only thing you have to do, if you are an American and a director of a company, is to put "U.S.A." after your name on the documents. That's all. Otherwise, you're treated as an Englishman. You pay your taxes like an Englishman. If you're in a high bracket, your tax is practically the same as it is in America. In a medium bracket, it's a little more. In a low bracket, the tax is very much more.

I would say that it's much easier to do business over here. Your competition is not as hard. England has great engineers, but they don't develop things the way they do in America. Refugees from all over Europe came to England right after the war, and became very successful in their own businesses. In fact, they went ahead of the English. I've been in other businesses here besides clubs. I opened a chain of stocking shops, and until a few years ago, I was also in the dress manufacturing business. I've always said that I couldn't have lasted in that dress business as long as I did in any other country. The unions are strong here. I think they are less responsible than they are in the United States. But, as I say, competition is very easy here. Anybody who has a little bit on the ball can come to this country and make money.

The Curzon House Club is your newest enterprise and, I gather, the largest. When did you get into this business?

ARONSOHN: To tell you the truth, I didn't want to get into it, but my partners and I had been together for so long, and they begged me to. "Just have a little piece of it," they said, "for old time's sake." So, I said, "All right." And here I am, working eighteen hours a day. Soon after the gaming law came into effect, in 1961, we took over this house, and spent about two hundred and fifty thousand pounds on reconditioning, remodeling, furnishing, and so forth. And we opened up in November, 1962.

This is primarily a gambling club?

ARONSOHN: A sporting club would be more accurate—a residential sporting club. We have just under three thousand members. It costs ten guineas a year—about thirty dollars—to be a member. New members have to be sponsored by an existing member. We're very choosy. If we weren't, we could be the largest club in London. I think at the present time that Crockford's makes more money than we do. As far as plush is concerned, I should say that the Curzon House Club ranks number one. We carry on the same tradition that we did in the Four Hundred. We have thirty-six bedrooms for members who want to live here. We have a very fine restaurant. We have a golf society. Also a motor rally. We have a resident bookmaker. Then we have all kinds of games of chance—bridge, poker, roulette, blackjack, *chemin de fer*, baccarat. We don't participate in the games. We charge a fee to sit down and play, whatever the game—bridge, roulette, blackjack, or whatever. But it's not like Las Vegas. We participate neither in the winnings nor in the losings.

Do you have to contend with the problems they have in Las Vegas—racketeers and the like?

ARONSOHN: We don't have anything like that at all. We don't have any payoffs. We don't have any security or protection. Nothing like that has ever happened in this country, and I don't think it will. We hope that some day we'll have government supervision of the gaming in this country. That would be a very, very good thing.

Aside from the slower pace of living, what are the other things that you find attractive here?

ARONSOHN: Of course, it has always been the people. The politeness of the people. They stay with you. If you treat them well, they appreciate it more, I think, than they do in America.

MISS HARDING: He's just pro-British.

ARONSOHN: Well, I suppose I am, no question about that. After all, look at the years I've lived here. You know, I think that most Americans who come over here don't like it at the start. But if they stay a little while, you can't chase them out. One thing they find is that it's cheaper to live here. The only thing I can think of that is as high here as in America is the price of hotel accommodations. Everything else is on a much lower scale. I can live here for one-third of what it would cost me to live in America in the same category exactly.

MISS HARDING: Does that apply also to business? I've always been led to believe that, comparably, it's better to work over there.

ARONSOHN: Well, of course, you get a much larger salary over there, but it costs more to live. One thing you can do better on is your flat. In California, you can pick up a little apartment, and have all the amenities and comfort of a modern flat at a reasonable figure. You can't do that here. But your food is cheaper. Services are cheaper. Amusements are much cheaper. It's only lately that the top price of a theater ticket has gone up to forty shillings—a little less than five dollars. It's nothing to pay twelve or fifteen dollars for a theater ticket in America. There's no such thing as ticket scalping over here. A fixed commission is added on, and it's very reasonable. If there's no ticket, there's no ticket. You couldn't pay any amount of money to buy one. I had an account with a ticket agency in New York, and I could come into town today and call up the agency and say, "I want a pair of tickets for the hottest show in town," and I would get them. And I would pay forty or fifty dollars for the pair.

Well, I don't go in for that any more. On trips back to America, I used to spend a few days in New York, seeing shows and so on, on the way to California, but now I try to miss it if I can. New York has no hold on me any more. I don't fancy it. Now I fly over the North Pole, and go right on to California. We used to go across on the boats—the Cunard ships. I remember we couldn't wait to get aboard and get our first cup of English tea. We've talked of retiring some time and where we would go. We talked about the south of France. We spend five or six weeks there every summer, but my wife didn't think she would like it the year around. We're too old to go back and forth to America. What we decided is that when the time comes, we'll just stay right here, in London.

> "In general, I would say I have less leisure here, but I lead a more leisurely life. Does that make sense?"

Lu Lubroth, a rather meditative, handsome man with an olive complexion, brown eyes, and prematurely white hair, is one of the few American architects practicing on their own in Europe. The son of an architect, he grew up in New York City, and went on to enroll at Chicago's Institute of Design, where he studied under such distinguished architectural innovators as Buckminster Fuller and Mies van der Rohe, and where he also met and married his wife, who is an artist. In their final year at the Institute, Lubroth told me in his office in a new building on the Avenida Generalissimo Francisco Franco, in Madrid, both he and his wife were awarded a Fulbright grant to study in Europe, she in Vienna, he in Paris. They arrived in Europe, for the first time, in 1951.

LUBROTH: I fell in love with Europe immediately. In Paris, I was supposed to study pre-stressed concrete, but I'm afraid I didn't do it very diligently. I just got enamored of everything. I started to study the history of architecture. I started to photograph. I started to write poetry. Europe affected me in a way that I had never expected. When the Fulbright year was up, I didn't want to go back, so my wife came to Paris, and I got a job in the Paris office of an American construction company—Brown, Raymond & Walsh. I was there for two years, working only on military projects—very uncreative. I thought I wasn't advancing professionally, and as my father and brother are both architects and have offices in New York, I thought I should go back, and we did.

Well, it just didn't work. Being a sort of lost romantic, I could never wake up in the morning without thinking of Paris and Europe, not in the way Americans did in the 1920s—dancing on tops of tables—but in a different way, which touched me very, very deeply. I refused to work for my father, and I went from job to job, but I just couldn't settle down to any of them. I couldn't manage there any more. I had to come back. After I'd been almost two years in the States—exactly twenty-two months, in fact—the company I'd worked for in Paris landed a contract to build American bases in Spain, and they made me an offer to come over and work on the project. Ten days later, my wife and I and the children—we had three small ones then—were packed up and on our way to Madrid.

That was in 1955. The job on the air bases paid a salary, of course, and as I was planning to stay on here and strike out on my own after that project was completed, I saved as much as I could to tide me over the two or three years that I thought I'd need to get established. The day I finished working on the bases, I rented a little room, and went out looking for business. In the beginning, I did a lot of work on speculation—an office building, a small art gallery, and other things—but nothing came of them. It took me two years to land my first paying job, which was designing an interior. I made five hundred dollars from it.

At times during those two years, you must have wondered if you'd made the right decision.

LUBROTH: I never doubted. Because I wanted to do it so much, I never doubted. After that first job, I just kept at it, and the business built up by way of reputation and mostly among foreigners—not only Americans but other foreigners. I found that I could express myself better with them. Spaniards are suspectful, always thinking that perhaps you're doing them in.

I always charged more than anyone else, because I thought I was giving more. Generally, Spanish architects turn out the minimum amount of drawings and specifications for a job. Their job is finished when the clients accept the drawings. The client then turns the drawings over to a contractor, and he does the job from then on. Because the architect has laid the thing out quickly and incompletely, so many problems arise on the site and have to be solved during construction that buildings that should take a year to construct may take two, three, four years. According to the American practice, the architect's work is nowhere nearly finished when he completes the drawings. He must go on to oversee every step of the construction, and make sure the client gets his money's worth. Obviously, the architect who works in that way is going to spend a lot more time, and he's got to charge more. Spaniards don't understand that.

Even so, I began getting more jobs, and when we had grown to the place where there were five or six drawing boards in that one-room office, we had to start looking for larger quarters, and wound up here. About a year ago, I formed a partnership with a Spanish architect, and we have since worked out an association with a Spanish construction firm. Besides my partner and myself, there are now five full-time people in the office and two part-time. So, things are working out. But it is only in the past year or so that I have felt secure about being able to live in Europe the rest of my life. It's been a long struggle.

That's a fairly common plight among architects starting out on their own just about anywhere, of course, but I suppose it was harder for you here simply because you are a foreigner.

LUBROTH: Yes, that's the main trouble. Spanish society is a closed society, both socially and businesswise. A foreign businessman who has some product to sell can have tremendous success here, but a professional man on his own has more difficulty. In my particular field, it seems that every Spaniard has someone in his family who is, or is about to be, an architect. Before the Civil War, it was very much the fashion for the sons in all the good families to study law. Now, the first choice seems to be architecture. It's become *the* fashionable profession. The Spaniards that I would have as clients are in the class that make their friends in school, and form their future business relationships there. Or they are formed through family or social connections. That kind of thing is very, very strong here, and, as a foreigner, I am outside all that. Even the passage of time won't change the situation. It could, perhaps, if you were very social, but one of the reasons I am so very happy here is that we can be *not* social. Oh, we do a certain amount of this. We have prospects and clients to dinner, but our social life is mainly for pleasure, and it's pretty well mixed—Spanish, French, Greek, American. When I first came to Europe, I thought I shouldn't spend any time with other Americans. At the outset, you want to be some sort of snob, but after a while, you mellow, and you find friends here, and you find friends there. You don't ask what they are. I can come full circle, and think perhaps the Americans are the nicest people in the world. They are the most intelligent. They open up more. You begin to appreciate the openness that Americans have. It is a wonderful characteristic. A Spaniard never opens up. You never know what he's thinking.

Does that have anything to do with the difference in language? Do you have any trouble communicating with him—or, at least, talking with him?

LUBROTH: No, it's not that. It's just part of his character. I can talk with him all right. I didn't study Spanish in school, so I have no basis for speaking it with grammatical correctness, but I can get along socially and in business without any trouble. Of course, if I go to the theater and it's a very deep play, I get lost. There's a lot of theater here, by the way, but it's pretty third-rate. It's overacted, almost like soap-opera. I've given it up. The cultural life here is almost a void, and if it weren't for having what I think is otherwise such a rich life, that would hurt.

What is it that makes the life rich?

LUBROTH: I think being able to live life the way you want to live it. There are less limitations. All my time is generally my own. I can devote it to my family, my wife, or I can be selfish and devote it to myself. I can live my life in a way that I can't in New York. You don't mold your own life there. Instead, things mold *you,* and you change. Even in the short time I was back working in New York, I saw a change, accepting things I wouldn't have accepted before. For example, not giving of myself to friends I really liked—not having the time or the energy or the nerve to do it, whereas I can give time to people here without rationing it. If they're in trouble, take them some place, do something for them. Just throw away time, and not have to think so much of it.

And you can do that because you have more leisure here?

LUBROTH: Well, no. I had more leisure in New York. There, I had the whole weekend to myself. Here, I have only one day, or a day and a half, because everybody works at least a half day on Saturday. But somehow you can make the time go further. There isn't the same kind of pressure. And there would be even less pressure if I weren't an American and felt obligated, when I give a client a date for completing a piece of work, to try to see that it is completed. My partner works longer hours than I do, but he's not under that kind of pressure. He says, "Well, if we don't finish until tomorrow, we don't finish until tomorrow." I'm still sort of on the American plan, but it works out differently. Here, you work twelve, fourteen, sixteen hours a day, go home, and are fairly amiable to your wife and children, and are ready to go out at night. In general, I would say I have less leisure here, but I lead a more leisurely life. Does that make sense?

I think so. Is your wife as enthusiastic about living here as you are?

LUBROTH: I think, in a way, she always agreed with me about it, intellectually, and for the past three or four years she has felt pretty strongly about it emotionally, too. Perhaps for different reasons. The fact that there are servants gives her the opportunity to teach and to paint, both of which she enjoys. She has a fantastic schedule. She teaches art in the mornings at the American School, so she's up and out of the house at seven-thirty. This year, she's taken on more teaching—some college students three nights a week. The other nights, and maybe on Sundays, she paints. She is one of two Americans whose work was exhibited in the Spanish Pavilion at the World's Fair. She had two pictures there.

How many children do you have now?

LUBROTH: Four. Two were born in Paris, one in New York, and the youngest here. Twelve, eleven, nine, and not quite seven. They all go to Spanish schools. It's not a perfect solution, but we thought it the best for us, since we plan to stay. If you're going to be here for two or three years, which is the case with most Americans, the American School would be just the thing. Because our situation is different, we send our children to a school called Estudio, which is influenced by the ideas of the liberal elements that existed in Spain before the Civil War. It's a well-organized school. Not very large—maybe three hundred and fifty students. One of the problems is that things are taught too much by rote. Also, not enough attention is paid to the contemporary world. Notes from thirty years ago are still being used. Since our children's school starts about six weeks later than the American School, we send them there every fall for those weeks, and they get English vocabulary and grammar, and they pick up other things. After his first day at the American School, my younger boy came home and told me what a wonderful new game he'd learned to play, using a stick and a ball, and I realized he was talking about baseball.

There are problems in bringing up children here. They don't know really what they are. They say, "Why are we Americans? We were born in France. We were born in New York. We were born in Spain. We live here. Why are we Americans?" And I think that might give them complexes when they get older. But if we can afford it, we will send them to American colleges.

What about their friends and social life?

LUBROTH: My older daughter's best friend is English. She doesn't have many others. She goes maybe half a dozen times a year to a Spanish friend's house. Practically all of the boys' friends are Spanish. They do see children of American friends of ours at the American School, but those friendships don't last. Their parents have a different life from ours. Timewise, we live a Spanish life, and that doesn't jibe with the American children's hours. Our children go to bed at eleven o'clock. They leave the house in the morning at a quarter of nine, and they're in school all day. They go five and a half days a week. So, you have pretty much complete control over their environment. If they're not at school, you know at whose house they are. You know they're not sitting around somewhere, smoking marijuana or something like that. I exaggerate, but you do have much greater control over their development than you do in the States. They go back there about every two years, usually with my wife. Those trips are wonderful for the children. They get a different kind of love from grandparents and uncles and cousins and aunts, which they miss tremendously here.

Do you think you're depriving them of something pretty important by taking them away from that?

LUBROTH: Oh yes, they're being deprived of that. Absolutely.

But in your view, that deprivation is being made up by other things they are getting here?

LUBROTH: Well, I don't put it that way. I've discussed this kind of thing with my wife often enough. I don't overstress the importance of living a life for the children. We're happy here. Very happy. More than I would be in the States. And that's enough for me. I'm not the sacrificing kind of parent who says, "My children will be happy in the States, so I must live there." Personally, I think they might be happier in the States. It's hard to judge. When they go there, they're treated like kings and queens. The grandparents and everybody else make a fuss about them. They have good manners and that kind of appealing superficial thing, and they're given lots of opportunity to do what they can. One plays the guitar, and he receives the cheers of the family. They receive gifts. Somebody says, "I'm your richest uncle. Here's a dollar." We shudder, but it impresses the children, of course. They think they've found a great new world.

Do they complain at all about not being able to stay in that world?

LUBROTH: They're too young to make a heavy complaint. Sometimes there are remarks, like "I wish we could take a ride and see Grandma." But their life here isn't unpleasant. It's true they work hard. They work two or three hours after school. I think if a child is brought up to work hard in school, it becomes natural. If everyone else is doing it, there isn't a problem.

You know, Spaniards really love children. We say all Americans love children, too. Well, we do, but we also have a don't-bother-me attitude. The old saw about their being seen but not heard. You go to a hotel here, and they put in extra beds for the children, feed them at half price. They can't do enough. Children are a class here. They're dressed well, even if they're from poor families. And they have nursemaids, who do all the menial work, which means that the parents have all the advantages of grandparents. The parents, too, can enjoy the children. They're not babysitting twenty-four hours a day. I tell you, that really helps.

Your children haven't been exposed to American life as you have, so they don't really know whether they are missing anything. But as for yourself, do you feel that you are missing anything by living away from the United States?

LUBROTH: Yes. For one thing, technical developments in the States. For another, the fellow next to you, pushing you to do better. Here, it is so easy to do well, as far as design is concerned. I know if I spend a day working out a design, it will be better than anything produced here. That's not a good situation. You get so self-satisfied. I try to be careful about that, but it's hard to avoid unless you have Americans working with you. I try to keep up by reading. Last August, I was in the States for two weeks, and I did nothing but study. I visited maybe thirty buildings around New York, and learned a tremendous amount. I was amazed by the generosity of the architects I called on—the way they helped me and put themselves out to show me new buildings and new developments. It was marvelous. I think it was partly the result of traditional American friendliness and partly because I was a foreigner to them. That gives you some aura. It's nice. And the fact that you don't have the feeling here of being just a number—Architect Number Six Hundred and Ninety-two—that's nice, too. It builds up your ego.

That may be a selfish kind of thing, but it's one of the reasons for being here.

Another thing that I like so much about Europe is the visual aspect.

That would be special for an architect.

LUBROTH: Perhaps, but I don't know whether I was so visual in the States. When I went back in August, which was the first time in three years, my vision was sharp. I think it's the difference that sharpens your vision. If you walk only in your own neighborhood, after a while you don't see anything any more. You go to another neighborhood, and you see everything. One of the great things about living in Europe is that you are only moments away from a completely new visual experience or a completely new social or historical experience. All you have to do is cross a border, and the people are different. The air smells different. Everything, just about, is different.

Another part of the visual attraction struck me when I was walking to work this morning—that in Europe, one is able to *see* a city. The human mind can only take in a certain scale, so what really matters is what happens on the ground floor and a couple of floors above that. If you want to see New York, you have to get on the Staten Island ferry, but all you have to do to see places like Paris and London and Madrid is to walk in them. You get a feeling of things opening up for you. There doesn't seem to be a great heritage of architecture in Madrid. If it weren't for the sun, I don't think it would be such a happy city. Nevertheless, you do get the sense that you can take it in with the eye, and that's one of the reasons why I like it here.

Another thing that I notice, which I don't recall having thought about in the States, is that here one is aware of a mixture of people and of things happening in the city. Old people. Young people. Rich. Poor. Business people. Everything is mixed together. I think that's a pleasant thing. It is the differences that exist side by side that make the city so attractive visually, and give the sense of always being *alive.*

You mentioned that you walked to work this morning. Is that your usual practice?

LUBROTH: Oh yes. One of the nice things about Madrid is the matter of communications. You can get anywhere in ten minutes, more or less. Out of this window you can see the roof of my house. It's a lovely place. We were very fortunate to get it, because houses are difficult to find here. Ours is on about three-quarters of an acre, and the property is full of olive trees and fruit trees. It has a swimming pool and a big terrace, where you can take the sun seven or eight months of the year. When we moved out there, people thought we were crazy. There was practically nothing around. There were thirty or forty caves in which gypsy families were living—right out there, where now all you can see are buildings, mostly apartment houses. The man who owns our house is in the Spanish diplomatic corps. I guess he'd like to see us move out, so he could raise the rent or sell the property, but we don't want to move until we can build our own house, and we can stay on indefinitely, because the Spanish rental laws favor the tenants. The property would be ideal to own, but it would cost around a hundred and fifty thousand dollars. Our rent, though, is very inexpensive—not quite a hundred and ten dollars a month. It's true that you can live well in Spain on less money than in the States. If you have an income of four hundred dollars a month, you can live very well here, and with enough left over to travel.

One reason, of course, is that you pay less taxes. How much did that consideration influence you in coming to live here?

LUBROTH: None whatsoever. It was never a question of economics. Never.

Are there things about living under a dictatorship that get on your nerves?

LUBROTH: Not constantly. Of course, you can't make any outward criticism, and you avoid all kinds of political declarations among your friends. You just put limitations on what you say. Things do come up where you're pretty well considered guilty before proving yourself innocent. For example, we had a problem about the licensing of our car. The law, which we had checked, was nebulous, and we were told that our handling of the matter would be O.K. Nevertheless, there was a reason to doubt, and one day the police just came and took the car and impounded it. It took me six months to work out the legal problems, and the car was returned to me with apologies, but it was a great inconvenience, to say the least.

The very fact of the absence of civil rights would be something hard to get used to, I should think.

LUBROTH: Oh, I wouldn't say one never thinks of it, but it's a minor thing. It doesn't affect my being contented or discontented.

Is not being a Catholic a handicap to a foreigner living here, socially or in business?

LUBROTH: There may be discrimination against Protestants. I don't know. We're Jewish. But there isn't the viciousness about religion and social differences that we see in the United States. Here, you can go with a Negro girl any place—any bar, club, pool, restaurant—and nobody will ever close the door. However, there may be some talk. There is no viciousness against the Jews, though everyone knows who is Jewish in Spain, and they say, "Well, he's Jewish." That's intended to be derogatory, though they will admit that 40 per cent of Spaniards have Jewish blood. There's this kind of subtle thing, but no doors are closed.

There is a synagogue here, but we don't go. I don't believe in religion, though I do send my children to a Sunday School that a group of Americans have formed. Our children are excused from the compulsory Catholic training in school because they are foreigners, but I want them to know Biblical history, and then if they want, they can go on and learn Hebrew. The Hebrew education helps to teach them who they are. Otherwise, they'd be terribly mixed up—more so than they are now.

What about your own parents—what do they think of your living here?

LUBROTH: Disaster. Both sides. However, my wife's parents were here once, and I think they understand. In the last two or three years, I think my parents have finally become resigned to the fact that we're here to stay. They may be resigned, but they're not approving. I've given up trying to explain.

They wouldn't understand, for example, that something else I like about Spain—not so much now for me, personally, but I think it's an important point—is that there is a masculine society here. It exists in France, too, and it appeals to me. We all know couples where we think the husband is great, but the wife is—oh, you know—so why the hell must you and your wife invite both of them because you like him? If you live here, you don't. Instead, the men get together and go out by themselves. For example, last night, I went to dinner with two friends. We had drinks, we ate, we talked, and we had a great time. There are a lot of reasons why you can't do that in New York. For one thing, you've got to be on your toes the next morning at nine o'clock, or the guy next to you, who architects almost as well as you do, is going to be moving ahead of you. There's a trace of this kind of masculine society during the summers in New York, when the wife and children go away for the summer, but it isn't the same. You call up friends then because you feel alone and at loose ends. Here, you call up friends and go out just because you enjoy their company.

Also, an important thing is that Europe, for me, is sensuous. America is not. It's sexy. I don't know how the dictionary distinguishes the two, but for me, the sensuous part is more romantic than the sexual part. This aura of romance that I find in Europe is one of the good reasons for my liking it so much. Women don't just give up when they're fifty. Neither do men. You don't have to be twenty-one, young, and beautiful to enjoy this life. In the States, a twenty-one-year-old girl goes out with a twenty-one-year-old boy. That's exaggerated, but I think you find the young with the young. Here, a twenty-year-old girl will fall in love with a man forty or fifty. It may last only two or three years, but it is a good relationship. That makes life here enjoyable. Not that I place much emphasis on sex as it is, but the aura is nice. It keeps you young. This has nothing to do with being in love with your wife or she with you. Nothing to do with it at all. It's just part of the atmosphere—another thing that makes the existence here more *alive*.

An American psychiatrist who's currently living in Italy told me that, without exception, the Americans living over here that he knew were running away from something. Do you think that applies to you?

LUBROTH: I've had people say that. Before I left, some of them said, "You're an escapist." They're right. I *am* an escapist. But I think you have to ask what you are escaping from and what you're going to. If I were escaping in the customary sense, I wouldn't be here. I'd be in some small town in Spain, just eking along somehow. Actually, I'm more involved with life than ever before. I'm simply living in a different atmosphere, one that I like better than the one I left. I don't kid myself that this one is idyllic. Life here doesn't have all that perpetual glow that it did at first, when we had no economic problems. The glow isn't as bright and constant, but we've found something else here that's richer, more real, more profound, and it goes in all directions.

> "Of course, the fact that all these people just happen to prefer to live here involves no compromising of their loyalty to home."

Douglas Fairbanks, Jr., actor, producer, corporation executive, and knight of the British Empire, has for many years been so familiarly associated with Great Britain, and, at times, with its ruling family that his friends have been known to describe him as the unofficial American ambassador to the Court of St. James's. His detractors, possibly envious of the fact that he has achieved the uncommon feat of having entertained Queen Elizabeth, Prince Philip, and other royal personages, describe him as an indefatigable social climber. Whatever his connection with the Court and however it was accomplished, Fairbanks is certainly close to St. James's Palace; his office is situated practically around the corner, at No. 10 Park Place. I visited him there one spring afternoon, and found him, though approaching sixty, still youthful-looking and full of vitality. Tall, lean, and quick to smile, showing those fine white teeth that he flashed in *Dawn Patrol* and some seventy-five other movies, he conducts his business affairs these days in a rather small, tastefully furnished room that has something of the aspect of a library in a private house. At the outset of our conversation, I said that I had read somewhere that his first trip to England had been made when he was five months old, and asked if that were true.

FAIRBANKS: Yes, it is. You see, my grandfather on my mother's side had been a sort of big nineteenth-century figure in the world of cotton and industry and so on. As a cotton financier, he had business interests over here, and there were also family connections between here and France. Also, my father had come over here as a young man, when he ran away from Harvard and joined a lot of other young fellows who worked their way over on a cattle boat. He made many friends at that time, around 1920. Then, when my mother and father were married, they had a house over here. So, what with my father's connections and my mother's family connections, it was rather natural that I was brought over in the summer of the year I was born. After that, my parents kept coming back and forth. Later on, when my mother and father were separated, I was brought up by my mother. I did some of my schooling in New York, but I was also tutored here. I went to school in France as well, and we used to come over here for holidays. This was always a sort of second base, as it were. When I grew up and started on my own, I picked up where I'd left off as a child. I started my own film-producing company here when I was very young. I was doing much the same thing at home, and each one was sort of dependent on the other. As I always enjoyed traveling, the two operations fell into place very conveniently.

When did you begin to make London more or less your headquarters?

FAIRBANKS: It has never been my headquarters, except in the public mind. New York has always been my headquarters. The other idea is an illusion, I think, largely due to the fact that I have had an identification here, and my existence has *appeared* to be more abroad than it actually has been. I have never changed my residence, or taxes, or anything else.

To turn to your professional interests, I gather that they are now mainly in the world of business. You've given up producing films and television shows altogether?

FAIRBANKS: Yes. After I had produced a hundred and sixty-four half-hour television shows, knocked out two story editors with heart attacks, and my general manager had had a breakdown, I thought I was going to be next, so I thought it best to stop while I was ahead.

Now I've got directorships in several companies. The one in which I have the greatest actual day-to-day participation is Fairbanks International, which is an Anglo-American company dealing with business developments and international trade. One of these was a company we started to introduce American bowling to Europe. Another was the Scripto pen company, which I have been a director of for many years as well as a shareholder. Then, we have a relationship with the Alcoa Company for their operations internationally. We will also take an interest in a housing development in Spain, package a merger of two companies, or undertake a variety of other enterprises. I started all this while I was still active in the film world so as to have an anchor to windward.

Meanwhile you have raised a family of three daughters. Did they go to school here or in the United States?

FAIRBANKS: They're all finished with school now. They've been on both sides, and they've been in France, and they all had a sort of finishing spell in Switzerland. My oldest daughter is married and has two daughters of her own. Her husband is an Englishman, and they live here. The middle one, who is in New York now, is a very promising painter. The youngest just arrived over here a couple of weeks ago. She's been in New York. Unfortunately, all of them had an education sort of like mine. We were all dragged up rather than brought up. I would like to have had some consistency about my own upbringing and I would like to have given my children some consistency in theirs, but it was awfully hard to manage, because things had to be geared pretty much to what I had to do, and it was hard to guess a year ahead what that was going to be.

When you speak of the children being dragged up rather than brought up, some people think that that kind of varied education can produce very good results.

FAIRBANKS: It has plus and minus values, but there is a great deal to be said for having roots and some consistency in terms of your schoolmates and the system of education. To counterbalance that, there's something to be said for the breadth of attitude and outlook that you get from being abroad. My children have grown up, as I did, being able to speak several languages. They're more tolerant of the world in general. They have a less insular viewpoint than some of their own group who have stayed in one place. They have found themselves well ahead in some subjects and terribly behind in others. I know what it's like. When I chose the Navy as a service—I'd always loved the sea and everything to do with ships—I was embarrassed to find that the one thing I was terribly deficient in was mathematics, and the Navy being a terribly mathematical service, I was always at a disadvantage in having to cram like hell so I wouldn't have to count everything on my fingers. It's true that I had the language proficiency, but that doesn't help you to navigate, you know. Of course, it did help in other ways, and that's the point. You get an education in which one advantage is counterbalanced by a disadvantage.

I suppose that would also be true if you were to compare living here with living in the United States. Out of your experience of living in both places, have you found basic differences?

FAIRBANKS: Well, for the most part, you find when you go from office to office or business to business, you're not terribly aware of being in one place or the other. Over a period of time, being on this side or the other side becomes quite normal, sort of like making the change from the East Coast to the West Coast or from North to South. I'm the least blasé person you've ever met, because I always enjoy what I'm doing wherever I am, and I'm always finding new things about New York and new things about London, but the impact of being in a strange place when I'm in one or the other has just worn off. So, for the most part, the two are interchangeable.

If I were pinned down to finding a basic difference in the business of living, I would say that there's a convenience in living over here that we don't have at home. It's the ability to get out into the country as a way of life. It's easier here. Furthermore, although London is a city of about a million more people than New York, it seems about ten million less. That's because London is a whole lot of villages put together, and therefore life is a little more casual. And yet it's more concentrated in terms of government and the various worlds of arts and sciences than we are at home. We're divided between New York, Washington, the industrial centers, and so forth. But there's a greater cosmopolitan sense in New York. More high-geared.

Of course, many Americans in Europe find the absence of that high-geared aspect very pleasant. They find the general pace of living on this side slower and more congenial. Do you notice a difference?

FAIRBANKS: Oh yes, though I think it's less noticeable nowadays than it used to be. In New York, the pace is set for you. Here, you can make your own pace. If you want to lead a terribly high-pressured life, you can. If you want to take it easy, you can. Just amble about and take your time—that's possible. It's more adjustable to your own taste. In New York, there's nothing much you can do about it. Life takes over from you. Here, life is very well organized in a subtle way for whatever you want to do. If you want to have a life of night clubs, theaters, and such, it's here. If you don't, if you want to lead a sort of sedate house life, you can do that. Or country life, or club life, or whatever—it's all here, with a minimum of fuss and feathers.

I seem to remember reading a few years ago about your social life here . . .

FAIRBANKS: I read about it, too.

I was thinking in particular about the coming-out party you gave for your daughter, Daphne, at Cliveden. As you remember, the newspapers made much of the fact that the Queen and Prince Philip attended as well as Princess Margaret, Princess Alexandra, and so on. Was that unique—having them among your guests?

FAIRBANKS: Well, I think it was really not so unique as it was an example of the fact that there is a sort of deeply imbedded public snobbism about theater people—that they're all mountebanks who are not allowed to be buried in hallowed ground, and therefore they should be separate from the rest of the world, and if they somehow happen to know or even be on speaking terms with anybody in any other kind of world, there's something spectacularly newsworthy about it. If a captain of industry goes to the White House, it's barely commented on, but if Sophia Loren goes, it becomes almost shocking, and a great deal is made of it. Why? It's simply a form of inverted snobbery.

Actually, I would say that we do no more than an average amount of entertaining—probably a little less than average. We have a lot of American friends here, of course. There's a surprising number who live on this side just out of choice and who really struggle to make it work. You also run across some surprising cases. I remember once when I was making movies, I got to talking to an electrician on the set, and it turned out he was from Texas. He'd been here since the First World War. He said he just liked it, and decided to stay. He'd married and settled down. I know a fellow who was a very successful and promising young banker in New York, but he gave that up, came over here, and joined a bank in the City just because he found he enjoyed this way of life more. Probably his rewards aren't as great, but he finds the existence here more satisfying. A couple of our particular American friends live here partly because the cost of living is less and partly because they find the life more enjoyable. Of course, the fact that all these people just happen to prefer to live here involves no compromising of their loyalty to home. That is something I think is often misunderstood.

It's a very funny thing. We get furious, on the American side, if we don't succeed in compromising the loyalty of foreigners who come to live with us. We say, "What are you doing here if you're not going to change your nationality?" But if you ask, "What about our people living over there?" the answer is, "Oh, of course, they shouldn't change their nationality." It's so inconsistent on our part. If John Smith, or whoever, wants to live in the United States, and he pays his taxes and leads a lawful life, why should we expect him to renounce the land of his birth? People shouldn't be expected to change their allegiance as a matter of principle, but only if they have some very deep political or economic or personal reason.

I suppose the American feeling stems from the fact that almost all of our immigrants arrived with the idea of becoming citizens, and we got into the habit of expecting everyone to do the same.

On another subject—you've lived among the British for such a long time I wonder if you can explain why they are unwilling to accept the fact that there is such a thing as winter. The other northern Europeans know it's going to get cold, and prepare for it. The British seem to like to pretend that cold weather doesn't exist.

FAIRBANKS: That's quite true. I think it's probably because the English always live in a kind of fairy-tale world. They very seldom get down to reality. They're illogical people, full of whimsey and imagination and fantasy. You know, travelers who came through here in the Middle Ages said that the people in these islands were so easygoing, so hated work, so loved sports and betting and having a good time that they really didn't pay much attention to the way the world wagged. The Romans also remarked on it. I think it was Tacitus, writing to Caesar, who remarked that the natives here were very amiable, and, being detached from the rest of the world by the Channel, were only sort of remotely aware of what was going on. They came gaily to pay their taxes. Took it as a sort of sport. They liked to grumble, but that was all. The only thing, he said, was that one must never force them to do anything. If you tried to push them around, they would dig in their toes and become uncommonly stubborn and difficult to deal with. It was always better to pat them on the back, and then you could get along splendidly. That was Tacitus, writing nearly two thousand years ago. And they still live in this fanciful, Alice-in-Wonderland world much of the time. Their late ambassador to Washington, Lord Harlech, once said a true and wonderful thing about his countrymen. He said, "They can never see the handwriting on the wall until their backs are to it." It's an awfully hard way of doing business. But it sort of adds to the charm of it all.

GALLERY NOTES

To be a career woman in Europe is the dream of thousands of American girls, a great number of whom arrive every year in Paris and London and Rome and other European capitals determined to make the dream come true. Their chances, thanks to the expansion of American business abroad and the proliferation of international agencies, are better than they have ever been. Even so, only a few of the hopeful arrivals—probably no more than one in ten—will succeed in finding a job that will allow her to remain and join the ranks of the Ameropeans.

The biggest obstacle to making the career grade in Europe is, of course, the extreme imbalance between the small number of jobs and the multitude of applicants. Furthermore, American firms abroad generally make a practice of filling from 90 to 95 per cent of their personnel requirements with citizens of the countries in which they do business. If the aspiring career girl is offered a job, it is not hers unless she can secure a work permit from the proper government agency. To do this is not always just a routine matter. In some cases, she and her prospective employer have to prove that the job she hopes to fill requires unique skills which she possesses and which no native applicant can duplicate. If the American girl gets over these hurdles, she will find that salaries in Europe are, as a rule, less than half of what they are in the United States and that living expenses for a single girl, particularly in Paris, London, and Geneva, are not apt to be much lower than they are in America. Then, too, she has to solve her housing problem, master (except in England) a new language, and make a new circle of friends. All in all, the challenge is rather formidable.

In addition to the Ameropean women who have found jobs with American or foreign firms, a number of others have created careers. Dorian Leigh, who had been a highly successful photographer's model (her sister is Suzy Parker, another famous model) in New York, moved to Paris in 1957, and set up a model agency, which she believes was the first of its kind in Europe. The agency has prospered, and Miss

Leigh now lives in style in a well-staffed ten-room apartment in one of the most fashionable sections of Paris. Nancy Holmes, the attractive former wife of a Texas oilman, moved to Switzerland with her two children after her divorce, and has since developed a thriving career as a photographer. "Before I was married, I had been on the staff of *Look*," Miss Holmes told me, "and I also did a lot of free-lance things for the magazine when I was living in Texas. After the divorce, I considered going back to *Look* as an editor, but that would have meant returning to New York, which I wasn't keen to do, and, since we'd planned to send the children to school in Switzerland, I decided to get my hat and go with them. I had to keep busy, so I revved up the camera, and now I'm all over the lot, taking pictures mostly for *Look* and *Venture*. Photography, I have found, is a wonderful profession for a woman, especially if you can work over here."

Acting is also a wonderful profession for a woman living in Europe, in the opinion of another Ameropean named Marpessa Dawn, the beautiful Negro actress, whose rise to stardom began abroad and who is probably best known to American audiences for her role as Eurydice in the film *Black Orpheus*, which won an Oscar for the best foreign film of 1959. Miss Dawn was born on a farm near Pittsburgh, later moved to New York, and attended New York State University. "I always wanted to be in show business," she told me, "but as I knew that was very risky financially, I decided to prepare myself for work that would earn money, so I was trained as a medical secretary. After graduation, I came to Europe on a two-month student tour. That was in 1953, and I was nineteen. I liked it here so much I decided I'd like to stay for a year or so. I had about ten dollars left. I went to the Embassy and everywhere else I could think of, looking for a job. Finally, an agency placed me with a family, where I was governess to six children. That was really a wonderful experience."

After that, Miss Dawn took a job as a medical secretary at the American Army Hospital, in Orleans, where she worked for about a year and a half. She customarily spent her weekends in Paris. On one of these, a friend got her a job working as an extra in a crowd scene in a film. "I thought, 'How wonderful to be in front of a camera!' " she has recalled. "I thought my career was made. I went back to Orleans, and on Monday, I quit my job. It was funny."

Returning to Paris, she joined an African dance group ("They taught me. All I knew was classical ballet, which I had studied when I was young.") that performed in Paris and then toured the provinces. While still a member of the dance troupe, she landed a bit part in a film whose director was a friend of Marcel Camus. He was then preparing the scenario of *Black Orpheus*, which he was also to direct. "One day he came to see me on the set, told me about the film he was working on, and said that he wanted me to have the leading role," Miss Dawn said. "I was thrilled, of course, but he was worried that I wouldn't accept, because the money was very little. I remember he wrote me a letter that said, 'If you do this film, I promise you glory.' It was wonderful to receive such a promise, and even more wonderful to have it come true. I enjoy being known. I haven't become blasé at all. I mean, I still enjoy meeting movie stars."

Since *Black Orpheus*, Miss Dawn has turned down many more film roles than she has accepted, mainly because most of those offered would have taken her to some foreign location, and she doesn't want to leave her family. She is married to a Belgian actor, and they have two small children. "I prefer the theater," Miss Dawn said, "because then I am free to be with the children during the day, and I work at night when they are asleep. I've been in half a dozen or more plays here. One of them, *Chérie Noire*, ran for years. Eventually, I'd like to do a Broadway play. As far as show business is concerned, it's easier here, because their standards—I don't want to say they are lower—but it's true you can do a lot of things that are mediocre and would never go over in the States, simply because people love you. They're very influenced by sentiment. From the moment they love you, they let you get away with murder, but I don't want that. I want to work in the States, where they know me from the film, but they don't have a big sentiment for me, and I'd be judged solely for my work.

"But I'm very glad that I had the opportunity to develop here. In the States, I was rather serious and more introverted. I wasn't pushing out at all. Here, I came out of my shell. This is where I bloomed."

To help her own and other children bloom through exposure to European life and culture was the reason that Mary Crist Fleming founded the American School in Switzerland, a private boarding school, situated in Lugano, that combines study and travel in a novel program. The school, which is widely considered one of the more interesting post-war educational innovations, has also enabled Mrs. Fleming, a stylish, vivacious, imposing woman, to satisfy her lifelong interest in education (both of her parents were educators) as well as her love of Europe, which dates from her teens, when she made her first visit there. "I'd always thought I wanted to go into the theater, being half ham at heart," Mrs. Fleming told me when I called on her in the beautiful, completely modernized, seventeenth-century villa that serves as the headquarters of her school, "but I found that I just couldn't help getting involved educationally with young people."

Her first such involvement, Mrs. Fleming continued, occurred after she had graduated from Radcliffe, married a businessman, and become the mother of three children. "We lived on a beautiful farm in Bucks County," Mrs. Fleming said, "and my husband permitted me to run a camp there in the summertime for children about the same age as ours. He tolerated this until we separated—we were later divorced—and since I was eager for the children to become bilingual—I had learned when I was about fourteen to speak quite fluent French—I took them to Aix-en-Provence and put them in the local schools." Her two daughters were then twelve and seven, and her son was ten. After a year in France, Mrs. Fleming moved with her family to Montreux, Switzerland, and enrolled the children in the local schools there. At the end of the second year, she was so pleased with the results that she decided to stay on. However, as the children grew older, she discovered that the Swiss schools at that time—the mid-1950s—had little knowledge of how to prepare students for American colleges, which is where she planned to send her children. Being unable to locate a school with a strong American curriculum, she proceeded to found one, providing four years of high school with emphasis on preparation for secondary schools in the United States. From an initial enrollment of twelve students, including the three Fleming children, the American School has now grown to a hundred and twenty, which is the limit of its capacity.

In 1958, Mrs. Fleming took another innovative step by launching what is known as the Post Graduate Program, a one-year course of study and travel open to high school graduates who want to have a European educational experience before enrolling in college. This program, like the high school, is coeducational and also has a hundred and twenty students, but is a completely separate operation. It has its own buildings, its own faculty, numbering thirty-five, its own director, an ebullient young American teacher named Ian David Mellon, and its own curriculum. "The classroom work is done here at the villa," Mrs. Fleming said. "Then there are the field trips, which are the heart of our concept. The school now owns thirty Volkswagen buses, and they are almost constantly in use. Periodically, with Mr. Mellon and others from the staff in charge, the students pack up and go out to see and to talk with Europeans about what they've been studying. They have meetings and interviews with political leaders, journalists, farmers, industrialists, students, workmen. They tour steel plants, coal mines, government offices, automobile factories. They attend political meetings, go through champagne caves, eat local foods, see how people live, and spend nights as paying guests with European families. Of course, they also go to places like Pompeii, the opera in Milan, the Louvre, and so on. They have very few idle moments." In spite of the cost, which comes to about five thousand dollars, including transatlantic travel, the program has four or five times as many applicants as it can accommodate. "In the early days," Mrs. Fleming said, "I had to spend at least two months every year in the States, traveling across the country as if I were campaigning for President, to sell the value of education in Europe. But no more. I think we can say that the idea has now been accepted."

Although going to Europe to pursue a career (and perhaps chancing to find a husband) has developed in the years since the Second World War into a popular way for American women to become Ameropeans, the traditional route to that estate has always been through marriage. The ranks of American women who have followed this course include many celebrated figures, one of the earliest being Miss Jennie Jerome, the Baltimore belle, who, in 1874, became the bride of Sir Randolph Churchill and later the mother of Sir Winston.

Around the turn of the century, when it became all the rage among the newly rich American merchants and financiers to try to move up the social ladder by marrying their daughters off to titled though frequently impoverished Europeans, there was a rash of transatlantic unions. Perhaps none attracted more public attention than that of Miss Consuelo Vanderbilt, of New York, and the Duke of Marlborough; the transformation of the railroad heiress into a duchess was accompanied, the newspapers reported, by the settlement of two and a half million dollars. During the same era, Miss Nancy Langhorne, of Virginia, was married to Waldorf Astor, the elder son of Viscount William Waldorf Astor (an eccentric American multimillionaire who had become a naturalized British subject), and eventually, as Lady Astor, had the distinction of being the first woman to sit in Parliament. Another American, appearing somewhat later on the British scene, was Miss Esther Cleveland, the daughter of President Grover Cleveland, who married a Guards officer during the First World War. Mrs. Esther Cleveland Bosanquet, now in her early seventies, lives today in Yorkshire. "I think by now I have pretty much absorbed the British way of life," she told a visitor not long ago, "but that does not mean that I forget for one moment that I am thoroughly American."

The most famous living Ameropean woman, the Duchess of Windsor (nee Bessie Wallis Warfield, of Baltimore), may no longer think of herself as *thoroughly* American, but she does visit the United States with her husband for two months every year and otherwise keeps in touch with her native country by reading a number of American magazines, such as *Time*, *Newsweek*, and *Life*. She also watches American television films, dubbed in French, of Bob Hope, Frank Sinatra, Westerns, and similar fare while taking dinner on a tray. She still buys her stockings in the United States (at a dollar and ninety-five cents a pair), and she has said she wishes she could buy in France the Sara Lee frozen cakes that she first found in American supermarkets. After three decades in France, she recently told a friend, she still misses not living among people who speak her native language.

The Duchess is not, however, completely isolated from those who do, for the circles in which she moves are full of other American women who have married Europeans, including Countess Edward Bismarck (who, as Mrs. Harrison Williams, was a noted ornament of New York society for several years), Baroness Philippe de Rothschild (nee Pauline Fairfax), the Countess of Sefton (nee Josephine Armstrong), the Duchess of Rutland (nee Frances Sweeney), Princess Chigi della Rovere (nee Marion Berry), Countess Alvise de Robilant (nee Elizabeth Stork), and, among many others, Marchesa Lily Gerini, who was born Lilly Poli, of New Haven, Connecticut.

The Marchesa, a tall, genial woman with dark brown eyes and a commanding presence, is the daughter of an Italian sculptor, who emigrated to America and eventually became what she calls a theater magnate. "I went to a number of convents in the United States and then to a number of finishing schools," she told me one day over lunch in Rome, "but none of them could hold me, so my parents sent me here for schooling." She met her future husband at that time, and after they were married, nine years later, in 1929, took up residence in the Gerini Palace, a sizable structure consisting of some three hundred rooms, in Florence. The Marchesa preferred living in a smaller place, so, with her husband's permission, she began remodeling an ancestral villa outside of Florence. The villa, which had not been lived in for a number of years, had a hundred and fifty rooms. It took some fifty artisans working full time almost seven years to complete the remodeling. "It was a beautiful place, surrounded by about five hundred acres of English parks," the Marchesa said. "We had some two thousand acres altogether and four hundred peasants. I always gave a Christmas party for them and all of their children, which involved buying an awful lot of presents. We had horses, and did a great deal of riding, and we also had a large shooting preserve. I suppose we had the biggest hunting parties in Italy. Tremendous lunches out on the field, expertly served by the staff. One met new people all the time, and there was a great deal to do. I loved it."

In 1947, after the death of her husband, the Marchesa moved to

Rome, where, at the time I lunched with her, she was living in a penthouse. She spends the summer at the beautiful seaside town of Porto Santo Stefano in a residence that she said was built on the foundations of what had been Nero's villa. Workmen, remodeling one of the structures on the property, found five underground rooms that were in the same condition as they were in Nero's time. A Roman bath has also been unearthed, and so many other things have been dug up on the property in the course of improving it that the Marchesa has a small museum to house them. "You plant a rose bush, and you come up with a Roman urn," she said.

Probably her cleverest building triumph was achieved recently in Rome, where she acquired two hundred acres on the Appian Way about twenty years ago. She immediately began a campaign to get permission to convert one of the ruins on the property into a residence or to build a new house there. "Of course, the officials said, 'Absolutely not!'" the Marchesa told me. "Regulations forbid changing anything at all. I had to have special permission even to plant a tree." She nevertheless persisted in her campaign, and by cajolery and other means at length received the necessary permissions to solve the problem in an ingenious way. With the aid of exceptionally talented architects and workmen, she has since completed, inside one of the ruins, an elegant, completely modern, two-story apartment—and without tampering with a single one of the ancient stones.

The majority of American women who marry Europeans do not, of course, marry nobility, though their husbands are often more prominent or more important in the world of affairs than the titled ones. For example, Jean Seberg, the actress from Marshalltown, Iowa, is married to Romain Gary, the well-known French author and diplomat. And Elizabeth Taylor is at present the wife of Richard Burton, the well-known Welsh actor. Sometimes, too, well-known American women marry unprominent as well as untitled European men. For example, Deanna Durbin, the former film star, some years ago married a French business executive and settled down to a comfortable, inconspicuous life as a housewife and mother in a village outside of Paris.

Altogether, there are probably between four and five hundred American women who are married to Frenchmen and live in France, according to Mrs. Phyllis Michaux, one of the founders and the first president of an organization called American Wives of Europeans. A native of Washington, D.C., Mrs. Michaux served as a WAC corporal, married a Frenchman who runs a customs brokerage business, and has lived in Paris for some twenty years. "One of the main objects of our Association, which has about a hundred and fifty members," Mrs.

Michaux told me, "is to work toward a relaxation of United States nationality laws. They now require that children born abroad of one American-born parent and one foreign parent must spend five consecutive years in the United States between the ages of fourteen and twenty-eight in order to retain their United States citizenship. The law as it now stands amounts to an economic restriction, because some parents can support their children in the United States for that period of time very easily, while others cannot do it at all." Another objective of the organization, Mrs. Michaux continued, is to open scholarship opportunities at American universities for young people with dual citizenship. In addition, the Association makes an effort to help American women who are living permanently in France to adapt to life there.

"A lot of these girls are very young," Mrs. Michaux said. "Many of them met and married their husbands while doing their third year of college abroad. Although the girls usually marry into an educated class, it is not an easy life. They have all the problems of a young married couple in addition to those that result from the girl's living in a country that is new to her. The young man has to finish his education, and even after he's embarked on his career, he and his wife have to contend with the fact that most European men make smaller salaries than Americans of the same cultural or educational level. Not earning the kind of income that is paid to Americans sent over here by American corporations, these young couples aren't able to send their children to American schools, receive paid home leave, and do those other things that give their children an American upbringing. Since the girls' parents don't always have the money to come here to visit, the girls are apt to get pretty lonely."

Furthermore, Mrs. Michaux added, the young American women who marry foreigners find themselves quite isolated from the American colony in Paris. "There is an organization here called the American Women's Group," she said. "It has something like four hundred members, mostly military, business, and Embassy wives. I've been to their luncheons. These ladies in their flowered hats make introductions all around, and say what their husbands are in, and then they say, 'And your husband?' When you say, 'My husband's a Frenchman,' they look sort of stunned. It's as if they were saying, 'Well, what's that?' So, there's not much there for these girls. If they spend their time instead with French couples of their own age, the American girl is not always one of that group immediately, either. Perhaps she doesn't speak French well enough yet, and she is usually asked all sorts of questions, which doesn't make her life any easier. When you live here, you are always in the position of explaining America to French people."

Looking back over her own life abroad, Mrs. Michaux said that she married when she was twenty-four. "I don't think I quite realized all that was involved in marrying a foreigner," she continued. "What I realize now that didn't occur to me then was the fact that one's parents are going to be growing old and that if you marry and move to Europe, they are not going to have the grandchildren to enjoy, nor are they going to have you. Those discoveries dawn on you later. One thing I would like to convince the American lawmakers of is that marriage has nothing to do with loyalty to one's country. The fact that I happened to fall in love with a Frenchman makes me no less loyal to the United States than if I'd fallen in love with a man from Milwaukee, Wisconsin."

> "In my own case, I feel that I have been sort of reborn in Europe. I have put together a new life here, and I don't want to give it up."

Beverly Putnam, an attractive, dark-haired, vivacious woman in her early forties, had had an unusually varied career in the United States before she undertook the building of a new one in Europe. Getting her first job in New York at eighteen, she worked successively as a secretary, hula dancer (in the Hawaiian Room of the Hotel Lexington), public relations operative for Scandinavian Airlines System, organizer and director of the First All-Girl Safari to Africa, and in a variety of posts for the Columbia Broadcasting System. "I was doing well enough, professionally speaking, but life was such a terrible bore," she told me one Saturday afternoon in her apartment in Paris, where she has lived since 1961. "Then there was a very unhappy romance. Nothing seemed to be going right, so I made up my mind to come to Europe and start over." She wanted to live in France, and, since she spoke very little French, decided that the first step was to get a good grasp of the language. On the advice of a friend, she elected to begin this study at the University of Grenoble.

MISS PUTNAM: I arrived in Grenoble at night. The people who were supposed to meet me weren't there, because I had become so enthralled with the French countryside that I had taken a slower train, and hadn't had a chance to let them know. I wanted to call them, but I had no French money. I had given a porter in Paris all my francs. I had some dollars, but I didn't know where to change them or how to find out, because I could speak scarcely a word of French. I was terribly tired, and there was nobody around who would help. All I could think of was, "My God, I left everything for this. Absolutely everything." I sat down on the baggage, and I cried. After a while, the stationmaster came by, and helped me, and I finally got settled in a tiny room of the pension of Madame Pinchard. I don't think I had ever felt as lonely as I did that night.

The next day, I enrolled at the University. I'd had twelve French lessons at Berlitz, and I was anxious to learn fast, so I asked to be enrolled in the hardest class. That was a mistake. I had terrible headaches at night, because I heard this new language all day, and maybe only a dozen words registered. In class, it was often embarrassing. I was the oldest one, and I made terrible mistakes. One day the teacher said, "*Mademoiselle Putnam, donnez-moi l'explication de l'amour-propre.*" Since "*l'amour*" was "love," and "*propre*" was "clean," I answered, "Clean love." Up went a roar of laughter. The right answer, of course, was "Ego." Oh, it was awful. At that time, I couldn't laugh at myself. Everything was tragic.

I came over with a little money, but I had to be very careful with it, because I wanted to stay in school until I could get along easily in the language. My room cost only a hundred francs—about twenty dollars—a month. I ate just two meals a day. There was a restaurant in Grenoble where you could get a good meal for five francs. For the other meal, I often just bought a bag of tomatoes and a piece of cheese. Sometimes I ate in the pension, but I was uneasy there. The other pensioners were students from all over Europe. They were about half my age, and their French was fluent. I was too scared to ask for the pepper.

When the summer session ended, in mid-September, my funds were very low. I couldn't bring myself to tap what I had left in America, so when I saw a sign at the University, advertising for grape pickers at ten francs a day plus room and board, I signed up. That was an experience. You're awakened at five-thirty. You have breakfast, and you're out in the vineyards by six-thirty. There is a short break at nine for bread and chocolate. Then you pick until twelve. Lunch, and you're picking again by one-thirty. You work until it's dark, have another meal, and die. The first night, my back hurt so I could hardly get up onto the bed. I lasted only four and a half days. They paid me for five, and sent me home with a bottle of their finest Beaujolais. They were wonderful people.

I wanted to stay on for another term at Grenoble—I wasn't ready for Paris—so I got a job at Berlitz, teaching English. I was paid fifteen dollars a week, which didn't go very far. The logical thing to have done, I realize now, would have been to live with a French family, been the assistant cook, made the beds, and done all kinds of other chores in exchange for the opportunity to live the language. Instead, I rented a room with a French family who lived in the suburbs. I was never a part of that family in any way. The only time I went into their quarters was in the morning, when I was allowed to go to the kitchen, heat some water, and take it up to my room for coffee. On Sundays, when the weather was good, the family would have their midday meal on a little patio right under my window. Not once did they say, "Come and join us," or "Come and have coffee with us." I would tiptoe around my room, because I was thinking, "I mustn't embarrass them. I mustn't let them think they have to invite me." I didn't know the French yet.

When I finished the second term at Grenoble, I took a temporary job with a family who were going to the country for the summer. I helped with the children, and met a number of country people, and that was very good for my French. In the fall, I decided it was time to come to Paris. I lived first on the outskirts of the city with a friend whose husband had been killed. I enrolled at the Sorbonne for courses in history, politics, and art—all in French, of course—and for more courses in the language. The first day, I went down to talk to the professor after a lecture and put my purse on the first row of seats, and when I picked it up, I discovered somebody had stolen my wallet. It contained only forty dollars, but it seemed like a tragedy then. In order to finish the eight months that I studied at the Sorbonne I had to draw on the money I'd left in New York. This now seemed all right—a kind of investment—since I had decided I was going to stay in Europe. I knew now I could make my way, if only by teaching English.

Two days after they gave out the diplomas at the Sorbonne, the wife of an editor at the Paris *Herald Tribune*, whom I had met, called to tell me there was a job opening at the paper. I hurried around and got it. The job was that of librarian, working from six in the evening until midnight. It paid a hundred and forty dollars a month. I was able to move into town and share an apartment with a French girl. There was no hot water and no bath, but it was within walking distance of the *Tribune*. For two years, I hadn't bought anything for myself or even looked in shop windows. Now I could begin to look again, though I was still squeaking along.

During those nights at the *Tribune*, I read all the want ads in the first edition, and before long I took on another job, this one with International General Electric. They were just beginning to sell their computers in Europe, and were bringing over a great many engineers, almost none of whom spoke French. They needed help finding lodgings and getting settled, and I did that kind of work. That job paid sixty dollars a week. So, from nine-thirty to six, I worked for General Electric, and then I went to the *Tribune*, which was just across the Champs Elysees, and worked until twelve. It was kind of a drain, but it felt good to be working hard. Also, the two salaries together came to a rather good sum, and I was able to get a nice studio and live by myself.

Then came my big, beautiful opportunity in Europe—the job I have now, which is with an organization whose name, literally translated, is the European Association of Proprietary Medicines. It's composed of both American and European pharmaceutical companies, and its object is to protect their interests in the Common Market, improve the image of the industry, and carry on other programs of that nature. I was hired when the Association was just being formed as public relations director. I am now the executive director, and it seems to be going very well. My salary is nine thousand dollars a year, plus expenses, which is high for a woman in Paris who is not a lawyer or a doctor or in some similar position. I can travel where and when I want to, and the Association also provides me with a new Peugeot. I can take the kind of holidays I like, and I now have many friends both here and in other parts of Europe. I really can't complain.

If you were giving suggestions to an American girl who wanted to come over here and make a career for herself, what would you tell her?

MISS PUTNAM: I'm not sure I would tell her to come. It's just too hard to find a job in Paris. However, if she's determined to try, I would say that she should come with enough capital so she can settle down for a while, meet as many people as she can, and attend as many parties as possible. That is the way I think you find a job in Paris—through contacts. You won't find one through an agency, and you won't find the job you *really* want in the *Tribune*. It's pitiful to look at the ads in the *Tribune* of people offering themselves for jobs. They're all looking for some way to stay in Europe, and they will accept anything. They do, and then they go a little balmy after six months, because it isn't at all what they're suited for. No, I think the only sensible way is to come with a little money and the thought, "I'm going to try it for four months. If I don't make it, I'll go back home, and no tears."

If it does work out for you, you don't think of going home. In my own case, I feel that I have been sort of reborn in Europe. I have put together a new life here, and I don't want to give it up. If I were to go back to New York, I would earn more money, but I would be desolate, looking for someone with whom I could share the experiences of these years, which have really been the best ones.

> "Here, you don't just rush by the little things in life, the very things that make daily living more enjoyable, that make it less monotonous."

Her Serene Highness Princess Grace of Monaco (nee Grace Kelly, of Philadelphia) has been, after the Duchess of Windsor, by far the best-known American living abroad ever since her marriage, in 1956, to Prince Rainier III, ruler of the ancient Mediterranean principality that comprises three hundred and seventy acres, or half the area of New York's Central Park, as an enclave in French territory and whose citizens, under an accord with France, pay no taxes. Although there have been occasional snide remarks in the gossip columns about the movie star turned princess, the consensus of well-informed people is that she has handled her role as the leading lady of Monaco with dignity, style, and industry. "Grace works very hard," I was told by a mutual friend, the wife of an American couple who live in Europe. "In the first place, she went to work and learned to speak almost perfect French. She is also a very good mother. She takes the kids with her everywhere. When she and Rainier came to visit us last year, she brought them along. They are fine children. She handles all of her official duties with aplomb, giving receptions and doing all those things, and she also works very hard for the Monegasque Red Cross. This is considerably different from the typical Red Cross activity in American suburban communities. In Monaco, just about all of the social service organizations are wrapped up in this one organization—the Red Cross. Furthermore, I think that many of the international events that are now held in Monaco to generate publicity and stimulate tourism were Grace's ideas, although she has never mentioned anything of the kind herself. Finally, I believe it is a very successful marriage. She has to be given some credit for that, too, doesn't she?"

Through correspondence, I had arranged an interview with Princess Grace at five o'clock one afternoon in mid-December. I took a taxi from my hotel to the Palace, which dates from 1215 and overlooks

Monte Carlo, and en route followed the old journalistic custom of trying to sound out the local temper by striking up a conversation with the driver. He complained, naturally, about the traffic. He said there are twenty-five thousand people in Monaco and twelve thousand automobiles. He had a few sharp words for Aristotle Onassis, then a very large property owner in Monaco, for opposing Prince Rainier's plans for developing the local economy. But when I asked about Princess Grace, the driver smiled. "Is good princess," he said. "First year, we didn't know—real princess or Hollywood princess? Now we know she is real princess. Is good mother. For Monaco people, that is everything. Is also hard worker—Red Cross, old people, orphans. French people, Italian people still say, 'Ah, Hollywood princess.' They just jealous of Monaco people, because Monaco people pay no taxes. *We* know she is real princess."

Arriving at the Palace, I alighted in front of an archway, on either side of which a soldier smartly turned out in a light blue helmet, black tunic, white belt, red-striped trousers, and white spats stood before a peppermint-striped red-and-white sentry box. An officer, whose uniform was made even more resplendent with an abundance of peppermint braid, appeared and saluted, and, upon learning the purpose of my mission, escorted me through the side gate and into a small reception room. There, a man with the appearance and manner of a reservations clerk at the Ritz telephoned the Princess's secretary that I had arrived. A few minutes later, a footman came to the reception room, and escorted me across the cobbled courtyard to the small private suite in the west wing of the Palace, where the Prince and Princess live with their family.

I was met at the door by an American woman named Mrs. Dale (her husband, I learned later, is employed by the Prince in a business capacity), who said that the Princess would arrive directly, and showed me into the sitting room, which is modest-sized, comfortably but not ostentatiously furnished, and artfully cluttered with framed family pictures and assorted ornaments and knickknacks. Among the conventional chairs and lounges I noticed a quaint antique blue-and-gilt love seat built for three. "The French call that an *indiscret*," Mrs. Dale said. In one corner of the room is a caged parrot that says, "Hello," when the phone rings, and, when cocktails are served, makes a noise like a person gulping from a whiskey bottle. Next to the sitting room and separated from it by wooden grilled doors is the dining room, which contains a table and chairs seating perhaps eight to ten people. Against one wall is a floor-to-ceiling cage in which a monkey-like animal with a long and brightly colored tail was cavorting on a large branch of a tree. The Prince, I was told, is very keen about animals, and has a large private menagerie.

Although I was aware of the way the Princess is properly addressed ("Your Highness" initially and "Ma'am" thereafter), I don't recall having used either form, because, from the minute she walked into the room, shook hands, and apologized for being late, until I left, nearly two hours later, she created an atmosphere so pleasant and unaffected that formal terms of address would have seemed out of place. She was wearing a handsome suit in a soft brown shade, a single strand of pearls, and a large pearl ring. She was carrying a pair of light-colored, bone-rimmed glasses, which she toyed with at times while talking but never put on. Maturity has, if anything, enhanced her beauty. Her complexion is magnificent, her eyes are arresting, and her voice is dulcet, adding interest even to her inconsequential remarks. Most engaging is her manner, which combines elegance with an easy casualness—a quality that has no doubt gone far in winning acceptance as a "real princess" by the people of Monaco.

After Mrs. Dale had left and Princess Grace and I had agreed that I would take notes, since, at her request, the interview was not being tape recorded, I asked what aspects of living in Europe she had found most enjoyable.

"One thing I enjoy is that people here take the time to live in a pleasant way," she replied. "They are not as rushed, not as hurried, as they are in the United States. For example, there is the midday meal, which the family takes together. This is a custom that I think is very pleasant. It is one part of taking the time to enjoy the days. Of course, this manner of living can also be carried too far and become annoying. It is really not too hard to change one's ways and become as lazy and indolent as any Mediterranean.

"A strong sense of values is another thing that one perceives here. In Monaco, there still exists a respect for authority. This is so important, particularly for young people. On television, in pictures, and in books there is so much effort expended in trying to be funny or clever, which often has the effect of actually tearing down the important qualities that young people should hang onto. It seems to be the case that young people who are in search of truth and reality are afraid to admit that something old can be something of value. I was just reading an article in which Margaret Chase Smith said that the word, 'square,' has become outmoded. It used to be one of the most respected words in our vocabulary. We talked about the 'square deal' and the 'square shooter,' and they were honored words. She said that nowadays the person who seems to get the attention and applause is the one who plays the angles. What we need today, she said, are more square people, more people who are dependable in the old-fashioned way.

"When you think of President Kennedy, nobody would have called him 'square' in the current derogatory sense, and he was greatly admired and loved by younger people. He was the All-American Boy, wasn't he? He was Jack Armstrong."

After dwelling for a while on President Kennedy and his popularity in Europe, Princess Grace returned to the subject of young people: "We're very fortunate with our young people here. They cause very little trouble. Of course, the French school system is so demanding that they don't have too much time to get into trouble. The schools here impose a strong sense of discipline, and the children respect it.

"Another difference is that in Europe there is more emphasis on manners. This has its good points and its bad points, but I think on the whole more good than bad. People here are generally more polite, and the children tend to follow that lead. I'm always appalled when I see parents intimidated by their children, and I must say that I see that quite often when I go to the United States. If I say something about the discipline in our household, they say, 'Can you do *that?*' Now, really. Parents do have to take a stand. They do have to put their foot down. So far, we've been very fortunate with our children. So far, so good. But, of course, they're not teen-agers yet. It is a problem with teen-agers everywhere. But how a teen-ager behaves depends very much on how he behaved before he was a teen-ager. People who are indulgent, overly indulgent, with babies often say, 'Oh, he's just a baby.' Babies, one finds, understand quite a lot.

"To get back to your question, I believe, as I've said, that perhaps the most enjoyable thing here is the tempo. Here, you don't just rush by the little things in life, the very things that make daily living more enjoyable, that make it less monotonous. For example, you can take the time here to set a table more attractively. That is a small thing, but it is indicative. The strains in modern life are such that there is so little time for the things that make it more satisfying. Nowadays, when the problem of help has become so acute, a young woman is obliged to play so many parts that she rarely has time to indulge her fancy in doing those small, perhaps unnecessary, but highly satisfying small things."

The subject of help having been brought up, I asked the Princess how many servants she has.

"If you mean the number who run the Palace, it would be over a hundred," she replied. "That includes the Prince's Cabinet, secretaries, a governor who overlooks the Palace, a *régisseur*, who is a kind of general manager, gardeners, personal staff, electricians, a curator of archives and his assistant, a woman who does bookbinding, a housekeeper, a man who is restoring paintings, upholsterers, carpenters, painters, and probably a few more. In our personal household there are a major-domo, three butlers, five footmen, my husband's valet, my personal maid, the women who wash and sew, a chef, and an assistant chef.

"Both the chef and his assistant are French, so we have mostly French cooking, along with many Italian dishes. We also have American dishes that I tell the chef about now and again. I have a collection of cookbooks, and I give him American recipes out of them. One thing he did recently, for the first time, was pumpkin pie. And he bakes American cakes now, too. They're quite different from European cakes, you know."

I asked if there were any aspects of American life—the pumpkin pie and cake situation being well in hand—that she did miss.

"One misses American efficiency, I think, more than anything else," she said. "The French—and I wouldn't be surprised if it were true of Europeans generally—have a way of complicating things that should be relatively simple. One does miss that fine American custom of saying, 'Of course, it can be done. Why not?'

"As for the things that I *do* like here, I must say that one is the custom of having babies at home instead of in a hospital. Perhaps it is less hygienic, but it's much more pleasant. Even if one has a baby in the hospital, the husband and others in the family can see the baby and hold it. That practice of keeping the baby away from the father, behind a sheet of glass, is so impersonal. As for the baby, to come from the mother's womb and almost immediately be placed in a room full of screaming infants—I'm not at all sure that that is a good practice. I feel sure that the system here is much better.

"Another thing: here, every salaried person has a full month's vacation with pay. I think that is a very civilized custom. In these modern, hectic times, everybody needs at least one month out of twelve to relax and restore his energies. Those poor people in New York who have only two weeks of vacation out of fifty-two—it just isn't enough."

A butler came into the room to deliver a message, and after he had left, I asked the Princess if she had retained her United States citizenship.

"Yes, I have," she replied. "On marrying the Prince, I became Monegasque. As I have never renounced my U. S. citizenship, I have dual citizenship. So do my children. Our son will, of course, have to renounce his United States citizenship. I would like to keep mine, because I am very proud of it and sentimental about it, too. If ever there were any political problem connected with my retaining it, I would, of course, give it up.

"You know, I find myself admiring American traits and characteristics, often without being aware that they are American. I try to incorporate these traits into my children's upbringing. For example, the hospitality for which Americans are so well known. People here are not hospitable in that way. You can know a Frenchman for twenty years, and never be invited to his home. He will entertain you very handsomely at a restaurant, but you won't see the inside of his house. To an American, this is very strange. An Austrian once said to me, 'Americans are so naïve. They believe people are basically good. We know differently.' Well, I don't agree with that, and I don't want my children to, either."

At this point, a door to the sitting room was pushed open by a small, gray poodle that entered and proceeded to prance back and forth in front of the lounge, barking.

"That's my daughter's poodle," the Princess said. "It goes through this routine every night. It means that the children are not far behind." They presently arrived, accompanied by two young women who were apparently governesses. After the children had greeted their mother and been introduced to me, they continued into the dining room, where they and the governesses carried on what sounded like a lively conversation while having their dinner.

Princess Grace had spoken to the children in English, and I asked if that was customary.

"Yes, I always speak to them in English," she said. "They have an English nurse. But they are completely bilingual. Their school is conducted in French, so they read and write better in French than in English. This summer, I have a young American coming to teach them English, so they can improve their reading and writing of that. I can give them a message to deliver to someone, and if it is necessary to deliver it in French, they translate it in their head without thinking.

"We have lunch with the children at least two or three times during the week, and always on weekends. We breakfast with them every morning, and we lunch with them on Thursdays and on Sundays and on any other day when they are free of schoolwork.

"The children here are in school until five in the afternoon, which makes a very long day for them. Our daughter is being educated at a convent. Our son studies at home with two little friends who come in. One day he has gym in the afternoon, and on Thursdays, he takes football lessons. In French schools, I think, the sports program is insufficient. The emphasis on sports may be carried too far in American schools, but there must be a happy medium. Here, there are not as many team sports, and I think that is unfortunate. It is so important for a child to learn to play on a team, to learn teamwork. Learning to get along with the other fellow—that's basic in life today.

"I would like our son to have a year as an undergraduate in England or America, and I would also like him to go to an American university. And I would like all of the children to go to summer camp in America. There's nothing like that in Europe, and summer camp gives children so many wonderful opportunities. I went to camp as a youngster—five summers—and they were among the happiest times of my life. One learned to do so many things—sail, play tennis, ride horseback. And it is so healthy."

Getting back to Monaco, I asked the Princess if she would tell me something about her official duties.

"As president of the Red Cross, I supervise all sections and departments," she said. "We have a secretary general as well as heads of the various services, but I see or review every case treated. We are now getting ready for Christmas, and I am in the process of going over all those plans with the people involved. Often, at Christmas, I visit the hospital or the home for old people. And I always go to the orphanage at Christmastime. I keep in close touch with the orphanage and arrange outings and similar things. I am honorary president of the Girl Scouts, and keep in touch with all of their activities.

"I am also interested in a committee that is preserving—or trying to preserve—some of the landmarks and other historic sites of Monaco. Some of the new architecture is far out of keeping with the original style here, and some of the original, I feel, should be maintained. Unfortunately, there are not a great many people here who are of the same opinion.

"In addition, there are the musical events, the ballet, and a variety of other affairs. We try to group the official events in November, December, and January. Lots of congresses and international groups meet here, and many are received in the Palace. Other duties are presented from time to time. When we celebrated the centenary of Monte Carlo, I organized the committee that carried out that program. Incidentally, I have never been inside the Casino. There is a ruling that no Monegasque can go there, but I could, of course, if I wished. However, it is the custom that nobody in our family does.

"As far as the daily schedule is concerned, the morning is largely taken up with matters pertaining to the running of the household and with the mail. The afternoons are largely devoted to Red Cross work and to the other interests and activities I've mentioned. The mail could take up almost all of my time if I were to let it. A great deal of the mail consists of requests for money or for help in getting housing. We have housing problems here, as nearly everywhere else. And there are requests for other kinds of help. Then there is the fan-mail type of correspondence—requests for autographs, pictures—that sort of thing. I try to supply what is requested. About half of the mail, I would say, comes from America.

"So there is something to do every minute—and more. I mean, I never sit around and say, 'I wonder what to do.' "

> "They know that I am not churlishly pro-American. Rather, that I am an American who lives in England and knows and loves two countries."

Mrs. Tom Montague Meyer, the chic, dynamic former wife of publisher Gardner Cowles, is now married to the managing director of the largest timber importing firm in the United Kingdom. As Fleur Cowles, the name that she continues to use professionally as an artist and as a writer, she became well known in the United States not only as a hostess, public figure, and world traveler but also as the creator and editor of *Flair*, a magazine that made publishing history during its short existence. Though she has curtailed her globetrotting activities ("I used to travel a hundred and fifty thousand miles a year.") since moving to England, her friends remain internationally diverse. She entertains them nowadays either in her London apartment, in Albany, or at Great Surries, the Meyers' informal country house, in Sussex. Her personal decorating idiom is apparent throughout the stunning Albany residence, as I found upon being invited there one summer day to lunch. I also found that Mrs. Meyer, like so many other Americans who now live in Europe, can recall the date of her arrival there as precisely as her birthday.

MRS. MEYER: I came here on November 20, 1955. It's a long time to be away from an accepted pattern of life, and yet not consider it anything but normal. So much has changed in me and in my life and in my personality, too, I think, but it doesn't seem like such a long, slow process. To me, this is the life. The other one I don't even remember.

How long did it take to feel as much at home as you do now?

MRS. MEYER: First of all, I didn't come here as stranger. I came into a world that I thought included a great many good friends. I had been terribly ill, and I was frail when I came here. Delicate, wan, and thin. In a funny way, this physical disability was a remarkably fortunate thing. I didn't come here well and full of the past. I came here frail and happy to get rid of the past. I didn't leave something so desperately active for something less active and feel any loss.

I'm busier now than I ever was, but not in the same way and not in the same pursuits. Not nearly so dramatically and therefore more pleasantly. Very definitely not publicly, if I can help it. I'm still on the board of the hospital that I helped to build in America, the Institute for the Facially Disfigured, and I still work in its behalf. I put all my money into a fund to pay for the transportation, nursing, and other care for mutilated children. Even now, all these miles away, the hospital is always on my mind and always on my desk, and I continue to raise money for it, operating from here. This is my main and great occupation.

Another is that I am chairman of the committee, which means that I am the working woman, to raise money for the American Museum at Bath. It is the only American museum outside of the United States. It was started by two American gentlemen. In one case, the family funds were made in England, and he had a feeling of obligation about returning some of the money here. The two of them bought this most lovely of all mansions, "Claverton," which is on the River Avon, a fabulous setting. The museum is not a dear little thing, but a thing of stature and splendor and rock and stone and so on. It has twenty-two rooms of absolutely authentic furniture and furnishings of each period of American history, from the landing of the Pilgrims on up. They have an old country store, which was entirely reproduced and which sells all the things that were sold at that period. They have an original covered wagon, so that people who have read and heard about the pioneers who went West in them can see with their own eyes how immense their courage must have been. One of the museum's founders was killed last year in a motorcar accident, and I am trying to raise a hundred thousand dollars to keep it going. I have decided that every American corporation with a British subsidiary should be attacked for a corporate membership of a hundred pounds. So, I have people to lunch. I write letters. I make telephone calls. I make personal calls. And all that takes a lot of my time.

I think the museum is very important, because the average Englishman judges us by "The Lone Ranger." The museum proves that we have a culture and that we have taste. I am so grateful to it, because when I find a snob, I say, "Stop all that nonsense. Let's take a look at America." And I almost literally take them by the scruff of the neck and get them to the museum.

Have you actually done that?

MRS. MEYER: Oh yes. I don't like snobs. And when they make sort of charmingly pretentious remarks about the Americans, I say, "You really don't know us. You've *got* to go to the American Museum in Bath. It's a small journey to the most beautiful city in England, and you will find out that there is a real America that you know nothing about." Then I get the museum director to call this person up, issue an invitation, and lay out the red carpet, and it works out marvelously.

Do you often encounter people here who have the kind of snobbish attitude that impels you to send them to the museum?

MRS. MEYER: I am not a good judge of what you're asking about there. My attitude is too well known. Everyone knows I am a practicing American. People don't take me on by mistake. If they take me on, it's probably because they don't like me. My position is very, very clear. Just yesterday, someone said, "Why don't you change your nationality and become English?" I said, "I'd lose my whole *raison d'être*." It's a joy to me to be the American in England—to love England but to represent America here in some silly, little way. Not in some coy way. If they want to talk American politics, I'm going to be as well informed as anybody. Believe me, I am.

How do you keep yourself informed on American politics?

MRS. MEYER: Number one—the mail bag. I probably have a larger mail than I ever had in my life. It's full of information. I'll come back to that. Number two—the people passing through. For example, Lew Douglas was in town for ten hours. His secretary said to my secretary, "Mr. Douglas will be there at four." My secretary said, "But Mrs. Meyer won't be." The other one said, "You better find her. He's going to be there." So, she found me, and he came here to check in. I love the old boy. He said, "What do they think in England?" I said, "What do they think in America?" There is this constant checking-in. I have the confidence of some good people, who will talk to me. And I read. I have, I think, achieved by now a political intuition, a very good one. I try to be sound about it. I care, and I'm interested, and I don't let an opportunity pass to garner information. When people make foolish remarks about American politics, I try terribly hard to have the actual facts. I think now my English friends expect me to, which is nice.

Also, I've learned to be absolutely honest. I can't bear to have an English person be the first to make an honest point about something bad that's happened in America. I want to make it first. I want to make it properly. I want to be able to say, "Of course, we are ashamed of this." And never to listen and then say, "But what about you? Maybe you have something to be a little bit ashamed of, too." That is a process that has no value at all. They know that I am not churlishly pro-American. Rather, that I am an American who lives in England and knows and loves two countries. Keeping informed, therefore, is essential. I have so many friends who write me from all over the world their news, forcing me to write back our news. This has helped to keep my mind active.

And that brings you to the mail.

MRS. MEYER: It is enormous and amusing and interesting and unexpected. Very often, the entire contents of the mailbag is all mine, and the mailman just leaves the bag here, and picks it up in the afternoon. Fifty letters a day would not be unusual. That takes a *lot* of time—all morning, as a rule, and I start on it early. We have breakfast at eight. Tom leaves here about ten after nine, after reading the morning papers, which we do from eight o'clock on. Then he goes to his desk, and I go to mine. The morning is taken up with handling the mail that can be taken care of by dictation and with getting together material needed to answer some of the letters. A lot of people casually ask me for information of one kind and another, which we may be able to get with a quick telephone call to the *Telegraph*, where I have friends, or we will carry the search wherever we need to. I have a very fast secretary on that. And I always have a second one when the pile of correspondence gets high. I handle it all myself. I have never yet turned a letter over to a secretary and said, "Tell them no." Also in the morning, I give my chauffeur a whole sheaf of things to do. They are always in writing. I'm the greatest notemaker on earth.

I hate going to lunch. I like to work right through, but I will go to lunch if I think I am going to find amusing conversation, which is not hard to find in England. Otherwise, I will eat at my desk. In that hour, while I'm eating, I will write twenty cards—short notes that take me a minute to write.

In the afternoon, I work on whatever project is scheduled for the day. It might be the museum. It might be the article for *Harper's*

Bazaar. I do a regular feature—interviews with famous or interesting people—for the English *Bazaar.* Or it might be some other article I promised to write. I'm always behind on that. I'm working on two books. One is a series of anecdotes, and the only thread holding them together is myself. The other book is called *The Bird, The Cat, and The Porpoise.* I have been regaling my house guests with these animal stories for a long time, and finally I was persuaded to put them into a book, which I'm illustrating. It's about half done. Eventually, I will also put down between hard covers my own personal, long-range, objective, non-violent, totally frank views on what happened to *Flair.* Another thing—I'm insane about the theater. It's really a hobby of mine. I put money into the theater in America, so I read plays all the time. Also, occasionally during an afternoon, I will work on a speech. I hate speaking. I do absolutely die when I have to, but I've never turned down the American Embassy, and they have asked me quite often. And I do speak at Oxford quite often, because I love students. Wherever I sit—at my desk, in a car, in bed, in my bath, in the garden—there is something for my mind to work over. Therefore, I say I'm busier than I've ever been. And all on matters of choice—the things I love—and all without tension.

And what about the painting?

MRS. MEYER: The painting goes on every weekend. I never paint in London. I sit there in the country with all my friends around me and carry on the conversation and meanwhile do my painting. I simply could not take myself to some gloriously quiet hideaway and do it. Let's face it: I may be the only artist we both know of who paints in this way but who would be a lot better if she didn't. What would happen if I went to a studio with north light and peace and quiet? I've often thought about this. But I don't care. I'm not trying to show the *best* I can do. I'm doing the thing I love. There's no contest.

As for there being no contest, don't you think that that is one of the things that has changed very much since you've been here? In New York, it always seemed as if you were constantly involved in a great many contests.

MRS. MEYER: But of course. Name me anybody in America in a top job who is not in a contest. You can't avoid it. I don't really care enough about the past to analyze it, and I hate looking back, so I don't. If I could take the time to think about it, I might come up with some simple half-truths, such as "What was your hurry?" Or, "You did better than anybody else could have in your spot." I don't know. I couldn't care *less*. What I do care about is that there are twelve copies of *Flair*. They exist. They are on shelves. I never go anywhere on earth that people don't speak to me about it. Every day. Wherever I go. That's great. That gives me joy. One person out of a billion associates me with *Look*. They forget, which is right, because even I have. But *Flair*—that's about the only part of the past that I think about, and because I love it so, I am going to write about it.

The difference between America and England is not only that there's no contest here. It's more than that. It's the total absence of scrutiny. That is the agony of America—scrutiny. And the categorization. You go through life, if you were I, thinking, "If I do this, I'm going to fall into the trap. They think I'm hard-boiled. This is going to prove it." Or they say, "She's glossy." By leaving New York, I exchanged the goldfish bowl for the incredible privacy of England—for the precious indifference, in fact, to whatever way you lead your life. After total exposure, how soothing. Everybody in America in top spots goes through life worrying, because they're under constant scrutiny. Here, you're under none. It's so easy.

Is that because people here have less interest in other people, are more self-centered, or because more respect is paid to one's privacy?

MRS. MEYER: All three. No real interest. They don't care. And a great, great premium paid on privacy *plus* individuality. For instance, if I never wore anything here except a green burlap dress, it would never occur to them as being strange. In America, I would be labeled "The Girl in the Green Dress." And I'd never get away from it. I'd *never* get away from it. Here, they expect a certain amount of eccentricity. They admire individuality. They don't even discuss it. They just unwittingly admire it. They take it *all* in their stride, and you have this lovely soft atmosphere in which to live.

Is the sense of privacy and of being able to live your life as you wish the best part of living here? Or what is the best part?

MRS. MEYER: I must answer that in general terms. If it were about me, personally, I would have to answer differently, because it involves Tom and all that. In general terms, I believe it is safe to say that once you have lived abroad, you're ruined. You're ruined because you can't do without it. You appreciate it to such a degree that it is a very real thing. You never forget it. That's the beginning.

I think, by nature, I'm happier abroad. I like the things that Europeans like, perhaps more than anyone suspects. I *love* conversation. I *love* good food. I *love* motoring. I *love* the change in people. These things I find here, and all this makes me happy, and I think it makes the average American—the kind that goes abroad to live—I think it makes him happy, too. Generally speaking, the American man or woman who goes abroad to live is ready to go. Once here, he's trapped by it.

You're trapped by the slower pace, by the remarkable changes in beauty in a short space. When we left for Petworth Hall last night, we left in the rain. As we approached south Sussex—an hour away but still our county—you could see deep, deep, deep penetrating rays of the sun, but you couldn't see the sun. When we got to Petworth, it was a hail of sun. And every picture, every drawing, every engraving, every painting of beautiful England was in that garden. This morning, I came from Sussex. It was hot and shining and bright, and in Brixton, which is twelve minutes outside of the heart of London, it was black, interesting, gray. Not just climatically, but the whole atmosphere of life had changed. England is good for my eye. I like what I see. America is so vast that you have to travel a hundred miles to see some small alteration, if you're lucky. I like change. And I think Americans who come here also appreciate it.

Some of them, of course, would appreciate a change that would bring them a little less rain and gloom and a little more sun.

MRS. MEYER: When the sun comes out here, I die. I'm very, very glad. I have a real sense of emotion. I don't take it for granted. I don't know that it's going to be sunny when I want it to be bright, and if it is, the joy is compounded. If it's terribly rainy, and suddenly the sun comes through—well, that is glorious. Anyway, I think bad-weather conversation is dull conversation. I'm not involved with the weather. I ignore it. Also, I'm not typical. I work at my desk. For me, it's beautiful wherever I am. This room looks sunny to me whether it's bright or black outside. I don't even mind driving in the rain. I think there is beauty in driving in the rain. I love what I see, wherever it is. I've learned to love the English sky, especially the one we get in the winter at midafternoon, just before it turns dark. The sun, usually hidden in grayness, burns through—a circle of gold in a blue-gray haze that puts Turner masterpieces before you. I've never seen it anywhere but here. It's just English.

It's clear that you are very fond of England and London. If you could choose any city in Europe to live in, would this be your choice?

MRS. MEYER: I couldn't live anywhere else. This is it, mainly because I've gotten to know the peoples of the other countries too well, and I don't find them as attractive. The French are cynical. They are desperately anti-social. They are not open-armed to the new face. It's a closed club, no matter what segment of society. If you have a dramatic name and a position, you will make it, but if you know you're making it on those terms, you don't want it. So, I don't like France.

Italy is a small village full of vice. I love to visit it, but I couldn't live in it. Madrid is enchanting—*so* beautiful, but it has no heartbeat. None. Any other capital would be out of the question to consider, except perhaps Brussels, because it has the Common Market headquarters, though the country is full of pretty stolid people. There is, however, a small community of pretty lively minds, and one could survive.

England I love. It has been good to me. It is good *for* me. England is a crossroads, and you can see your pals. Conversation is taken for granted. England is a paradise for talkers, and I include myself among the peculiar breed. That you like to talk and do it well is not unique. It's general. Certainly the people I spend my time with love it. No matter what happens in the news, it's chewed *to bits* here. And when I went to America, it broke my heart, because nobody asked me anything, except, "How do you like living in England?" and "Where are you going on your holiday?" and "Have you seen this play and that play?" and so on. There's so much more to it here, because it's in the national habit pattern to devour the newspapers and discuss them. Don't let me suggest that everything you hear is brilliant. I've heard some pretty stupid remarks. But it's taken for granted that everything you read—the "Letters" columns of the *Times*, the offbeat stories—everything will be discussed. Somebody may take a good hour to discuss whether or not a Beatles' song contains some fugue that has never been in any other piece of music. And I love it. I love it. It suits me.

You've been to the United States fairly recently, I gather. How often do you get back there?

MRS. MEYER: On the average of once every nine or ten months. I never go except for a show of my paintings or for some similar reason. Never just for a visit. At first, I thought I had to go back to keep myself American, but that's over. I go now only for a purpose.

When I lived in America, I was examining Europe. Now that I live in Europe, I am examining my own country, and I am distressed by the scrutiny I make of it. My heart breaks on occasion, because of what look like seriously hideous omens. I am a little bit ashamed, although I shouldn't be, because we, in the United States, are only larger portions of the same elements that exist in other places. We have such large percentages that they loom larger. I do think when I go back that I see more and more violence on the march, and I see more and more ugliness. This is true all over the world. I must keep saying that, because it is true. For example, the extreme right-wingers make such an impact in America, because there are so many of them. The few that are here just mark up the walls. When I come back, I say, "Look at America," but then I say, "No. Look at the world." What upsets me is that what I see anyplace in the world is so exaggerated in America. And in America, everything is speeded up. More money. More power.

One also notices, of course, that everyone is on edge. Everyone is pushed too hard. In New York, one has to race at such high speed to take everything in. And, of course, everything does have to be taken in. Here, I do all the things I want to do—the theater, the Tate, and so on—and I never have the feeling of being rushed or pressed.

I think there are two reasons for that. One is that there are not too many things going on at the same time, which is the absolute opposite of the situation in New York. The other is that—I don't know whether it's England or just that I have become intelligent—I don't *care* what I miss here. Actually, this insistence of the American to be in on everything is intensely superficial unless it's very carefully guarded. To be out of a lot of things makes you much more connected with the things you are in. Tom and I don't mind what we don't see. In America, if you don't get there—somewhere—Oh Lord, it's disaster. If you set those people down and if their life depended on it, they couldn't tell you what they've seen, what they've been through. They don't know. They go to the opening of an art show, and they have to get through it so fast to get to something else that they don't know what they've looked at. To me, here, art is not just an opening of a show. I go to the colleges. I watch the kids painting. I spot a talent on the make. I keep my eye on it, become a friend. Buy something from time to time. A *real* connection. And, of course, I take such pride if these kids go anywhere. And in the years here, I've had lots of such charming experiences.

In the years here, have you also had the experience of feeling that you are missing something by being away from the United States? Or is there anything about America that you still miss?

MRS. MEYER: Nothing. I can't think of a thing. I would have to do a lot of prowling through my mind to answer that. The things that so irritate most Americans who come over don't irritate me. They say they can never get anything done or anything repaired. As far as things for the home are concerned, I can always get everything done. It's a mixture of great good luck plus efficiency plus compassion. For instance, I find a man who does upholstery well. First of all, I try to be American, and I pay my bills very promptly, which is very unusual here. Fantastically so. It's the national habit to work on overdrafts, which we Americans don't even understand. If someone does a good job for me fast, that person gets plenty of business through me. And the next time I need him—bingo—I get attention fast.

Well, so much for the housekeeping problems. It does seem that your settling into English life has been unusually complete.

MRS. MEYER: Look, but I am unusual. I'm not the bank vice president's wife or the officer's wife who comes here. I'm a professional woman with contacts around the world, who loves the arts, who comes to a cultivated city, which people pass through. What could be better? I say I am unusual. Well, I have the benefit of all this material that comes with me, so I cannot be compared with the others. Also, people say to me, "I find the English so hard to crash." Well, I knew so many before, so I'm not usual in that sense, either.

What I meant about the unusually complete way of settling into this life was that in many respects—not only in your professional interests but in more casual things, such as taking an interest in young painters in the colleges—you seem to have a deeper involvement than you did in New York.

MRS. MEYER: Oh yes. Deeper. Much deeper. You can't even put a question mark on that one. There is no debate. It's sad, in a way. I mean, there I was, but how far down did I really reach? Never had time, really. I made, I now think, an unusual amount of friends on my staff. Some still-not-locked-away naturalness allowed me to respond to some people I liked. But—oh dear me—flying always at high speed on top—that was it.

I want to say something else, though. Very, very important. My American experience—the pleasures, the glamor, and the tragic side of that New York experience—it took that to make this work. I would hate ever for anyone to think that I discount that or slur it off or that I don't realize its usefulness and purpose. I am sure if I had come here twenty years ago or fifteen years ago, I might well have been one of the Americans who hated it. All life in essence is timing. When I did come here, *the timing was right.* And for the American background I left behind I have nothing but gratitude, *immense* gratitude. It formed my tastes. I didn't have them. It formed this remorseless, permanent, relentless pursuit of the arts, which will never, never, never be drowned. The love of information was also formed in America. And actually marriage to Mike Cowles. He wants to know. This is marvelous. It helped. I promise you that the life I led there prepared me to judge what I fell heir to and to utilize it with care. I mean, I now have judgment. I recognize when a thing is good and that I am in a position of true luck. I recognize it. I know it. I never *not* know it. I say, "God, this is good! Lucky me!"

"The French seem to understand me in some mysterious way."

Olivia de Havilland, the film actress, has made her home in Paris since her marriage, in 1955, to Pierre Galante, a senior executive of the French magazine, *Paris-Match*. Although they were legally separated in 1961, both remained, until very recently, discreetly silent about their marital situation, and they have continued to live under the same roof, a civilized arrangement permitted by a French law enacted at the end of the Second World War, when the severe housing shortage made it practically impossible for parting couples to find adequate separate quarters. "Strictly speaking, this is supposed to be the initial stage prior to divorce and therefore only a temporary arrangement," Miss de Havilland told Geoffrey Bocca in 1966, "but I doubt if we will ever get around to completing the formalities. Pierre and I are no longer obliged to each other, but we are very close friends, without any of the previous tensions." Since the separation was not publicly known when I talked to Miss de Havilland, it did not enter our conversation, which began one morning around eleven in the beautiful, four-story house overlooking the Bois de Boulogne that she shares with her husband, and ended at one in the afternoon, when M. Galante, a tall, slender, handsome man, wearing a gray suit, a black tie, and a black handkerchief in his breast pocket, came home, as most French husbands do, for lunch. During the previous two hours, Miss de Havilland had ranged over a number of topics, including her career, her meeting with M. Galante at the Cannes Film Festival, and her book, *Every Frenchman Has One;* but her most interesting comments, it seemed to me, came near the end of our conversation, when she talked about what she considers the advantages of raising children in France—she and M. Galante have a daughter, who was then eight, and Miss de

Havilland by a previous marriage has a son, who was then fifteen—and about some of the other reasons why she prefers to live in France.

MISS DE HAVILLAND: Bringing up children here is infinitely easier than it is in the United States, because life in France is much more traditional and conventional. You're not fighting the society around you if you impose a life of absolute regularity and security on your children because you think it is best for them—a life in which certain rules are not to be broken, and if they are, certain privileges are withdrawn. Here, these things are made quite clear, and parents show that they know how to defend themselves. If parents don't defend themselves and the rules they have made, children know that when it is necessary, the parents will be equally ineffective in defending the children. I don't have to fight an entire society which lets its children stay up until two o'clock in the morning and where girls of fifteen give big parties for boys of fifteen. That's unheard of in France. In bringing up these children, I've got it all going my way here, and I know they will be much better for it.

So, for the children's sake, I prefer to live in France, but in the future I would like to spend a lot of time in the United States, because I am increasingly happy there. Really, how strange that is. Possibly it is because so many of my hungers have been satisfied from living in France. The French seem to understand me in some mysterious way. Damn it, I never was understood in Los Angeles. They never could get *anything* straight. If you tried to be well-mannered and considerate, they thought you were weak and soft. They misinterpreted absolutely everything. The French know the complexity of the human personality, and they know how to read it. You come to France, and people start reading you right, and you begin to read yourself right, and then you learn how to be comfortable with yourself.

"This is another curious thing about England. When they say it is a man's country, they are right."

Mrs. Kenneth Alexander Keith, who is known to her friends as Slim and who was formerly married to Howard Hawks, the film director, and to Leland Hayward, the theatrical producer, is now the wife of the deputy chairman and chief executive of Hill, Samuel & Co., Ltd., the largest of London's merchant banks. "I didn't get tired of America, and I didn't come here to escape taxes or anything of the kind," she told me. "I just got married. My husband lived here. Now so do I." The marriage took place in 1962. In London, Mrs. Keith, a beautiful and witty woman, has added to her reputation as a celebrated hostess. During tea in her Eaton Square flat, which has a Rouault on one wall and an exquisite Chinese cabinet against another, she talked about many aspects of living in England, including some of the more entertaining differences in social customs.

MRS. KEITH: I wasn't engaged to get married before I came here, and when we said, "Let's take the dastardly step," I did think more than five minutes as to whether or not one could readjust to another country and another life. When you live in a place for a long time and are around friends, you have a language with them. You don't have to translate. So, I found the hardest thing of all when I first came here was that I couldn't understand a single thing they were saying, and when I could finally understand their language, I couldn't understand what they were talking about. I was awfully quiet for a year or more. One eventually catches on, but I made all the usual mistakes.

Oh, there were some marvelous ones, and there would have been more, except that I fell into an absolute dish of cream, because, working for Kenneth when I married him was the greatest living man in the world. His name is Mordecai, and he is the butler. He looks like he's from Central Casting. He was trained at Hatfield, which is a very grand house, and he's just the greatest servant and the funniest, dearest, nicest man. We're great friends, but I remember the first dinner I gave here. I'd been married about three days. It was a dinner for Henry and Anne Ford. I had been doing this sort of thing fairly well, you know, for a number of years, and I said to Mordecai, "We'll have cheese with the salad." Well, this caused a crisis. He called up the office and told Kenneth's secretary, "She wants cheese with the salad. We've never served cheese with the salad in our whole career." Here, you see, you serve cheese and crackers—that is to say, biscuits—at the end of the meal. You have earlier served the dessert, which is known as the sweet or trifle, which is always followed by port. It goes on and on.

How did you resolve the original cheese-with-the-salad crisis?

MRS. KEITH: It was very simple. I had hysterics. When Kenneth came home, I said for openers, "That *idiot* butler! *Really!*" With that, Kenneth stomped out of the house. Honestly, it was like two kids twenty years old having their first fight as bride and groom. Then he came back in again, and said, "Look, I've got a word of advice for you." I said, "What's that?" He said, "When in Rome. . . ." I said, "O.K." Then I showed him the plan for seating the dinner, and he glanced at it, and said, "That's fine." Well, I'd been in the flat three or four times, and I'd always entered the dining room from the little sitting room in the back of the flat, and I seated the dinner from that entrance. The only trouble was that when you have a dinner party, the guests enter from the opposite side of the room, so all I'd done was seat the entire dinner backwards.

Then, before the first Christmas, Mordecai came to me and said, "Madam, we should go over our list of what we must get for Christmas." I said, "Well, I've not only made my list. My shopping's all done." He said, "Oh, madam, I mean about all the other things. For instance, what kind of crackers do you want?" And I said, "Well, the kind we always have. I think the crackers that come with the cheese are fine." He said, "I'm sorry, madam, but that's not what I meant at all." So I asked what he did mean, and it turns out that crackers are like those things at kids' birthday parties that you pop. At home, we call them snappers. Here, snappers are things used to fasten clothes. Snappers are also called poppers. I got completely lost. But one gets on to it all.

There are absolutely marvelous things about living here. It's easier in many, many ways. I think it's simply that the tension is less. I find when I go to New York, which I do two or three times a year because my child is there and because I love it, that I'm wound up as tight as one can be. I do twenty things a day. Here, I can't make myself wind up. I do four things a day—two in the morning and two in the afternoon. Then it's time for tea, and I read the newspapers. After that, it's time to take a bath. Then it's time for dinner. Here, by the way, one is absolutely on-the-button prompt. If you're asked for dinner at eight-fifteen, you're *there*. I think that's so sensible. The food is better, because it's not kept waiting while people stand around and get drunk and eat those awful sticky things.

In New York, as you say, you do twenty things a day, and here you do four. Are you satisfied to reduce your activities all that much?

MRS. KEITH: Certainly. I'm going to live longer. When I lived in New York, I remember, you would order your food and do all the household things in the morning. Then you'd go to lunch, and from there to a shop for a fitting, perhaps, or to a gallery to look at some paintings. You'd then go some place for a drink. You'd change, and either go to the theater or go out to dinner—and that was *every* night. Then you'd go to El Morocco, and wind up at P. J. Moriarty's for a hamburger. You'd be home at three o'clock in the morning, and you'd get up at nine. It seemed possible and easy. Whether it's a terrible strain and you pay the price finally, I don't know. I suppose one does.

It's true that one seems to see more people of an advanced age here than in New York. For example, my husband's father is seventy-nine years old. He drives his own bright green Jaguar, which is lined with green leather. He plays eighteen holes of golf twice a week. He shoots during the shooting season, and is a fantastically good shot. The man who looks after him has always looked after him. His clothes are taken care of. He has what he wants to eat when he wants it. He lives exactly the way he wants to live. And it's been that way since he was a young man.

Kenneth is an exception to that pattern, in a sense, because he works very, very hard. He's a high-powered fella. In addition to being head of Hill, Samuel, he's on every board you ever heard of, including the National Economic Development Council. He's a very strong Common Marketer. He is, actually, a man of no small influence in the country. He seems to me, compared to the other people one sees in his world, to be much more like an American than an Englishman. But that's when he's in London. You drive out of town and start toward the country and he becomes like all the rest. The only thing that matters in his life then is shooting birds.

We have a shoot, in Norfolk. Kenneth absolutely adores it. He also farms, and he adores that, too. The farm and the shoot are the same, by the way. The reason he has the farm is so that he can have the shoot. He's not going to say that, but that's the way it is. The house in the country is very, very old. The cellar is Roman. Kenneth has done marvelous things to it. Central heating and all that. It's divine. The place has twenty-five hundred acres. You see things there that are almost feudal. There are about sixty or seventy people who work on our land. They live, I think, in the most primitive way, judged by American standards. I mean, they don't have iceboxes. Kenneth says, "But they've never had iceboxes." They adore him. They adore what they're doing. It's what they've always done. The man who runs the farm has been there since he was a boy. His son works there, and his grandson works there.

How often do you get to the farm?

Mrs. Keith: Every weekend. Well, next weekend, we're going to Blenheim. We occasionally go someplace else, but what Kenneth cares about more than anything else is that place. It's also a great big business, and it makes a very, very good profit. For instance, we have a dairy, where they milk about a hundred and eighty cows twice a day. It's all done with electric milking machines, and then a truck comes and takes the milk to Campbell's Soup factory, which is up the road. The place is a responsibility, but Kenneth would go right up the wall if he had nothing to do on a weekend.

And, of course, there's the shooting, which is his passion. Grouse begins on the twelfth of August—the "Glorious Twelfth." From then until the first day of February, one's life, if you're married to this kind of Englishman, is absolutely dominated by bird life. If Kenneth doesn't shoot at our house, he goes to someone else's house to shoot, and he does exactly the same thing there. This is an absolute way of life.

We have about four or five shoots a season at our place. The arranging of it all is fantastic. It begins toward the end of June. By that time, the head keeper—we have enough land so that we need three keepers, who watch out about the eggs, gather the ones to be hatched in the incubators, and so on—the head keeper knows how many birds there are going to be. He will say, "I think you can have one partridge day and four pheasant days." Then Kenneth and I sit down with the book and work out the dates for our shoots, which have to be selected in such a way as to leave him free to go to the other shoots he's keen about. The goings-on about this you wouldn't believe.

When we're making all these arrangements, I always say, "I don't want to have just people who are good shots. I want to have people who are amusing." You know, some of those good shots talk so you can't understand anything they say, and if you could, you wouldn't give a damn. Well, you settle on the dates and the people, and you always ask them with their wives. Very often, if it's a weekend, the wives come. I think they like to come to our house, because it is very comfortable, and it's run more like an American house, so there is enough of everything. There are plenty of matches and things like that. And they eat quite well.

When we have shoots, I must have at least three people in the kitchen all of the time. This is just too strenuous for the cook we have here in London, who is marvelous and a darling, but I couldn't put her through that, so, for the shoots, I usually bring a chef and two helpers. I also bring another butler—a man who works in Kenneth's office, where they have a dining room. Then I have three local ladies who come in to make beds and so on. I talk to the chef long before the season starts, and order all the food I'm going to have all the way through to the end of February. On the day of a shoot, I will feed something like a hundred and twenty meals. Let's say there are ten people staying in the house, including Kenneth and me. Let's say you have two or three men who bring their own servants. They bring their loaders. Some of them bring a loader and a chauffeur. You have to plan for all these people, put them up. You've augmented the staff, and you have to take care of them as well. Since we are ten in the house, which means five guns—five men who will be shooting—and since you usually have seven guns, you ask two extra people for the day of the shoot. They are locals, and they also bring their loaders. I have a separate kitchen and a separate dining room, which I use to feed the loaders.

Once I've talked with the chef about the food, I don't have to think about that again. The booze is also done that way, long ahead of time. I think there's nothing more dreary than a fidgeting hostess. "Oh, we've run out of vodka." There's just no excuse if you've planned well. I keep a book, so I know who's been there before and when and what they've been served. I never repeat the food for the people who were there the year before. Although they probably don't remember, I *think* they do.

So, it all gets rolling. The guests arrive on Friday evening, and they all arrive at once, so there is a great deal of scurrying-around and unpacking, and then everything settles down. There is a rather quiet evening on Friday. Everybody goes to bed quite early. The men get up at the crack of dawn. They have their tea brought to them in their rooms, and then they come down to breakfast. The men don't like the wives to come down to breakfast, so the ladies are served in their rooms. I'm up quite early, but I don't come downstairs until about twelve o'clock to check that everything is in order, see how the ladies are doing, and ask if they would like to see one drive before lunch. If they do, we find the guns, and watch them shoot birds, and then we come back, and we lunch.

On Saturday, you have extra people for lunch. The neighbors who come bring their wives, so you have sixteen, eighteen for this meal. The food one eats at a shooting lunch is almost always the same. You always have steak and kidney pie. You always have Stilton cheese. You always have fresh celery. You always have sloe gin at the end, and it must be passed around the table clockwise. You can't pass it across the table. If you did, they would look at you as if you'd done some terrible thing. After lunch, the men go out and shoot more birds.

I gather that the women don't shoot at all.

Mrs. Keith: They don't. A woman would have to be an absolutely marvelous shot to shoot here. In Spain, for example, it's different. I've shot there with Kenneth. But not in Norfolk, which is sort of the heart of the shooting country.

For Saturday night, you try to import two new faces, or four new faces, if you can, to perk up the cast. I have a movie machine, and I run movies, and that helps tremendously. I get ones I know are good from Rank, MGM, Columbia—all those. I show the movies in the drawing room, and I run the machine with a lot of swearing and all that, and every time a reel has to be changed, a lot of drinking goes on. Whenever the movie is finished, that winds up the evening, and people go to bed. That's the big night of the weekend.

Usually, about half the people stay for lunch on Sunday. They are almost always all gone by teatime. Very often, Kenneth has another shoot on Monday, which means that the entire house has to be changed immediately and all the guest rooms done all over again. Oh, it's very trying. Actually, it can all be great fun. And I do enjoy myself if I'm allowed to have anything to say about the cast. It makes a better weekend if you have one American couple or somebody who isn't that much a part of the shooting world. Something new.

Does the conversation run mainly to shooting?

Mrs. Keith: Almost entirely. Of course, one wouldn't invite a guest who didn't shoot. You wouldn't take up a bed with someone who wasn't a gun, you see. You wouldn't be allowed to do that, unless it was a pretty girl or something like that. So, the conversation is not what you would call wide-ranging. They talk about *their* birds and how many pheasants *they* got and whose shoot is good and whose shoot isn't and what's the best cover and so on and on.

In the nature of things, most of the people you see socially are English.

Mrs. Keith: Almost completely. My cronies, the people with whom I'm most relaxed, are Americans. One just gravitates toward them because of the language. You know, when English people come to my house to stay, they find it an oddity, because it runs in a way that theirs doesn't. And when I go to their house to stay, I also find it strange—at least in some of them. Kenneth's uncle is a man called Captain Alexander Keith, and he lives in Northumberland in a great pile of stone called Chesters. Uncle Alec has a grouse moor. A grouse moor and a pheasant shoot are two quite different things. A grouse moor takes thousands and thousands of acres of land. It is all heather and terribly hard to walk on. It's just unbelievable. Kenneth took me, the new American wife, there for the grouse. Well, I had a feeling it was going to be a disaster, and it was.

First of all, Kenneth said I would have to get up for breakfast. The wives do that at Uncle Alec's. I said, "Very well, I'm delighted. I'll be there on time." And I was. But none of the women spoke. This is another curious thing about England. When they say it is a man's country, they are right. As a woman, you are not considered—your comfort, your ease, anything. On a weekend, the men's dinner coats are pressed and laid out, and your dresses are not touched. It's different in my house. Women get taken care of there.

Uncle Alec is married to a lady called Aunt Daphne. Aunt Daphne, I suppose, is sixty-five. On a shoot, she goes out on the moor with him, and she walks from nine-thirty in the morning until five-thirty in the afternoon. Almost everybody else rides across these moors in Jeeps. Aunt Daphne walks, every bit of the way. Uncle Alec is eighty, and he walks. He is a great shot. To shoot a grouse is very difficult indeed, because they go like a bomb—about sixty miles an hour. You do the shooting from something called a butt. A butt is a little hole in the ground, usually lined with stone, and big enough for the man with the gun and one other person. The other person is always the loader. It is not the poor new American wife, whose feet hurt. She is made to sit outside the butt with the dogs, and the dogs are crying, and I'm crying, and it's just hell.

The first time we did this, Kenneth said, "You'll love it. You'll love it." We climbed up this incredible hill. Then you walk across the heather and you can't see what's under the heather but it's all holes. So you're falling down, and it's just murder. We arrived at the first butt. I had said to him earlier, "What do I wear?" He said, "Oh, just a pair of pants, and take one of those coats you wear at home for shooting." That's all I took. It was now freezing cold and getting ready to rain. I was allowed to sit on a rock, and the keeper handed me an envelope. It looked like a sort of plastic cushion, and I sat down on it. Then it started to rain, and he said, "Pardon me, madam." And I said, "Yes?" And he said, "May I have what you're sitting on?" It was an envelope full of rain clothes—rain trousers, raincoat, rain hat, rain everything—for Kenneth Keith, who was then covered up with all this cellophane and plastic while I sat there, soaking and *furious*. The loader kept passing me candy to keep me quiet, like I was a bad animal. It was just unbelievable.

Of course, I also learned that you're not allowed to look up during a drive, because if the bird sees your face, he's going to go somewhere else. I said, "What the hell did you bring me for? You won't even let me look at the damned birds." "God damn it, keep your head down." And I'm crying, and I'm furious, and I'm swearing. And I hate England, and I hate him more than England. Oh God, it was just hell. Finally, on the last drive, I was invited to sit on the ground in the butt, which by now was solid mud. And I thought, "In order to do this, we come here in our airplane—that's a plane with two pilots—and we send by ground a Land Rover with two men in it. One is to drive Mr. Keith, and one is to load his gun. Two dogs. Two changes of clothing. Two guns. Two thousand bullets we send. For this. For *this!*" It was a day the like of which no one will ever know. And I longed so for someone to be near me who knew how funny it was. You know, so you could say, "How about this cockeyed country? I mean, *really*."

Do you find that the kind of rigidity that marks the shooting way of life something that also turns up in other aspects of life here?

MRS. KEITH: It does in the country. It doesn't necessarily in London. There are things about the structure that we as Americans don't understand. In our South, maybe, there have been faint similarities, but nowhere else. For instance, how you address a servant. Our man, as I've said, is called Mordecai. When he was a footman, his name was Edgar. Now, if he were the headman in a great big house like Blenheim, he would be called "Mordecai" by the Duke and the Duke's guests, and "Mr. Mordecai" by all of the other servants. We have a chauffeur, Dawson. I call him "Dawson." Mr. Keith calls him "Dawson." But he gets upset if Mr. Keith's secretary calls him "Dawson." He thinks the secretary should call him "Mr. Dawson." It's all very curious. There's a whole system. I get it all wrong most of the time.

You mentioned that there seems to be a slower pace here, but yet there seems to be a great deal going on, a lot of action.

MRS. KEITH: There is a lot going on, but so much is devoted to the most wildly unimportant things, it seems to me. Wearing what hat to Ascot, and it must be a hat and be absolutely ridiculous and made out of flower petals and all that. Now, I can't see, if you spend all that time having your hair washed, and it's all nice and fresh and clean, with a good dress and a good coat, why you have to wear a hat. But you do, of course, on account of the Queen. Tonight, we're going to a reception at St. James's Palace, and it says on the invitation, "Black tie. Decorations, Miniature." I read in the paper yesterday that the men are furious because they can't wear their sashes and their ribbons and their necklaces. Considering the miniature decorations and so on, I didn't think I would have to wear anything on my head. But about an hour ago, Mordecai came to me and said, "Madam, I've spoken to General So-and-So, and it's *essential* that you wear your tiara tonight. I'm on my way to the office to get it out of the vault." This breaks me up.

One thing you find here that you never find in America is the amazingly trustful attitude on the part of shopkeepers and other people one deals with. For instance, I went to the Antique Dealers Fair the other day, and I saw a chair that I liked very much. It was very expensive. I thought it was expensive in dollars and, of course, the price was in pounds. I don't understand numbers at all, unfortunately, so I'm always figuring in dollars and thinking I'm getting a big bargain all the time. At any rate, I said, "I'll have that chair. Will you please send it?" And I gave the address. The dealer didn't say, "Would you put a deposit down, madam," or anything of the kind. They never do. You can go anyplace in the country and walk into a shop and say, "I'll take this with me. Send me the bill." Which is unheard of at home. The manners in that respect are absolutely marvelous.

In fact, I think manners here, generally, are infinitely better than in America. There are several things that strike you as different. For instance, here, if you're invited to something, you're usually invited by card, which requires an answer. Or, if I call someone and ask them if they will dine with us on such-and-such a night, and they say they will, a reminder card is sent to them. Another thing: I had a dinner party for fourteen people a week ago, and I've had a letter from every woman who came to the party, and flowers and a card from the extra men. This is always the case here. It is not true in New York at all. Maybe they do more writing here than is necessary. I suppose getting all those little cards going back and forth helps the postal system. They sell more stamps. But there is a kind of politeness and courtesy in the custom, which is very attractive.

There's another curious thing they do here, which we don't do at home. They seat the dinner both before *and* after. It goes something like this. After dinner, the ladies go out and powder their noses, and the men stay usually too long in the dining room. When they come out, you say, "Now, Mrs. X., will you talk to Mr. Z., because you sat next to Mr. Y. at dinner." You seat them all. Then, after a while, you switch them around. Unless you move them, they just stay where they are. I was staggered when it first happened to me. "How dare this woman push me around. I'm doing perfectly well where I am." I hate it, but one has to do it.

Do you use this system now at your dinners?

MRS. KEITH: I don't. If I see two people who have been sitting there talking for forty-five minutes, I go over and break it up, or I kick Kenneth, or something. But I don't make them all get up and musical-chairs around the room. Usually, there's a tray of Bitter Lemon and things like that. I always have a bottle of champagne. It works better.

That's an innovation in your house?

MRS. KEITH: In a sense. There are a lot of innovations. But people seem to enjoy them. When it comes to eating out, one finds that the food here now is as good as it is anyplace. I mean, the Mirabelle is as good a restaurant as there is in the world. One eats terribly well. You may miss corn on the cob—and I do—but California has never grown a strawberry that tastes like those you get here. And the asparagus. At home, you can have strawberries the year round. You can have them instead of plum pudding on Christmas Day. Here, you have strawberries for two months, and you eat them until you're covered with spots, and then you never see them again until next year. And the same thing is true of the asparagus. There's something wonderful about that.

Aside from corn on the cob, is there anything else that you are conscious of missing?

MRS. KEITH: In the beginning, I always felt a sort of deep-seated frustration, because I couldn't reach out and do what I wanted to do when I wanted to do it. Now, it's easier, since I know my way around a bit more, and I'm used to the slowness. For instance, if you go in June to the tailor who is going to make the coat for your winter shooting life, and you ask when the first fitting is, you can expect to hear him say, "Two months from now." And you'll be damned lucky to get the coat by Christmas. To get anything mended is a career. And the telephone system—the domestic service—is enough to drive you absolutely insane. At the same time, the men who handle the long-distance calls are so wonderful. When I tell them that I want to call America and talk to my daughter—her name is Kitty Hawks—they're thrown into paroxysms of laughter. I say, "Well, don't laugh. I'm her mother." They go to work, and keep at it until they find her. They are absolute darlings.

There are other things that are better here, and I suppose you become more keenly aware of them when you're away from them. When I go to New York now, I feel like the place is strangling to death. Where you could go and get your hair washed and get out in an hour and a half, it now takes two hours and forty-five minutes. You can't get a taxi, no matter what time of day or night. They are either going home, or they just don't stop. "Off Duty," you know. For instance, we were living in the St. Regis Hotel the last time we were there, and it rained part of the time. We'd have to go uptown to have a drink with somebody and come halfway back downtown to have dinner with someone else, and there was only one way you could do it, and that was to hire a car. You have to have dough in New York now. Everything is more expensive there than here.

I just found New York not as attractive to me as it was the first time I went back after coming here. This now seems more like home than that, and so this becomes easier and that becomes more difficult. For instance, the last time I was in New York alone, I dined at 550 Park Avenue, which is Sixty-second Street. I was staying in the Regency Hotel, which is Sixty-first and Park. I was going back to the hotel, and my hostess would not let me walk alone from Sixty-second Street to Sixty-first Street, on Park Avenue, at eleven-thirty at night. The butler came with me. You know, this spooks you. Here, you're perfectly all right. At least, one thinks so. I suppose you can get boshed on the head here, too. Or "coshed," I think, is the word.

But, you know, when I get off the airplane in New York, and I walk through that Immigration Control, and the man says, "Welcome home," I *just go to pieces*. Kenneth says I have the American flag tattooed on my—well, on my back, which is probably right, because I do love it. It *is* my country. And I think we do everything better than anybody. I used to say so a lot. I'd say, "I don't understand why you have to have seven different kinds of electric plugs in the same room. At home, you can buy a lamp in California and plug it in in New York, and never change a single plug. What's the matter here?" This doesn't go down terribly well. I've learned to be much more controlled about this sort of thing.

All in all, I have a marvelous life here. I'm married to a remarkable man, and it's an interesting new life. I get lonely, as anybody would. I get lonely for my child. I get lonely to call up Truman Capote or some other crony and talk nonsense for half an hour. But for the age I am and for the time of my life this is, it couldn't be more right.

"Here, one somehow always feels as if one is somebody. You don't feel like a grain of sand on a beach."

The Countess of Romanones, who is the wife of a handsome, rich, and talented Spanish nobleman and is also the Madrid editor of *Vogue*, a successful businesswoman, and an embellishment of Spanish society, began life as Aline Griffith, of Pearl River, New York. The eldest of six children, she attended the local schools, graduated from Mount St. Vincent, a Catholic women's college, and a few months later, joined the Office of Strategic Services. In January, 1944, she was sent by the OSS to Spain, where she served as an agent until the end of the Second World War. Not long afterward, she met her husband, whom she refers to as Luis, and they were married. The owner of several ranches and other business enterprises, he is also a successful artist, an accomplished horseman, a fine shot, and an expert golfer. In addition to his country estates, he owns a very attractive secluded house in Madrid. That is where I called on the Countess one October afternoon at six o'clock. A strikingly beautiful, very Spanish-looking woman, with black hair, dark brown eyes, and olive complexion, she was wearing a handsome dark blue suit, a pale blue sweater, a single strand of pearls, and a white silk headband. She gives the impression of being well organized, determined, rather intense, and indefatigably enthusiastic, and she speaks at a torrential pace. Some of her friends say she has become more Spanish than the Spanish. She thinks they may be right.

COUNTESS OF ROMANONES: When I first came to Spain, I fell so in love with the country that I hated the thought of ever having to leave it. I didn't, in fact, go back to America for three years. When I did, I found that I still had all my admiration and appreciation of the United States, but I also remembered having been so much more comfortable in Europe. I was almost frightened that something would happen to keep me from coming back. Now I've lost that fear, and I love going back to the States. As a rule, we go to America about twice a year, usually just for pleasure, and stay three or four weeks. It's a great contrast and most enjoyable, but I've been here so long, and have made such deep roots, and live so much a 100 per cent Spanish life that I certainly wouldn't want to live anyplace else.

What is there about Spain that you find so attractive?

COUNTESS OF ROMANONES: I think Spain is a little different from other countries in Europe. Unfortunately, it's changing very rapidly. Spain had the advantage twenty years ago, ten years ago, five years ago, and being a country that was small enough and life was led at a slow enough pace so that everybody had time to be friendly with everybody else. Here, one somehow always feels as if one is somebody. You don't feel like a grain of sand on a beach. You don't feel like one lost human being in a mob, being pushed around. The shoemaker is somebody, and has dignity. When I arrived here new, I was so impressed by that little bit of extra attention that one received, by the pleasantness and the smile and the politeness on the street. Whereas our country is so big and powerful and people are in such a hurry that none of us count at all, really, in New York.

And the hours we keep here, which the Americans hate so much, are delightful when you get accustomed to them. I suppose that takes a while, mostly because you get hungry. When you've learned how to have tea in the middle of the afternoon, you've learned how to manage. Here, the rich man and the poor man alike can enjoy the sun in the middle of the day, or go for a walk in the park, or play a game of golf. It's marvelous the way everything stops in midday, and then you go back to work when the sun is getting a little lower, and you don't mind being in a dull, old, closed-in place again.

I like the outdoors, and that's another thing that's nice about Spain. This climate is so good all year around. We have four seasons, just as in New York, but it never gets as cold as New York. In more than twenty years here, I think I've seen snow twice in Madrid, and it lasted for maybe one or two days. The sun is so strong that even though it's a cold day, you like to be outdoors. I go riding almost every day of my life, if I'm not shooting. We do a lot of shooting in Spain. It starts at the beginning of October, and goes through to the beginning of February.

Had you done these things before—riding and shooting?

COUNTESS OF ROMANONES: No, I never had. I've learned all that here. For several years, I used to play golf, when my husband dedicated himself to golf. Almost everybody who lives here has some sport or hobby that keeps them outdoors a certain part of the day.

The place where I ride is just ten minutes from here, from the center of the city. If you arrive in Madrid by plane, you notice that the city stops quite abruptly, and beyond is wild, open country. On the western side is an enormous tract of many thousands of acres that is owned by the government and called *Casa del Campo*—"The House of the Country." It's as savage as if you were a hundred miles away from the city. I keep my horses there. Ten minutes after leaving this house, I'm on my horse, and one minute after that, I'm in marvelous open country.

Is it as arid and barren as it appears to be from the air?

COUNTESS OF ROMANONES: I remember when I first arrived and looked down, I thought, "It looks like the end of the earth." After having come from Lisbon, which is all very lush and green, you look down at Spain, and it appears baked-out, barren, and sandy. One doesn't see many cities. It looks awfully lonely and sad and dreary. That impression is completely the opposite of what it is when you get on the ground. It has great character—this earth. The colors are violent and marvelous—bright reds and bright yellows. Incredible. You have mountain ranges all through Spain, and there are live oak trees that are green all year round. It's an agricultural country, and there are great fields of wheat and vineyards, particularly around Madrid. When you walk in those fields, everything comes alive. There is an enormous number of birds—not the ones you shoot—but all other kinds and varieties. It has something special, this country, that gets one, even more than those countries that are easy to like. Somehow, this countryside reflects the character of the Spanish people. It's strong. It has power.

To turn to your own life here, do you have children?

COUNTESS OF ROMANONES: I have three boys—twelve, fourteen, and fifteen. They are all trilingual. When you live abroad, your children have to speak at least three languages perfectly. But that's easy enough because governesses are so easy to get. I've always had a French governess for the boys, so their French is as good as their Spanish. And I have taken turns sending one of them to America in the summer, so they speak English. They stay with my mother and father or with one of my brothers. I have an enormous family.

My family are all terribly Spanish now. If you go into my parents' house in the States, it's too funny, because everything you see is Spanish—furniture, rugs, paintings. My mother and father come to visit us every other year, and all but one of my brothers have also been here with their wives. My husband says that he always thought he was so clever when he married me, because he would have no in-law problem. Instead, the in-laws not only come to visit, but they move right in, and stay for three or four months. Of course, my husband and my parents love one another, so it works out fine.

I wonder if you could tell me what a more or less normal day would be like for you.

COUNTESS OF ROMANONES: My life here is quite different from what another American woman's would be, because I married into a

Spanish family, and immediately took up Spanish life to such an extent that I am now really at least half Spanish in the way I think and feel.

As for the average day, to begin with, we never wake up early. It took me years not to feel guilty about staying in bed until eleven in the morning. That is the hour I wake up. Most of my Spanish girl friends wake up around twelve. I usually spend an hour and a half or two hours with my secretary, dictating. She is English. We cover a variety of matters in that session.

One thing, of course, is the management of this house, and there is also our country house, which had been in Luis's family for seven hundred and fifty years or so. He had no interest in it, and nothing had been done to it. That's the one I have transformed, and I am terribly attached to it. It now even has a swimming pool and an airport, but it's still not finished. The building is enormous, and whenever I get a few extra pesetas, I remodel another wing, adding a few more rooms and a few more bathrooms. My husband thinks I'm crazy. "What are you trying to do?" he says. "Build a hotel?" But as it is away out in the country, it's pleasant, particularly when we have shooting parties, to be able to put up twenty-five or thirty friends.

I am also very fond of this house. Here, you're right in the city, and yet it's quiet, which is amazing. When we moved in, it was a house of only two stories. As we started to have children and as Luis wanted a studio, we added a third floor. Then we needed more room on the first floor for parties, so we have just added this room. A larger house and a bigger family means more servants to manage. I have two men who are both chauffeurs and butlers and four women. One of them cooks, and the others are maids. That's six people who live in, and you feed them and supply their uniforms and look out for them.

I suppose the main reason that so many servants are needed here, aside from the fact we've only recently begun to get washing machines and similar equipment, is just that one is accustomed to not doing anything for oneself in this country. If you want something, you have a button right next to you, and you call someone to bring a match from there to here. One doesn't do a *thing* for oneself. You are even practically dressed. I have to nearly kick my maid to keep her from putting on my shoes and socks. When I was first married, I used to get hysterics, because my husband didn't have a valet—he had a maid whom he's had since childhood, and she would dress him and undress him—practically wash him in his bathtub. "Oh Luis," I said, "you cannot have a woman in our bedroom, dressing you and putting on your socks. That's impossible." He looked at me as if I were crazy. He'd never put on a sock in his life. Or a shoe.

Servants here may not be as efficient, but they actually do more, because they have unlimited hours. If you give five parties a week and people stay until five o'clock in the morning, the servants stay up, too, and never complain. We take them back and forth to the country with us or wherever we go. They're much more dedicated than servants you could get in another country, where they keep certain hours, and you have to have dinner at eight, and they won't stay later, because they want to get to their television set.

Really, as it turns out, running the household doesn't take too much of my time.

I'm on the board of directors of two Spanish companies, and there are letters and memos to dictate in that connection. Or I may be doing something for *Vogue*. As Madrid editor, I cover the collections, and when I see anything especially interesting or unusual, I write the New York office about it. Once or twice a year, we do an article with pictures on Spanish fashions, which means a week of intense work with photographers sent from America. When there's a big ball or something special going on, I arrange for a Spanish photographer to cover it, and send those pictures back to New York. Or the magazine may want to know what is the best shop in Spain for leather goods or whatever. The work for *Vogue* is not something that I do every day.

If all of my other tasks are up to date, I may have time to do some dictation on the book I'm writing. It's a novel, but it's based on an incident that happened here during the war when I was with the OSS. The book is written in the third person, and I am not the heroine. It hasn't amused me to think of a title for it yet.

I often do other things while tending to these various interests, because I can take my secretary with me to the hairdresser, for example, and she has to sit next to me while I'm under the dryer. I can also dictate to her while fitting clothes. Or I may have to go to a government office to see a minister, and as they usually make you wait a few minutes, I can dictate while waiting, and I don't have to lose time on the way there or back, because the secretary can take dictation while the car is moving. No matter what else I have to do, I never slight my business responsibilities.

And what about the companies whose boards you are on?

COUNTESS OF ROMANONES: Ah, yes. That came about because I'm awfully restless and because I'm American, I guess. When I was first married, I begged my husband to let me look into some of his business affairs, and I found two companies whose board meetings he never attended and which he didn't think much of, but it seemed to me they could have quite a future. I said, "Let me go to a board meeting." He finally agreed, and I went to the meeting, and the gentlemen on the board were just charming. It was only a dusty little factory, where they manufactured electric condensors—machines that cut down the reactive energy in big factories. As soon as I started looking into the company, I saw clearly that we could cut down our cost if we could enlarge our production. So, I had the chief engineer in the company teach me how to calculate the *coseno de fi*—I don't know how you say that in English. There are all sorts of words I don't know how to say in English. I haven't had a baby in English, either.

At any rate, I learned how to do that mathematical calculation, which is very simple and measures the reactive energy, and then I had the nerve to go to Bilbao and Barcelona, where most of the big factories are, to try to sell our product. For a woman to do this was unheard of then. I went dressed as neatly and simply as I could, and I was terribly well prepared. When I called at a factory and got to talk to the president, which I could easily do with a card from my father-in-law, the president would be so overwhelmed to hear me asking about his *coseno de fi* and such matters that he would immediately have to call in one of his engineers, because he naturally didn't know what the reactive energy was or what it was costing him. Then I would go ahead and explain about our product.

Going to those big companies wasn't fun, but it amused me terribly —the feeling of going ahead and getting something done. I managed to sell an awful lot in the two years or so that I worked on this. Now we've got a great big modern factory, and we can't produce enough to fill our orders, and we're branching out into all sorts of other things.

The other company is one that manufactures machines used in hospitals and in laboratories to make medicines. I could explain this in Spanish, but I don't know all the words in English. We are the only ones so far who can make these machines in Spain. We have just bought several acres, and we are building an enormous new factory. So, my two companies have done wonderfully well, and I am now president of the board of directors of the first one.

I don't expect to get into any more businesses, but I think the opportunities here are enormous. Whatever sells well in America is going to do the same here. There is now a buying power in this country that didn't exist before. Salaries have gone up. Suddenly, everybody has money to spend. It was unheard of, a short while ago, for anybody except awfully rich people to have a car. Now the man who sells me newspapers has a little Seat the same as mine. It was unheard of for people to have even small radios, but now you find the most humble families have a big television set. They also have a refrigerator. All these things they buy on the installment plan, which didn't exist before, either. In these circumstances, almost any little business that one starts up is bound to be successful.

To get back to your day . . .

COUNTESS OF ROMANONES: I was still working with my secretary. The poor secretary. I have my breakfast, dictating to her. I have my bath, dictating to her. We rush out to the hairdresser. We rush out to a business meeting. Then I will come home about two-twenty. We try to have lunch at two-thirty, if we're not having guests. If we have guests, it's about fifteen minutes later. As the children are away at school all day, I have lunch with my husband. I don't like to entertain at lunch, because I think that breaks up your day, and one eats more than one would like to. Also, I like to exercise after lunch–ride, or golf, or go out for a walk.

Then I have a literary club that I stop in on every now and then in the afternoon. It isn't a club in the American sense. Actually, it's called a *tertulia,* which is a kind of informal gathering of people who have similar interests and who get together to talk and exchange ideas and information. Usually, they meet in an old-fashioned café. There may be writers in one *tertulia*, people interested in history in another, those interested in bullfighting in yet another, and so on. It's like meeting with a group of friends. I go to one that is composed mostly of historical writers and bibliographers and Latinists. That group meets in the Café Leon, on the Calle Alcala. You spend whatever time you have–thirty minutes, an hour, two hours. It's charming, and it's fun.

On other afternoons, there may be a tea for a benefit. I'm trying to start a school for young boys, and often get together with other ladies to work on that. We're trying to get enough money for a school for a thousand boys, the very poorest ones. There aren't half enough schools in this town. The city has grown so rapidly that it's been impossible to keep pace with the building of schools. In workers' areas, there are just none.

After you have attended an afternoon meeting for a benefit of some kind, how do you carry on?

COUNTESS OF ROMANONES: Sometimes the tea is not for a benefit, but just a meeting with friends. I find, being American in the Spanish world, that I am constantly being asked by Spanish friends if I know someone in America who would be helpful to them in this way or that.

It may be a business matter, or travel advice, or any number of other things. I do spend an awful lot of time as a kind of agent or adviser.

Also, in the afternoon, I often go to art exhibits, because my husband is interested in painting. We know a lot of painters, and we're always helping them out or seeing them. My husband is soon to have an exhibition in New York. He loves painting. He always has, and has always had very nice paintings. That very nice Goya on the opposite wall he just inherited from his grandfather.

Now that the afternoon is about over, one may plan on dinner. If one is invited to dinner here, you are invited at ten-fifteen, and arrive about ten-thirty. That still gives you time, before bathing and dressing, to go to a concert or the theater. The matinee here begins at seven o'clock, and ends about nine-fifteen. The evening performance at the theater begins at eleven. If we don't go to the theater or out to dinner, I like to have an early, quiet dinner, which means dining at eleven-fifteen. Then I'll go to bed around one, say, and spend an hour or two reading the newspapers—Spanish, French, and American.

So, really, I go pretty strong from eleven o'clock in the morning until two or three the next. And that would be on the nights that I go to bed early.

To listen to your schedule, one would think that you work as hard and under about as much pressure here as you would in New York.

COUNTESS OF ROMANONES: Somehow, if you're an American, I think you could go to the middle of Tibet, and you'd end up working like a bee all day long and seeing a hundred more things that you'd think you ought to be doing. I think that we're brought up to enjoy working so much that it ends up being relaxation. Spaniards are not like that. They will live longer than we will.

GALLERY NOTES

The Ameropeans who probably have the deepest roots in Europe are the painters, sculptors, and writers. Their spiritual ancestors go back to the first group of Americans who returned to live in the Old World—a band of painters who settled in London, starting in the latter half of the eighteenth century. The doyen of this pioneering colony was Benjamin West, a native of Pennsylvania, who departed at age twenty-two for Italy, where he studied for three years before taking up residence in London. He had immediate and lasting success, was appointed historical painter to the King by George III, and served as a friend and mentor of other American artists who came to live in London, a distinguished group that included John Singleton Copley, Gilbert Stuart, and John Trumbull. During West's lifetime, Robert Fulton and Samuel F. B. Morse were also members of the colony before they abandoned England and painting for America and inventing. West never returned to his native land, nor did Copley, whose son, having taken British citizenship, became a noted jurist, and ended his days as Baron Lyndhurst.

With the death of West, in 1820, London ceased to exert its former attraction on American artists. In the next half-century, they tended increasingly to choose either Rome or Florence as their home away from home. Then, lured by the excitement stirred up by the emergence of the French Impressionists, the American painters were drawn to Paris, which, by the opening of this century, had become the favorite city of American artists living abroad. It still is, though Rome in recent years has become increasingly popular.

Of course, neither Paris nor Rome is any longer the art capital of the world. New York is. Why, then, do American artists want to live in Europe? To a certain extent, for the traditional reasons—to study, to absorb the cultural atmosphere, to look for inspiration. "My motives for moving to Europe?" James Metcalf, an American painter and sculptor, remarked in Paris. "To find more ancient roots. And then there was also the romantic attraction of being where Modigliani and Brancusi had worked. For an artist, that seems important, in the beginning. But mainly, for me, it is the association with the more ancient things that makes the attraction of Europe. Being surrounded by buildings that date from the twelfth century gives me the feeling of being more in the human flux than a kind of pioneer setting does."

There are other reasons that are also important, though perhaps not so easily defined. For example, John Levee, a young painter from California who has lived for several years in Paris, has explained that he would rather live in Europe than in America because "the scale in America is inordinate, excessive, and really outrageous. The countryside is enormous. Automobiles are enormous—*everything* is enormous." This makes it difficult, he added, to measure the relationship of man to his environment. By way of illustration, he recalled that he and his wife, who is French, once visited the United States and set out to drive from New York to California. "In New York," he said, "we bought a picnic basket and all the wonderful things you can buy in delicatessens, because we thought we would picnic. And we drove for ten days and five or six thousand miles, and we never found a place to picnic. That's what I mean by scale. I have to say that I find I function better in a scale which is more *a l'echelle humaine*."

Though the artists were among the earliest Americans to live and travel in Europe, the writers have always been the most conspicuous. The reason, of course, is that they generally use the experience as grist for their literary mills. Washington Irving pioneered the way. Moving to Europe in 1815, he remained there for seventeen years, meanwhile producing some of his best work, including *The Alhambra*. He has been followed over the years by every American writer of stature, with such a small number of exceptions that they can be counted on the fingers of one hand: Thoreau, Poe, Whitman, and Emily Dickinson.

For some of the literary pilgrims, including Longfellow and Melville, the sojourn was brief; for others, including Hawthorne and William Dean Howells, both of whom held consular posts during part of their residence abroad, the stay was extended. Emerson made the journey for the high-minded purpose of seeing, as he wrote, "what is uppermost that social man has done." Mark Twain went to observe and record the foibles of some of his innocent countrymen abroad—and, as it turned out, to make his reputation. Stephen Crane and Bret Harte went looking for inspiration, and failed to find it. Robert Frost went in search of an appreciative audience for his poetry, and did find it. James Baldwin, in his book, *Nobody Knows My Name*, has reflected on the reasons that contemporary American writers feel the need to live abroad. "The American writer, in Europe, is released, first of all, from the necessity of apologizing for himself," Baldwin wrote. "It is not until he *is* released from the habit of flexing his muscles and proving that he is just a 'regular guy' that he realizes how crippling this habit has been. It is not necessary for him, there, to pretend to be something he is not, for the artist does not encounter in Europe the dangerous suspicions he encounters here. . . . This lack of what may roughly be called social paranoia causes the American writer in Europe to feel—almost certainly for the first time in his life—that he can reach out to everyone, that he is accessible to everyone and open to everything. This is an extraordinary feeling. He feels, so to speak, his own weight, his own value. It is as though he suddenly came out of a dark tunnel, and found himself beneath the open sky. And, in fact, in Paris, I began to see the sky for what seemed to be the first time."

To see the sky, to find their separate identities, and for many other reasons, American writers continue to make the pilgrimage to Europe. Although the majority nowadays tend to stay for a relatively short period of time, some remain, and become Ameropeans.

"Living here as I do, I have an isolation which I need and which, when I wish, I can go out and break."

James Jones, the author of *From Here to Eternity*, *The Thin Red Line*, and other successful novels, is a stocky, athletic, unaffected man in his middle forties, who was born in Illinois and had, as he once remarked, a childhood that was so much like Thomas Wolfe's that he decided that he, too, must have been cut out to be a writer. Before embarking on that career, however, he served a long stint in the Army ("My formative years were spent being shot at and being scared to death and trying not to admit it."), which has provided the background for most of his major works to date. After the publication of his first novel, he took up residence in New York, and lived there for a year or so. Since 1958, he and his wife have lived in Paris, where they have a lovely apartment on the quiet, beautiful Ile St. Louis, with enchanting views from every window. Owing to a contretemps in connection with my original appointment, it was necessary to make another, the only mutually agreeable—or at least possible—time for which was early on a Saturday morning. Despite the hour, Mr. Jones, who welcomed me in pajamas, slippers, and a Japanese-style dressing gown, was cordial and responsive. After he had asked the maid to brew a pot of coffee, we sat down in the living room, and I mentioned that I'd read the night before in *Time* that he had recently signed a new publishing contract guaranteeing him eight hundred thousand dollars for rights to his next three books.

JONES: Well, the sum involved is not quite that much, but it's roughly in that area. We've just returned from New York. The main reason for the trip was to finalize the new contract, but we were there for a couple of weeks, doing other things. I found it took me about three days to get accustomed to New York again. That's probably because I've only been back a couple of times. Once when I finished *The Thin Red Line,* and then this time. It's been two years since the last trip. Everything looks very rich. That's the first thing you notice. Very rich and very efficient. I mean, the machines work, and the electricity works. I think it's largely because we created most of the modern machines, which Europeans just don't seem to be a natural part of. We are at home with them.

I love New York. I love to go back there. I think the people are essentially more friendly in America. Even strangers—faces—that you meet on the street look much more open and friendly than they do in Europe. In spite of all our present troubles, I don't think we've learned to mistrust each other quite as thoroughly or quite as deeply as Europeans have. Of course, the pace of living in New York is killing, compared to Europe. Much more hectic. Much more of a strain.

Was the killing pace of New York one of the reasons you left there?

JONES: Well, I didn't mean to stay away when I first left to come over here. That was in '58. I'd never been to Europe before. When we came over, we meant to spend about a year and a half. I had an idea for a book I wanted to write—a novel, which would be built around the life of Django Reinhardt, the jazz guitarist. First, we meant to spend a couple of weeks in London, and then go on a three-week tour of Russia, which we had all fixed up through Intourist—Moscow, Leningrad, Stalingrad, and Rostov, where we were going to meet Mikail Sholokhov, the man who wrote *And Quiet Flows the Don.* Well, we were on our way to Russia, and then my wife had a miscarriage in Copenhagen. We had heard such horrible tales about Russian hospitals from John Gunther that we decided to cancel the Russian trip and go back to London. We spent the summer there. Then we came on here, in August of '58.

I guess we'd been here a little over a year, and my wife got pregnant again with our little daughter. We had a tiny apartment, and we wanted to get a bigger place. Renting an apartment here involves paying key money, which means that, since apartments have a fixed price, you have to pay the person who has the lease a certain number of francs to get it for yourself. It runs into quite a lot of money. My Middle Western thrift was against the key money business, because, should they ever change the rent controls, you're stuck. The second choice was to buy an apartment, which I decided to do. When I found this place, which I liked very much, I told my wife that if we bought it, we would have so much of our available money tied up that we would have to stay here quite a while—at least ten years. So, we thought about it, and decided that we wanted to stay. That's something else—why we wanted to stay. The deeper reason.

I'd wanted to spend some time here, and I had this book, so I had a sort of good moral excuse. I never did get around to writing it. It's one of a number I have planned. The way I figure now, I'll be a hundred and twenty-eight by the time I finish all the books I've got planned. But we fell in love with Paris. There's something about Paris that catches you. I don't know what it is. There's an ambience about it. It's really the first of all international cities, I think. We did think of going back to London for a time, but I wouldn't want to live there. It's really very insular. We spent a summer and part of a fall here in Paris, and didn't like it very much. Then I bought a little car, and we drove to Italy—about a two-month trip to Rome and all around. I didn't dig Rome too much. The atmosphere there is sort of rural decadence. When we got back here, you know, we suddenly discovered we were home. It had all seemed strange before. It no longer did. Part of the strangeness is the language problem.

Did you speak French when you arrived?

JONES: We both had a tutor in New York, but we didn't have very much French when we got here. We just sort of picked it up. I never studied it. My wife did. When I got through working, I was usually too tired and keyed up to be able to sit down and spend two hours studying French. I still make lots of grammatical errors, and I don't have the vocabulary that my wife has, but I can get by. I can hold a serious conversation now.

Somewhere along the line, when you were making up your mind about living here, I suppose you came to the conclusion that Paris was good for your work. How does living here affect your work?

JONES: I'm so American that I could live just about anywhere, and it wouldn't influence me. People are always saying that if a writer lives abroad, he loses contact with his roots and that sort of business. There may be people that that does apply to, but I don't think it applies to any writers here that I know of. As for the working schedule, I seem to work about the same wherever I am. It takes me about an hour after I wake up to get my head in gear. I have a little office, separate from the apartment, in the back. I go in there and work five or six hours. That's about all I think anybody can take in one day—writing, you know. After that, I read and mosey around. I love to walk, or I take the kids to the Bois or somewhere. They're four-and-a-half, both of them, but they're not twins. The little boy is adopted.

While I spend practically the same number of hours a day at the typewriter here as I did in New York, other aspects of working in this city are very different. I think Paris is much more conducive to writing or painting than New York is. As we said, the pace is a lot less hectic. The kind of predatory search for success is much less noticeable here, and has much less effect on me. If you become a successful novelist in New York, you're sort of jerked bodily from one group and planted in another, and there's very little contact between the two. Here, you go to a party at Calder's or Max Ernst's or some other place like that, and you see a lot of successful people, and right alongside them are five or six fellows in blue jeans and old leather jackets, who obviously haven't got any money, and they're helping themselves to the buffet because they need it. There's not that sense of social separation. They seem to realize here that you may be up this year, and they may be up next, when you may be down. It's much nicer this way. Also, there isn't the separation of writers and painters the way there is in New York. We see a lot of painters when we're in New York now, largely because we got to know them here.

The artist has got some sort of honor here, you know. They do name streets after writers in this town. There is a feeling in Paris that promulgates art in any of its forms, which you don't really get in New York. When you get up here in the morning, you have the feeling that everywhere in this city there are people with the same problems and the same miseries who are getting up to create something. You're one of them. In New York, even a successful writer, if he's serious about writing, always has the feeling of being a little bit on the outside of everything. Here, that isn't true. I think the physical ambience of the town has something to do with it, too. It's so beautiful. In New York, when a building gets old enough to be beautiful, they yank it down and put up something else. Here, it's like walking through a perpetual painting.

Another thing that figures in the "why" of our being in Paris is that I'm sort of free of the Literary Establishment here. It's like a prospector, you know. He hunts and hunts around, and finally he finds a stake, and he stakes it out. He's then got his little vein of ore to work. That's what I want to do. Living in New York, it's pretty hard not to get involved in the literary politics of the day. That's another reason I like living here. I've got the work I want to do, and I'll go down the line doing it. I don't give a damn about the critics much, but when you're there, you get involved with invitations and non-invitations, all of which has nothing to do with the critical world as much as it has to do with jockeying for position in the Literary Establishment. For the time being, I'm very satisfied to live here and write my novels.

When did you buy this house—or do you call it an apartment?

JONES: It's an apartment, really. It's sort of like a co-op in New York. We own two floors in this building. There are other people on the three floors above us. I bought it in the spring of 1960. Before that, we lived right over behind Notre Dame, which is only a short distance from here, and I used to walk a lot around this island. I've always loved this particular island. It's got a little *esprit* of its own, which Ile de la Cité doesn't have, maybe because there are a lot of municipal fortresses over there. People who live here seem to have a curious identification with this island, as though it were a little village of its own right in the heart of Paris.

Anyway, I was just walking around, as I often did, and I saw a sign out front, so I came in and looked it over, and then brought my wife to see it. What we bought originally was two and a half rooms. Later, we managed to get enough together to buy the floor below us. We couldn't have afforded to buy what we now own all at once. Real estate values, I understand, have not gone down on this island since about 1680, so it's a pretty good investment. As a matter of fact, our place has just about doubled in value since we bought it.

Did you invest more in this apartment than you would have had to if you'd bought the same number of rooms in a somewhat similar location, if there is such a thing, in New York?

JONES: I should think not. Probably closer to two-thirds or five-eighths of what it would have cost us in New York. Actually, this location is comparable in a general way to Central Park West, in New York. One difference, in the matter of apartments, is that after you buy a co-op in New York, you still have to pay almost as much as you'd normally pay in rent for the maintenance. Here, all you have to pay is a share of the heating and of the electricity for the lights in the hall and so on. It's nothing like what you have to pay in New York.

Speaking of all this, I suppose expense has something to do with our being here, too. We couldn't live on this scale in New York. We just simply couldn't afford it.

But people keep telling me that the cost of living in Paris is so high.

JONES: I think people who say that are comparing it to what it was six, eight, ten years ago, when it was very cheap. Even today, restaurants, for example, are cheaper here than in New York, except for a very few places. A stranger can walk down the street and pick any one of five restaurants without knowing anything about them, and four times out of five he'll get a very good meal, which he'd probably have to go to Pavillon to get in New York. There is also the matter of help, which is much cheaper here than it is in New York. And I think food is cheaper, when it's bought in the shops. I know a lot of people say otherwise, but I really think living is cheaper here than in New York.

So, our being here is partly happenstance and a combination of a lot of other things. There isn't any one big reason.

What part does the tax situation play in your being here?

JONES: Well, that doesn't help me very much, because generally all my taxes are paid on royalties, and they have to be paid the same as if I lived in America. The tax situation does help when I do a film job, because a part of that income is tax-free. I've worked on about half a dozen film scripts since I came here, and the money I've made off them has helped pay for the apartment.

You do have time for considerable leisure, I gather. How do you spend it?

JONES: Reading, mostly, and walking. And we sort of follow the French habit of taking a month off in the winter and going somewhere to the mountains, usually, in our case, to Klosters, and then a month off in the summer, when we go somewhere to the sea. Last year, we spent the month of August in Italy. We may go back there this year. Or we may go to Biarritz. We have friends who are going there. One of the nice things is you have so much choice. When we go away for the month in summer and winter, I take my typewriter with me, get up at seven, and work the same number of hours as I do here. And then I spend the rest of the day swimming or skiing or whatever.

I've heard that Sunday evenings at your apartment here are something of an institution.

JONES: That started simply because it's the maid's day off, and we had to stay home with the kids. My wife, who's Italian-American, makes marvelous spaghetti, which isn't terribly expensive, so she'd make a huge pot of spaghetti, and we'd get two or three cases of beer and some red wine, and slowly the gatherings grew. At one point, Jimmy Baldwin brought his sister, Paula, over. She spent almost a year in Paris, and we were sort of commissioned to look after her, so we more or less organized these Sunday nights around her. She was studying haute couture, and she'd bring a lot of young writers and kids from the Latin Quarter. Kids who had no money and lived very close to the bone. There are a lot of them. It's fun to talk to them about what they do and to see how they think about things. As far as I can tell, a small percentage are rather serious, and the rest are just kind of drifting. It's the same as in any college town at home, I think. Like any young generation, they're trying to find a place for themselves.

You have a reputation for helping many of the young writers here.

JONES: I do what I can, when I can. I've helped a couple to get publishers in the States. Both are working on novels, so things seem to be working out pretty well there. I'm also asked to talk to kids at places like the American Students' Center. I'm not a good speaker, because I get very nervous, so I usually just let them ask me questions, and try to answer them. One thing I tell them—it's erroneous to think you can sit down and dash off a novel. You can't. It takes an apprenticeship at least as long as it takes to become a reasonably good doctor. Unfortunately, most American parents aren't willing to subsidize their children for seven or eight years so they can become writers.

I don't know how the kids feel about what I say—whether they like it or think I'm a pompous old ass. Probably both. Of course, they want to knock me down. It's a natural reaction, and I don't blame them. I guess I feel a bit guilty about having made a good bit of money at writing. It is not my primary purpose. That, of course, is to write. But you can't fault somebody for wanting to live well while writing, if that's possible.

An American psychiatrist who's living at present in Europe told me that all of the Americans he's met over here are running away from something. Does that seem like a sound observation to you?

JONES: I think everybody's probably running away from something all his life, one way or another. Certainly, most people I knew when I was a kid who had adjusted to the society they lived in in the Middle West are basically running away from knowing themselves. So, I think his reasoning may be a little specious. But, God, I don't know. Maybe I'm in a peculiar position, because I have plans for what I want to do, and it seems to me the best way I can do it is to be as free as I can from pressures that are not important to my work. Living here like this, I can do that a lot better than if I were at home.

Is there anything that you do miss by not being home?

JONES: As a matter of fact, I was thinking about that the other day. One is popcorn. Another is pro football, and—I can't remember what the third one was. It was a little less prosaic. You know, bullfighting is a good sport, but I still don't think it's as beautiful as pro football. We went to Pamplona year before last for the festival. It was all right, but I wouldn't care to do it again. I don't get any of the mystique about it, either the bullfighting or the drinking. I like to drink, but it's not a mystique with me. Those kids who were there—it seemed as if they were mainly Yale boys and Smith girls—were trying to be something they really weren't, and it just didn't come out right. It was all distorted, like an El Greco portrait.

By this time, do you feel that you have become rather a part of this community where you live?

JONES: I don't really. I'm pretty isolated, but I like that. You know, when I'm working hard, it takes me six or eight hours after I stop to begin really to see people. The characters get to be so real that the people I'm with afterwards, except for my family, I can hardly see. Living here as I do, I have an isolation, which I need and which, when I wish, I can go out and break. It's not like living somewhere off in the woods or in the country, where you have to go a hundred miles to break your isolation when you need to. Here, you can just walk out the door. So, you have the best of both situations.

When we lived in New York, it seems to me that we were out every night. It didn't bother me. I was getting up and getting my work done just the same. But there didn't seem to be any tranquil periods in between. That is still true, judging by what I've seen when we've been back. There seems to be something about New York—for me, at any rate—which keeps calling me out to parties, to restaurants, to see somebody. I don't have that here. There are no parties at Norman Mailer's or Dwight Macdonald's or wherever, and I think the absence of all that is good for my work. If anybody from the United States gets in touch with me, it's for something specific and usually important. It's not just to chew the fat. This also helps to make a more tranquil life.

But, God, I do love New York. We have a marvelous time when we go there. When we get old, I suppose we'll move back home and maybe buy a place in the country fairly close to New York. Bill Styron has a place in Connecticut, where we've visited a lot, and they have a pretty good system. They can stay out in the country by themselves when they want. When they feel like it, they can come to town for a few days or a week, and it's not much of a drive—maybe an hour and a half. I'd like something like that.

What do you mean when you say, "When we get old"?

JONES: Well, maybe fifty-five or sixty, assuming I live that long. What I mean by getting old is when I've worked my way through the middle period of my life, my work. You know, when I get ready to diddle around with memoirs, autobiographies, and sundry stuff like that. When I feel I've done enough so I can finally relax, that's when I'd like to go back.

"People come here for different reasons.
Mine was for art and liberty."

Beverly Pepper, a tall, slender, vital woman, is a Brooklyn-born artist whose work, first in painting and later in sculpture, has received international recognition. Trained at Pratt Institute Art School, she had quick success as a commercial art director in New York before moving to Paris to study painting. In addition to being represented in important collections in Europe and America as well as in Israel and Japan, she has recently completed a number of architectural sculptures, one of the most impressive of which is the one-ton, seventeen-foot-high arabesque of stainless steel that stands in the entrance loggia of the United States Plywood Building, on Third Avenue in New York.

Along with these talents, Mrs. Pepper is also a cook of considerable renown, the author of four cookbooks, the mother of two children, and the wife of Curtis G. (Bill) Pepper, who is chief of the *Newsweek* bureau in Rome. The Peppers are among the best-known Americans in Rome, and take a certain pride in the number of celebrated visitors they have entertained in their attractive residence, in the Monte Mario section of the city. When I called there late one afternoon, Mrs. Pepper was working on a metal sculpture in her studio, a large, separate building behind her house, and was wearing blue jeans and a blue work shirt. Since her living room was being painted, she suggested that we walk back to her studio, where she talked about "this happy, lovely life—in quotes," beginning with a description of an ancient house they had recently bought in Trastevere and were in the process of remodeling.

MRS. PEPPER: The new place is quite special. Sixteenth-century. Right by the river. At the moment, it's an apartment house, but the whole building is ours, and we will use all of it. We'll have three floors, four terraces, five levels. That house will be heaven to live in. But there's so much to do we'll be here for quite a while. That's why I decided the other day to paint the downstairs rooms. In three days, they will all be finished. And it will cost next to nothing—less than a hundred dollars to paint all three rooms. That's one of the joys of living here.

But getting along on little money is not the reason to live here any more. It was once. That was the reason we first came to live in Europe. To go back a little further, I was one of those very bright children who graduated from art school at nineteen, and six months later, I'm one of those very bright New York art directors, and I'm really making money. I handled some big jobs. I handled Coty. In five years, I was making twenty thousand dollars a year. And I hated it. Just hated it. Couldn't bear the whole advertising life. And after all that money I'd made, I had about four or five thousand dollars left. And I'd had nobody to support. It was ridiculous. Idiotic. It was true I had a wardrobe of clothes et cetera, but that was not the reason for living.

So, one day I decided to be a painter. I quit my job, and went to Paris to study with Fernand Léger and André L'Hôte. Then I met Bill, and we were married, and I've never been back to America to live, except to have Jorie, our daughter and first child, who was born in New York. After that, Bill and I stayed on in New York for about six months. I worked for a while as an advertising consultant, and then I wrote a cookbook, which was called *Glamour After Five*, and became a best-seller. When that happened, I decided to go to the Cordon Bleu to study cooking.

Meanwhile, we had returned to Paris. I was painting, and Bill was writing. He was working on a book, and he also wrote a lot of short stories. None of them were published. The money was running low. It got to the point where we were so broke we had to steal food out of the baby's supply. You see, when we went back to Paris, we were so concerned about the baby's future and our uncertain financial outlook that we brought back enough food and everything else she would need for a full year. We had two trunks full of canned baby food and another with the formula things, the clothes for the next stage, the Dr. Spock—the works. We felt so guilty when we'd open those strained carrots or strained peas. At one point, I remember stealing that awful canned spinach, which Jorie hated anyway, and making a spinach soufflé, because we happened to have a couple of eggs.

Eventually, we ran out of money. Bill got a job working on some films in Italy, and within six months, we had put aside enough to let us go away and live somewhere while he finished his book. We decided to go to Positano, which was very cheap in those days. We paid fifty dollars a month for an enormous house. Beautifully furnished. Two floors. Big garden. Overlooking the sea. Even on our limited budget, we had been able to bring our maid from Rome, and we hired a local there. The house had no telephone, of course, and no central heating. We didn't care. It was heavenly.

We would have stayed on forever in Positano, I think, but neither of us could work there. The trouble was that the place was too beautiful, and you had to be constantly on guard against the temptation not to work. For instance, we would never go to the beach until we thought everybody had left—say, at the time of the siesta, because we didn't want to get involved with a lot of people and be distracted. Of course, we had lots of visitors from the outside world, as we have here, but I think the basic thing about living in Positano is also true of living in Rome. If you become a part of the Rome society and join the circle that moves constantly from place to place, it's very hard to work. So, we live on our own terms. Once I've started to work, I personally never answer the phone until four or four-thirty. Also, we almost never any longer see visitors who are friends of friends, unless the friends send us a letter in advance, or the visitors send us a note from the hotel. If they do that, we never fail to see them. But if they trap us on the phone—no, because we were getting onto our tenth round of seeing our friends' friends' friends' friends.

The problem seems to be general. Over the whole range of time you've been here, have you had generally good or generally bad luck with the people who have been sent to you?

MRS. PEPPER: Oh, it's been good. One of the reasons for living in Europe is that you meet the most heavenly people. But until you've learned how to defend yourself, it's almost a reason not to. People think that it's all *la dolce vita.* They don't realize that we get up every day at six-thirty. Every day. Of course, there's nothing wrong with the practice of sending friends to friends. We do, all the time, but we always send a letter. And we love to meet people who are sent to us that way. You are an island for them. If you click, it's like a shipboard love affair. You become very close friends very quickly.

How many children do you have now?

MRS. PEPPER: We have two. Jorie, who is thirteen, and Johnny, who is nine. If somebody asked me the main reason for living in Europe, I would say, "For the children." If you consider that in ten years the flying time between here and New York will be two and a half hours, and less than that between here and Russia and between here and Africa, then just about the most important asset a child can have will be languages, and this is the place to learn them. Our children speak English, French, and Italian. They also read them and write them. Next year, they both start German. Of course, you can learn these languages in America. The difference is that these children have no accents. This summer we will go to France again—it's like going to Maine if you live in New York—and their accents will get more polishing. Next summer, we will probably take them to Austria, or to the German-speaking part of Switzerland, or send them to a German-speaking friend's family, and they'll pick up their German.

We travel all the time. Bill travels for his work, and I travel for mine, and then we travel for pleasure. One summer, we took a camping trip all through northern Italy and into Austria.

For pleasure?

MRS. PEPPER: Well, that's what we'd hoped. As a matter of fact, we put the tent up the first couple of nights in regular camping areas. After that, we stayed at people's homes, and put the tent up on their lawn for the children to sleep in. Lady Berkeley will never get over our arrival at her place. When she saw all this gear, she said, "I know a lovely place to camp," and we promptly put up the tent on her estate, and moved in with her. We finally got fed up with the whole tenting idea, so we hired a man to drive the car and all the equipment home, and we flew from then on, staying with friends or in hotels. We came home with a great sense of defeat, because the Germans, in every camp we saw, got everything up in three seconds flat, and the English did almost as well. We practiced before we left, so we wouldn't look bad, but we did. And we took our maid to do the dishes. It just wasn't right.

Now, in addition to the advantages for children, I will tell you why artists, especially sculptors, should live in Europe. For one thing, the fact that the artist has always been respectable in Europe is a very persuasive reason for living here. Furthermore, the art market here is exciting. And as for bronze casting, there is no place in the world that can compete with what is offered here, both in quality and in cost. Beautiful casting. Brilliant casting, done in the way Cellini did it. And cheap casting. The steel that I work with costs more than in America, but the cost of helpers, of renting a factory to work in, of transporting castings—all these things are less.

As for prices generally, you will find that electricity costs much more than in America. So does heating. You may rent a house for very little, and then wind up, if you want heat the way we like it, spending a fortune keeping the place warm. The cost of food is now about the same, except if you're an American and want canned foods, then it's more. But if you go to a restaurant, it's about half the price, because the labor, the table linen, and the rest of the service cost so little. For example, Bill and I saw how the house was upset today because of the painters, so we ran down to the *piazza* and had a lovely lunch. It was a very splurge kind of lunch, and the whole thing cost five dollars.

Aside from the matter of costs, do you think, if you were obliged to return to America, that you could work there as easily and as well as you do here?

MRS. PEPPER: Well, had you asked me last year or the year before, I would have said, "I couldn't possibly work there." But now I have. I worked there on the sculpture for the U. S. Plywood Building. It was the first time I had worked in America in fifteen years. I found that the equipment is extraordinary. The technological help you can get is not to be believed. As a matter of fact, I think I have made as much progress as I have because of my trips to America and being able to observe processes and materials there.

It sounds very immodest, but I'm an inordinately efficient woman. I never realized that until I understood that you can't do what I do without being orderly. This realization became very clear recently, when for the first time in ten years, I was without a cook, and I had to do the running of the household. American-trained women, by God, know what they're doing. Italian friends of mine, getting into that situation, fall apart. I discovered that all my food closets were in order. All the tomato cans were in place. All the meat was there. Fruit was there. So that I could, every morning, do the meals for the whole day. Even in Italy. So, I know now that I could function in America.

But would I like to live in America? No. I couldn't afford it, artistically. It's easier for me to work here. And I couldn't afford it as far as my children's education is concerned. There's another reason. When you live in a foreign language—and I'm using the word, "language," not "country," on purpose—you always have one aspect of yourself that you keep to yourself. You always have an area of fantasy. You don't always have to be yourself. If you don't express yourself properly, or you're a little harsh, or you're a little overpolite, you have a kind of self-protection, because you live always on two language levels. It's like playing a game, and I would miss it. Now, if you asked me if I *never* wanted to go back to America, I would say, "I couldn't bear it." I do make trips to America about three times a year—the whole family goes back every third year—and I love every minute I'm there, but I'm always so glad to get back to Rome.

There's no question that life is easier here than in America. For me, the good thing is to be able to go through the day without involvement in menial tasks. I can do that here, although it requires much more help than it would in America, because we just don't have the equipment. For example, I have to have a full-time laundress, who does washing every day, whereas in America I would have a washing machine and do the laundry once a week myself. I have a man who drives the children back and forth to school, and cleans, and does other chores. And I also have a woman who cooks and helps around the house. In America, with all that equipment, I could probably run a house this size with one maid—and I'd no doubt have to pay her almost as much as I pay these three together.

I think a really important reason why life is easier here is that in the middle of the day everything stops, and you have to stop, too. You have lunch. Incidentally, we drink no wine at lunch, unless we are with friends. We drink almost no liquor any more—only wines. This also makes life easier. After lunch, I usually go to sleep for a couple of hours. That nap changes the whole day. It really makes two days out of one. In New York, I don't have the nap, and I find that I'm exhausted before the day is over. Also in America there is a what-makes-Sammy-run atmosphere that everyone gets caught up in. You find yourself constantly moving about and spending precious hours with people in whom you really have no interest, nor they in you. Here, we only see people that we really care about.

What kind of people do you really care about? Are they Italians mainly or Americans?

MRS. PEPPER: All kinds. I'm one of those persons who has a hundred best friends. Though I do have some intimate friends here, most of them are in America—people who have lived in Europe and gone back. That's another aspect of living here—it's like living in a railroad station. You have deeply intimate, really sharing relationships with people for two or three years, and then they're gone. That's hard, but I suppose it strengthens you in a way. I think that Americans who live in Europe usually have more good friends than those who stay at home, but that doesn't apply to the Americans who have lived here for years and can't speak the local language. As a rule, these are people with a certain amount of money. I think they live here because they don't want to face their responsibilities.

People come here for different reasons. Mine was for art and liberty. Bill needed a certain amount of freedom. And we both fell in love with Italy. Paris was my first love affair with a European city. Rome has something quite different. Rome is an inviting city. It's a permissive city. There's a kind of eternal maternity here—a sense that you may do wrong, and you will be forgiven. No one remains angry.

Another wonderful thing—there's very little physical violence here. I have never seen grown Italian men strike each other. Here, in fact, men kiss each other, as you notice when you see them at the airport, greeting one another or saying goodbye. In their attitude toward women, Italian men are the most disrespectful in the world. This takes a while to get used to. When I arrived here from France, fifteen years ago, I still had my American clothes. It was the year when we wore sun-back dresses. The first morning, I put one on—no shoulders and very low cut—and in my complete naïveté, I walked out of the Excelsior Hotel and started down the Via Veneto. I realized that someone was following me. I was very concerned. You know, in America, how you feel if someone follows you. Before long, I realized that there were now two men, following in sort of Indian file. Well, I got very nervous, so I went into a bar, and ordered a *caffè*. I thought if I sat down at a table, they would go away. They came in and sat down at another table. Nobody said anything, and when I got up and started out again, there were three men, Indian file. So I walked up the hill to the Excelsior, and there was a policeman on his little stand. I went up to him, and said, with slight hysteria, "Monsieur, there are three men following me." The policeman got off the stand, bowed very low, and, replying in French, said, "I'm terribly sorry, mademoiselle, that I am busy working, or I would follow you, too."

As I know now, the average Italian woman in my milieu would never make a scene about a man following her. She would just think, "Oh, he's just feeling *gallo*"—you know, like the cock of the walk, and not be upset at all. One talent these men do have: they can make any woman feel beautiful. It's true even about me. I never go to a party where it doesn't happen. It's very different from America. You can't flirt with an American man, because if you do, you're committed. It's for real. Here, it's a game. You can play with all your feminine charms, and you don't have to pay the piper, because you know that the man who flirts with you doesn't have to ask you to dinner the next day or even remember your name. It's very pleasant. It's another reason to live here.

There used to be things about America that I missed very keenly. No more. I'm at home wherever I am. Maybe if you're a creative person, it's easier to feel that way, since you can relate to things around you more quickly and easily. And to people, too. That, perhaps, is the rarest privilege of Europe—all the marvelous people you get to know. And along the way, you also get to know a great deal about yourself and not a little about life.

> "Now it's not town and country—it's Europe and America. Between them you can work out a wonderful design for living."

I had planned to interview Mr. and Mrs. Pepper together, but found that he had had to leave Rome unexpectedly on an assignment, so I returned a few days later to talk with him. A compact, active, articulate man, he made his first trip to Europe in 1938, when he took time from his study of art and architecture at the University of Illinois to spend about a year on a bicycle tour of the Continent. Of all the countries he visited, Italy made the deepest impression, and the feeling was intensified during the years that he served there during the Second World War. He decided then that he would return when the war was over, and he did. After studying at the University of Florence under the G.I. Bill, he married, and not long afterward embarked on a journalistic career, the underlying purpose of which, he explained, was to enable him to continue to live with his family in Europe.

PEPPER: I think one very important element in the concept of living abroad is that here you get a margin for living. Hundreds of Americans have come through here—heads of businesses, political figures, professional people of all kinds—sat in that chair and said, "Gee, if we could only live in Italy." I say, "Why? Why do you want to live in Italy instead of the States? What's the difference?" They say, "Well, here you really live." And I say, "What do you mean—here we really live? I work about sixty hours a week here. You work about sixty hours a week at home. The difference is that when you are here, you aren't working, and so it all looks marvelous."

This is what happens: they arrive, and they go out and have lunch, and they have wine with their meal. Then they go back to their hotel, and they do something they never do at home—they take a nap after lunch. They get up about four o'clock, and come down and sit at a sidewalk café. They have a double *caffè espresso*, thinking it's American coffee. They're pulsating with caffeine. It's generally summertime, and they look at these girls in their summer dresses, and they suddenly feel young. They're happy as clams. They have been forced by the very fact of being here into a pattern of living that revitalizes them.

There's another element in living abroad, and that is what the people who do it are escaping from or what they are looking for. I think the key to that is beautifully put in *Time of the Cuckoo*. Do you remember the place where the woman who runs the *pensione* in Venice asks Leona, the American woman, "Why did you come here? What are you looking for?" And Leona says, "Maybe somewhere way *way* in the back of my mind I was looking for a wonderful, magical, mystical miracle." This is the thing they come looking for.

Of those you have observed, have you seen many who have, in fact, found a miracle?

PEPPER: Well, you remember in the play, Leona found it, and she destroyed it, too. The seeds of destruction she brought with her. I think a lot of the people who come here seeking the magical thing have within them the seeds of their own destruction, which wrecked their living at home. They come over here, in a way, as misfits, rather than as adventurers on the frontier of knowledge. They're not Dodsworths. Dodsworth was successful in his own world, and then came looking for another. These are incomplete Babbitts, many of them. There's a difference between those two categories—the successful and the unsuccessful—but I think both of them are drawn here because they want to find in our time a place where they can have a margin for living, where they can stabilize their income and outgo.

I think also that there's a certain amount of illusion around a person living abroad. This is less true today than it was years ago when I first arrived, but it still exists. Somebody comes over here, and he says he's a writer. Well, damn it, in the United States, if a man's a writer, people say, "What did you write?" Here, if you're introduced to someone who's a *scrittore*, and you've never heard of him and have some doubt about him, you would never think of asking him what he's written—that is, if you want to maintain a social relationship. In Italian society, you do not ask a question of a person or put him in a position conversationally where it reduces his dignity.

So, here is this American writer, and since people don't know that actually he is only a would-be writer, he automatically becomes a *scrittore*. He has a name. He has a title. He suddenly becomes dignified. Well, this is very satisfying for some people. It helps them to restore illusions. Everybody likes it, and everybody benefits. For example, if you're invited to someone's home, and your host can introduce you as *Scrittore* So-and-So, instead of just *Signore* So-and-So, it not only makes you look good, it makes your host look good, too. It's a little bit like a Pirandello play, in which the whole nation takes part. But why not? Why not pretend we're all more important than we are? It makes life much more bearable.

Many of your friends think that the life that you and your family live here is bearable indeed. They usually describe it as the Italian way of life. Is that the way you think of it?

PEPPER: Well, I don't know whether it's an Italian form of living or an international form of living. For example, our meals would be the same whether we were living here or in Idaho or New York or somewhere else. The people we see are an international group. We have here in this house a physical plant, where the operation of our lives can take place and be effective. We can write, we can sculpt, we can paint, we can raise a family, we can have servants, and the children can go to school and be trained. The way of living is more graceful, and it's fuller. I'd have to make five times as much as I now make in order to live on this level in the United States.

Now, there are drawbacks to it. There are premiums that people pay, and I don't think everybody can do it. The ones who do it best are the people who produce, who work—artists, writers, and so on. There are a few of the wealthy who don't produce, but contribute—the graceful rich, if you want to call them that. They're just as rich and just as graceful here as they are in America, and if they're intelligent, they're just as much a pleasure to meet here as they are there. There are a few of them in town. The person who comes over and retires on his pension is usually just as uninteresting here as he is there, although perhaps his existence here has a little more flavor than it would have back home.

I think it takes a special kind of person to live in a positive, constructive way, not as an expatriate but as—well, as whatever the word is that describes us. I don't feel any less an American because I live in Europe. I feel very much an American, but not in a provincial sense. For example, this house could very well be on Long Island, but if it were, we would see fewer Americans in it than we see now. College presidents, corporation presidents, scientists, senators—everybody has been through this house. Hubert Humphrey and Beverly formed a new political party in our living room while doing a jitterbug. The party was going to be called Liberation Through Vibration. That wasn't serious, of course, but I can't begin to tell you the people who have come through. These contacts very often are fuller than if they had been made in the United States, where things are much more rushed. The encounters and conversations in Rome are done with much greater leisure, and the relationships are much more civilized. It's as if one would call a conference on learning or business or on some other topic at a remote spot in the Appalachian Mountains, where people could come for a weekend and be able to sit and talk and reflect. This is what we have here permanently. So, you see, it's a rich form of living.

Mrs. Pepper said that you also do a good deal of traveling and that you get back to the United States—the whole family—every three years, I believe.

PEPPER: Yes. On home-leave, and that's wonderful for the children. I feel very strongly—I don't know how to say this without sounding nationalistic—I feel very strongly that you should have a sense of what it is to be an American. And I think that sense of being an American should be so strong—about the good and powerful things about America—that you feel secure when you find something displeasing there, and can fight against it. Part of the grace of living is having an identity somewhere. And I think your identity as an American is very, *very* important. God, I grew up in America. I was taught to ride by the Indians in Oklahoma. I've been all over the country. I know it backwards and forward. The knowledge of what is America and what is an American is very strong in me, and I want my children to have that. We've taken them there, and exposed them to America from coast to coast.

When we took them by car across the country, I told Johnny all about the cowboys and Indians, about the Cherokee Trail of Tears, and about the Five Civilized Tribes and about how the real cowboys tried to help the Indians and all that. On our way out through the Oklahoma Panhandle, we saw the first cowboy. He's on his horse, and he's dragging a fence line along. I said, "Johnny, there's your first real cowboy. Look at him. He's putting up fences for pastureland. He's not killing anybody. He's not shooting any guns." And we got out of the car, and I said, "Mr. Cowboy, this is my son, John. He's never met a real American cowboy before." So he shook Johnny's hand, and said, "Would you like to take a ride with me?" Johnny said, "Yes." So he pulled Johnny up on his horse, and said, "I'll take you over yonder, where I killed three Indians this morning." Well, it took me two days to unwind that one.

I gather from what Mrs. Pepper said that you have no plans to go back to the United States to live.

PEPPER: I think the balance of our life will be arranged so that we will always spend some time here. We have bought the house in Trastevere, and then we also have land in West Virginia. I think we'll probably live the major part of our time in Europe, but I think there will be a continual returning to the United States. It's so easy to go back and forth. It's not an either-or question. Why not both? You know, it's the town-and-country concept carried onto the international scene. The magic in the term, "town and country," is that you have the leisure of the country and the richness of the town. And only the wealthy could afford that way of life. Now, it's not town and country—it's Europe and America. Between them you can work out a wonderful design for living. And the great thing is that you can do it without being rich.

"I have never believed there was any one way of doing anything. Or that anyone should do anything. Or believe anything."

Paul Bowles, the well-known composer and writer, who is now in his middle fifties, made up his mind to live abroad when he was eighteen. He was then in his first year at the University of Virginia. "It seemed to me that time was going by very fast and everything was happening in other places, so I ran away," he recalled not long ago. "I had never been to Europe, but I had been published there. When I was sixteen, I wrote a poem and sent it to *transition*, and they accepted it. Although I was attending a New York high school at the time, I considered myself from then on a part of the Paris group, and so Paris was the natural place to go. Since I didn't have a passport, friends got one for me illegally, saying they were my guardians. I arrived in Paris in the spring of '29. The whole Montparnasse scene was going then, but I didn't meet a soul. I did go around to the offices of *transition* one day, but as I stood there in the hall, I suddenly realized that I looked even younger than I was. I decided they wouldn't be interested, so I didn't knock on the door."

After a few months in Paris, writing poetry and supporting himself by working as a telephone operator at the Paris *Herald Tribune*, Mr. Bowles returned to the University of Virginia, and began the study of music. "I finished out the first year. It pleased my parents. Then I said, 'I can't stand this any more. I'm going to be a composer. Goodbye.' I went to Berlin." There he studied under the distinguished American composer, Aaron Copland, and for many years made music his career, composing scores for *My Heart's in the Highlands, The Glass Menagerie,* and numerous other productions. Though he still occasionally writes music, he has become known primarily during the past couple of decades as a novelist. His first novel, *The Sheltering Sky*, which the New York *Times* has ranked among "the dozen or so most important American novels published since World War II," appeared in 1947. That was also the year that Mr. Bowles began to maintain what he calls "a more or less fixed residence" in Tangier, the Moroccan seaport opposite Gibraltar. In those days, when Morocco was still a French and Spanish protectorate and Tangier was an international zone, it was a world headquarters for smugglers, money-changers, black marketeers, and spies, whose operations gave the city its reputation for wickedness, mystery, and romance. All has changed, according to Mr. Bowles and other old residents, since 1956, when Morocco gained independence and absorbed Tangier, thus bringing to an end its international status and the basis of much of its glamor.

To anyone like myself, who hadn't known Tangier in the old days, it is still apt to seem like a pretty colorful place. Though it is only a two-hour ferry ride from Gibraltar, one realizes as soon as he steps off the boat and sees Arab men in cloaks and veiled women in robes that he is in a quite different world. ("Bob Hope country," a middle-aged American near me observed.) One is immediately assailed on every side by aggressive strangers with something to sell, ranging from hotel accommodations and native artifacts to propositions involving money-changing, kif, and women. Tangier, as I later learned, is a city of about a hundred and eighty thousand people. It is made up of the European district, which has modern stores and apartment buildings, broad boulevards, and sidewalk cafes, and the Medina, or Arab quarter, an immensely crowded, labyrinthian world of dwellings, bazaars, and tiny shops—all very exotic and straight out of an old Humphrey Bogart movie.

Since I was new to the city, Mr. Bowles, a tall, slender man, gracious in manner and ironic in spirit, kindly picked me up at my hotel, and we took a taxi to his apartment. On the way, he said that among the other American residents of Tangier were Mary Rogers, the daughter of Will Rogers; Eugenia Bankhead, a sister of the actress; Princess Marta Ruspoli, a native of Cincinnati who is married to an Italian; and William Burroughs, author of *The Naked Lunch*. "He's in St. Louis right now, doing a piece for *Playboy* about his old hometown," Mr. Bowles said. He added that Barbara Hutton, the much-married Woolworth heiress, also maintains a local residence, which is in the Medina and was constructed of what had formerly been seven separate dwellings. She usually occupies the house for three months of the year beginning in June, and does a great deal of entertaining, including one lavish party with an orchestra and entertainers flown down from Paris. Mr. Bowles remarked that he doesn't participate in the local social life. "I don't go out," he said. "Oh, I go down to Casablanca for holidays, or I go visit a friend in Marrakech, or somebody comes through, and I take them to the Sahara. That's always great relaxation for me."

Mr. Bowles's apartment is in a rather new building, and differs from the conventional European or American counterpart in the relative scarcity of windows and in the use of heavy matting instead of doors between interior rooms. A fire was burning in the living room fireplace when we arrived (it was early February, and the weather was chilly), and Mr. Bowles kept it fueled during the rather long interview, which he called a "seance." After he had remarked that he had lived in his present apartment about ten years and that his wife, Jane, who is also a writer, occupies the apartment above his, I asked why he had decided to live in Tangier.

BOWLES: It wasn't my idea. It was Gertrude Stein's. She used to come here in the summer, and she thought I'd like it, too. She was quite right. I loved it. I came here first in '31, but I didn't stay long. I moved all the time in those days. I went back to Paris. Then I was in Italy. Then in Spain. Then I came back here in the spring of '32. Caught typhoid, and went back to Paris. Was in the American Hospital five weeks. Then I went to stay in Grenoble. Then I lived in Monte Carlo for several months. Then I went to Algiers. Then I went down to the Sahara. Stayed there for several months. Crossed to Tunis. I came across North Africa to Tangier in the spring of '33. Stayed a while. Shipped out from Cadiz to Puerto Rico. I went up in the hills and stayed there. Then I went to New York and stayed there for about six months. Then I came back over here and went down to the Sahara again. Then back here. Another ship out of Cadiz to Colombia, South America. Went up in the Andes. Then to California. Then to Chicago. Back to New York. An odyssey. But it's always that way. My whole life has been moving from country to country. Came back here in '47, and bought a little house up in the native quarter, and began fixing that up. It took about two years. I later gave that house to a maid who had worked for us for a long time.

In 1949, about the time I'd finished fixing up the house, I started going out to India and Ceylon. In 1952, I bought an island off the coast of Ceylon, in the Indian Ocean, and began living there six months of the year. The other six months here. Persephone deal. I got the island cheap, but I sold it for half what I paid for it. The reason is that Ceylon has been going to wrack and ruin ever since independence. They're all anti-American there now, which is the case in Asia generally. It's almost a mark of the educated man all over the world now to be anti-American. Fortunately, there are very few here. This is the kind of country, really, where one can say that the fewer educated people there are, the better off everyone is. A nice, reactionary statement.

After having lived so long in foreign countries, what do you think it is that makes a person want to live away from his own country?

BOWLES: I don't think it ever has anything to do with what's in the country one chooses to live in. It all has to do, naturally, with what's inside oneself. When I was a very small child, I learned the difference between the family and neighbors. It's always better to be with neighbors, because you have an intrinsic value for them. They want to know all about you. You are a person. But with the family you don't have any value at all, except as part of a group. I always hated that. Your family thinks it owns you. It expects certain things of you just because you are one of the family. This can all be extended to governments, of course. I suppose, really, that this passion for living away from the place where one is born is probably a childhood neurosis. If you speak to real expatriates—I don't mean those who are just over here on a kind of extended vacation—you will very often find they had unsuccessful childhoods. In any case, if you live in a place where you are a person and have an intrinsic value, I think you have a much better idea of yourself.

Of course, one becomes a different person to a certain extent the moment he sets foot in a foreign country.

BOWLES: Just as any object looks different when it's taken out of its context and put among other things. Not with hundreds in a row but all by itself. Then you can really see it.

No, I don't think anything in the places one elects to live in really determines one at all. Choosing Morocco was just an accident, really. If Gertrude Stein had sent me to Greece, I'd probably be in Greece now. But it was wonderful here in those days. Above all, it was very cheap. There were hundreds of small hotels run by the French where one could live very cheaply without losing face with the natives. The great thing after the war was that the exchange was so good. All over Morocco, one dollar was a lot of money. You could take a taxi to a restaurant, have a drink and a good dinner, and still not have spent a dollar. The same thing would now cost at least five times as much, if you could find it. A good restaurant no longer exists here. There used to be enough Tangerines to support a couple of good restaurants, but too many of those people moved away after independence. If you want to eat well, you have to eat at home. Good food here is not cheap. And you have to go personally to the markets—you can't send servants—and you have to be a regular customer, and you have to be nice. In fact, we have often invited the butcher for drinks with friends to keep in good with him. He's Italian, and he's interested in experimental cinema, so he comes around and talks about Fellini and Antonioni and the various other directors. Even if you're nice to the tradespeople, you don't get anything half the time, because they don't have anything to sell. The idea in this country is to be economically independent, so you have to buy the local products. For example, the only rice you can buy in the market is Moroccan rice, which is very big and full of stones. You can't eat it. Bootleggers come around selling imported rice, which is forbidden. Nothing has remained cheap here, except labor. We have two maids full time. One gets the equivalent of fifty dollars a month, the other, twenty-eight dollars. We pay much higher wages than most people here, because Mrs. Bowles insists on it.

No matter what you pay them, I don't think any Moroccan servants are very good. To be a good servant, you've got to think of yourself as a servant, and that's not the way Moroccans think of themselves at all. One has to realize that they are in no doubt whatever that, being Moslems, they are far superior to the rest of us. We're savages, dogs, pigs. Of course, we're damned, utterly. We can't get into heaven. And it's a great concession that a true person, a Moslem, spends any time at all with a savage. That's really the way they think about us. You can't admonish them, upbraid them. They won't take it. They get into terrible fits of temper. You've got to be extremely careful and handle them with suede gloves. You speak to them like one of their family. The employer-employee relationship isn't so good. It's better to be the uncle. They're funny people. They all believe firmly in black magic, even the educated ones, and work black magic on one another. I like them very much.

They have their drawbacks, like everybody else. I suppose cupidity is the worst one. They're so grasping, but, again, that's conditioned partly by the religion. It's all right to have relations with non-Moslems, if you can prove to God, which is to be able to prove to yourself, that you did it for business reasons. So, they will often talk to you in the street and be very pleasant, and then suddenly say, "You couldn't let me have fifty francs?" You know, a dime. That's simply to clear themselves in the eyes of God for having spoken to you. They've done something pretty bad, but if you give them *anything*—it doesn't matter what or how little—then it's all right.

Considering this situation, it must be very difficult indeed to have Moroccan friends.

BOWLES: It's almost impossible. I am speaking of the Moroccans of my generation. I don't know how the new generation feels. I don't like to know the younger ones anyway, because they're too much like Europeans. They can read and write. Why come all the way here to associate with people who can read and write?

No, the charm of the Moroccans is that they are illiterate. An illiterate person has no point of reference except his memory, so his mind works completely differently. It works in a natural fashion, without the *aide-mémoire* of making notes and so on. He has to remember everything, so he's extraordinarily good at recalling every detail of his life, everything he's seen, and he's very alert. When he knows how to read and write, he feels that everything can be done somehow outside his head, and his head remains almost empty. He begins to fall for prejudices that are against his own culture. He denies that certain things exist, which do exist, and he pretends that other things exist, which don't exist. For example, you speak to a literate Moroccan, and he'll tell you Morocco is a large, flourishing, industrial country, because he would like to see it that way. He will quote misleading statistics to prove his point. He has very little rationality and no logic at all. Everything he has to say is to impress Europeans. These Moroccans are worth zero to me. How am I going to get the truth from people who won't even recognize it when they know it? And they get very angry when you tell the truth in print. It's best not to write about Morocco since independence. Of course, I always hoped they would get independence. I was 100 per cent in favor of it. I think colonialism is a menace. But things don't necessarily work very well right after colonialism is finished. The sad thing is that the illiterates seem to think that things were better before. Like the one who said, "How long is this independence going on, anyway?"

Even though things may not work very well at this stage, you're still here, so I assume the country still fascinates you.

BOWLES: Ah, yes. It hasn't been ruined by any means. Tangier has been ruined for many years, of course. The decline began about 1937, I think. We were in Mexico then. We spent about four and a half years there, wandering around. I like Mexico very much as a place to live, but not nearly so much as here. Mexico is too dirty. You get sick too often. The last year I was in Mexico, I spent six months in a hospital and sanitariums. The water and the food were the trouble. Of course, you can catch all sorts of things here, but you're not so likely to. You have to worry about typhoid here—I've had it twice—but you can live pretty cleanly.

What does one do here if he gets seriously sick?

BOWLES: That is a problem. There's no good hospital here, and there are no first-rate doctors left. You can't get any American, British, German, or Swiss medicines now. Only French. I don't trust anything the French do, except their perfumes and their wines and their fashions. You can trust them to be chic. But I don't worry too much about medicines and doctors and all that, because my sicknesses are the sort of things I can take care of. Liver attacks. I've been having them for decades. I'd rather take care of them myself than go to a doctor.

It's not only doctors that I feel that way about. The only way you can be sure to get anything done right here is to do it yourself. You can't rely on anybody. A small example: some English friends of mine were traveling through Morocco a while back, and in Marrakech they bought about a hundred dollars' worth of a kind of floor covering made of woven reeds. They turned it over to an agent, and paid him to pack it and ship it to them. That's the last they saw of their purchase. They were indignant. They said it was a reputable firm, but they got no answers to their letters. Well, there's no such thing as a reputable firm. That's the whole point. In America, if a shop says they will send something, nine hundred and ninety-nine times out of a thousand they will. Here, it might be a hundred and twenty-five times out of a thousand. I'm not sure it's always a question of cupidity. I think it's often just neglect. I got a letter last Friday that had been mailed in Italy six weeks earlier. It had been in the post office here almost all of that time. They just hadn't put it in my box. That sort of thing happens all the time. Everything that has to do with the organization of human life is almost bound to go wrong in a country like this. The French always treated the Moroccans as babies, and so babies they remain.

Apparently the fact that things go wrong all the time doesn't irritate you a great deal, or you would live somewhere else.

BOWLES: If you live here, you either go crazy very quickly, or else you become more or less philosophical. You learn how to arrange your life so it isn't always catching on these particular nails. For instance, I'd like to see a movie occasionally, but I never go. In winter, the theaters are freezing cold, and in summer, they're so hot you come out dripping wet. In all seasons, they're full of fleas. But it's no problem for me, because I just don't go. All these nuisances would drive most people out of the country, but if you are accustomed, as I have always been, to doing everything yourself and providing your own amusement, then it's just as easy to live here as in Nairobi or Calcutta or wherever. You see, once you've gotten used to not having anything done for you, you want to go on that way. You don't want to move in rhythm with the outside world. You want to move only in your own rhythm, so that what began as a drawback eventually becomes your desire.

There's a theory that creative work is promoted if there is a certain abrasiveness in one's existence, and it would seem from what you say about the problems of living here that Tangier supplies the abrasive quality in abundance. Of course, many people also find that in New York.

BOWLES: There's always friction, wherever you are. Being alive gives you that. But it's nice to be able to choose your abrasive substance. New York, I think, wears you down. It doesn't give you any ideas. I have friends there, but I have never been much stimulated by talking to people. I get much more stimulated by sitting alone, thinking, reading, taking walks. I don't take in impressions very readily, I'm afraid. I suppose it's a mark of a stubborn, closed mind. One of the reasons I liked Tangier so much was that there was absolutely no sign of European cultural life here, and nothing ever happened. You couldn't get any books in those days. You couldn't even get any newspapers. There were no radios, of course. Very few automobiles. Never any theater, ballet, opera, exhibits—nothing. You didn't have to put up with all that nonsense. I like to go to museums on occasion, but I'm not a museum hound. I'd rather go to the circus or a flea market. Museums depress me, like cathedrals. I don't understand how anyone who isn't an architectural student or professor can possibly spend two hours in a cathedral. Some European cultural things have been introduced here over the years. Tonight, for example, there's a ballet. My wife is going, but I'm not.

I didn't choose Tangier just because it was free of European culture, nor did I choose it because of its climate. I chose it because of its proximity to many places that I liked. Spain is two hours away. We are near Algeria, which I used to like before the new regime was installed. Paris is not too far. We are beautifully near the Sahara, which I always repaired to when the cold weather came, and we're near all of Morocco, which is the most magnificent country in the world, for me. Nobody is as interested in Morocco as I am. Nobody is obsessive about it the way I am. Everything about Morocco has always fascinated me—above all, the simplicity of the life, once you get away from the cities. But now, you see, one is immured in the city unless he has a car. I used to have a Jaguar and a chauffeur, but I had to get rid of them. It was too much of a drain, financially. We had to fill the tank every day because the chauffeur used the car every night, taking girls out, and it was always full of scratches and had to be painted. Once, he told me a jinni, an evil spirit, had gotten in the car and that we had to go through a complicated ritual to exorcise it. I said that was nonsense, and refused. The next day, I sent him off for something, and he came back with a face as white as a Moroccan's can be, and said, "It's happened. The jinni has smashed the car up. He drove it right into the bridge." I went to look at the car, and the whole side was toothpicks. He said, "Next time there's a jinni, we've got to do what's right. You Christians don't know about such things." After that, when evil spirits came, I let him do just what he wanted, but there were still lots of accidents. He was always backing into a telegraph pole, or something. I was spending thousands of dollars every year just to maintain that cursed car. I finally had a good idea. I gave the car to the chauffeur. He sold it, and used the money to take a local American lady on a holiday to Rome.

Without a car, you can't get out of the city or go to the places that have a good climate. It's too much trouble. So, actually, most of the reasons for my having come here originally are gone. The biggest reason for staying is that I'm here. And, being middle-aged, one doesn't feel all that eager to pull up stakes and go looking for new adventures. I want to be left alone. I want to write books. And I want to die. It's a negative request, but not likely to be granted. I have a feeling I won't die here. In fact, I don't subscribe to any magazines or papers, because I always think I won't be living here six months from now. That goes on year after year.

Have you ever speculated on how your career as a composer and writer would have been affected if you had remained in the United States?

BOWLES: It might have been better. It might have been less good. It would certainly have been different. I would never advise anybody to leave his country and live somewhere else, nor would I advise against it. Who knows? Everyone is different. I don't think there are any rules that can apply to anybody about anything. I have never believed there was any one way of doing anything. Or that anyone should do anything. Or believe anything. It wouldn't be very easy to live according to that philosophy in America.

GALLERY NOTES

Anyone who has traveled in Europe during the last twenty years could hardly fail to notice that one of the most conspicuous groups of Americans in the Old World these days consists of young people. Most of them are in their early or middle twenties. Taken as a group, the men outnumber the women. In either case, they can usually be recognized by their dress: for the women, a sweater and either a skirt or slacks; for the men, khaki trousers or blue jeans, boots or loafers, and a jacket of some sort—and often, a beard. In the cities, their favorite meeting places are the American Express offices, where they receive their mail, socialize, and study the bulletin boards, which are vast collages of notices advertising living quarters to rent or share, cars, motorcycles, skis, and other quick-cash items for sale, and offers of share-the-cost transportation, as well as a variety of personal messages ("Bootsie: I have gone to Nick's. Meet me there. Bring poetry. Poopsie").

The young Americans in Europe are made up of three main groups: students, sojourners, and beatniks. There are certain overlappings, so it is not always easy to distinguish the members of one group from another. Furthermore, changes occur within the three groups. Students sometime become sojourners, and sojourners sometime become beatniks. The process almost never works the other way.

Of the three groups, the largest is made up of students. (Anyone who has stepped inside a lecture hall in a European university is apt to call himself a student.) While it is true that Americans in Europe to pursue their education are not a twentieth-century novelty, those who studied there before the Second World War are but a trickle compared with the flood that has poured in since. Among the principal causes of this scholastic inundation have been the G. I. Bill of Rights, the Fulbright Act, and the proliferation of university junior-year-abroad programs. At present, more than half of the liberal arts colleges in the United States sponsor their own junior-year-abroad programs, or allow their students to participate in those offered by other universities. Several thousand American students sign up for these programs every year. (In this group, the proportion of women to men is about two to one.) In addition, educators estimate that for every student enrolled in a junior-year-abroad program there are two others attending school in Europe on a program of their own devising. The ranks of students abroad also include those doing graduate work; they are a small minority.

Considerable difference of opinion exists among both undergraduate students and educators about the tangible academic value of the year of study abroad. It is well known that for the most part American students in Europe do little actual studying, at least compared with what they would do at home. But there seems to be quite general agreement that the experience confers intangible benefits in the way of broadening the students' horizons and adding a dimension to their personalities.

It is also generally agreed that study abroad presents many problems beyond the initial ones of getting along in a foreign language and finding living accommodations. For one thing, European universities provide practically no supervision of their students. Attendance at lectures is almost never required. Examinations are infrequent. Furthermore, except at Oxford and Cambridge, where the tutorial system is used, there is no personal relationship between the European professor and the student. Also, the level of instruction is high, since it is geared for students drawn from the upper 5 to 10 per cent of secondary-school graduates. The American students who solve these problems most successfully are those doing graduate work; next are those enrolled in supervised junior-year-abroad programs; the least successful are those studying on a program of their own. The casualties in this group are highest not only scholastically but personally. Every year, about a hundred young Americans studying in Paris are admitted to the American Hospital there with serious emotional disturbances; four out of five of them are studying on an independent program.

Many American students who find, to their dismay, that university work in Europe is far beyond them quietly give up trying, but as they are reluctant to go home, they become sojourners. They may make some pretense of continuing their studies, hanging around the university and perhaps attending an occasional lecture, but most of their time is spent in socializing, sightseeing, or traveling, usually in the company of other dropouts. As a rule, they continue to receive an allowance from home, the practice being to leave their status vague in letters to their parents. The sojourners often become the kind of people who are seen in the cafes in the forenoons.

In addition to the dropouts, the sojourners also include a large number of students who are taking a year off not to study but to travel, to see the sights, and, as they often say, to discover their own identity. They are also usually on an allowance, but some take jobs for a while. They tend to be industrious sightseers, covering a lot of territory, often by hitchhiking. I talked to a number of them that I picked up in various countries. They were generally agreeable young people who felt that they were getting a great deal out of their European experience. They were usually quite vague about their future. Hardly one knew what career he intended to follow. "I know exactly the job I want," a young man sojourning in southern Spain told me. "The only trouble is, it hasn't been created yet." One thing they were all sure about: they were not going to be businessmen.

Among the sojourners' most popular ports of call is the beautiful Italian seaside village of Positano, whose American residents include a film editor named Norman Schwartz (he spends about half the year working in Rome or Paris), who is in his early thirties and for some time has been an interested observer of his young itinerant compatriots. "These kids are war babies, and they seem to me to constitute something new in American life," Mr. Schwartz remarked one day when we lunched together. "One factor fairly common to this group is that life has always been made easy for them. Even now, they're all getting money from home. Often, it's a kind of bribe, especially when the parents have been divorced. When the kids are over here, they are sort of out of the way. It seems to be a mutually satisfactory arrangement. They're different in many ways from the European kids of the same class who come here. For one thing, if the European kids have rich parents and the kids can't stand the bourgeoisie, they come here and spend all the money they can get their hands on, living it up. Not the American kids. They're strange. They don't spend a great deal of money, and you have the feeling that even if they had it, they'd cudgel it and stay here rather than go to Paris, say, and live a little larger than life.

"During the three years I've been here, about fifteen kids who grew up together in and around Westport, Connecticut, have settled here for a while. From what I've gathered, their parents are generally in publishing, advertising, television—those kinds of jobs that require business sense but also a little taste, a little art. These parents are not the conventional Babbitts. They're the sort of people you would expect to be politically liberal, have Picassos on the wall, and so forth. And yet their children want to reject whatever it is their parents are. They are in revolt against something. It seems to be more than just the idea of suburbia. It's as if they all feel that there's some great hypocrisy about making thirty or three hundred thousand dollars a year writing advertising copy, or doing something similar. They are never very clear about what they're revolting against. In general, they don't have the same depth or intensity or interests that you find in Europeans of the same age. Some of the American kids paint. Some don't do anything. They do read the Paris *Herald Tribune* almost cover to cover, and they take an interest in American politics and international politics, but in a kind of secondhand way. They don't seem to absorb a great deal of Europe, although they do take a little interest in the local people. Essentially, they form their own little core, almost like high school bohemians. It's as if they had formed an alien camp outside of Westport and are taking potshots at something back there that they don't quite understand. At this distance, that's a very safe thing to do."

Unlike the sojourners, who have usually not decided on their life work, the beatniks have already found a career, such as it is. The beatniks, known to many Europeans as the American Flea Market, are easily recognized by their studiously unkempt appearance, their shuffling gait, and their air of aimlessness. Whether in Trafalgar Square in London, on the Spanish Steps in Rome, on the Ile de la Cité in Paris, on the Greek island of Hydra, or on the Spanish island of Ibiza, or in any of their other favorite gathering places, they exude the same spirit of leaden indifference as their counterparts in New York's Greenwich Village. They give the appearance of living hand to mouth, and many actually do (including one in Tangier who exists on twenty cents a day), but many others receive money regularly from relatives. However low their finances, the beatniks are usually able to keep themselves supplied with marijuana, *kif*, or hashish, which is part of their way of life. They drift in large numbers to Tangier, because the stuff is easily available there and cheap.

"When the beatniks started coming to Morocco," Paul Bowles told me, "the local people at first thought they were a religious group, and loved them. The chief of police went around saying, 'Isn't it marvelous that these people of the olden times, with their beards and simple dress, are coming here? They are so peaceful. All they want to do is sit and talk. And their women don't wear makeup. They're not like those European whores who come here all painted up with lipstick, and they only speak when the men tell them to. The men know how to treat them. They don't let the women go around alone. When they're tired of them, they take them home and lock them in. Then they go out and amuse themselves. They're very fine people.' That was his first reaction.

"But before long the beatniks misbehaved, as they have a way of doing. They started entering into competition with the Moroccans, selling *kif* in the street. Then they began renting out their girl friends to Moroccans at so much an hour. That didn't go over very well with the authorities, so the police stopped being so hospitable. But the beatniks still come in droves, after receiving letters from their fellow beats that tell how they're living here on ten dollars a month. Yugoslav ships bring them over from New York for about a hundred dollars. By the time they get here, their fellow beats are probably no longer on the scene, because nowadays the police go out about once a month and round up all the tourists who are not well dressed. They are taken to the police station, where their wallets are examined, and unless they have a considerable sum of money, or can prove that they have access to a considerable sum of money, they are kept in the police station overnight, and shipped out the next day on the ferry to Spain, with orders not to return. The local people don't see anything very religious about them any more."

The image of the beatniks was slightly improved after the latest disastrous flood in Florence, when a sizable number of them converged on the city and donated their efforts to rehabilitating damaged manuscripts and other treasures. Generally, however, their contribution to the social welfare tends to be commensurate with their talents, which seem to be confined for the most part to a primitive ability to pluck the guitar and to sing folk songs of a sort and to make crude crayon drawings on the sidewalk. Some beatniks make ends meet by performing these skills on the streets of European cities and taking up a collection. Others who are not that gifted or energetic cadge or beg. One of the latter was once asked why he didn't work. "It would be a waste of my youth," he replied.

One of the sources I consulted about young Americans in Europe was David M. Davis, executive director of the American Center for Students and Artists, in Paris. The Center, a private institution founded some thirty years ago by members of the American community in Paris, occupies a former mansion, complete with swimming pool and extensive other recreational facilities, located on what was once the estate of the noted writer and diplomat, François Chateaubriand. In addition to serving as a social headquarters for young men and women of thirty-five nationalities, the Center carries on a vigorous and varied program of cultural activities. In the opinion of many Paris-based Americans, the Center ranks as one of the most successful American enterprises in Paris, thanks largely to the energy and imagination of Mr. Davis, who has himself made another life in Europe.

Before moving to France, in 1961, Mr. Davis and his wife had lived in New York, where he had been administrator of the Foundation for Youth and Student Affairs. "I had run that foundation for years," he said, "and after a certain point, when you've solved most of the problems, you've had enough. So, I decided to retire and do some writing. We came over here and settled on the Riviera, and then a couple of years later, I was approached to take on the job of rejuvenating the Center and running it, and the challenge appealed to me so much that I accepted. I have always been interested in work that will bring us into better relationships with other countries, and will present America in its best light, and I think I can do that much more interestingly here than I can in New York. Anything I do here, if it's well done, is exciting, whereas in New York, one can do something well, and it just gets submerged. Here, the possibilities of doing something creative, even unique, are high.

Paris has always held out that possibility, Mr. Davis continued, and that is still probably the most magnetic force that draws young Americans there today. "A studio in Paris has the same glamor for them that it had for the members of my generation when they were young," Mr. Davis said. "It hasn't worn off. Maybe it never will. Of course, this is a fascinating city, and one of the things it has, which we don't have, is an appreciation of the artist himself. In the States, 'egghead' is a term of opprobrium. Not here. A politician in France is not handicapped by having a superb intellect and a magnificent education. Léon Blum, for instance, or De Gaulle himself. After all, he is a very civilized man. But those attributes were against Stevenson. They were even against Kennedy, though he came closer to overcoming them because of his good looks and certain other qualities.

"I think another reason young Americans come here is to get away from the pressure for conformity. Despite the fact that France is not exactly a democracy these days and that there is a censorship and various other things, nevertheless one is freer here in some ways than in the States. In the first place, you're freer to live as you wish without your neighbors caring or being interested. There's also less pressure for conformity on the political scene. Look at the number of Communists in France—something like one out of every four voters. You can't be a Communist in the States unless you want to be an outlaw, while here, if you go to a dinner party, anybody you meet may be a Communist. In the States, it's all right to be far Right but not far Left.

"Finally, there is the matter of money. The junior-year students don't have to be much concerned about this, because they get enough money from home, and so do many of the independent students. But there are a great many other young Americans here who have to earn part or all of their expenses. Some give language lessons, others teach painting. Then there is quite a colony of actors and writers and other young people who do pretty well by dubbing movies. Living costs here are terribly high, but if you're on the student level, you can still probably live more cheaply here than in America. If you're enrolled at the university, you can eat in a student restaurant and have lunch or dinner for twenty-five cents. It's adequate. It sustains life. But you have to be young."

It should probably be noted that my conversation with Mr. Davis, as well as my interviews with students and other young Americans in Europe, took place before the riots and lesser manifestations of student unrest erupted at the Sorbonne and at other European universities.

"Smith College is a very fine place, but I wanted to experience a different atmosphere."

Approximately 10 per cent of the juniors at Smith College spend their third year abroad, studying either in Paris, Florence, or Geneva. Among those in a recent class who chose Paris were two bright, attractive young women named Katharine Townsend, who comes from Montclair, New Jersey, and Sarah Jane Eigerman, who comes from Brooklyn. Through a mutual friend in Paris, I arranged to talk to them together at my hotel one afternoon after they had finished classes.

KATHARINE: I am majoring in French, and I think the only way to learn the language is to come over and speak it all of the time. We live with French families—that's part of the program—and all of our courses are conducted in French, and we write all of our papers in French. So, we are able to use the language almost exclusively and have a chance to really learn it.

SARAH JANE: I am a theater major, and I also wanted to learn French and to see something of the French theater. Furthermore, I don't plan to go to graduate school, so my only chance to come here as a student was now. I had never been to Europe, and I didn't want to see it just as a tourist. Smith College is a very fine place, but I wanted to experience a different atmosphere.

How does the work here compare with the work at Smith? Is it harder?

KATHARINE: Since everything is in French, I think it was harder, at least in the beginning. What was really hard, at the start, was understanding the French system, which is completely different from what we were used to in the United States. Here, they have the *exposé* system. Everything is done according to a very rigorous plan. You tell what you're going to say in the beginning. It doesn't have to be *your* thought. It doesn't have to be an individual thought. In fact, it's better if it isn't, whereas in the United States, if you write a thesis, you're supposed to have an original viewpoint. Here, they don't care if you say what people have said for five thousand years, as long as it's a rigorous plan. In a way, I think this system is all right, if you also have the American system.

SARAH JANE: It's a matter of giving back what they want. As Katharine says, it's not supposed to be original. I think it's better if you're encouraged to have a certain curiosity, but that is something they don't seem to like here. The idea here seems to be that you adapt yourself to the system. You don't try to change it. You're not encouraged to try to think things out for yourself.

Another thing—in the United States, students are used to having quite a close rapport with their teachers, especially in small colleges. Here in France, the teachers don't like you to approach them. The professor comes to the lecture hall, delivers his lecture to five hundred students, and leaves. That's as close as you ever get to him.

How does living with a French family work out?

KATHARINE: I live with a wonderful family. There are five children, and the apartment is large. I share my room with another American girl from our group, and we have all our meals there. We don't do any chores, really. They have integrated us into the family. They include us in their birthday parties, and they gave me a birthday party, and made me a little present. At Christmas, they took one of my shoes, and put it under the tree. Little things like that make you feel much more than just a paying guest.

SARAH JANE: I also live with a family that has five children, one of whom is away at boarding school. Both parents work for a plastics company that is owned by Americans so there is a good deal of talk about how fantastic American methods are, or how America is invading Europe, or other topics of that nature. The conversation is always very amicable. On the other hand, I wouldn't say I was very much integrated into the family, nor is the other girl from Smith who shares my room. We are very much guests. We do help with the dishes after dinner, and so on, but if personal problems are being discussed, we go quietly to our room.

What do you do here for social life?

KATHARINE: In the first place, it's very hard to meet French people. Of course, you *see* a great many people at the Sorbonne, but they all have their own little group, and they're very hostile to strangers. What helped me was going on a tour of Prague and Budapest at Christmas with a French university group. On that trip, which lasted ten days, I met many French students, and when you're with them that long, they accept you. Since then, there have been several parties of that whole group, and I've been invited to all of them. I'm going out with one of the students I met on the tour, a law student. If it hadn't been for the tour, I wouldn't be going out at all.

SARAH JANE: I've joined a group that's going to make a tour during spring vacation, and I hope that will mean something. Also, I've just begun taking acting lessons in a group. They seem very friendly, and I hope I'll make friends that way. French society really is very closed. For example, the girls in the family I live with belong to a neighborhood club—both boys and girls are members—that meets on Sundays to play bridge and to dance afterwards. They meet at each other's houses on a kind of round-robin system. One Sunday, they met at the house where I live, and my roommate and I were invited. It was very nice, but that was it. We weren't invited again. But there are things to do. We go to the movies, the theater, museums, go for walks, and so on. Also, I take guitar lessons—and sometimes I do my homework.

What do you think of the French boys you've met?

KATHARINE: I like them. I really do. You have to sort of get used to them. Their sense of humor is so different from what we're accustomed to in the United States. They laugh at everything. In the beginning, it sort of shocks you. For instance, when we were in Budapest, we were visiting the monument to the Russian soldiers killed in the Hungarian uprising. The French students started making jokes about them and laughing. Well, you can make jokes about some things, but I thought that was in very poor taste. But they just laugh at everything, including themselves. They make fun of De Gaulle all the time, and President Johnson, and just about everybody else.

SARAH JANE: The few French boys I have met have very set ideas about how girls should look, how they should dress, and how they should act. They're very quick to judge you, and they expect you to say something brilliant, almost as soon as you're introduced. They have a terribly superior attitude toward Americans. That's true of the girls, too, and maybe of all the French. When we arrived in France, we spent the first six weeks in Aix-en-Provence, where we had a kind of orientation course—lectures on French history, grammar, and so on. We stayed in pensions, and I remember the woman who owned the one we stayed in informed us very early that France was the most cultured country in the world. There were three French girls living in the pension. One was going to secretarial school. Another attended high school. The third was studying in a university. All of them were really very rude to us. They snickered whenever we tried to speak French, and they made sarcastic remarks about everything we said.

KATHARINE: At dinner, when I said I was going to major in French, they all started laughing out loud. That really broke them up. Of course, the French are very critical of the United States. Vietnam they bring up all of the time. They can't stand Johnson. They think he's sort of a hick and not very bright. The racial troubles in the United States are another thing they bring up constantly.

SARAH JANE: They talk about racial troubles as if we were the only country that ever had them. I was talking to a boy at the bridge party I mentioned, and he said he didn't like the Latin Quarter any more, because he sees so many Africans there going around with white girls. In the next breath, he was criticizing Americans for their racist attitudes. And always there is the refrain about the superiority of French culture.

KATHARINE: Some of them are quite chauvinistic, but then Americans are, too. There is so much about this country that is quaint and appealing—people walking down the street carrying those long loaves of bread, the markets, the statues all over. I see a style of life here that I think is very attractive.

SARAH JANE: Before I came over, I was warned by my brother, who lived here for two years, that the French were very rude and that they didn't like foreigners, especially Americans. I think those things are truer in Paris than in the provinces. In Aix-en-Provence, the people were not only nice but happy. The sun seemed to be shining on everyone. It seems to me that the French people are just like people anywhere else, perhaps a little brighter. Not necessarily more intelligent, but sharper. Their reactions are quick. There is also an authoritarian strain in life here that I don't like. The paterfamilias notion is carried to an extreme. If the father is out of sorts, the whole family walks around on tiptoe. If there's an argument between a husband and a wife, the husband says, "You're stupid." The wife doesn't object to this. She tries to justify herself. She says, "Well, I really meant to say such-and-such." The husband just keeps saying, "You're stupid." This is not, to me, a relationship between equals.

You'll be going back to Smith before too long. Do you look forward to that?

KATHARINE: In the beginning, I thought it would be horrible to go back, but now I don't think it will be too hard. One reason is that I love the library at Smith. The libraries here are terrible. You have to go through a tremendous amount of red tape every time you want to use a book, and you can't take one out without paying a deposit. You can take out only a certain number. It's a mess. Also, I like the Smith teachers very much, and I think we'll find we have profited from this year tremendously. One of the important things, I think, is that it has given us a chance to see the United States from a different perspective. Also, after observing the political situation in France, where De Gaulle, as many French people have told me, is a virtual monarch, I have begun to have a new appreciation of the American system of government.

SARAH JANE: I don't think any of my basic ideas have changed since coming to Europe, but many of them have either been reinforced or modified as a result of being away from the United States and developing more objectivity toward it. I have always been critical of the foreign policy of the United States in general, and so I have been quite surprised, when I've found foreigners agreeing with me, at the vigorous way I defend the United States. There's been another unexpected effect of living here: I don't take myself so seriously any more.

If you were giving advice to students planning to spend their junior year here, what would you tell them?

SARAH JANE: I would say, if they're coming with an American group, that the most important thing is not just to stay with them, but to get out as much as possible by joining French clubs and other organizations. They can go to the Sorbonne, and join folk-singing groups, choral groups, mountain climbing groups, or any number of others. They should do this as soon as they can. That's the only way—or at least, I think, the best way—to meet French people.

KATHARINE: Yes, that's true. I would also give them a few hints on what is considered polite behavior in this country. For instance, if a Frenchman pays you a compliment, you never say, "Thank you." Instead, you're supposed to blush and say, "Oh, it's just an old dress," or something of that nature, depending on the circumstances. You say "Thank you" only when somebody gives you something material or passes you something at table. When you are introduced to someone, you don't say, "How do you do, Mrs. Smith." Using the person's name is considered vulgar. You say, "How do you do, Madame." These are small things, but knowing them makes it easier to make the change. It's quite a big one, really, when you come here and, I suppose, when you go back. Friends who have gone home by plane say it's too big a shock. I'm going back by boat, so I'll have five days to change from this life to that one. I wonder what it will be like.

"I thought if I took a year out and came to Europe and just got everything out of my system, I'd be in a better position to decide what I want to do."

Andrew Loughrin, a tall, good-looking, nineteen-year-old high school graduate from Southern California, was sojourning in Europe while I was there. We met by chance in Paris at the apartment of a friend of mine whose son had known young Loughrin in California. In many ways, he seemed a typical sojourner, though perhaps more self-possessed and articulate than most. We met again, by plan, at the same apartment the following afternoon, and he talked about the life he had been leading since finishing high school.

LOUGHRIN: My dad had promised me college, but I didn't want to start right away, because I was just not ready for it. I would certainly have flunked out, and the money would have been wasted. I really wasn't sure what I wanted to be. I used to think I wanted to be a dentist, but a pilot who lives up the street from us gave me a few flying lessons in his own plane, and he thinks I would make a good pilot for an airline. Within ten years, about 90 per cent of the commercial pilots, who were trained in the war, will be retired, so there will be good opportunities, and you could get a good seniority number. Pilots make a good living, and I could live just about anywhere I wanted. But I wasn't sure, and I still don't know. I thought if I took a year out and came to Europe and just got everything out of my system, I'd be in a better position to decide what I want to do.

Where did you get the money to make the trip?

LOUGHRIN: I've always had jobs, since I was a little kid in the fourth or fifth grade. The last business I had was leasing bicycles to retired people who live in a place called Fair Haven Leisure World. There are at least ten thousand old people in this one little compound.

It's a great market. The old people will buy anything with the right charm. Anyway, before I left, I liquidated the business and sold the bikes, and that gave me seven hundred and ten dollars, which I came over with. Then my brother owes me a hundred, and my parents owe me two hundred, which I can have when I want it. I drove across the United States in my old Citroën, and left that in New York with some friends. I flew over on Icelandic Airlines, which is the cheapest. It cost a hundred and sixty-seven dollars and eighty cents from New York to Luxembourg. That's the cheapest city to fly to, even though it's further than London or Paris. I suppose there's a cheaper landing tax.

On the plane coming over, I met an American fellow named Barry, who's doing about the same thing I am, and we started palling around together. In Luxembourg, we stayed at the hostels, which are really great. You really meet a lot of nice people and have a lot of fun, and it's cheap. A bed is forty cents for the night. You get as much as you can eat—and the food is usually pretty good—for seventy cents a day. Also, you can keep your travel expenses down if you hitchhike, which is really great.

We stayed in Luxembourg for four days, and then we decided to go to London. We started out at ten o'clock in the morning, which is a bad hour if you're hitchhiking. People who are going a long distance leave much earlier than that. Anyway, we got a ride to the outskirts of Luxembourg, where we were picked up by a man who spoke only French and German. We spoke very little French, but we found out he was some sort of Braille teacher. He goes to houses of the blind and writes letters for them. Every town we went through, he stopped in a café and bought us coffee and cognac, and insisted on paying for it. Couldn't have been nicer. After eight or nine stops, you're feeling pretty good. He went a hundred kilometers out of his way to take us to the outskirts of Brussels. Then we got picked up, even before we put our thumb out, by two Scandinavian girls who travel around selling nylon products to stores. They were just fabulous. We almost lost our minds there. They took us through Brussels and way out in the sticks and dropped us off. We got picked up almost immediately by a truck driver, who spoke no English. He gave us a pillow, so we could get some sleep in the cab, and tuned the radio to an American Armed Forces station just to please us. Took us right to the docks in Ostend, where we got a boat to Dover. In England, we got a ride from Dover all the way to London with a man who said he was a commercial traveler in sweets. Maybe you know that means he was a candy salesman. He took us right to the subway depot and told us which train to take into the center of London. Hitchhiking doesn't happen like that all the time, but when it does, you can't beat it.

How long did you stay in London?

LOUGHRIN: Just a few days. It was wintertime, and the weather was miserable. We were staying at a hostel, and it wasn't heated, so we decided to leave and go back in the springtime. One reason we went to London was that someone at the hostel in Luxembourg told us you could buy used English Army motorcycles there for practically nothing. Well, we found the military bikes had a lot of charm—little baskets and lights and spinners, very unique-looking—but with the license and tax they cost about eighty dollars. We decided to spend more and get new bikes, so we each bought one that cost a hundred and twenty dollars. I'm sorry now that I got that motorcycle. I hope to sell it and get some of the money back. It's more fun to hitchhike, especially if you're traveling alone, which I've been doing since we came back from England. Barry went back to Luxembourg. He's scheming on some girl there. I came to Paris. You get lonely when you travel alone.

Where are you staying here?

LOUGHRIN: In a little hotel over on the Left Bank. The hostels are too far out of town. The hotel I'm in costs eight francs a night. Around the corner there's a kind of cafeteria, where the students eat. You can fill yourself up for three francs. If I can keep away from the pastry shops—those pastries kill me—I can keep the expenses down to about three dollars a day. Of course, it costs more when you're traveling, but I've been stretching the money pretty far. I've been spending about a hundred and fifty dollars a month, according to the ledger I keep. I also keep a journal, which is a day-by-day account, usually a page, of where I've been, what I've done, people I've met and talked with. It will be fun to read over. There have been a lot of experiences.

One night when we were in London—Barry and an Australian fellow named Peter and I—we were walking through Soho, past all those strip shows and things. We were just contemplating what we wanted to do. We had been hitchhiking and sleeping in cold rooms and hadn't had a bath in about two weeks. We were pretty miserable, and were looking for something to cheer us up. We were thinking about going to one of the strip shows, but then we changed our minds and said, "No, we'll go to a regular show." There were a lot of good ones in town. Then some girl hopped out of a doorway and said, "Are you looking for girls?" We weren't sure what we were looking for, so when she invited us to go upstairs and talk, we went upstairs to talk. There was another girl up there. Both of them were neat and clean and not terribly bad-looking. They said, "We're hostesses. Would you like to come to our place and spend the night? We will give you comforting." We said, "Is your place heated?" They said it was. We said, "Is there a shower? If there's a shower, we'll take it." They said there was a fine shower. We could stay all night, and it would cost one pound, two and six for each of us. We figured, "Great! We're getting a shower and a warm bed plus comforting for about three bucks." Which wasn't bad.

So, we each gave them one pound, two and six, and then they said, "Now you buy us drinks." We said, "Wait a minute. We don't want a drink." They said we didn't have to drink it, just buy it, and they handed us a little folder called *Rules for Hostesses*. It said something like, "You are required to buy each hostess two drinks and one drink for yourself." Well, I went out and cashed a traveler's check, and when I came back, the girls said it was time to buy another drink. We said, "Now, look. Tell us again what we get out of this. Spell it out for us." They went through the whole thing again about going to their place and the shower and the comforting and so on. Then Peter went out and cashed a traveler's check. We were dead tired. We just wanted a place to sleep. Finally, after cashing a couple more traveler's checks, we began to get the pitch that this was a real Mickey Mouse operation. We realized we weren't going anywhere. By that time, they'd gotten about nine bucks apiece out of us, and we were pretty mad, but there's nothing you can do. When Peter went out to cash a traveler's check, he also went to the police department. They said they don't like what the girls do, but they have a legitimate business going, and they can't be touched. They're hostesses, and that's all they are. They will sit and talk with you or play cards, or you can take them to a bar or walk around town with them or some other thing like that. They give you their company, and that's it. They're just great con artists. They play it up big and make you think you're going to get something more. We didn't get a thing. We didn't even get a shower. Well, it's an experience you learn by.

How have you been spending your time in Paris?

LOUGHRIN: I spend a lot of time walking around. Get on the subway and go to the American Express and then walk back to the hotel by a different way every time. I went to the Louvre one day. I've heard of some museums I plan to see. I read. Before, I never liked to read. Since coming over here, I've started to enjoy reading, and I do quite a bit of it. I suppose that would have happened eventually wherever I was. Anyway, now I appreciate a good book.

Of course, the fabulous thing about being here is that I can do whatever I please. I'm free. I had a lot of freedom at home, more than most kids, but there are always small things, like your parents telling you to get a haircut, you know, and different things. Here, if I want to stay up all night, I can. I'm my own boss. I never drank until I came over here, and I don't do it much now, and I never smoked or anything. This year, if the opportunity arises, I want to do anything that comes along. This year is my year.

Where do you plan to go after you leave Paris?

LOUGHRIN: I'd like to go to Switzerland to ski. Two fellows I've talked to told me how cheaply you can do it. You can stay at hostels, and get your bed and dinner. For breakfast, you just grab a loaf of bread somewhere. These two fellows went to different places, and besides bed and dinner, they rented skis, boots, and poles, and they paid for their lifts. One did it on four dollars a day, and the other did it on four-fifty. That sounds really great.

Then I'd like to go down to Spain. We had a Spanish maid, and I learned to speak a little Spanish from her. From Spain, going the other way, I'd like to get as far as Egypt. Everybody says it's great to see, and you can travel about five hundred kilometers for a dollar or so on the train, and you can live on twenty-five cents a day. Have steak and everything. From what I've heard, it's really great out there.

After that, I'd like to see Italy, and then come back here. I really like this city. It's so beautiful. It's just fabulous. Every time you turn around, there's more history hitting you in the eye. I want to come back and take my first year of college here. I think I can convince my parents that that would be a good idea, because then it would be easier to get into the college of my choice at home. I want to learn French, which is a fabulous language, and also take some art and history courses.

What do you think of the other young Americans you've met over here? Are they getting something out of it, or are they just bumming around?

LOUGHRIN: Oh, you can't go through this experience and not get something out of it. You learn about different peoples and cultures and civilizations, and it gives you a better outlook on life. I think what you get out of it depends on the person. Many of these fellows come over just to ski, and you see a lot with beards and long hair down their backs and wearing old trench coats. I'm not sure what they are getting out of it. I suppose they're just looking, as the saying goes, to find themselves. Which everybody's doing. I plan to find myself in many ways. I've learned how to enjoy reading and how to manage everything by myself, so I think I'll have better study habits and be a better student. And I've seen so much. Before, I'd always thought when I settled down, I'd live in San Diego, but now I don't know. I don't think I'd like to live here permanently, but I'd like to stay for a while and learn French. And if I do become a pilot, which is very appealing, because they are free and they have unlimited travel, I think it would be great when I get married and have children, to live three years in Paris and have the children learn French as the French do, and then go to New York, say, and fly out of there for a while, and then go to South America or somewhere else. Which you could do if you worked for a large airline and had a good seniority number. That would be my utopia.

> "It's sort of easy living. I mean, everything's sort of quiet and easy-going. No rush."

When I visited Positano to interview Joseph Jay Deiss and other Ameropeans living there, I found among its other charms the fact that the local telephone service is in such a primitive state that messages are generally delivered by hand. Consequently, to give me instructions on how to reach his residence, Mr. Deiss sent his son, Casey, to the hotel where I was staying. A tall, slender, rather shy young man with long black hair and beard, he was wearing dungarees, a striped sweater, sandals, and one large, pirate-style gold earring in the lobe of his right ear, when he arrived on a motorcycle, which he drove with one hand while eating an ice cream cone with the other. Riding behind him on the motorcycle was another dark-haired young man, who was also wearing dungarees, a sweater, and sandals, but he was clean shaven, his hair was shorter, and he wore no earring. His name, I learned on being introduced, was Robin Bagier, and it developed that he, like the younger Mr. Deiss, was also an artist. At my request, the two young men agreed to an interview, and we made a date to meet late that afternoon at Mr. Bagier's place.

Like the Deisses' villa, Robin Bagier's house is situated "on the top" and built into the mountainside. When I arrived there, he showed me into the casually furnished combination living and dining room, introduced me to his wife, a very good-looking Italian girl, who speaks no English, and proudly showed me their child, who was sleeping in a crib in a corner of the room. "He's six months old," Robin (he suggested that I call him by his first name) said. "He's got a great name—Juan Wolfgang Bagier." On the walls were a number of collages and wooden constructions, some of which were mechanized, and featured fingers that rang bells, eyes that winked, and so on. Many of the pieces were very clever and amusing. Robin said that he had been making objects like these since he was a boy in Los Angeles, where he was born, grew up, and finished high school.

BAGIER: Then I went to the University of Mexico, but I did only a year and a half. After that, I went into the Army, and served most of my time in Germany. When I got out, I lived in New York for a year. I was painting, actually, but I had a nighttime job at Schrafft's. During the day, I would paint, then go uptown and do my job, and then go back and paint some more. It got to be a real drag, so I came over here. I first lived in Salerno for about five months, where I learned Italian. I lived and ate with an Italian family, and then I moved to Positano. I found it nicer here, and there were other people with whom I had things in common. I lived here about a year, and then I met my wife, and we were married.

My idea, when I came over here, was to continue painting. But after a while, I realized that the things I was really adapted to were assemblages and constructions. I did my first constructions when I was about thirteen years old. I used to collect driftwood around Los Angeles and Santa Barbara and make things out of it, using brass and other materials. I've always done them for fun—constructions—and lately I've been doing them just about exclusively.

Can you sell enough of them to make a living?

BAGIER: Not exactly. I get some income from the United States, and for four months during the summer, I work at the art school here—the Positano Art Workshop. It was started by an American woman, Edna Lewis, and she still runs it. People come to the school from all over, old and young. I do some assistant teaching, but the main job is running the store that supplies the paints and other materials. I also do all of the hanging of the shows. With the summer work and odd jobs during the winter and what you could sell, you could probably make it go if you were a single man. But not if you're married and have a family.

What about rents here—are they high?

BAGIER: I pay fifty dollars a month for this house. It also has a whole downstairs, where I have my studio. That part of the house has another kitchen, a living room, and a bathroom, which I rent out to a writer, an American fellow named Will Brumbach. You ought to meet him. I'll go ask him to come up in a minute. There's also another separate room downstairs, which I rent out during the summer. So, the house comes out costing me about twenty-five dollars a month. Which is very good.

[*Excusing himself, he went downstairs, and came back with Will Brumbach, who, like the other two young men I'd met, had not been near a barber in some time. He was wearing baggy trousers, a beat-up gray sweater, the conventional sandals, and glasses. He said that his family lives in Westport, Connecticut (his father is employed by a New York market research firm), and that he had worked for three years after graduating from high school.*]

BRUMBACH: I worked for my father, and I worked for a cabinet-maker for six months, and then I worked for about a year as a carpenter, actually constructing houses. After that, I went back to school —N.Y.U. for a year, the New School for a year, and then Columbia for a while. Then I decided to come to Europe. Originally, I had planned to study at the University of London. I arrived in London in December, 1962. As you remember, that was the worst winter they'd had in many years. There was about half an hour of sunlight a day. Literally, about half an hour. I decided to come to Positano for Christmas, and I never went back.

Since you have been here, have you been writing all of the time?

BRUMBACH: Not all of the time. I went to the University of Perugia, and learned Italian, and I've continued to study it on my own. At the moment, I'm trying to develop a new method of teaching Italian to English-speaking people.

BAGIER: Will's a genius at languages. They'd never seen anybody do what he did in three months at Perugia. Now he even reads books in Italian dialects—Neapolitan and others that are almost completely different languages.

I gather, Will, that it was the good weather that brought you here in the first place. Is that the best thing about living here?

BRUMBACH: I suppose so. The sun. The sun and the sea.

BAGIER: It's sort of easy living. I mean, everything's sort of quiet and easy-going. No rush.

BRUMBACH: There's no economic advantage, really. The cost of living, excluding a house, is higher here than it is in Rome. On a year-round basis, you can rent a very large house, three stories, for a hundred dollars a month. If you go to the next town down the coast—it's not considered fashionable, you know—the prices are a third of what they are here. A friend of ours there has five rooms plus two bathrooms, a kitchen, and a terrace, and he pays sixteen dollars a month. You can see the town from here. It's only about three miles away, but nobody wants to go there. It seems so far away.

But here, don't you avoid other expenses that you would have in Rome—laundry, dry cleaning . . .

BRUMBACH: Dry cleaning—what's that?

BAGIER: There isn't any dry cleaner around here.

Are there no economic advantages besides the low rents?

BAGIER: Oh sure. You don't spend money anywhere. There's just one movie theater, and it only runs two times a week, and then it costs only thirty cents. Since you can't go more than twice a week, you're saving money there. We can live—my wife, the baby, and myself, and with the automobile—we can live on about a hundred and fifty dollars a month very comfortably. Actually, on two hundred dollars a month, a person could live really well, and have enough money to get out—you know, go to Rome and get around. Really feel free.

BRUMBACH: Oh yes. That would be ample. Worked out on a year's basis, I probably get by on about a hundred and twenty-five a month. If I just stayed here, didn't take any trips, I could manage it quite easily on just a hundred a month. Of course, that wouldn't mean throwing it around. For example, cigarettes consume a tremendous amount of money.

BAGIER: You don't even think of smoking American cigarettes. Even Italian cigarettes cost between thirty-two and forty-five cents a package, and that really eats up the money.

When we were talking down at the hotel, you said, "Positano is a nice warm womb. It would be very hard to leave it." Would you, in fact, want to leave it?

BAGIER: It's very difficult to get away from here. Geographically, you're sort of closed in. The cliffs behind you, and the ocean in front, and just the one road out. Some people come down here from Rome, and they feel claustrophobic, and they never come back. But if you just look out to sea, you don't have that feeling.

Do you ever manage to overcome the geography and get out?

BAGIER: It's very difficult, but you do. To Rome, to Naples, to Salerno. But to drive to Salerno and back is really a day's hard work, and it's only fifty miles round trip. It would be almost like going downtown, if you lived in a normal place. But it's nothing but curves around these cliffs. So, we don't make the trip very often. Before we do, we plan it for months. We haven't even considered it the last couple of months, because the road has been closed. A whole cliff came down, and just took the road with it. So, you would have had to go the back way—from Salerno up to Naples, and come down from the north. That's too much.

If it is so hard just to get to Salerno, how are you ever going to go back to the United States, or do you ever plan to? How far ahead do you plan?

BRUMBACH: A couple of hours.

BAGIER: Oh, I do get up to Rome to buy supplies and to see an aunt who lives there, but, as I say, it is difficult to get out, and it usually winds up to be pretty expensive.

When you live here, in this remote setting, and are your own boss, how do you manage your work? I've heard people say they just couldn't work here, because it's too beautiful. They had to move away.

BAGIER: You just have to discipline yourself. If you want to sit around all day, you can. Nobody is going to stop you. During the winter, there's nothing else to do except work. Not because of the weather. Except for that one year, the winter weather has always been good. We go swimming all the time. Winter or summer, I like to work in the evening, and I work until one, two o'clock, so I wake up late.

BRUMBACH: I got up late this morning, because I was up late last night, but normally, in the summer, I wake up about seven or seven-thirty, but there's no rush to get out of bed. I get my best work done in the evening, so I often don't get up until ten. At the moment, I'm not writing very much. I'm doing a great deal of catching up on reading. I have developed a great enthusiasm for Immanuel Kant, but he's difficult enough to understand in English, let alone Italian, so I order those books from the States, and it takes a couple of months for them to arrive. At one time, I contemplated writing a book about Italy, but I haven't been out of Positano for so long, I don't know what the rest of the country's like.

Cut off as you are, geographically, do you ever feel that you are in kind of a backwash here?

BRUMBACH: I've never felt any sense of that.

BAGIER: I'll tell you the truth. I think it's a good place for a young person to live for a couple of years or so. After that, I think you'd just get old and sort of lazy. I think it would be a perfect place for a writer, say, who's made a name and has a lot of contacts, and just wants to settle down. But I think a young person, after a couple of years, should sort of move on.

[To Casey Deiss, who had quietly come in and sat down on the floor] Do you think that a young person ought to get out of here after a couple of years?

DEISS: I don't feel like going anywhere. I just feel contented.

How long have you lived here?

DEISS: About three years here in Positano, but I've been coming to Europe since 1956. I went to school at the International School, in Geneva. Terrible school. At one point, it was probably good, but now it has become a sort of meeting place for all the children of American businessmen, military, and diplomatic corps. It's no longer truly an international school.

BRUMBACH: Talking about getting out of here, Casey and I did take one significant trip. We went to Czechoslovakia. We drove up in a little Fiat. That was very worthwhile. And Casey takes trips alone on his motorcycle all over Europe.

BAGIER: Quite a lot of American guys come cruising through here on their motorcycles. There's one named Les. His real full name is Leslie. He has a black motorcycle, which is his home. All he does is drive around Europe. He wears the big black leather jacket, tight blue jeans, black boots, and motorcycle cap—you know—the kind the big gangs wear, with badges and things on it. And he stands at the bar, looking cool, just like those guys in *On the Wild Side*. Man, when I first saw him standing like that, I thought, "This is it. There'll be bottles flying in a couple of minutes." But then he starts to talk, and you know, he's real sweet. He's got a very soft southern accent. You get to talking to him, and he says, "I wasn't accepted in the United States as an American. They always thought I was a foreigner. So, I decided to *be* a foreigner. Now Europe's my home." He's been riding this bike around for three years. He drives it about two miles an hour, like an old lady. He collects wild flowers, and presses them between leaves of a book. He also makes gravestone rubbings. He sends a lot of that stuff to his mother. He looks just like somebody out of one of those tough movies, but he's very sweet and nice, and he gives out over things. He came here and spent a whole afternoon just looking at my collages and other work. He's really groovy.

(*It was time for me to leave. I said goodbye to Will and Robin. Casey said he would go along with me to my car. Walking along in the dark, he was much more talkative than he had been inside.*)

DEISS: After I finished school over here, I went back to the States, and worked there for about a year. I lived in New York, on Twenty-fourth Street, and I walked to the place where I worked, which was on Fiftieth. Every day, walking back and forth, I saw the ashen look on the faces of the people I passed on the street. I figured that was no way to live. And there is so much hostility in the United States. You can't walk on the city streets without being afraid of encountering violence. It's very peaceful here. Also, if you want to be different—wear your hair differently, or a different kind of clothes, or whatever—nobody pays any attention. Nobody cares, which is another reason why I like living here.

> "These young people are looking for something that will open their eyes, that will make them much more alive than they have been."

Dr. Sidney L. Werkman is a Washington-based psychiatrist, who was living in Florence when I was there and whose views on young Americans abroad I found of great interest. We first talked about the subject one afternoon at a reception at the American Consulate, where we met. Dr. Werkman, an affable, outgoing man in his middle thirties, agreed to come to the hotel where I was staying at eleven o'clock the following morning to talk about the topic further. He arrived precisely on the hour, and it was evident soon after he had started talking that he had arranged his thoughts beforehand and also, since he had said that he would have to leave at twelve-fifteen, that he intended to impart them with a minimum waste of time.

WERKMAN: First, I had better give you some background. I am a psychiatrist at the George Washington Medical School, in Washington, and also in the Adolescent Clinic at a hospital in Washington. In addition, I am a senior psychiatric consultant to the Peace Corps, and have been for some time. Last year, I had planned to write a book on certain aspects of teaching psychiatry, but Peace Corps work took me to India and Nepal in February and then to Malaya in August, and while both trips were delightful experiences, they kept me from making any real progress with the book. Furthermore, I found that even when I was in Washington, between my professional work as a teacher, the government work, and the telephone, it was almost impossible to set aside time for writing. So, I arranged to come here to work on the book for a whole year, and right now, I'm thinking of staying longer, if I can. Florence has very much bit me.

I had been here before, and I have close friends who are Florentines. When I first arrived, I stayed with them for three weeks in a marvelous villa overlooking the town, had my breakfast brought in every morning, and enjoyed many other advantages that made the transition to Florentine life very easy. Coming into any foreign city is tough, if you're going to stay a long time, unless you are a student. As a matter of fact, the easiest entree into a way of life is the way of the student.

Fortunately, I was able to make use of that entree myself to a certain extent here. I studied Italian at the University for about a month in a rather desultory way, and I got to know a great many of the young people who are here, since I was in their classes, and the teacher treated me just like one of them. She was quite a bossy woman—and a total delight. She would say things like "Sidney, stop talking to Jean." Or, "Sidney, if you can't keep quiet in your chair, come up and write this on the board." Out of a class of fifteen, there were two other men and myself, and the rest were girls, almost all from eighteen to twenty. I learned about the interests of these girls through talking with them, and we made quite good friends. Age barriers are much less rigid here in Florence than they are in the United States—quite an important observation on why people come here and why, once here, they stay.

There are English girls here and American girls and Dutch girls—that is, those were the nationalities in our class. The English girls tend to come here and go to supervised schools, whereas the American girls go to school on their own. As a rule, the American girls have either finished junior college or taken one or two years of college and dropped out. A few have come from boarding school, and a few have finished actual college. They go either to the University of Florence or to the Centro per Stranieri—the Center for Strangers—which is the same idea as the university for foreigners in Perugia. The Centro is actually a part of the University of Florence. You make friends there when everybody is new in Florence, and, if not slightly bewildered, somewhat uncertain. And you find that the people you meet there remain very warm friends.

What were some of the reasons that brought the American girls here? To go to school, of course, but why here?

WERKMAN: I've talked to them at considerable length about this. Because of being a psychiatrist and because of the Peace Corps background, I am quite interested in why people do things. The girls here I am very impressed with. I think they have many of the same kinds of motivations that Peace Corps volunteers do, with some significant differences. Their backgrounds, almost entirely, are those of upper middle class families. I have found them universally to be gay, delightful, vivacious. In addition, they are girls who are dissatisfied with America. You have to push to hear this from them, or know them fairly well. They found that they were on a treadmill. They didn't want to go up to Yale for another weekend. They'd gone there and seen the drinking parties and perhaps had a good time at football games and whatever, but found there was an awful sameness to what occurs at Yale or at most of the other colleges they knew.

Most of the girls who came here, I should add, are attractive. They recognize that, being attractive and being part of a country club society in Darien, Connecticut, or Lake Forest, Illinois, or wherever, that they will probably meet a pleasant man and marry him. They're not frightened by that so much as appalled by it. They know that existence would be pleasant, but they are not attracted to it, partly because that is what their parents did. There has been a continuity and a regularity in their parents' lives, but often, in the eyes of these eighteen- and nineteen-year-olds, there has also been a pervading dullness. And they don't want that, even though the life is perfectly comfortable.

So, these young Americans are not coming to Florence for the reasons that the Italians of the 1890s came to America—to look for opportunities to make money and get ahead. These young people are coming to Florence to find life—to find something that will put meaning into their lives. And I think they choose Florence instead of Rome, for example, partly because they are looking for some artistic aspect to life. I think that the girls who go to Rome are looking for a jazzy time. There are exceptions, of course, but the general feeling here is that those who choose Rome are mainly interested in finding a movie actor with dyed hair to stand around in a bar with or go swimming with, et cetera. Quite a number of the girls here have been in Rome, and have had a wild time, and have had enough of it. After a while, they see that Rome has a kind of stale, hangover quality. In the minds of the girls here, Florence has much more solidity. It gives them much more reason for being. They really hope to learn about pictures, about architecture, and about the Renaissance.

Is the thing that concerns these young people most—and brings them here—the desire to avoid a life as full of dullness as their parents'? Dull, at least, as the children see it?

WERKMAN: The dullness is one of expectation. It is not necessarily lack of activity, but rather that one knows exactly what will happen over the next week, the next year, and the next ten years. The wish to come here is a rebellion against that. It's much more a seeking. You remember Salinger's "Frannie"—that short story about the girl, who is seeking something, and pulled away from her boy friend, saying time and again, "God have mercy on us." In psychiatric terms, she really retired from the world. She didn't try to look further into it. These girls are more vivacious, less philosophic, and less turned in upon themselves. They want to find something that will give them more real thrill. Many of them use the word "ecstasy," not in a cheap way but in the sense of "What will really make me stand on my toes?" These young people are looking for something that will open their eyes and make them much more alive than they have been.

Do you think they are finding what they came for?

WERKMAN: I think they are. Again, being a psychiatrist, I am much more attuned to the fact that I know a lot of them who sit at home at certain times and wonder what in the world they are doing in Florence. They wonder how they could be so lonely. Or they wonder whether they are really accomplishing anything.

I must say I've been surprised that many of the young people here have not gone into the Peace Corps, where I think the motivations of some of them would be better served even than in Florence. I believe one reason why they are here instead of in Nepal, for example, is that they come from environments that have been comfortable enough and self-centered enough so that they haven't really developed the concept of helping other people in a strong and enduring way. It's not that they don't want to. Their problem is that they are afraid they wouldn't be able to live in difficult surroundings for two years, and do all the other things that would be required of them in the Peace Corps. On the whole, I think they are a little less strong than Peace Corps volunteers.

In Florence, these young people are living in a city whose people are much warmer, much more overtly delightful, than the people in general that one knows, say, in Washington. The Florentines delight much more in small things in life. They are able to subsist without the sense of significance one needs in the United States. Here, the day-to-day workings of the world are of very little importance. The talk is much more about the pleasantries of life—a lovely party you attended, what the skiing was like on your holiday, where you are going at Eastertime. Among the settled families of Florence, one never talks business or work or about how much one has or hopes to have. People here are not weighed down with the question of whether they've been successful or not successful. The bitch god of success doesn't really exist in Florence, on my level of knowledge.

The warmth that runs all the way through life here goes beyond whether or not you're successful or particularly bright or witty or whatever. These things are incidental. What matters in the world of Florence are the relationships among people. I live in Arcetri, a tiny village outside of Florence. It is the village in which Galileo lived. It looks like something Rouault might have painted. The single street is very narrow and angulated, and on it is a *trattoria*, the only one in town. In the front is a delicatessen, and I have found that the owner is just as interested in selling fifteen cents' worth of delicatessen to me as he is in serving dinner to his most important customer. That attitude is general here. The result is that you feel that you are taken quickly into the community of Florence. If you didn't have a real friend in this city, you still could subsist by going to the delicatessen, the shoe repairman, and so on, and feel that you belonged.

Of course, the element of time is very different here. The fact that you're late for an appointment is not so important as it is in America. Actually, you don't make any appointments as such. For example, I am a musician, and I may want to get some old music. I don't quite know how to lay my hands on it, but I have a friend here, a Florentine, who would know. I also know that the chances are I'll run into him on the street in the next three or four days. When I do, I say, "Let's have a coffee," and we sit down and talk about the music. Now, this man is a working person, but in a completely impromptu way he'll take half an hour to talk with me, which would be most unlikely in any large city in the United States. Incidentally, the music is very good here, and I play a lot. Chamber music—string quartet and piano.

I have heard it said that the cultural level of a community can be gauged by the length of time it takes a newcomer to form or be admitted to a chamber music group.

WERKMAN: If that is so, it might be interesting to note that I was here only three days before I was playing in someone's house.

Going back to the young people, I gather from what you say that as a group they are here because they are seriously searching for something. Do you think that they are also running away from something?

WERKMAN: I think that all Americans living overseas by choice, myself included, are escaping from something. I think that many of us, in the course of our careers, whether we're eighteen or twenty-five or thirty-six, as I am, come to a point at times when we want to make a decision about what the next step should be. It is at these times that your usual ways of living seem most dull, most set, most unfortunately expectable. To say that you want to escape is true. I think it is a more admirable thing that what one attempts to do at that time is really to reconstitute, to look in, to look at what life is really about.

You can do that on many levels. You can become a hermit. You can go into the Peace Corps. You can enter a monastery or a nunnery. You can become a wild person. Et cetera, et cetera. But there is a point, either in words or in activity, where you find yourself saying, "This is not for me at this time and forever." The psychoanalyst, Erikson, has coined the term, "psycho-socio moratorium," for this. He spoke of it mostly in regard to college students—those who have the capability to finish college and get jobs after graduating but find themselves unaccountably stopped, as if they were an automobile that had just turned itself off. When that happens, they can either stay in Cambridge or Washington and stew or, perhaps more wisely, go away and get a better view of themselves. I think that the escape, to a very great extent, is the hope to elevate oneself, to have the sense of elevation. Not to get ahead, but to be able to realize a keener, higher, more sensitive way of living.

Coming to Florence offers this possibility to people, and, I think, gives it to them. I think Florence really pays off very well in helping one to deal with these questions of how one can enjoy every moment of life. Not necessarily that one wants to become a novelist or painter or whatever. Most of the girls I know here don't have tremendous ambitions for setting the world on fire. They do want to live. And they hope that Florence will offer this possibility to them. They will return, I think, better people.

As far as your own work is concerned, do you feel that you are making satisfactory progress on what you came here to do?

WERKMAN: I am, because I have a very charming and delightful secretary, and I feel guilty if I don't have work for her to do. Seriously, I think that one reason the work has gone well has to do with the matter of identity. In Washington, I am identified as a psychiatrist and as a person who works with people, not as a writer. So, I am not allowed to do things I can do here. For example, I have given up dinner parties here at the last moment, or said I wouldn't be able to go out with someone, because I am working. "Of course, I understand," the person here will say. They don't understand that in America, partly because their own time is considered to be so important. Here, there is that wonderful open sense of time.

One other thing: the attempt to live the life of the senses, though it's now a discredited concept, still exists here. And I would say very strongly—it's something I hope has been changed in me and will continue—that here you do look for pleasure in all kinds of art—in the art of the eye, the art of the ear, the extreme appreciation of sense experience that, unless you're a working artist in the United States, you find easy to forget. In America, you go to a gallery only because there is an opening or because a visitor has come to town or for some similar reason. Here, one doesn't need to go to galleries. You live in a world of art. You're in a world of delight everywhere.

GALLERY NOTES

"In Liverpool indeed, the Negro steps with a prouder pace, and lifts his head like a man;" wrote Herman Melville in *Redburn*, a work dealing with the voyage he made in 1837 as a youthful sailor from New York to Liverpool, "for here, no such exaggerated feeling exists in respect to him as in America. Three or four times I encountered our black steward, dressed very handsomely, and walking arm in arm with a good-looking English woman. In New York, such a couple would have been mobbed in three minutes; and the steward would have been lucky to escape with whole limbs. Owing to the friendly reception extended to them, and the unwonted immunities they enjoy in Liverpool, the black cooks and stewards of American ships are very much attached to the place, and like to make voyages to it." Melville further remarked that because he was very young and inexperienced at that time and also unconsciously swayed by prejudices "that are the marring of most men, and from which, for the mass, there seems no possible escape, at first I was surprised that a colored man should be treated as he is in this town; but a little reflection showed that, after all, it was but recognising his claims to humanity and normal equality; so that, in some things, we Americans leave to other countries the carrying out of the principle that stands at the head of our Declaration of Independence."

Today, a century and a quarter later, it is as disheartening to observe that the first principle is still not being carried out in America as it is to realize that Melville would nowadays be unable to comment with such approbation on the racial situation in England. Within recent years, there have been race riots in London, and barriers have been erected against colored immigrants. Those who do settle in England experience increasing difficulty in finding jobs and in renting living quarters not only in London but in many other English cities, including Liverpool. England is not the only European country to become infected with racism. It has happened in France since the massive Algerian immigration. It has happened in Russia since large numbers of African students were brought there to study. It has, in fact, happened to a certain extent in every country on the Continent, with the possible exception of Holland, where the number of colored residents is very small.

In spite of these developments, many American Negroes prefer to live in Europe. The reason is that while they may encounter prejudice, they do not encounter it as often or in forms as virulent as they do in the United States. It is a matter of degree. In Europe, Negroes still have a better chance than they do in America to have their claims to humanity and normal equality recognized.

With very few exceptions, the Negro Ameropeans are either writers, artists, musicians, singers, dancers, or in some other profession. (There is practically no opportunity in Europe for the unskilled American, either colored or white.) Among the handful of Negro Ameropeans who make a living in non-professional fields is Ray Hamilton, a thirty-five-year-old former Brooklyn car salesman, who now operates a chain of Laundromats and publishes an English-language newspaper in Augsburg, Germany. He is married to a German girl, whom he met while serving in the Air Force in Germany, and they have a son named Patrick. Life in Europe appeals to Mr. Hamilton not only because he has had to contend with little racial prejudice but also because his business enterprises are bringing him an income of about twenty-five thousand dollars a year. A young Negro Ameropean named Dolores Francine Rhiney, who was a drop-out from Washington Irving High School, in New York, is currently a popular model in Rome, where she is known professionally as Bambi. "I prefer Rome to any place I have ever lived," she has said. "No one gives a damn here if you are green, purple, or black."

The prevalence of this attitude was also remarked by a white American businessman named Herbert Lattes, who has lived in Rome since the end of the Second World War (he devotes mornings to his work, which is exporting marble, and the rest of the day to his hobby, which is photography) and who has a wide acquaintanceship among the American Negroes who have settled there, for many of whom he has provided financial assistance. "I have been willing to help them, not because they are a minority group but because I have found many friends among them," Mr. Lattes told me. "One of them is a dancer who is happily married to an Italian architect. They have two lovely children. Another of my Negro friends is a writer, who is married to an Italian woman. They also have a family. Nearly all of the Negroes here are in some branch of the entertainment business. They are dancers and singers or would-be dancers and singers—those whom I call 'the talented untalented.' They have talent but not enough to make it in the United States. Here, it's much easier. In Italy, if you can move two feet in a sort of rhythmic way, you're a dancer. Life in Italy is not so realistic as it is in the United States, so it is easier for the Negro entertainers here to nourish the illusion that success is just around the corner. Also, in Rome, they can sit at a sidewalk café and brush shoulders with a Hollywood director and maybe get acquainted —something that wouldn't be possible in New York. As for prejudice, I would say that it's nil. Negroes can live wherever they wish, so long as they are responsible tenants. And even the most conservative Italian, seeing a white man with a Negress, would not bat an eye. Instead, with the typical Mediterranean attitude, he would probably say, 'How lovely she is.'"

Economic opportunity is very seldom the reason that Negroes move to Europe. On the contrary, they may have to reduce their standard of living. William Gardner Smith, a novelist who moved to France in 1952, once remarked on the economics of transplantation. "I had been offered a job just before I left the States with a magazine, for a lot of money," he recalled. "And I said, 'No, I'm going to France.' The magazine editor came over here, and he saw me living in a little room in a hotel with cold water and horrible flowered wallpaper, and he said, 'You turned down my job for *that?*' And he didn't really understand when I said, 'Yes, exactly for that.'" Seven years ago, Providence Jenkins, who is thirty-eight, gave up a good-paying job as a hospital chemist in Cleveland to settle in Paris. He now lives in a sixth-floor walk-up apartment, and makes a precarious living as a translator. He does not regret the move. "I am not as afraid here," he says. When Edward Barnett, another Negro Ameropean, was a factory worker in America, he earned between five and six thousand dollars a year, lived in a three-room apartment, and drove a sports car. In 1960, when he was twenty-eight, he moved to Paris, where he earns considerably less as a free-lance photographer, has no car, and lives in a one-room apartment that has neither a bath nor a telephone, and costs him ten dollars more per month than the apartment he had in the United States. He nevertheless prefers the new existence, because he feels that it allows him to lead a more normal life. "Nobody is surprised here because I am black," he says. "I can meet Americans in all walks of life here, on neutral ground, and we can have a chance to get to know each other without the pressures of society trying to divide us."

The fact that the divisive pressures are less strong in Europe than in America has been remarked by other Negroes, including James Baldwin. Referring to his relationship with white Americans in Europe, he has written: "The fact that I was the son of a slave, and they were the sons of free men meant less, by the time we confronted each other on European soil, than the fact that we were both searching for our separate identities. When we had found these, we seemed to be saying, why, then, we would no longer need to cling to the shame and bitterness which had divided us so long." William Gardner Smith has recalled that the bitterness that he felt in the United States reached the point, after he had written three books, where he was unable to write any more. "I just didn't want to write, because I didn't want to communicate," he has said. "To communicate means you like the other person. You want to explain something to the other person." After living for a while in Europe, he found that his desire to communicate had returned, and he was able to write again.

The sense of expansiveness that springs from living in Europe has also been remarked by Gordon Heath, a personable Negro actor and singer who made his first trip to Europe in 1947 to appear in the London production of *Deep Are the Roots* and not long afterward settled in Paris, where he still lives. "When I arrived in London the first time," he told me, "there was that feeling of not knowing you had had a headache, but, finding it gone, you realized you must have had it all the time. I felt a kind of freedom, which is intensified about 2000 per cent in Paris. It's an extraordinary feeling to realize for the first time when people look at you, they don't begin by thinking, 'He's a Negro.' After a couple of years on this side, I suddenly felt that I could be a Negro, and it was rather fun. In Paris, it was regarded as an interesting attribute. In America, I had always been terrified of being a Negro. You know, avoiding fried chicken and watermelon and all that. I think the trouble with my generation was that they tied themselves up in knots, trying not to be Negro. In France, one doesn't feel that way. The atmosphere allows you to be yourself."

Probably the most conspicuous group of Negro Ameropeans consists of musicians, most of whom play jazz. One of the few exceptions is Mattwilda Dobbs, a beautiful, forty-two-year-old soprano, who has sung in most of the famous European opera houses, including La Scala (she was the first Negro to sing in that house), Milan, Covent Garden, and was the third Negro (after Marian Anderson and baritone Robert McFerrin) to be signed by the Metropolitan in New York. She sang for the first time at the Metropolitan in 1956, as Gilda in *Rigoletto*. The fifth of six daughters of a railway clerk, Miss Dobbs is a native of Atlanta, Georgia, where she early showed a remarkable aptitude not only for music but also for academic studies, and later received a number of musical scholarships that enabled her to study in New York and in Europe. After making her operatic debut at La Scala, in 1953, she was married to a Spanish journalist, who died not long afterward. Her second husband, to whom she was married in 1957, is a Swede named Bengt Janzon, who was then the public relations director of the Royal Opera of Stockholm; he gave up that job to become her impresario. They divide their time among three residences—an apartment in Stockholm, a house in Hamburg, Germany (Miss Dobbs is the leading coloratura of the State Opera there), and a villa on the Spanish island of Majorca. She has the reputation of being the most modest of all the prima donnas, and scarcely ever mentions that she may be the only one among them who has a masters degree. She earned it at Columbia University.

The number of jazz musicians among the Negro Ameropeans is so large that their moving to Europe has been called "the third greatest migration in the history of jazz." The first migration, from New Orleans to Chicago, took place during and in the years soon after the First World War. The second, from Chicago to New York, occurred around the turn of the thirties. The third, from America to Europe, has largely been a phenomenon of the period following the Second World War. Those who have made the third migration include several who would have to be included in any history of jazz—among them, Bud Powell, Kenny Clarke, Albert Nicholas, and the late Sidney Bechet. Paris has always been the favorite city of the jazz musicians as well as of other Negro Ameropeans (altogether, some fifteen hundred live there at present), but Copenhagen has also become popular, and so have Amsterdam, Munich, Berlin, Madrid, and Rome.

The fact is that every large city in Western Europe now has a colony of Negro Ameropeans. When asked why they prefer living abroad, they usually say, at first, that the life there is more comfortable, more relaxing, or something of the sort—the standard reasons, as William Gardner Smith has called them. "I can give the standard ones," he has said, "like I *do* like that cliché of the sunset on the Seine, I *do* like coming home late and seeing the light at five o'clock in the morning. And I like waving to the coal bargers when they pass the Vert Galant. 'I like the twisting streets,' Gordon Heath says, when he's asked why he stays in France instead of going back to the States, 'I can't stand straight streets.' And I like the slowness. It's not really slow, but what I mean is, I was delighted when I first came here and discovered that after a while, I didn't feel guilty any more when I sat on a cafe terrace all afternoon. At first, it was horrible. And I notice when Americans come over now, and I say, 'Sit down and have a drink,' they sit down, and after half an hour they get nervous, and say, 'Shouldn't we go and see a museum or go someplace?' " But, behind the standard reason, Mr. Smith pointed out, lies the real one: to escape the effects of racial prejudice in the United States. This applies to all Negro Ameropeans. "They are our new pioneers," Janet Flanner remarked when we were talking in Paris. "They went east to find freedom—or at least, a greater measure of freedom."

> "It's not cheap to live in Paris any more,
> and I don't earn fabulous sums, like in
> Las Vegas, but I get along better here."

Hazel Scott, the Trinidad-born concert pianist and singer and former wife of Congressman Adam Clayton Powell, Jr., has kept an apartment in Paris since 1958. "I'm sort of a wanderer," she remarked when I called on her there one afternoon. "I work all over Europe, the Near East, the Middle East, South America. In 1961, I was in Brazil. My son met me there, and we went back to Paris. He said, 'Well, here we are. I think we should stay.' And we did." Her son, Adam Clayton Powell III, who is known as Skipper, was then fourteen. He attended school in France for two years, and then returned to the United States, where he graduated from prep school, and entered M.I.T. when he was seventeen. Miss Scott stayed on in Paris, again at her son's suggestion.

MISS SCOTT: At that time, he said, "Look"—we have always been very frank with each other, a wonderful relationship—"I want to tell you something. You know, Mops,"—he never calls me "Mother" unless it's a crisis—"there's something I've noticed about you, and it's even more marked since you've been in Europe. You were never one to mince words or to bite your tongue about anything that came up—much to your and our regret sometimes—but on the whole it's been a pretty good thing, because it's taught me the value of respecting the truth, in spite of what may happen. At the same time, you've managed to have a certain tact that living in the United States does force you to have. While living in Europe, though, you've gotten used to coming out with *exactly* what you feel like saying, *exactly* when you feel like saying it, and devil take the last fellow over the fence. I think, Mops, that the best thing for you, actually, would be to stay in Europe and, you know, fight the battle from over here, because you just don't have the weapons that we need any more."

He was telling me in a very sweet and extremely sort of tactful way,

"Darling, this is a new generation, and while I know I'm young and all that, I'm still a bit more with it than you are at the moment. You're used to coming out and saying, 'Well, now, what is this? What's going on? Why is this so?' Instead of that, one now says, 'This is not going to be thus and so any longer. I intend to do exactly this about it. There is no chip on my shoulder. There is no need for it.'" That is the essence of what he was saying, and I understood. I remember he also told me, "You'll make a lot less money in Europe, but you'll be a lot happier."

Well, that's the way it has turned out. It's not cheap to live in Paris any more, and I don't earn fabulous sums, like in Las Vegas, but I get along better here. The best part about life here is the thing that, according to my son, spoiled me for living in the States: the feeling of freedom, of being able to say what you think and to live wherever you wish. The *only* thing that would prevent you from living *wherever* you might wish would be not having enough money. Nothing else stands in your way. That is wonderful.

Of course, to a certain extent, prejudice exists everywhere. In England, there is a great deal. I couldn't live in London unless I had to work there. I certainly wouldn't enjoy it the way I enjoy living in France. I could even live easier in Germany than I could in England. The Scandinavian countries I love. Italy? Charming. But there's something very special about France. Still, even the French have a racial feeling about a North African or an Arab. I was in a restaurant last summer where they were talking about the freedom in France, and one of the men said, "Yes, but what about the Algerians?" And the whole picture fell into a million pieces, because the other man said, "That's different. They're not people." I said, "*What?* How can you *say* such a thing? You just got through telling me how my qualities are appreciated here without your having to look at my skin, and then you do a complete about-face in the case of the Algerian. How is that possible? How is that logically possible?" He said, "Oh, you just don't understand." I said, "No, I don't understand. I'd like you to help me." He couldn't, of course. Blind prejudice can never be explained.

I had my own way of dealing with the problem in the United States when I was on a concert tour. I insisted on playing in the South, and at first I insisted on having in my contract a clause which provided that if the audience was segregated, the manager would forfeit half my fee, and I wouldn't have to go on. Later, when I was represented by Columbia Concerts, it was considered unnecessary to include the clause. I played the Deep South, and I had only one incident. That was at the University of Texas, where there was a misunderstanding, because the local Columbia man hadn't followed instructions. I didn't get any fee, and I had to pay my train fare and other expenses, but that was that. The misunderstanding resulted in a lot of publicity, which I didn't like, because I had been managing things very quietly. A lot of people may not have agreed with my way, but it seemed right to me. I have no taste for going to jail. I don't think it's chic to go to jail. I don't think it's good. I don't think it's right. I am *willing* to go to jail, but I wouldn't enjoy it for a minute. So, in order to avoid being arrested in the South, I wouldn't use the "Colored" entrance, and I wouldn't use the "White" entrance. I used the Yellow Cab entrance. I was always met at the theater by several people of whichever group happened to be giving the concert—white or Negro—and they would be in front of whichever entrance they were going to use. I would just have the taxi stop in front of the group that was meeting me. I would join them, and we would go on in. I always stayed with a Negro family, because, of course, I couldn't have a hotel room, but my concerts were completely desegregated. I did that from 1945 on. In those days, a great many people in the South said, "You're out of your mind. You're bucking a system that will never be broken." That's why today I laugh. It seems ironic.

Actually, as you have said, you were working for civil rights before it was called that, and, of course, you still are. I wonder how the current racial situation in America strikes you from here.

MISS SCOTT: Seen from over here? Of course, it's very close to me—my son's in the midst of it all. You do feel a little removed, but you can keep informed here, if you watch the telecasts. Naturally, every country slants the news their way. This is universal, but if you read certain newspapers and periodicals, you can keep abreast. I've looked at that television screen and seen these people who are quietly kneeling and praying and singing "We Shall Overcome." They're not preaching violence. They are not preaching racial hate. And they are being attacked. In other words, if I am to understand anything at all out of this madness, the people who are preaching hate are correct. But I don't *believe* in violence, in racial hate. My God, I don't see what can come of it. It's war. It's total war.

I once met Malcolm X here in Paris. He was coherent. He was concise. He was deliberate. He was articulate. He exposed ideas that had never occurred to me, and he elaborated upon things I had first heard as a little girl of four, when I was brought to the United States from Trinidad. My mother was preparing me, though I didn't realize it, for the inevitable clash with the outside world. We lived in an all-white neighborhood at that time, and it was explained to me that I was different, but not why or what difference that made. My father, on the other hand, was a great admirer of Marcus Garvey, who was extremely militant as a black man. My father was a black nationalist in his heart and in his thinking. I inherit a great deal of that from him. On the other hand, I inherit my mother's humanity. The two, I think, go toward the making of a good amalgam. As a result, I can feel as much pain, and, momentarily, I can feel as much hatred as any black nationalist. But my motivation is not hatred. I cannot be guided by that. I cannot be led by that. I have a much longer, more all-embracing view and one that's much more involved than simple blind hate. That's too easy. Hate is too easy.

How do you manage when you're with French people or other Europeans and they criticize the United States on racial grounds?

MISS SCOTT: Oh yes, it's a bit painful. You find yourself defending the entire United States. As a black American, it gives you a strange feeling, because they look at you as if to say, "Are you *mad?* Are you completely out of your mind?" It's sort of like a family. You say, "Let me say it. Don't you say it." It's that sort of feeling, you know. I won't let anybody who's not American condemn America. I just won't have it. No, no.

Actually, since the assassination of President Kennedy, I have tried to keep my mouth shut. There the world lost a statesman. It lost a fine human being. And I lost a personal friend. Since that happened, well, I have just not had much to say about America to anyone. I just say to my French friends, "Let's change the subject, shall we? Let's talk about something else, because I really do not want to discuss it." Which is the best way when you cannot say that they are wrong. There's no point in going on endlessly with people who are fixed in their ideas and whose ideas happen to be sound and with whom you secretly agree. If you cannot agree with them out loud, well, then you're a hypocrite, so forget about it, and talk about something else. No, I don't discuss politics with Europeans any more. Oh dear.

Do you have any plans ever to return to the United States to live?

MISS SCOTT: I was first asked that question by my son in a radio interview in Boston. He's news director of WUBS—University Broadcasting Service—at M.I.T. When he asked if I thought I'd ever come back to America to live, I said, "No." He said, "Definitely?" I said, "Definitely." I could come back to visit, but I could never come back to live. That's terrible, isn't it? But it's true. You see, I'm quite comfortable in Paris. It's very accessible. I've seen more friends since I've made my headquarters in Paris than I would normally run into in the States in years. Everybody comes through here, and, of course, I have a lot of good friends who live here. There is no single American settlement—everyone is sort of scattered—and that's one of the things I like. You have the right to be an individual. That is worth almost anything. If I get a job in the States, I'll go back and work, but no matter how long the duration, I'll return to Europe. I'm not European, but I'm Parisian. It's funny, isn't it?

"Over here, one gets a little perspective on a lot of things."

Harold Bradley, a tall, well-built, handsome Negro, who speaks slowly and softly in a deep voice, was a professional football player until he made his first trip to Europe, at the close of the 1959 football season, and liked what he saw so much that he decided to remain. An art major in college, he has made his living in Europe partly by painting and partly by singing and acting—a considerably different life from anything he had known at home. He lives with his wife, a dark-haired German girl whom he met in Italy, and their two very fair and beautiful daughters—the elder is three and the younger, eight months—in an apartment consisting of two rooms and a hallway in an old building in the Trastevere section of Rome. When I called there, the baby was sleeping in the family bedroom, so Mr. Bradley, his wife and elder daughter, and I sat in the rather crowded living-dining room. Throughout our conversation, the daughter either sat quietly in her father's lap or stood beside his chair, listening attentively. Mrs. Bradley, who busied herself with sewing and other chores, also listened in silence until, toward the end of my visit, she added some comment of her own to her husband's observations on living in Europe. Before that, he had talked briefly about his life in the United States and about the development of his multiple careers.

BRADLEY: I started painting when I was four years old. That interested me. My father wanted me to be a football player. He thought sports were a wonderful thing. As it turned out, both art and football became my means of expression. I wasn't always the most willing football player. When I got my nose bumped the first few times, I was not so enthusiastic about it. My mother wasn't, either. She used to cry. My father didn't push me. He didn't say, "Come on, we'll go out and run a mile today." I did it mostly on my own. After you get over a few hard knocks and a few kicks in the face and a few teeth missing, you keep going. I suppose you feel it can't get any worse. I was a slow starter at football. I'm still a slow starter in whatever I do, but after I've gained a certain amount of experience, you can't beat me too easily.

I was an art student at the University of Iowa—a painter. I suppose I do portraits best. I could probably make a living as a portrait painter. Of course, I also played football in college. I graduated in 1951, and went right into the Marine Corps. I played football in the service, too. After that, I played five years of professional ball—one with the Philadelphia Eagles and four with the Cleveland Browns. I was a guard on offense. That was my field, in a sense, my money-making field. But I didn't neglect the other career. When the football season was over, I went back to painting, and in Cleveland, I also taught painting and drawing.

I came over here originally to paint, and I also wanted to absorb a little of the old Europe before it changed too much. The subject matter that had always appealed to me most in the States were the things that abound in tradition—the old sections of cities, the old gingerbread type of architecture, and other things that had that special quality. So, the environment here—the monuments, the architecture, the sense of history—naturally appealed to me. I decided to stay for a while. I thought I'd use the G.I. Bill to go to school and study the history of art, but you couldn't study the history of art unless you knew the Italian language. The best place to learn it, I found, was at the university in Perugia, where they have a school for foreigners. So, I went there for two years, and I am now fairly fluent in Italian. That's where I met my wife—at Perugia. She was also a student.

Where had she come from?

BRADLEY: From Berlin. She's German. She had learned English before we met. Otherwise, we probably wouldn't have become acquainted. In Perugia, I established myself as a painter. I was painting and exhibiting in Perugia and Florence and Spoleto. One thing I missed was the environment of the night clubs I used to go to in Chicago, which is my home town. My father had gotten me interested in jazz music. He had a record player, and he and his friends used to listen to jazz music and discuss it. It was for them a fountain of artistic endeavor.

Was your father a musician?

BRADLEY: No, he was a government employee and an amateur athlete. His interest in music was just for his own pleasure. In Perugia, I missed music so much. I missed bathtubs, too, in a sense, because they didn't have too many around there. Well, I couldn't do anything about bathtubs or night clubs, but I decided to do something about music. I started singing. The only song I knew at that time was "Old Man River." The Italian friends I'd met at the University encouraged me. I sang on programs at the university, and I met musicians there, and I also met some jazz musicians in Florence. Next thing you know, I was singing all over the place. *I* enjoyed it, at least. That was the main thing—that I was enjoying myself.

My life in Perugia took on another dimension that I hadn't expected. I got introduced to the film business there. They were looking for extras to participate in a film they were doing in Assisi—something about the life of St. Francis. Several of my friends said to come on over and see if there would be anything for me. I did, and I was chosen for a Saracen role, of all things. The next thing, I had everybody on the set pretty excited, because the part called for a leader-type, and I always considered my face pretty good for expression. Also, the director felt likewise. And a lot of other people in the production tried to talk me into coming to Rome and getting into acting. I did come here, in the beginning of 1961, and I have since worked in many films. I got typed as a strong, mean type—one of the bad ones—but I took it all in my stride, being good-natured about these things.

It was after I got to Rome that the singing also became of some importance. Originally, I had intended to settle down here and make a living as a painter. I found a studio that I divided with a sculptor friend. Then I met an English fellow who had a good voice, and we teamed up and began singing in a restaurant in Trastevere. We didn't keep at that very long, because the boss seemed to think we wanted to sing just for the pleasure of it. After that, I gathered together a number of my friends who played guitars and were interested in folk songs, and we started meeting in my studio—just friends. Little by little, people began hearing about us, and they started coming to listen. To give them something to sit on, we used to borrow benches from the local churches and chairs from the bars. We didn't charge admission—just passed the tambourine around the way they do in certain churches on State Street in Chicago. We decided that that was a little humiliating, so we organized the place as a private club. That way, you can avoid all the licenses and so on that you have to have if you open a night club. We decided to call our club Folk Studio, because its purpose was primarily to further the cause of folk music. It's been two years now since we opened it.

Is it doing well?

BRADLEY: Pretty well. Recently, I brought most of my painting equipment and materials back here to give us more space at the Studio. Although we have folk music mainly—I am master of ceremonies and one of the mainstays—we also have poets and actors who recite things. We've had a lot of famous people come and perform there when they're passing through town—Bob Dylan, Langston Hughes, Pete Seeger, Odetta—and *Time* published a nice article about the Studio. We get quite a lot of people, but it doesn't bring in much income. Our life here is a struggle.

It must have taken a good deal of courage to give up that steady, good-paying job with the Browns to come over here to pursue a career as an artist.

BRADLEY: Well, I am always interested in developing my sensitivity as an artist, and when it took on other dimensions, such as acting and singing, this excited me. Those were talents that I wanted to develop, and you never know what can happen here. If you go back to the States, you can make good money, all right, but now I have a wife and children, and if you go back there, you have that horrible situation —the prejudice and the race hate. You never know what effect that will have. Here, you don't have any of that problem in this sense. They have never had the problem, naturally, that we have had in America. They've never had Negro slaves. They've never had a mass population of Negroes to deal with. If they had, they might have reacted in the same way that Americans, unfortunately, have traditionally reacted. I would say that the European is too complacent in his attitude about the Negro.

Too complacent?

BRADLEY: Too complacent in the sense that he thinks, "Well, we don't have to worry. We don't have that problem. We love everybody." I have often asked an Italian or a Frenchman, "What would you do if you had a mass of Negroes, because, instead of having developed a race of white slaves, as you did in medieval times, you had had Negro slaves?" They don't really know, and I don't know. They just say, "Oh here, there's no problem." That's all very true on the surface, but underneath there may be some questions. I don't think very many Europeans are willing to marry Negroes, either, especially when the mass of people have a provincial mentality. They don't easily break the boundaries.

They have many stereotypes here, too. Kids come up to me and say, "Bongo! Bongo!" They have gotten a stereotype through the comic strips, so when they see a dark face, they think of this idea of savages cooking a white man in a pot and dancing around and saying, "Bongo! Bongo!" And in the films they see here, the government doesn't screen out the places where the Negro is seen as a savage in the jungle.

Do you think that the idea of coming to a country where discrimination is so much less widespread and severe than it is in the United States played an important part in your decision to come here?

BRADLEY: No, because I didn't ever have a problem in the States. I mean, I am a mixture of several races, though I am certainly considered a Negro. In a sense, I was never too aware of it, you know. Living as an athlete in the States, you have a different frame of mind. In Chicago, I attended a mixed high school—Englewood High—and we used to have little romances with girls of any color. No problems there. When I was at the University of Iowa, I tried to date a girl or two of some other color, and it wasn't the most comfortable feeling, even in a place like Iowa City, where I was pretty well known and where I always thought I could go back and be elected mayor, but personally, I never had a problem there. I never had the problem as football player, either. I was just another American. Sure, I've been called a black bastard sometimes when I've been playing, you know, to intimidate me. Never fazed me too much. I just thought, "I'd like to give that guy a punch in the jaw, if I can." I tried to stick to my responsibility as a player. That was the main thing with me. I've always tried to stick to my responsibility in all these things—as a painter, actor, singer. I've always tried to keep that first in mind, and the other thing comes after. I've always been able to calm myself emotionally.

Over here, one gets a little perspective on a lot of things. The distance, or the perspective that you gain through your experiences, helps things to mature. It's like when you're too close to a painting, too involved in it—you don't really see it. Get five meters away, and the frailties start showing up, and so do the good things. You need that space to see things clearly. I needed that space to decide whether to stay here or go back. You know, I wasn't getting any younger. I'm thirty-four now. I always thought I could go back and play football until I was forty, because I never drink or smoke or anything. When you're a football player, when you're making eight, ten thousand dollars a year, and you're single, you don't have too many problems. You certainly don't have any contact with the everyday problems that normal people have. Over here, I started to face those problems. What was it I wanted to be? Should I accept the challenge over here or in the States? I decided to stay here, because I had an opportunity here to do things artistically that I probably couldn't do as easily in the States. I think perhaps my maturity as a man has started over here. I have started finding out what people really are. And I think, too, that I have become a little more Negro here than I was in the States.

What do you mean?

BRADLEY: I have found that my roots—well, I've dug my roots a little deeper. I've sort of transplanted myself inwardly further down into Negro lore. It gives me a little more purpose, because I am one who is tied up mentally with the good and the bad and the just. I am looking for justice, no matter what a man's color is. I think justice is the one thing in the world that is the least realized.

My father's philosophy is quite concise. He says, "Do something for the race, son." And when he says that, he means it. He's very dark, and he married a very light-skinned woman. He said, "Now I've done my part. I've got some beautiful children. If everybody got together and married without any hesitation about color and just went ahead and had children, that would solve the race problem." I'm sure he'll be very happy to see his grandchildren. He hasn't yet, but my mother has been here. Of course, the typical attitude in the United States toward intermarriage is that this leads to the mongrelization of the race. There has always been that sort of fearful, stupid, thoughtless attitude about intermarriage among the races. This apart, I met my wife, and I like her for what she is. I'm not trying to do anything for the race in that respect. I'm sure my father would be pleased. But it just happened that way.

Some people have said that discrimination against Negroes is practically non-existent here. Have you found that to be the case? Have you had any trouble, for example, in renting an apartment?

BRADLEY: No, but foreigners generally may be having a little more trouble with landlords here because of the beatniks, who run off without paying their rent. We have had no difficulty renting an apartment, though rents are high. For this apartment—just two rooms and an entrance hall—we're paying sixty-five dollars a month.

As for discrimination generally, I would say that, superficially at least, the situation is good. One can have a certain prestige here as an actor or an entertainer. I'm in that position now. A lot of people like me because they have seen me on the screen or on television. I get along pretty well. I think I've made some of the first real friends I've ever had in my life here. Of course, I made friends in the States, too. Most of my buddies there were athletes, but I never felt real friendship until I came here.

And these friends are all Italians?

BRADLEY: Yes. As I say, if you're a Negro entertainer or an actor, there can be a certain kind of hero-worship, but I think the Italian must also ask himself, "Would I let my daughter marry a Negro?" or, "Would I let my son marry a Negro girl?" The Italians went to Ethiopia, you know. And they didn't go down there to love thy neighbor. It was a short war—a kind of thirty-day excursion tour. They don't remember that, of course. In places like Somaliland, where the Italians have remained as rulers or administrators, they have done a certain number of things for the people. They have tried to lead them to government, and they have intermarried down there. You know, superficially, the Italians and Negroes have a lot of the same sort of interests. The Italians are noted as musicians and singers. They also have a sort of open quality, which is also a stereotype of the Negro. They both have a relaxed nature. Then there is the interest in sex. The great lovers are supposed to be Italians. And so on.

Maybe the Italian is basically a good person, but he certainly deludes himself. I mean, he has never won a war, and he has really been a fascist himself, but if you look at the Italian films, like *Four Days in Naples* and a lot of the others about the war, you'd think they were our allies during the Second World War. There's such a paradox here. The whole history of this nation must perplex historians, if they come here and live with the Italians and get to know them. How can they believe that these are the people who created the Roman Empire? My God, the whole story must be a fabrication. At least, it has been very badly misunderstood by the historians, because you find no trace of those great qualities that built the Roman Empire pervading life here today. You find no traditions here that are strong and good. The whole scheme of things here is decadent. There is such a lack of sensibility and purpose and virility. The traditional theater here is nothing. I have been acting with a private group, the Teatro delle Arti, but it's very hard to run a theater here. You have to have state support, belong to the right set, and all that. There's the same lack of sensibility in art. I think Chicago probably has better painters than Rome—more sensitive art than I find here.

Have you considered going back to Chicago?

BRADLEY: I don't really think about it, because I'm so tied up here. I miss my parents and my grandmother and some of the stores and sights and smells. I yearn for them, but I have other things here. As an observer and as an artist, perhaps I don't miss things as keenly as people in other fields do. I feel pretty much at home here, and I'm making ends meet—just. Some months are very good, and other months are pretty low. I depend altogether on income from the work I am doing, especially in the field of acting at present, and that's chancy. I sold one painting recently, but I haven't exhibited my paintings here. I don't have an agent or a gallery here, because they are not reliable. The Italians promise you the world, and nothing happens. It's not only that they are not reliable, but they tend to take advantage of one another whenever possible. You encounter this attitude in every walk of life, even among foreigners living here, because it's a contagious thing. You can trust no one. You get so fed up with it. The little twists of things to do you out of something. The little papers they put under the meat on the scales to up the weight. The television set in the apartment when you rent it, and then before you move in, they remove it. "Oh no, that doesn't go with the apartment." All the little gyps. That is one of the reasons I would like to go back to the States and stay six months or so every now and then.

But you have not actually been back at all, have you?

BRADLEY: No, not since I came over. I tell my wife sometimes that we should go back. Financially, it would be better. I know that. I could play football. There would be no problems. There are intermarriages there. She doesn't really want to go, though. The Americans she has met here in Europe, generally speaking, she doesn't care for. I defend Americans as much as possible. I say, "You must go and see for yourself. You can't base your judgment of Americans on the American who comes to Europe, either the serviceman or the tourist."

MRS. BRADLEY: We have very nice American friends, whom I personally appreciate very much, but if you start a little digging into their backgrounds, you find that the nicest ones have had European educations, or originally came from here. They are naturalized Americans. The nicest people tell me, "Oh, you must go to the States. You will love it." They talk about all of the Europeans who are taking advantage of all the comforts of living there. Well, I don't know whether that's the most important thing in life—comfort. I was brought up under very strict rules. I cannot, for instance, think I could follow a saying like, "Take it easy," or "Keep smiling." If something goes wrong, I'm feeling bad. I can't take it easy, and I can't keep smiling. My whole personality is like that. I am different, you know. I have had a terribly classical education, so I think I can participate in any kind of conversation, no matter what the speciality is of the person I'm talking to, whether he's a lawyer, a medical doctor, a historian. Whereas if you get a lot of Americans who have had the same amount of education I've had in the same situation, they are lost. Americans say they don't know, but they are willing to learn. That's very nice—to be willing to learn—but it's better to know.

So, as your husband has said, the experience that you've had with Americans generally has not been such that you would be encouraged to think it would be pleasant to live among them.

MRS. BRADLEY: Oh, I am sure it could be pleasant living there, but I am not a pleasant liver.

Perhaps I should have said that you would not expect to find the life there congenial.

MRS. BRADLEY: It's not so much congenial. Only financial. Look, if I had money in the safe, I am sure I could get out of the States what I get out of living here. I know that dressmakers cost more, but with the right kind of money, I can get myself a Dior model as well in Chicago probably as I can get it here. And be elegant all the same. But if you aren't able to make a good living here, why should I go to the States? Here, if there are financial problems, I can quickly go home.

And also I have maybe not so much racial trouble. I am a little bit scared of this, because I have had a lot of this in my own life, when I was young. I've been through it, and I don't feel like going through it again. I married my husband because I love him, not because of any race, but I'm not feeling up to fighting now. Here, it's different. My husband's home country is not the same as mine, but here we're both treated as foreigners, and foreigners are expected to be a little crazy.

BRADLEY: There are so many misunderstandings in Europe about the real America. It's Utopia in a sense, perhaps. At least, the good things about America are utopian in nature. The mixture of all the races is what created what's true about America. A lot of things about America are false, and America is on shaky moral and spiritual legs in many ways, but there is so much good about America to be taken in a missionary sense to other countries. I didn't live as a family man in

America, but the virtues of America I understand and know, and they are worth fighting for. I would like to be in that fight for integration. But I think the greatest fight in life is the fight against ignorance, which is the cause of segregation and racial hatred. There's a great deal of ignorance in Europe and a great deal to do right here where we are. If I can do that and somehow make a living—my wife is comfortable here, and she's helping me fight—and if my children can grow up without too much struggle and strife, and we can help them beat the ignorance rap, then we'll stay here. I can fight as much for America right here in Rome as I can in Chicago. Here we are, and here we're going to stay, at least for the time being.

> "Here, you can go where you want to go, do what you want to do. You can even forget you're a Negro, if you let it happen to you."

Mae Mercer, a tall, slender, attractive Negro singer in her late twenties, grew up in Rocky Mount, North Carolina, where she began singing professionally at the age of eight. "I began as a spiritual singer," she told me. "I had a group in church, and I started appearing in different churches, and then on the radio, and it just went on from there to night clubs, records, concerts." In the spring of 1962, she signed a contract to appear in a Paris night club called the Blue Spot, in the Rue Saint-Séverin. "I had a contract for three months, and I'm still here," she said. "I've done night clubs and theaters and movies since I've been over here, but I won't work in any more cabarets. It's too hard. I do only concerts now. You do an hour show, and you're finished. It's a more normal life. I go all over on concerts—the Middle East, London, Spain, Copenhagen, Israel—but I've kept my headquarters here." When I called on her, she was living in an apartment on the top, or fifth, floor of a building near the Place Madeleine. The elevator happened to be out of order, and the lights in the hall were out—conditions that had prevailed for a couple of days, Miss Mercer told me after I had negotiated my way to her pleasant, rather casually furnished apartment. She was wearing a skirt and a flowered blouse and a sweater over her shoulders. It was a chilly morning in early spring, and a fire was burning in the small fireplace in her living room. We sat opposite each other in front of the fireplace. Miss Mercer has a fine, engaging smile as well as a steady, direct gaze with which she fixes one when she is talking about matters that are close to her. I asked her if she had had any trouble renting a place to live in Paris.

Miss Mercer: No, there's no problem about that, if you're willing to pay. The people over here are grabbing for every cent they can get. Actually, they are picking up a lot of habits from the Americans over here. They've spoiled so many things. The rents in many places were cheap once, but now they're very expensive. It's because Americans didn't care. They wanted a place, and they would pay whatever they had to. I don't live that way any more. I find places to live through my French contacts, so I don't pay that ridiculous rent. And I shop for food like the French do. I go to the market myself whenever I have time.

I've always had my own place here, except for a couple of months when I lived with Jean Seberg and her husband, Romain Gary. There's a real American girl—Jean Seberg. You don't find them like her every day. She's one of my good friends. She came to a club where I was working, and we started talking. I'd just come back from the Middle East, and was looking for an apartment. She said, "Why don't you come and live with us?" It wound up that I did. She and her husband are lovely people. I was working, I could have afforded to pay, but they wouldn't let me.

Had you been in Europe before you came over to sing in the Blue Spot?

Miss Mercer: I'd never been out of the States. After signing that contract, I decided I didn't want to go through with it, because I'd be so far from my family. But, of course, I had to, and now I'm glad that I did. Life is better here. You work hard, but you can relax more than you can at home, because in America we don't take time for anything. We don't have sidewalk cafes, because we don't have time to sit down for a minute. We're too afraid we're going to miss something—some business. We sit up in the office and have lunch. Just running all the time. Over here, you just have to stop rushing.

Also, you're more comfortable, because you don't have to say to yourself, "Who is this I'm talking to?" You can say anything you want to say, if you choose to. In the States, it's supposed to be so free, but you can't say what you want to say. I know, because I experienced a lot of things in America when I was sixteen years old, in Florida. I know quite a bit about the life over there. Here, you can go where you want to go, do what you want to do. You can even forget you're a Negro, if you let it happen to you. You can actually forget it.

It's also true that my career has blossomed here, and that is a very agreeable thing, but I wouldn't say I'm going to live here the rest of my life. I'm going to the States for a concert in July, but I will come back. In a way, I'm looking forward to going to America, and in a way, I'm afraid. I don't know how I will react. I've been away for a long time. Actually, I'm very afraid of it. With the way the situation is in the States now, I don't know how I can get accustomed to living home again, and really be happy.

I wouldn't say that you get away from everything over here, because there is prejudice all over the world. I didn't come here for that reason. That didn't influence my decision to come here at all. But since I've been here, I have felt completely different about it.

How does prejudice show itself here?

MISS MERCER: First of all, there's the prejudice against Americans.

Do you think the French are ruder to you because you are an American than they are to other Europeans or to Asians or as they are to one another?

MISS MERCER: Not all of the people in France are rude. If you know how to handle them, they aren't. You just have to tell them this and that, and they'll go along with you. I haven't had but three arguments since I've been here. Those all happened soon after arriving, and had to do with the landlords putting keys in my door and coming in. I told them, "I'm paying my rent. Don't come into my place, unless I ask you to." You can't be nice, saying it. You have to be as rude as they are. They like to argue. I think their greatest thrill is arguing. But they can be very nice people.

Were you able to speak French when you arrived?

MISS MERCER: No. The French they teach in America is no good when you get here. I must say we're behind on that. The way I learned the language was just listening to the people talk. Now I can understand what I want, and I can say what I want, but I prefer not to speak it too much. If people ask me if I speak French, I usually say, "Just a little," because if people think you don't speak the language, you learn more. You can listen instead of joining in. I know some songs in French, but I don't sing them, because I am an American singer. Incidentally, on the last tour, I did twenty-four one-nighters in a row. I haven't had a vacation in two years.

So you haven't been in America and seen what's been going on for quite some time?

Miss Mercer: No, but I have friends who are constantly coming through, and they say the situation is very bad. It will improve. It's got to. Being an American, I am actually ashamed. You feel that you're carrying the whole weight on your shoulders. The people just don't love us any more. They're very angry, all over. They don't like us, because, first of all, we don't treat other Americans as human beings. We're fighting against one another when we should be together.

Another thing—we're trying to change the ways of other countries when we should be changing the ways in our own country. Vietnam. What business have we got there? Stop being concerned with other people's problems. Think about your own. Or your own will get out of hand. Look at what's happening now. What we have is a civil war, a civil war right in our own backyard. What kind of living is that? Everybody's a human being. Everyone can live in the same country and be happy. It can easily be done.

People come up to me and say, "Why are you going back to America? I think America's just terrible." I get tired of hearing that. Tired of their saying that.

What do you say to them?

Miss Mercer: I just look at them. They say, "Don't you hate the American white man?" I say, "No, I don't hate him. I pity him. I pity him, because he's just ignorant. So I have pity in my heart for him."

All the time, I'm asked this question. All the time. It makes me nervous. It makes me sad. But what can you do? We're supposed to be the leading nation of the world, but we can't live together. White and black persons should be able to live together. It's not the color of your skin. It's your heart that matters.

My mother was Cherokee Indian. She came from the reservation. I've seen so much happen to her in North Carolina because of being an Indian. My father was a Negro. I've seen my mother cry. She said, "It's not over with. Bad things will happen to you kids." I've seen her sit and cry. I've seen things happen to her, which made me cry, too. But she had no hate. No indeedy. I can't hate people for being unintelligent. I have to pity them. It affects me when I work. They come to my dressing room, and they're constantly speaking about that problem. Constantly. I don't want to discuss it. The way it affects me is that it makes me nervous. I asked my doctor, "Why am I nervous all the time?" He's a doctor here, a French doctor. He said, "Because you work so hard, and you were born with a nervous strain." I asked him, "What strain?" And he said, "Because you were born a Negro in America."

And yet you are planning to go back there to live eventually?

MISS MERCER: Well, it's my family. And America is my home. I can't continue living the rest of my life in another country. I have found, if you live away from America very long, you will become very critical of it. I feel guilty about being away from the United States. I'm not doing anything to help the cause. And I miss my family and my friends. I've been looking out for myself and my sisters and brothers since I was twelve years old. There were nine. There are eight now. I was the oldest girl. My mother died quite young. My father was a very sweet man, but that was a very hard thing, keeping nine children together. He's still living. I'm looking forward to seeing him. My family used to worry quite a bit about me. I don't think they do any more. But there's enough for all of us to worry about.

GALLERY NOTES

Along with the Ameropeans who left home for racial reasons is the small but interesting group who left for political reasons—the refugees from McCarthyism. During the late senator's dark reign, when hundreds of Americans, particularly those in the entertainment industry, found themselves blacklisted and hence unemployable, a comparative few were able to move to Europe and go about trying to resume a more or less normal existence. They were, of course, more fortunate than most of their fellow victims, who, because of family obligations or lack of money or for some other reason, couldn't manage this escape from intolerance, and many of whom have never since been able to piece together their personal and professional lives. Even some who have, from all appearances, successfully established themselves in Europe, and intend to remain there, prefer not to talk about that segment of their lives, apparently still fearing some threat to their security.

Among those who are willing to speak of their exiled life and times is Jules Dassin, the director, who, like a few other victims of the blacklist, made his reputation and fortune during his enforced residence in Europe, where he turned out a number of very successful films, including *Never on Sunday*, *He Who Must Die*, and *Topkapi.* After some fifteen years abroad, he returned to the United States in 1966 to direct his wife, Melina Mercouri, whom he married abroad after his first marriage had ended in divorce, in the Broadway musical, *Illya Darling*, adapted from *Never on Sunday*. I called on Mr. Dassin, a courteous, soft-spoken man in his middle fifties, with gray hair and gentle eyes, late one afternoon in his apartment on upper Fifth Avenue, and learned that he grew up in Harlem, one of seven children of a barber, and that, like his brothers, he went to work when he was ten. "It was tough, but happily, we had a family where everybody loved everybody else," Mr. Dassin said. "Seven kids, and each one ready to die for the other. That's pretty strong armor against anything that can happen to you in Harlem or anywhere else."

From childhood, Mr. Dassin continued, he hovered around the theater, and when he was sixteen, began spending his summers on the borscht circuit. "That was real theater," he said. "God, we used to do seven shows a week." About five years later, he began devoting his full time to the theater, and eventually wound up as a film director in Hollywood. He also made pictures abroad, and it was while working in Europe that he read in the newspapers that his name had been submitted to the House Un-American Activities Committee as being a subversive. As soon as he had finished the picture he was working on, he returned to the United States so that he would be available to testify before the Committee. "I was here for about six months or more, thinking I would be called," Mr. Dassin said. "At one time, they asked me to appear, and then it was postponed. Finally, they said, 'Never mind.' I went back to Paris, and got a job, making a film with Fernandel. Just a few days—literally, just a few days—before we began shooting, the blacklist reached into Europe, and threats were made to the producer that if he kept me on the picture, it would never be released in the States, and there would be other dire consequences. That project instantly fell apart, and then I was out of a job for five years. Five years of stark unemployment."

"How did you live?"

"I don't know. I couldn't possibly tell you. It's a mystery."

I asked if the five years were so unpleasant that he had actually blotted them out of his memory, or if perhaps he preferred not to remember.

"Well, it's really mysterious," Mr. Dassin said. "I remember once I was working in the theater here in New York. I'm going back now to when I was about twenty-one. That's when I made my first real association with the theater in a permanent sense. It was with the Artef group, a Yiddish theater. That was a marvelous theater. Did brilliant, brilliant work. We were the darlings of the intellectuals, and the press adored us, but the paying customers were few. We were a collective, and at the end of the week, we would split whatever money there was not, and yet we kept that theater alive for six years. I don't know how. There are mysteries, you know, about some things. That's the way it was during the blacklisting. We did have a little bit of money. Very modest. We lived in a place about thirty miles from Paris. The problem was to keep the kids warm. Just physical problems. We had three children. They went to the local schools, and were playing in Moliere three months after they arrived, so that was all fine. Then, too, we had friends who would help out with a little loan, but we would have to give that back, you know, the following Monday. I don't know how we managed. It was just one of those things where people survive because they want to and have to."

Though it was a difficult and confusing time, Mr. Dassin continued, he was able to do some writing. He turned out a play and a musical comedy, though he had a market for neither. "I was also learning languages like mad," Mr. Dassin said. "It wasn't all dreary and bitter. There was even fun in it. Then, after five years, I got a job. That was *Rififi.* I got the job, first of all, because the man who hired me knew I would work for nothing. I wrote the script, directed the picture, and did a producer's job for eight thousand dollars. But I was very happy about it. From then, there was no problem about work."

Mr. Dassin said that while he feels there are certain advantages in working abroad, he believes that the kind of director he is finds it difficult to work removed from what he knows—his home and background. "A lot of you just doesn't function," he remarked. "Actually, for a number of years, particularly for the last five, I've been anxious to come back here. I've been homesick. I have a lot of friends and family here, and I have a *big* affair with New York. Of course, there are things that I will miss. I don't think—my American friends disagree with me, and some get angry with me—but I don't think we've yet come near the cultural levels that have been attained in Europe. On the other hand, I don't think it's all roses there. There is much that I dislike. There's a cynical attitude that I can't deal with. Here, it's true, we had the McCarthy illness. It was a pretty ugly business, and it did inestimable damage. But I never did consider it more than an illness. It is not in our character. I've now traveled a good deal, and I don't know any nicer guy than the American. He's generous. He's open. There is a directness about him that I treasure very highly. But he's a naïve guy whose very naïveté is a danger. It makes him a chump for demagogues, for slogans, for that goddamned box—that television—which is ten times more dangerous to America than Vietnam or anything else. But he *is* a nice guy. I like him better than most of the people I've met elsewhere."

In addition to the racial and political exiles, a third category of Ameropeans who left the United States because of dissatisfaction with contemporary American life consists of the men and women who might be called the cultural exiles. They have a good deal in common with the artists, writers, and intellectuals who fled the United States in the 1920s, although today's emigrés are usually less specific in singling out the springs of their discontent. However, some of these have been described by a cultural exile named T. S. Matthews, a former managing editor of *Time*, who has lived in London for the past several years.

"For this is not my day in America," Matthews wrote in his autobiography, *Name and Address*. "This day belongs to the 100-per-centers, the Madison Avenue Boys, the professional patriots, the organization men, the hard-eyed herdsmen of political Yahoos, the dogs that eat dogs. If they have really taken over America and taken it over for keeps, then I think the American experiment has failed. The dinosaur, its tiny brain still dreaming of paradisal forests, is plodding witlessly toward the asphalt lake."

As a rule, the cultural exiles are not as outspokenly critical as Mr. Matthews, the probable reason being their awareness that an American who finds fault with America is generally regarded by his countrymen as ungrateful if not unpatriotic. Ameropeans are especially vulnerable in this respect, for, as Mr. Matthews has also remarked, "It's only when you're thought to have cut the umbilical cord that binds you to your native land that your Americanism comes into question." Even though the cultural exiles, along with most of their fellow Ameropeans, tend to speak in muted tones when discussing what they feel is unrewarding or unpleasant in American life, it is obvious that they all feel that, for them, something in America is at present out of joint. They also feel—and very strongly—that it is a sign of rank immaturity to equate a preference to live outside one's country with a lack of loyalty to it. Mrs. Gerald Brennan, a native of South Carolina, who is married to the distinguished English writer and has lived in Europe for many years, told me that she has never met an American living abroad who had turned against his country. "The people I have met who have turned against America are people who are still living there," she said.

Historically, it is true that the patriotism of Americans is not diminished but, if anything, enhanced by residence abroad. "I had no idea until I came here," the famous nineteenth-century preacher, Phillips Brooks, wrote from Europe, "what a tremendous American I was." His contemporary, the writer and editor, William Dean Howells, was similarly affected. In a letter written from abroad, he asked, "Is it not worth the journey thither to learn that the Fourth of July orations are true?" The same sentiment is echoed again and again by contemporary Americans living abroad. "Only a person who does not live there truly knows how wonderful America is," Herman Wouk, a novelist who has lived outside the country for many years, has remarked. Another American writer, Lee Pogostin, told me, after he had lived with his family in Spain for several years, "I've come to love my country more since being away from it. You tend to be a critic of America while you're there, but as soon as you move away, you become a defender." The truth of the Fourth of July orations was also revealed to Mrs. Phyllis

Michaux, one of the founders of the organization called the American Wives of Europeans, as a result of living abroad. "I am an American of eight generations," Mrs. Michaux has remarked. "Throughout my childhood, I was told that America was the best country in the world. You have no reason to doubt it, but after you've lived here, all of a sudden you find yourself saying, 'It's true—America *is* the best country in the world.' In America, a man's son can go higher than his father. That, to me, is *the* great thing about America."

Actually, the problem faced by Americans living abroad, as far as their patriotism is concerned, would seem to be not how to sustain it but how to keep its expression within socially acceptable limits. "One thing that's difficult for somebody who has lived abroad a good deal and who really belongs to America is dealing with the American superiority complex," Jules Dassin told me. "We think we're so much better, so much faster, so much brighter. And it isn't true. I'm talking now about things like technique in mechanics, inventiveness, technical efficiency, and so on. They're damned good over there, you know. They don't have as many toilets, but you can make a movie, manufacture an automobile or an airplane, build an airport, or put up a house with as much skill and speed there as you can here—and sometimes, more."

To recognize the existence of the American feeling of superiority is one thing. To change it is quite another, for it has been a part of the American character for a very long time. In 1786, Abigail Adams, the wife of the first American minister to the Court of St. James's and second President of the United States, wrote to her sister from London: "Do you know that European birds have not half the melody of ours? Nor is their fruit half so sweet, nor their flowers half so fragrant, nor their manners half so pure, nor their people half so virtuous; but keep this to yourself, or I shall be thought more than half deficient in understanding and taste."

Considering their built-in feeling of superiority, it is probably not surprising that of the many thousands of Americans who have lived abroad throughout the history of the country, only a bare handful have taken foreign citizenship. We remember those who have—Henry James and T. S. Eliot are probably the two best known—because of their singularity in this respect. No matter how long Americans stay away from their country—Edith Wharton and Bernard Berenson lived most of their adult lives in Europe, and so have Janet Flanner, Maria Jolas, Man Ray, and many others less well known—they seem as jealous of retaining their citizenship as they do of their name. Even the racial and political exiles, who have departed in anger or bitterness, seldom exchange their United States citizenship for that of the country where they settle and where they feel they are treated more justly.

I asked Jules Dassin if, during the years when he was blacklisted, it had occurred to him to take foreign citizenship. "Well, a number of countries offered me what they called honorary citizenship," he replied, "and I must admit that in the difficult moments during those years when I had no passport, I thought of accepting. But I couldn't. Why? Couldn't possibly explain. I distrust patriotism. I think it's all a snare and very often inhuman. So, it's not patriotism. It has to do with where I was born. And the streets and my friends. And the fight to live. Harlem, where I grew up, was a bloody jungle, but I loved it. I don't know why. I know people who have renounced American citizenship, and whereas I certainly wouldn't think of criticizing them for it, that path was not for me."

Although I was constantly on the lookout in Europe for Americans who had become citizens of another country, the only one I found was John Huston, the film director. I also interviewed an Ameropean in London who expects eventually to take British citizenship. John Huston and Jules Dassin both told me that Elizabeth Taylor once began the process of becoming a British citizen, but found that she couldn't overcome her misgivings about taking the final step. Mr. Dassin said that he knew "about half a dozen" political exiles who had become citizens of France or of another European country. "I don't want to say who they are," he told me, "because I think they're embarrassed and a little unhappy about it."

> "If it hadn't been for the blacklisting,
> I might not be living here in London,
> and that would be too bad."

Carl Foreman is a film writer and producer whose work includes such highly praised and successful movies as *High Noon*, *The Bridge on the River Kwai*, and *The Guns of Navarone*. In 1952, as a result of encounters with the House Un-American Activities Committee, he left Hollywood and moved to England, where he has since continued to make his residence. I called on him one beautiful May morning in his office, a large, comfortable room filled with photographs of friends and other personal mementoes, on Jermyn Street, in London. Dressed with somber conservativeness, as is his habit, in a dark suit—the corner of a white handkerchief protruding discreetly from the breast pocket—a white shirt, and a black tie, he opened the conversation by saying that he had given a large party the previous Sunday to commemorate the anniversary of his arrival in England.

FOREMAN: I'm very sentimental about that date, and usually mark it with a party for all my friends. I arrived here May 12, 1952. It was a day something like this but warmer. As soon as I had checked into my hotel, I jumped into a taxi and went down to see the Houses of Parliament, then to Westminster Abbey, then up to Fleet Street for lunch. It was fabulous. I loved it. I stayed here for three weeks—I was alone—and the weather remained lovely. It was glorious. Then I went to the Continent, and while I was traveling about there, it was raining here. When I returned, in July, the weather, with typical perfidy, was lovely once more. After that, the rains came, but I had decided to stay. And I never went back.

When you did that traveling on the Continent, were you scouting other possible places to live, or had you made up your mind to settle here?

FOREMAN: I came to England shortly after the Un-American Activities Committee investigations in Hollywood. I was blacklisted in Hollywood at that time. I was called before the Committee in 1951, while I was making *High Noon*. Once that film was completed, I was finished in Hollywood. I had a very unhappy divorce from my associates, Stanley Kramer and George Glass. We had been partners in the company that made that film and four others for United Artists, and we had made a new deal with Columbia Pictures that called for twenty films to be made over a period of five years. Then I was out. There was no possibility for me to work in Hollywood.

Were you actually forced out of the company, or did you and your partners mutually decide to dissolve it? What really happened?

FOREMAN: It worked something like this. I was originally subpoenaed in May of 1951, as was George Glass. Stanley Kramer was not called. Almost immediately after Glass was subpoenaed, although I didn't know this until later, he indicated to the Committee that he would be a co-operative witness, so he was all right. That just left me. We had many meetings about this, obviously, and I explained my position and my feeling about the Committee and why I felt I couldn't be a so-called co-operative witness, or informer, about friends that I had known ten or fifteen years earlier. I tried to explain that I was perfectly willing, if not happy, to tell the Committee anything it wanted to know about myself, but I didn't want to involve anyone else. They were all right in the beginning. A bit frightened but all right. I made it plain at the time that if my position embarrassed them at a later date that I would voluntarily leave the company.

My feeling was that my situation could not affect us as a company, because we, in our short period of existence, had been very lucky. Our films had been very successful. Oddly enough, the content of the films, although they were the Hollywood New Wave of the time in terms of production techniques, low budgets, and the kind of subjects we approached—for example, we made the first film on race prejudice, which was an adaptation of *Home of the Brave*, in which we substituted a Negro soldier—that sort of thing, and as I say, oddly enough, these films, besides being very successful, had been very well received by the Establishment. I felt that our record was such that nobody could accuse us, or me, of using the Hollywood screen as a subversive channel. We had about three hundred awards attesting to our Americanism. I thought that if anyone had a chance to fight what was going on, we did.

However, as time went by and my appearance before the Committee kept being postponed, my partners became more and more jittery. We had other associates, who were somewhat more conservative politically, and as the date grew closer, they became very frightened, and finally offered me an ultimatum, saying that I either had to co-operate or I would have to go. I reiterated that I was completely willing to go but that I felt the issue was bigger than all of us, to coin a phrase, and what I wanted was to make my appearance before the Committee on my own terms and then wait a period of thirty or sixty days to see whether or not in fact everything would fall apart. They agreed to this, under pressure. They had to, because I was an officer of the company, and there were other things involved. I did make my appearance before the Committee. My partners didn't want to wait, and they ousted me. And that's the whole story in a nutshell.

So you decided to pack up and move to Europe?

FOREMAN: Not right away. There were some legal matters, such as settlements, that had to be worked out. Meanwhile, I went off to New York for a rest. I saw a lot of New York theater. It was pretty bad that year, and I began to think, "I could probably write as bad as some of the things I've seen. I'll move to New York, and try to become a playwright." Well, on the way back to California, I began to feel that this was the wrong way out. One should try to make a fight of it. So I decided to give it another six months.

I opened my own offices, and started to prepare the making of a film.

It was surprising the number of people who came around and offered sympathy and encouragement. In fact, one day I really broke up. I had offices at an independent studio, where our company had formerly been located, and a friend invited me down to the set of a film he was making. The entire crew were the same people who had worked with us on many films. The leading elements came around, and said, "We're just waiting for you to get started, and if you have any problems, we'll work for nothing." Wonderful. But then the message came down from on high that anybody who worked for me would be similarly blacklisted. That was why, finally, at the end of April, I knew I'd had it. I thought I'd better come over to Europe and see if I could work here.

Now, to answer the question that started all this—No, I had no intention of staying in England, particularly. It was the first port of call. I came, ironically enough, on a ship called the *Liberté*. Even more ironically, *High Noon* had just come out, and was getting marvelous reviews. It was being called not only a great film artistically but a contribution to good citizenship.

Well, I arrived here on the beautiful day I mentioned, and everybody was terribly nice to me. The film people told me how wonderful it is here and talked about all the things we'd do. I was also getting messages from the Continent, saying "Come on over," so I went to France, Italy, and Germany. That made me realize I couldn't function there because, unfortunately, I was provincial. I had forgotten all my high school French and German. The movie business is enough of a jungle, even if you understand the language. Here, I could reasonably communicate. So, I fled back to England, and I've been here ever since.

Did you bring your family over then—after you'd fled back here?

FOREMAN: I brought them—my wife and daughter—over in late July. Since I liked England so much, I naturally wanted them to like it, too, so I was very anxious to find a nice place. This turned out to be a serious problem, because in '52, the British were just beginning to come out of the war, and the places that were for rent at that time were pretty horrible. Finally, I took a flat in Hyde Park Gate, just across the street from Sir Winston Churchill's home, in a building owned by an Indian gentleman, whom I should have been wary of, but I was desperate. It was a very large flat, complete with service, and it had a very ornate cocktail cabinet that lit up when you opened it. Our electric power bills were fantastic. Not because of the light in the cocktail cabinet, but because we found our landlord had gone into the electricity business, so to speak. He was secretly adding a very stiff surcharge to our electric bills. There were other problems, so we moved out rather fast. For the next several years, we lived in other furnished flats, most of them quite nice, and then three or four years ago, we bought an apartment and furnished it ourselves. It's in the Bayswater area. The best way to visualize it, I suppose, is to think of Central Park West, in New York. However, in our area, you can take a walk at night and not be afraid you're going to be attacked. That is a great comfort. The apartment is what in America we call a duplex; here, they call it a maisonette. It has its own gardens as well as a marvelous view, overlooking Hyde Park.

After all the moves, you and your wife find this apartment—or maisonette—perfectly satisfactory?

FOREMAN: Not my wife. My wife actually never did like England. Oh, there were times when she liked it, but most of the time, she didn't. She didn't like the weather. It depressed her. We had other problems, and we are now separated. She's living back in California. My daughter is graduating from Beverly Hills High School next month, and I'll be going over to see her. My wife did a very good job of decorating the apartment. It's large—ten rooms—so we had space to install a Finnish sauna bath, which is a marvelous luxury to indulge in in my old age.

How do you get from the flat to the office—and around the city generally?

FOREMAN: Well, somewhat embarrassingly. After *The Guns of Navarone*, which was a great success, Columbia Pictures showed their appreciation by offering to buy me a Rolls-Royce as a present. I come from poor but honest parents in Chicago, and I'm just not the Rolls type. So, I settled for a Cadillac, which turned out to be a big mistake, because it's even bigger than a Rolls. I have a driver, whose name is Jack. He was a taxi driver when I met him. A very interesting chap. He also looks after my clothes and laundry. Does my shoes. Brings me a cup of tea first thing in the morning. Wonderful. It makes Jack very happy to drive the Cadillac, but I must admit when we're going through narrow streets and people look at that enormous car, it makes me very self-conscious, particularly when it's raining or at the height of the traffic and people are lined up in tremendous queues, waiting for buses. I try to get somebody to ride with me so it won't look so bad. Surprising, though, what a large car can do. I have some friends who are Members of Parliament, and occasionally when there's something doing, they ask me by to have dinner at the House. Normally, you would drive up to the public entrance, and get out and walk in. With that Cadillac, you can drive right in through the Members' gate, and the coppers never bother you. Big deal.

Had you been in Europe many times before you came here to live?

FOREMAN: Never. It was quite a change. Still, when you're in the film business, you find that the people you work with are basically the same wherever you go, and everybody here was wonderful to me. One problem was that most of the people who met me for the first time were prepared to be terribly sympathetic precisely because of my situation. They *wanted* to hear me say all sorts of lurid things about my country. I found myself in the ironic position of having to *explain* the United States. It wasn't easy, because the people here never understood the whole phenomenon. They just knew the word, "McCarthyism," and that was all. In point of fact, McCarthy never came out to Hollywood. At any rate, I had had time to think on my way over, and I had decided that I wasn't going to be a martyr. It might be personally gratifying, but a martyr wears out his welcome all too soon. All I wanted to do was work.

Furthermore, during all that period, I never had the feeling of outrage against the United States as such, or felt that I was being singled out for bad treatment. It wasn't just the film colony that was affected but other areas of the nation's culture and education as well. I felt that I could understand why this was happening. The reason was the bomb. We had possession of this terrible weapon, which made us all extremely uncomfortable, and, understandably, the nation was in a state of great tension. The idea that anyone was being disloyal, when tied up to the terror of the bomb, was just too much to withstand. I never felt that what happened was truly within the real spirit of American psychology. Even at the height of it, I remember, there were always people who came around, and sent you things, and wrote to you, and told you how much they felt for you. It's true that the writers and actors suffered tremendously. But you couldn't blame the country at large. I never did. I did feel that the whole thing was embarrassing and ludicrous and disgraceful and humiliating.

Although I had rejected the martyr role, I was full of anger and self-pity. That was my major problem, and it hurt my writing terribly. Every time I sat down at the typewriter, I found myself writing an angry letter to the editor of the New York *Times*. It was very bad. In 1952 and '53, I didn't write anything. It wasn't until the latter part of

'54 that I really began to try to write a film script. I had tremendous difficulty doing it, and I knew it wasn't good. That was a terrible blow. I realized then that I would have to—well, being a prizefighter, I use the metaphor—I would have to go back into the gym and get my timing back.

What exactly does that mean—"to go back into the gym"?

FOREMAN: I'll try to explain. A lot of jobs were being offered to me, but I didn't like any of them. While the big film operators were very anxious to get people like me, they also saw an opportunity to make a deal very cheaply, you see, and I had the feeling that I ought to hold out, both in terms of the content and the money. There was an exploitation element involved, even though it was well meaning. I was lucky, because I had retained my interest in *High Noon* on a hunch. So, I was able to go along for several years.

However, quite a lot of other displaced persons—friends and associates who had come over here a while after my arrival—were not as well off as I was. They needed the work, so when these jobs were offered to me, I would say, "I can't do it, but So-and-So can." The operator would say, "Well, I don't know him." And I would say, "I promise you he can do the job, but if by any chance it turns out he can't, I'll come in and do it for nothing." I soon discovered that practically all my chums were having precisely the same trouble I was. They couldn't turn out a good script. As a result, I found myself working very hard, and instead of being exploited for little money, I was getting no money. However, it was very good for me, because I could at least see what they had done wrong. I did about two years of that—patching and doctoring and fixing—all for free. But it was worth it. At the end of two years, I had my timing back. That's the point. When it came around to *The Bridge on the River Kwai,* I was able to do a pretty good script. So, I've been very lucky, I must admit, and I'm no longer full of the anger I had when I first arrived.

Of course, I found the life here terribly congenial right from the start. The most surprising thing was that they knew of me as a screen writer. It had never occurred to me that a Hollywood screen writer would be known outside the Screen Writers' Guild. But they knew here, and the same thing was true on the Continent. What I'd done were just movies, but I was here as a *writer*. That was wonderful balm for troubled spirits. It made me feel so good that I didn't even mind the weather, after a while, and if I did, there was always the south of France. That's one of the places I used to go to write, or I would rent a chalet on Lake Lucerne, which is also pretty hard to beat. But now I have a place to write that I like even better—a little shack on the Thames. It's only thirty-five minutes from here, on the new road to the airport. It also happens to be ten minutes from Shepperton Studios, where I do most of my shooting. I love the river, and I love being in that place of mine, even when it's raining. It is very modest—a wooden frame building with two bedrooms, a living room, a kitchen, and a sort of glassed-in loggia, which is the dining room when the weather is warm. It has a garden and about forty-five feet of river frontage. I have a small boat out there. It's funny. I have always liked boats, but when I lived in America, although there are marvelous places to boat within reach of Hollywood, I never got around to it. I was always too busy. And when I first got here, I was too busy, but then I ate enough of those lotuses to make me feel that I didn't have to be quite that busy and that I could afford a Saturday and Sunday off, like everybody else.

When did you begin to notice the difference in the change of pace and to take advantage of it yourself?

FOREMAN: I noticed it almost immediately, of course, because people you wanted to talk to about business would always disappear on Friday afternoon, and you wouldn't see them again until Monday afternoon. It didn't shock me, exactly, but it was completely alien. I couldn't understand it. For quite a few years, I continued to live and work as I always had. I must say that it was no hardship. When I began to write again, I had a tremendous amount of energy, and all that frustration had to be worked off. It was a kind of sickness. On Saturdays, the secretaries didn't come in, and that gave me a chance to sit here quietly, ponder the events of the week, go through my post—you see, I even talk English now—and make plans for the next week. Well, I don't work on weekends any more, and I get just as much done. You learn to organize your time better, it seems to me. Now, I usually spend weekends at the shack.

You mentioned earlier that you had several friends among the M.P.'s. When did you begin to make friends among the English —that is, among the English who were not in the film business?

FOREMAN: Well, the screen people have fairly wide contacts themselves, and I suppose that is the way it began. The first M.P. I met was a sensational fellow—Nye Bevan. I met him and his wife, Jennie Lee, at the home of Ben Levy, a playwright whose wife is an American actress named Constance Cummings. I had read Bevan's last book on the boat coming over here—a very exciting piece of reading—and it was wonderful to meet him. Nye had the aura of greatness about him.

and Jennie is a marvelous woman. Not that I saw them very often, but the association lasted over the years. After Jennie became Under Secretary of State for Science and Education, one of the first things she did was to get me appointed to the Board of Governors of the British Film Institute. I am undoubtedly the only American who has served in that capacity.

Do you spend most of your leisure time, when you're with people, with Americans or with English?

FOREMAN: Actually, with both. I have a great many English friends, but there are always a lot of Americans coming through, and there's also a very large American colony here. Most Americans, when they come here, either like it very, very much, or they hate it. The ones who like it go through a very difficult phase. To begin with, there is the honeymoon period, when everything is marvelous, and that's very worrying, because if it's all so wonderful, you know there has to be a great and agonizing reappraisal. But first they develop a British accent. That takes about six weeks. When they begin saying, "bawth," you know the virus is beginning to work. And then, of course, they start going to all the pubs they possibly can. They're convinced the pub is the world's greatest institution. Then, there's the theater, which is so much cheaper than it is back in New York. And they're eating roast beef and Yorkshire pudding, and they're doing all the sights, and it's marvelous. They keep saying, "And the people are so polite," as indeed they are. "And the taxis are so much cheaper than New York, and the drivers are wonderful. And *everybody's* lovely and marvelous." Well, they are. But, you know, after a while, things begin to develop. You're going to run into the occasional rude taxi driver, who will say, in effect, "Yank, go home." It will happen.

Has it happened to you?

FOREMAN: Not the "go home" bit, but I did have an altercation with a taxi driver. I was coming home one night from work—I'd let Jack go—and I was tired and somewhat irritable. Sitting in the back, I could see the meter, so I knew what the fare was when I got out, but unconsciously I said, "What is it?" The meter was opposite the side I got out, and the driver upped the fare by thruppence or sixpence. I was just annoyed. He had destroyed my faith in London taxi drivers. I said, "Nonsense," and one word led to another. I told him he had let down the whole fraternity. He was very angry with me. He ultimately refused to take a tip. That is the only time anything of that nature has happened during all these years. Not bad.

As I say, for the Americans who come here and fall in love with everything, disillusionment is almost bound to set in. If it's winter, it may get a bit cold in the flat, particularly if there's no central heating. Then they get the feeling that everything here goes very slowly. When they dial the telephone, it seems to take longer than it does back home. They get a bit tired of the diet, and start to get a little bitchy about that. And the weather depresses them a great deal, especially women and most especially women from the West Coast. During the winter, it begins to get dark here about three o'clock in the afternoon, and by four o'clock, it's pitch dark. Then there's the fog. The first time, it's a great adventure. "Oh," they say, "it's just like those Sherlock Holmes films." It's marvelous—if it goes away the next day. If it hangs on for a week or ten days, it loses its charm. That can happen any November, and you see these new arrivals getting progressively depressed.

Then, too, in the department stores, American women are apt to become a little annoyed after a while by the sort of *laissez-faire* attitude on the part of the staff. They're very polite, and will call you "sir" or "madam," as the case may be, but they may not be all that concerned about what's in stock. Or a woman will go into a store and say, "Oh, I love that dress in the window. I'd like to have it." And the clerk says, "Oh no, madam. We can't take it out of the window." The men run into something of the same kind with secretaries, who don't want to make the slightest change in the routine way they've always done things. And in time, both men and women are going to become aware of what could broadly be called anti-American feeling. You couldn't put it in the same category as anti-Semitism in the United States, but you come to notice it in the press and in political statements. However, on an individual level, except for, say, drunken arguments that get out of hand, there's no question that the British like us.

You mentioned anti-Semitism in the United States. What about anti-Semitism here?

FOREMAN: In all my years here, I have never been aware of it. I have never found people telling me so-called Jewish jokes under the impression that I wasn't Jewish, which happens to me very often in the United States. My daughter certainly never felt it, whereas I—just as we sit here talking—I remember back in Chicago, coming in from Division Street one day and saying to my father, "Some boys just came down the street, and they called me 'sheeny.' What does that mean?" He told me. Now, the fact that I have not been aware of it here doesn't mean that it doesn't exist. Unquestionably, it does to a degree. It's more restrained—let's put it that way.

Considering how things have turned out—the ease and pleasure with which you live here, the professional success, and everything else—have you ever thought that the blacklisting was a blessing in disguise?

FOREMAN: Yes. I think the blacklisting was a lucky thing. If it hadn't been for the blacklisting, I might not be living here in London, and that would be too bad. It's true that those blacklisted years were a bit difficult, partly because my passport was revoked a few months after I got here, and it took me three years to get it returned. This made things a bit awkward, because you can get claustrophobia in any country, no matter how big it is, and this isn't a big one. But if the blacklisting hadn't come along, I would quite likely have stayed in Hollywood, and in time gotten fed up with it. I had lived there for eighteen years. I quit the University of Illinois in my last year, when I was nineteen, because I was a movie bug, and couldn't wait any longer to get to Hollywood. I arrived with fifty-seven cents in my pocket. Hollywood had great sentimental attachments for me. But, while it has the best craftsmen in the world—it still does to this day—the inevitable isolation of the film colony is stultifying. I would have found myself, like many of my friends, coming over to Europe once every three or four years as a tourist. And you can have that. No, I like to live here. Really, I have been much happier here. This isn't to say that I wouldn't go back there to make a film. In fact, I am getting ready to do just that. Furthermore, I have family there and a great many friends, but I don't think I could live there again.

I feel much freer here. For one thing, I have many friends here who are not in films. That's impossible in Hollywood, unless you want to make friends with the rich real estate operators and others who have moved into Beverly Hills. If you want to sit around all night, talking money and investments with them—O.K. I don't think that's the way to live. I prefer it this way. I get out here. It's broader. And if I want to stay home and have a game of chess with my driver, I can do it, and that's the way I often spend an evening. He's a good chess player, and we're on pretty even terms.

The freedom that one feels here works out on two levels, it seems to me. On a personal level, this country is the home of eccentricity. As long as you don't go about being too destructive, nobody is going to bother you. If I felt like taking a walk in my pajamas, the police wouldn't pull me in. They might speak to me politely and say, "What are you doing, sir?" I would tell them I was taking a walk, and they might ask how far I planned to walk, and I would tell them that I was just going down to the corner and back, and they would say, "Very well. Good night." Nobody here is afraid of the police. That's nice, particularly for somebody who comes from Chicago. Of course, the police here don't carry guns. It's an eccentricity that appeals to me.

There are other eccentricities, and not all of them are appreciated by some of my American friends who have gotten uncharmed. Take this building, for example. On this side, you're on the fourth floor. If you walk down the hall and *up* a flight of stairs, you'll find yourself on the third floor. It's the way the building is put together. You've got to adjust to it. After a while it has a certain charm, and it seems to me that this sort of thing pervades the whole country.

On a working level, I also have marvelous freedom here. I don't have to contend with the system, as I did when working for a major studio in Hollywood, of making films by committee. Here. I'm on my own. I'm an independent film maker. I have a wonderfully amicable relationship with Columbia Pictures, who supply the money for my films. I deal mainly with their administrative offices, which are in New York—three thousand miles across the ocean. Very good. I don't care what happens over there as long as they run their company efficiently and continue to treat me decently, as they do. Where it's difficult is that I don't have the facilities here that I would have there. For example, they have a research department. You press a button, and somebody tells you what the population of Istanbul was in 1923, or whatever you want to know. I miss that, but I don't really mind.

Is there anything else about the United States that you do really miss?

FOREMAN: Well, yes, but on a very mundane level. I miss delicatessen food. I was brought up on it, and one of the things that makes me very happy is a corned beef sandwich or a hot pastrami sandwich or a hot dog. They can't quite make it here. They're trying. Everyone must give them credit for the effort, but they can't do it. They have a thing called salt beef here, which is almost like New York corned beef, but it misses. It lacks the flavor and the texture. Pastrami is unknown here. Most of their hot dogs are pork hot dogs, which are all right if you're at a baseball game or football game, where you don't care what you're eating particularly, but when one has been brought up on a good beef hot dog, that is the sort of thing you have in mind. They've got rye bread. They can't make good cheesecake to save their lives.

Now, for a New Yorker or a Chicagoan who knows about bagels with cream cheese and salmon, you have in this country a contradiction that drives men mad. On the one hand, the smoked salmon here is the best in the world. Unquestionably. On the other hand, the bagels may be the worst. They call them "bye-gulls," because most of the Jews here seem to have come from Poland, and they have a different accent. The point is that the so-called "bye-gulls" are inferior in construction. They're thin and bony—almost scrawny, one might say. They lack the fullness of the American bagel. You just can't do much with them. And, of course, they're limited to just the one flavor, whereas in New York, if you want a pumpernickel bagel, for example, you can get one. I say this in a spirit of libertarianism. I don't like pumpernickel bagels. I'm a simple man. But the fact that you can get one if you *want* one is the important thing. And onion rolls—you can't get them, either.

All of this makes a problem, of course, but one overcomes it if one has friends who are constantly coming over from America. Very early on, I set up a kind of Care package system in this department, so that, fortunately, I can say that over the years my little home has never been without a salami hanging in the kitchen. At the moment, the freezer in my apartment contains one pastrami, one corned beef, a dozen knockwurst, a cheesecake from Reuben's, and quite a few other delicacies. You've got to work at it, but if a thing is worth doing, you do it well, don't you?

Your complaint about the bagels is novel among the Americans I've talked to here, though quite a few have complained about the slowness of the services. Does that ever bother you after all these years?

FOREMAN: Oh yes. It can be very aggravating. For example, I've been trying to get an awning for the shack. They promised it in three weeks. It's now six weeks, and still no sign of it. I can get very impatient at things like that, and I'm very outspoken about them. I've been here so long that I feel I don't have to be polite any more, and can speak frankly.

At what point can you cease to think of yourself as an unofficial American ambassador, as the State Department suggests, and start being yourself?

FOREMAN: That depends entirely on the person, I think. In my case, I've been here so many years, and people who know me are aware that I'm here because I like it that I no longer have to be on my good behavior. There is so much I like about the country, and it's been very good to me, and I feel that I can express myself about it.

However, I can't do it in terms of films. That's where I have a block. As a writer, that is the greatest single problem I have here. When I was young, in America, most of the films I worked on or cared about were concerned with contemporary life—things that I felt keenly about. I can't do that here. I never have since I arrived. This is a tremendously interesting country from a social as well as an economic point of view. They're having peaceful revolutions here every year, and life goes on just the same, but those developments I have not been able to write about. I rationalized this by saying, "Well, I'm just a guest here, after all, and they've been wonderful to me, and I shouldn't criticize. It's like being somebody's house guest and telling them how to raise their child. One doesn't do that."

Whatever the reason or rationale, I don't get into those areas, and this limits the kind of films I can make. It has pushed me into making the big film, the international film, whereas I would really be happier if I were making a film about the color bar, for example, or some other subject of consequence. I don't, and that is a problem. I find, though, that I can live with it.

> "I found myself living there, and I got to love the place and the people. As I kept going back, it got to feel more like home than America."

John Huston, the film director, producer, actor, writer, painter, art collector, raconteur, and Master of Fox Hounds, was born in Nevada, Missouri, in 1906. In 1964, having made Ireland his main residence for many years, he became an Irish citizen, and now lives in considerable splendor on an estate called St. Clerans, sixteen miles inland from the western seaport town of Galway. The main house, a twenty-six-room structure built of gray granite, is usually described by American visitors as a Georgian mansion. According to Seamus Kelly, the Irish drama critic, the house has been altered and added onto over the years and now has "a Georgian core, a touch of Regency, a bit of tolerable early Victorian, behind a handsome neo-classical portico." Mr. Huston told me that the house had originally been a tenth-century monastery. "It was just walls when I got it," he said. "Everything had to be made over, restored to what it had been in its Georgian period. However, the interior is not furnished in Georgian style. It's furnished from every place in the world—a mélange."

It is a mélange at once dazzling, rich, and comfortable, reflecting the owner's taste, culture, wit, vitality, and love of things. Paintings abound—a Monet in the drawing room, a Juan Gris hanging next to three Jack Yeats in one of the bedrooms, an El Greco in the master bathroom. Most of Mr. Huston's noted collection of pre-Columbian art is housed in a gallery in one of the converted cellars. Also on display is his imposing collection of African sculpture, which vies for attention with a T'ang horseman, an Italian tapestry Pierrot, a Grecian horse's head in marble, and, among other treasures, a medieval French Christ in wood. The mixture of furniture is also impressive: eighteenth-century French pieces along with Gucci chairs, made of antelope hide stretched over a steel frame. Some of the bedrooms, including the owner's, have Napoleonic four-posters, while another has a bed with a headboard that was once an altarpiece in a Mexican cathedral. All of the bathrooms are designed along the lines of private sitting rooms, and contain well-stocked bookcases and large, comfortable chairs upholstered in terry cloth. Perhaps the most unexpected feature of the house (and what one of the owner's Irish friends has called "John Huston's greatest contribution to gracious living in the County Galway") is an imported Japanese bath, complete with sliding Shoji screens, a shower, a sunken heated pool, and a sand tray. In addition to the main house, the property also contains a tastefully furnished small residence that was formerly occupied by Mrs. Huston (now amicably separated, she lives in London), a trout stream, a shooting bog, and sizable stables, whose lofts have been converted into rooms capable of accommodating some twenty guests.

In a typical year, Mr. Huston told me, he is able to spend five or six months at St. Clerans. During that time, he is usually preparing a script. The rest of the year, he is generally off in some other part of the world, shooting a picture. After several unsuccessful attempts to arrange a meeting in Ireland or elsewhere abroad, I finally caught up with Mr. Huston at the end of a brief visit that he made to New York, and was invited to call at his hotel one evening. A tall, loose-limbed, fit-looking man, with blue eyes, a shock of brindled hair, a tanned, expressive face that is picturesquely wrinkled, grooved, and creased, and a strong nose whose bridge was broken years ago during a stint as a boxer, Mr. Huston was wearing slacks and a suede vest, having a Scotch, smoking a long, thin cigarette the color of a cigar, and preparing to depart for Rome on a plane leaving around midnight. A man of immense charm and impeccably skilled in handling the role of interviewee, he succeeded—almost—in giving the impression that there were few things in the world he would rather have been doing just then than to talk to me about living in Europe. He said that he had been making his residence there for some fifteen years, the initial reason being that the pictures on which he worked were made in Paris or Vienna or in some other location abroad.

HUSTON: No matter where I was working, I used to take every opportunity I could to run over to Ireland and get on a horse's back and hunt. All my holidays I spent there. I used to stay with friends, and later on, I rented a house in County Kildare. I lived there for two years. Then, one time, hunting out in Galway, the pack ran over this particular land, and I saw this house that was going to come up for sale. It hadn't been lived in for some time. It was just a shell. I bid on it, and got it. That was about twelve years ago.

I have heard that when the remodeling was under way and the workmen left for the day, it looked like the end of a shift at a Ford assembly plant.

HUSTON: Well, there was a lot to be done, and it took quite a long time. In fact, it took about three years. But things proceed slowly in Ireland. It's still a country of craftsmen—fine joiners and carpenters and cabinetmakers. There is nothing, or very little, that's prefabricated.

And I suppose the cost of the handwork is less.

HUSTON: Certainly no more. I probably spend as much on living in Ireland as I would in the United States, but I get much more for it. I couldn't live in the United States the way I live in Ireland. I couldn't possibly. My place has only a hundred acres, but I've got some twelve people in the house and on the land. I do a little stock breeding, and keep hunters and a few head of cattle. The number of horses varies. Usually, there are six or eight hunters, a couple of brood mares, and their foals and yearlings. Last year, we sold our first thoroughbred stock. And I did very well.

I understand you are also Master of Fox Hounds of the Galway Blazers.

HUSTON: That's really an honorary title in my case, because I'm home so little. Fortunately, I have a great Joint Master of Fox Hounds. We're both MFH's, but in this instance, we're Joint Masters. He hunts superbly well. Even if I were able to hunt hounds well, I wouldn't be there enough to manage properly. But it's great sport.

The life in Ireland obviously appeals to you, but you could have enjoyed it without becoming an Irish citizen. Why did you do it?

HUSTON: I didn't do it out of principle or anything like that. I found myself living there, and I got to love the place and the people. As I kept going back, it got to feel more like home than America. After having lived there for some twelve years, it was proposed that I become a citizen.

Who proposed it?

HUSTON: Some of the Irish. They said, "You're one of us. Why don't you stay here and be an Irishman?" And I said, "Yes."

What is the process? Is it complicated?

HUSTON: Most uncomplicated. I thought at first that there would be some red tape, but a friend of mine called the Minister of Justice, and said, "John Huston is thinking of becoming an Irishman. How should he go about it?" And Charley Haughey, the Minister, said, "Tell him to come down and get his Irish passport." It was as easy as that. Now, this doesn't hold for everyone. I mean, I'd lived there for all that time, and I knew people in the government. Normally, one would take out papers, and go through the same processes he would here.

There was one aspect that was rather, not distasteful exactly, but it gave me a bad moment. I had to go before an American consul and renounce my American citizenship. It was just a matter of form, but still, the act of renunciation—it's almost disclaiming loyalty to the United States. It has a kind of unpleasant ring.

Have you ever encountered people who have expressed a disapproving view of your having taken that step?

HUSTON: No. Some of my American friends advised me against it. I think they felt there would be a public reaction against my becoming —against anyone's ceasing to be an American. It's all right for an Irishman to become an American, but the very idea of someone doing the opposite shocked them. They were afraid, I suppose, that motion picture goers would resent it. Of course, I imagine if I had become a Panamanian citizen or a Swiss citizen or something of that kind, it would have been a different story.

While we're on this subject, I think it's rather interesting that on the second anniversary of my becoming an Irish citizen, Eddy Gilmore, of the Associated Press, came over and did an interview. It was published in a great many papers in the United States, and the response, in letters, was enormous. One would have thought there would have been several denunciatory letters, you know, accusing me of a lack of patriotism, but there wasn't a single one. Not one. In the interview, I had said that

I would always feel very close to the United States and admire it, but that a lot of things about America that I had known and loved as a young man no longer exist. When I was a kid, you didn't have to go very far to get out into the country. It was pretty simple and easy to take a rod or a gun and go fishing or shooting. It isn't any more. Places that I used to fox hunt over are factories and developments, and to get to the kind of places I used to like to go to—and that I like to have my kids go to—are harder to get to nowadays than to get to Ireland, where everything is right on my front doorstep. It's more like the America I used to know and love.

The fact that so many of these things no longer exist in America—that was what the people who wrote seized upon. That is what they also felt. There were at least a couple of hundred letters. They came from people of varying social and economic backgrounds. Some were from farmers, asking if it would be possible to buy a small acreage. Others inquired what kind of education they could get for their children. Several asked about Trinity College. The letters came from all over the country. I would have expected them to come mainly from urban centers, but they came from small towns, too, as you could see from the postmarks. One would also have thought that the people who wrote would have been moved by sentimentality, but at least half of them didn't have Irish names. All in all, it was quite an interesting experience. We answered each of the letters, supplying the information and advice that seemed to be required.

What did you tell people who asked about educating their children in Ireland? How have you managed that for your own children?

HUSTON: There are two. Walter Anthony, called Tony, who is fifteen, and Anjelica, who is thirteen. They went to grade school in Ireland, and now they're both in prep schools in England. The girl is in Town and Country. The boy's in Westminster. They'll probably return to Ireland—Trinity College—to finish their education. They love it here. When school is out for a holiday, they're back that same day, if there's a plane.

They have just become Irish citizens themselves. I've never tried to influence them one way or another in any of these things. I would have been delighted for them to go on being Americans, but they came to me individually with this request.

What did they say? Why did they want to do it?

HUSTON: It's just their great love of Ireland. Of course, they've lived here since they were infants. Their affections are Irish now.

It would have been almost impossible, by the way, for me to have raised my children in the United States the way I have here. From the time they were four or five, they've been on horses' backs. The boy fishes. He is also a falconer. They've both had that wonderful childhood in deep country that's very hard to get now in the United States along with an education. Wherever they go, they will always carry with them that wonderful, deep association with Mother Nature.

Going back to your own decision to become an Irish citizen, I would like to ask what part taxes played in making that decision.

HUSTON: Almost none. I pay practically the same taxes now as before. There are certain advantages and certain disadvantages, and they weigh out quite evenly. The Irish tax system is based on the English.

Is it that high?

HUSTON: It is that high. It all compensates. It all works out to be just about even. May I say, by the way, while you're on the tax issue, that in the United States, the taxpayer is regarded as a tax evader, someone who is trying to get away with something. He's suspect, and he's scrutinized, apparently with the idea that he's doing everything he can to keep from paying his taxes, so that if he files an honest return, he's all the more suspect. There's an air of criminality, and perhaps it leads to behavior that's not untinged with dishonesty on the part of the taxpayer in the United States. This, may I say, does not exist in Ireland.

Doesn't anyone question your tax returns?

HUSTON: They don't. They take it for what it's worth, and certainly I, nor anyone I know, would try for a moment to practice dishonesty with them. The American practice of always looking for loopholes is not the atmosphere of Ireland at all. I don't know at firsthand, because I have people who handle these things for me, as I did in the United States, but I have the feeling that the tax structure in Ireland is considerably simpler. The atmosphere is a lot clearer, and the system seems to be easier to understand. It's one of the nice things about living in Ireland, coming around to that point again.

Since we're back on that subject, what are some of the other things that you enjoy there?

HUSTON: I will go into one other little avenue, if you wish. Despite the religious climate of the country—they've been accused of bigotry and so on, mostly by their own prophets and writers—a wonderful tolerance exists in Ireland. They may be against mixed bathing—and I think that's one of the lesser causes for anxiety on the part of the Church, because that ocean is the coldest goddam sea south of the Aleutians—but there's great understanding and tolerance towards a man and his right to his viewpoint. For instance, when people in the United States who were against Senator McCarthy were afraid to express themselves, and great injustices were being done because of that fear, the people of Ireland were outspoken in their criticism of him. None of the press failed to express the fact that they had very little use for this Irish descendant. And when people with names and reputations actually went to jail as a result of his persecutions, this was not understood in Ireland at all. I shouldn't say "not understood." This was deplored.

You know, I'm for all kinds of countries and nationalities and differences among peoples. I'm all for frontiers that are ever so easy to cross, and I'm dead against passports. So, I don't think what country you live in makes very much difference. I think *where* you live—your instant location—does make a difference. There are people who like to live in cities. There are people who like to live where it snows. There are people who like to live in the tropics. In Connemara, which is the northern part of County Galway, where I live, the people have an identity with their land that is quite remarkable—something that doesn't exist, as far as I know, anyplace in the United States today. A Connemara man knows every rock on his land. They've lived there for generations and generations—ever since Cromwell drove them out. It's harder to buy that unyielding, rocky land than the bluegrass farms of Kentucky or the wonderful limestone farms of County Kildare, because that land is *theirs*, and they are that land. That is a wonderful kind of identification. They aren't Irishmen. They are Connemaramen.

These Connemaramen who are your neighbors—are they your friends? Do you entertain them? Do they entertain you?

HUSTON: Oh yes. Certainly. And again, the so-called lowliest farmer—his behavior as a host couldn't be surpassed in sheer elegance and hospitality. It's a country of *real* democracy. One man *is* as good as another. There's never been any racial discrimination in Ireland. No Jew was ever chased down a back alley in Ireland. No Negro was ever discriminated against because of his color. A man is as good as he does.

Are you conscious at all of what strikes many visitors to Ireland as rather widespread poverty?

HUSTON: No. There is no poverty in Ireland today. The people are very well off compared with what they used to be. It's a relatively prosperous country, Ireland. In the one city, Dublin, there is a kind of slum area, a lower-class area, but that is the nearest thing to poverty in Ireland. There's not the middle class or bourgeoisie wealth that one sees in the United States, but people are well fed, well clothed. The government has made great strides in this respect, maybe at the sacrifice of some of the charms of Ireland.

And the climate—many visitors are not very favorably impressed by that, either.

HUSTON: Oh, it's a fine climate. It rains a lot, but it's a wonderful climate, really, and ideal for the things I like to do. It's rather better than British weather. The Gulf Stream curves around the southern part of Kerry, and laves it warmly. There are even palm trees in Kerry. Very little snow in Ireland, except the hilltops, and usually, in the course of a day, you at least glimpse the sun. That doesn't happen in England, where the skies lower leadenly, and remain just over your head for weeks on end.

Is there anything about the United States that you do miss?

HUSTON: Friends. But they come over and see me. All through the year, whenever I'm home, people drop in. At first, I missed a favorite dish, Jailhouse Chili, but then I arranged with Dave Chasen to send it over. Now my cook has worked out the formula, and her Jailhouse Chili is so good I think we'll send some to Dave.

Another thing about Ireland—there just isn't that violence that we see so often in the United States. I also detect here in America a kind of harshness and aggressiveness in the voice and actions of the people generally. I don't know the reason, but the sense of aggressiveness is everywhere evident, and I find it altogether unattractive.

And, you know, there is no murder in Ireland. I assure you, you could send two little girls across Ireland by themselves, sleeping in haystacks, and they would be as safe as if they'd never left home. I don't know of what other country you could say that.

> "The American pace of living may be more stimulating and productive, but the British pace is much more mine."

Ben Duncan, a native of Birmingham, Alabama, arrived in England in 1950 to attend Oxford University, and, upon completing his studies there, decided to make England his home. This decision, he found, was more easily made than implemented, for the Home Office inexplicably refused him permission to remain in the country. He thereupon undertook a campaign to make the authorities change their collective mind. "By any standards under the sun, I was doing something pretty strange," he later remarked. "Coming from a country the whole world was trying to get into, I was struggling stubbornly for the right to live outside it." His struggle was successful, and he is still living in England, at present in a fifth-floor apartment on Hertford Street, diagonally across from the London Hilton Hotel. "I can afford to live in such a grand neighborhood," he told me as I arrived at his apartment late one afternoon, "because, as you have no doubt just painfully discovered, this building has no lift." Soft-spoken, extraordinarily tall, with dark hair and brown eyes, Mr. Duncan was wearing a blue suit of conservative shade and cut, a white shirt with French cuffs, gold cuff links, and a quiet tie. From his dress and accent, it seemed to me, he might easily be taken for an Englishman. I asked him if that often happened.

DUNCAN: I have lived here long enough so that I wear English clothes, and get my hair cut by an English barber, so I suppose I do look rather like an Englishman, but I don't think, whenever I have opened my mouth, that I have been mistaken for one. There are certain perfectly clear signs that I am not. I still say, "ask" and "can't," whereas every Englishman, except some who live north of the Humber, says, "ahsk" and "cahn't." That particular "a" sound, if nothing else, would give me away, and although my "r's" may sound English to your ears, to the English they sound either American or Irish. I think Irish is the most frequent guess. When I first became conscious that my accent was changing, I made a very strong effort *not* to change it. I never in the least wanted to, but if you work in an English firm and know mainly English people, as I do, it's bound to happen. And you can't go on using the American names for things. If you don't know, after all these years, that it's called "petrol" and not "gasoline," it would be a terrible affectation.

I know that you came to England originally to go to Oxford, but I wonder if you could tell me briefly how that came about.

DUNCAN: I was born in Birmingham, but I didn't grow up there, because my parents traveled around a good deal. My father was a clerk in hotels, and was moved from one to another. My parents died when I was eleven, and for the next seven years I lived in a series of orphanages and foster homes in various places in the South. Then I was drafted into the Army—that was 1946—and spent about a year in it. When I came out, there was a splendid thing called the G.I. Bill of Rights, which paid for me to go to school anywhere, and I chose, of all unlikely places, the University of New Mexico. One reason was that I didn't want to stay in the South. I had never liked it, if the truth be told. The other reason was that the eastern universities were crowded at that time, and New Mexico was more or less empty. So, I went there, and graduated with a major in English.

During my last year at New Mexico, I heard about the Henry Fellowships, which are something like Rhodes Scholarships but without the emphasis on athletic ability and the well-rounded personality. The Henry Fellowships were set up by an English woman in memory of her husband, who was an American. They provide funds for five Americans to go to Oxford or Cambridge every year, and five Englishmen to go to Harvard or Yale. I applied for one of the fellowships, which I later found had never been awarded to anyone west of the Mississippi, had the great good luck to be given one, and set off for a year at Oxford. That was the first time I had been outside of the United States. It was a fairly overwhelming experience.

What did you study at Oxford?

DUNCAN: English again, though, in fact, it was a different English, because in the English language and literature course at Oxford, you don't officially read anything published after 1832. Aside from the study of Anglo-Saxon, I enjoyed the whole experience of being at Oxford, in particular the part of my studies that I did with my tutor, J. I. M. Stewart, who writes mysteries under the name of Michael Innes. I would find it very difficult to say whether I enjoyed Oxford more than New Mexico or even to compare them, because they are so terribly different. In fact, I never tried to compare Oxford, when I was there, with any single place in America that I could imagine myself going back to. What I did compare was being in England generally with the whole chunk of my life in America, and on that score, I was 100 per cent sold on living in England.

At the beginning, though, I was extremely lonely and unhappy. I think it is one of the faults of Oxford and Cambridge that if you are foreign and don't have introductions to people, you will simply be left alone for a very long time. I was very miserable my first term. I didn't really like England very much. It seemed to be cold and dirty and unsympathetic in every sense of that word. I was almost always terribly cold, and I didn't get enough to eat. What I did get I didn't think very good. One has to remember that this was 1950. The food rations were not only still in effect but the lowest they had ever been, even during the war. I had come from a place where there were no shortages to a place where you got one egg a week and a weekly ration of meat the size of a matchbox. And I couldn't see why England was thought a beautiful country at all. It seemed to me incredibly ugly, and I thought the people were strange-looking, not at all attractive. My attitude was also affected by the fact that I had been thrown into a very aristocratic college, Christ Church, and the aristocratic young men there didn't lay themselves out to please or be friendly, particularly at the beginning.

When did your feelings about Oxford and England begin to change? I suppose it was a very gradual process.

DUNCAN: It was, and one of which I think I was myself more or less unconscious until about halfway through the third and final term of the year, when I was suddenly faced with the prospect of not having a second year at Oxford. Then I realized—well, I thought I couldn't live if I didn't have the other year. The feeling had obviously been building up all that time. My fellowship was, in fact, renewable, but I didn't discover that until too late. However, I did manage to find a way to stay at Oxford. A rich American woman given to philanthropy happened to be in Oxford, and an American friend of mine there told her I was in dire need. She had various scholarship funds set up in America, and evidently because she thought mine sounded like a worthy cause, she passed the word to one of them, and they sent me the money. So, I was able to stay on for the second year, and get my degree.

Had you decided, while you were still at Oxford, that you were going to stay on in England?

DUNCAN: I had begun toying with the idea. Before that, I had always imagined that I was going to be an academic of some sort, and after Oxford, would go back to America and get on with my studies. When I actually changed my mind I couldn't really tell, but when I left Oxford, I knew, even though I had practically no funds left, that I wasn't going back to America for a bit. That meant getting a job, of course. I applied to be a schoolmaster and for a variety of other jobs, but nothing worked out. Finally, I got a job in an advertising agency as a copywriter. I had never done anything remotely like that. In fact, I disapproved of advertising, and accepted the job only because I was quite desperate by then. I am still in advertising, although that isn't the only kind of work I've done here.

Getting onto that subject brings me to a terrible period in my life. I have written about it in a book called *The Same Language*. Briefly, having gotten permission to live and work here for one year, I then had the greatest difficulty in getting permission to live here for another year. The reasons are very complicated, and I won't go into them now, except to say, as I remarked in the book, that the whole subject of aliens is kept so dark in this country that you don't know half the time what you're supposed to be doing, even if you want to do what is right. What one is up against, I found, is a kind of nightmarish situation that works something like this: to get permission to stay here, you need permission to work. To get permission to work, you need permission to stay. The Home Office doesn't stop you from working. The Ministry of Labor doesn't stop you from staying. But between them, they stop you from doing either.

The upshot, in my case, was that I was threatened with deportation. Eventually, I was faced with the choice of going back to America or taking a job in what is called an undermanned occupation. These are the jobs in England that are so nasty that nobody wants to do them. I took one, and became a hospital orderly. I remained an orderly for two years, working in an eye hospital in the East End of London. It was a fairly harrowing period of my life, but I said I would do anything to stay here, and I very nearly did.

Part of your problem in staying, as I understand it, was that you had to earn an income, so you had to get permission to work. Would your situation have been different if you'd had your own means? In other words, can one live here as long as he wishes, if he doesn't take a job?

DUNCAN: It's not even as simple as that. The Home Office has very strict regulations about who may come in and who may not. Basically, the regulations are designed to discourage immigration, so they make getting permission to work here very difficult indeed. The company you expect to work for has to make out a very good case for hiring you. It has to prove that the job you are going to do could not be done by an English person. If you can manage to work here for four years, then you are allowed to stay on as long as you like and do whatever you wish. You have sort of worked off your indenture. But, of course, getting a job in the first place is the hurdle.

To try to answer your question—no, it is not always possible simply to come here to live and support yourself with funds from somewhere else. Even the promise that you will be bringing dollars into the country is not enough. In fact, people with private means are quite often turned out. I know of a retired American couple who came here for the Coronation, found they liked living in England, bought a house, and prepared to settle down. Then, for reasons they could never understand, the Home Office said, "You must go." When I was in my most desperate stage of trying to get permission to live in England —my case, by the way, had become a great cause in England—a wealthy American here suggested a solution. Since I simply wanted to stay here and write, he offered to support me until the troubles with the Home Office were worked out by giving me the same sum of money I had received from the Henry Fellowship. I would thus not be taking a job from any English person, and I'd be bringing dollars into the country. As proof of all this, I showed the Home Office the check that my American benefactor had given me. But still they said, "No."

Aside from this American, who else became interested in your case?

DUNCAN: Who didn't would come closer. At various times, the list included a Conservative M.P., Charles Fletcher-Cooke, and a Labor M.P., Roy Jenkins, who later became Chancellor of the Exchequer. A number of solicitors got involved as well as some clergymen and scores and scores of other people. I think my most tireless champion was [Sir] Roy Harrod, a don at Oxford, who also sits on some of the Home Office committees that decide immigration policies. Once I had enlisted his support, he went on and on and on, arguing that in the light of those policies the decisions that had been made in my case were wrong. In the end, I think, the Home Office's resistance was simply worn down. Suddenly, at the end of two years, they said, in effect, "All right, you can stay. You can stay and work." As a result of my sufferings on behalf of immigrants to England, I am told, there is now a classification at the Home Office called the "Duncan Category," under which certain Americans who want to live here and write, as I did, or paint are allowed to. So, something may have come out of that terrible period.

And the reason that you had been willing to go through it was purely the very strong attachment you had formed to this country?

DUNCAN: Actually, my reasons were mixed. First, of course, was the desire to live here, and, once having begun to seek permission to do so, not wanting to be put off. Exactly what proportions of each of those motives were involved it would be impossible for me to say. My determination to stay certainly grew as it became more difficult. When one becomes a public cause like that, one's own motives cease to be of very much importance. It would, I thought, have been betraying people if I hadn't gone on. In fact, all through the time that I was being threatened with having to leave, I was appalled by the idea of going back. It was partly that I had no place to go back to. The places that I had lived in the longest were the ones that I least wanted to return to. Nothing on earth could have persuaded me to go back and live in the South, and, having grown up in the sticks, I was slightly alarmed at the prospect of going to a place like New York.

To balance against that, I had, by the end of three or four years in England, begun to have more feeling of roots here than I ever had in America. The Oxford friends whom I went on seeing after I had come to London I felt closer to than I had to very many people in America. There is no doubt, too, that once I had broken through their reserve, there was some sort of reaction between me and the English, which was almost chemical. I knew inside that basically they were more like me than my fellow Americans. It wasn't a matter of liking particularly some of my own faults that they share. I think in some ways my fellow Americans have more admirable qualities, but I happen not to share them. I think Americans are more genuinely openminded. I think the English are inclined to cling to their prejudices, and I am, too. I approve of the American attitude, but I share the British. Also, the American pace of living may be more stimulating and productive, but the British pace is much more mine. If it is possible to isolate the single most appealing facet of life here, it is that.

There is another quality that I sense and respond to in the English. This is a quite commonplace observation but one which I happen to feel the strength of. When I first made friends in England, I had always the suspicion that the fact that I was an American visitor who was here for a short time and would soon depart for my own shores meant that the people were more friendly to me than they would have been otherwise. I discovered that this was quite the reverse of the truth—that, in fact, the longer I knew my English friends, the closer I was to them, the more loyal I felt them to be. The English are not given to welcoming strangers, God knows, but if you can survive the initial unfriendliness, you find they are very loyal indeed.

What kind of social life does an American have here, when his friends, as in your case, are mainly English?

DUNCAN: Mine is fairly sedate. I am a bachelor. I share this flat with an Englishman, and I also share a rented cottage with him down in Cambridgeshire, although I'm in the process of building a small house there on a very beautiful small tributary of the Cam. Down there, in the country, which I love, I have an extremely pleasant, absolutely informal life, which is spent largely with two or three families who live nearby. One is a don, who lives in the same village and has a wife and five children. In the next village lives the elder brother of the man who shares this flat, again with a wife and family. We go to meals with them, or they come and have them at our cottage. People come down from London and stay the weekend. Other friends, who have more children than we can put up in our tiny cottage, come down and spend the day with us. In London itself, I go out to dinner with friends, I suppose, one night a week.

What I really enjoy most are the weekends in the country, particularly in the spring. I don't know why the English spring should be so much more lovely than it is anywhere else, but it is. I think that the really incomparable English spring had a lot to do with my deciding that England was not ugly but beautiful. I think also that one must develop a certain eye for seeing the point of England. I always regret that any tourist should come here and stay only a week or so. I think, at the very least, he should pay fortnightly visits spaced over a period of years, because the lights and shades in England are so delicate and so subtle that they cannot really be taken in unless you work at seeing them over a period of time.

On my holidays, I have recently started going to Ireland, and I love it. I have a curious feeling that in certain parts of Ireland, one feels, as an American, curiously at home in a way that one doesn't anywhere in England. Bits of Dublin are very like bits of New York. Some of the simple habits of the people are alike. In London, you don't see people actually standing in their doorways, even when the weather is good, and greeting people who walk by. Of course, this happens in certain areas of New York, and it happens in Dublin and in provincial cities in Ireland as well. In Cork, I could have closed my eyes, walked around a certain corner, and persuaded myself that I was in New York or some other American city.

When, in fact, were you last back in America?

DUNCAN: A terrible admission—I've never been back at all. In 1960, I decided that it was ridiculous not to have gone back and that I must, and I got myself all set to go. I arranged to take off two months between jobs, but as the day of departure drew near, I began to feel that I didn't actually very much want to go. It was going to cost a great deal of money to get there and to live there. I also had the feeling that it was all very well to go back to America, but where exactly would I go after getting there? Should I go to New York, where I would be very much like a tourist? Or should I try to visit various relatives scattered all over the country? Whether I lost my nerve or whether my better judgment prevailed—whatever the reason—I went instead to Greece. I spent the two months there, and enjoyed them very much.

As far ahead as you can see, England is going to be your residence?

DUNCAN: Oh, certainly. I am in no doubt about that at all. I have never for a moment regretted the decision to live here. I think, really, my only regret is that I would have been happier in an academic life than in the commercial world. But at the same time, the sort of books I write are not the sort that earn incomes people can live on, and the job I do is, of its kind, a very congenial one for me. So, I suspect for quite some time I shall go on doing what I'm doing, which is holding down a fairly exhausting job—I still write copy, but I am now an account director as well—and at the same time trying to find time to write.

In view of your fondness for this country and your plans to stay on here, have you considered becoming a British citizen?

DUNCAN: I have been forced to think of it by the troubles I've had living here. My first chance to become a British citizen came after I had worked here for the required four years. I realized then that by taking British nationality I could, once and for all, eliminate being caused any further troubles by the Home Office. But I thought, "No, the hell with them. They put me off long enough. I can perfectly well live here and keep my American nationality, and so I shall." I don't doubt that one day I will, in fact, take British nationality, but what still rankles is that when I embraced England so wholeheartedly, they rather shied away. I think that's the only reason. I don't think I have any very sentimental attachment to the idea of an American passport. Certainly, on practical grounds, it wouldn't make the slightest difference, since I'm going to live here forever.

GALLERY NOTES

It may be true that when good Americans die, they go to Paris, but rather few native Americans go there or anywhere else in Europe when they retire. Probably the main reason is that by the time a person reaches the usual retirement age, he is not apt to have the vigor or the interest to accommodate to another way of living. He prefers to stay in familiar surroundings, near his family, his friends, and his doctors. Except in a relatively small number of cases, the spirit of adventure is no longer in him.

The majority of retired Ameropeans fall into one of two general categories. The smaller consists of men who were able to retire in their forties or fifties, while still possessing enough zest to undertake the building of a new life, and did so, usually in company with their wife and family. Among this group is Truman Monroe Dodson IV, a very hearty, ruddy-faced retired executive of a Pennsylvania coal company, who lives with his wife in Positano. Since their children were grown, Mr. Dodson, who is in his early fifties, said that he and his wife were able to live wherever they wished after he had decided, at age forty-six, to retire. "As a youngster, I traveled a fair amount, and I learned to love Europe," he said. "It just drew me back when I decided to stop chasing the Almighty Buck. Initially, our thought was to have a hat-rack somewhere in the Mediterranean area, and from there do a great deal of traveling. The hatrack grew into our home. We like it so much here we don't go away very often. Climatically, it's hard to beat, and we love our little house, which was a series of tiny rooms when we bought it. I designed and managed the reconstruction, which involved some rather unusual features, such as carving space for a new kitchen and a bath and dressing room out of this solid rock mountain, using only a hammer and chisel. The whole job took a year and a half. It was fun. My wife plays a good deal of bridge, but I prefer to go out in my little launch with a couple of friends and do some diving. You might have noticed on the terrace those two old anchors. We brought those up from the sea. They're probably upwards of two thousand years old. Now we're going after an old cannon, a Roman anchor, and some other things we have already marked. All this intrigues me. When I first came here, after working for all those years under the usual pressure in the States, I found that the unwinding period lasted about six months. The first thing you notice is lethargy. You have never been so sleepy in your life, day in and day out. Gradually, that leaves, and you begin to feel alive again. You begin to be aware again of time going by. Now it goes by almost too fast. You don't know where yesterday went. Time just flies. It's fantastic. But it's glorious. It's all glorious."

The larger category of retired Ameropeans is made up of men whose professional life required that they live abroad a good deal of the time. Some were businessmen, others were in the foreign service, and quite a few others were attachés of one of the armed forces. Not only did they become accustomed to life abroad but grew to prefer its attractions, in particular the relatively lower cost of living, and so becoming an Ameropean after retirement was, for them, a quite natural step. One of these, Henry T. Jarrell, is a tall, tanned, silver-haired, broad-shouldered former United States Navy captain, who spent most of his professional career in the Far East before being appointed, in 1955, naval attaché to the American Embasssy in Madrid. By the time he retired, three years later, he and his wife had become so attached to Spain that they decided to remain there. Since then, Captain Jarrell has opened an insurance agency in Madrid that represents a number of American companies and caters primarily to English-speaking residents.

"It's not always easy to explain why one elects to live abroad," Captain Jarrell told me in his office one beautiful fall afternoon. "Just before I went off active duty, the admiral who was then our commanding chief made a visit here, and I told him that I planned to stay on in Spain after retiring. He said, "What's the matter? Isn't the United States good enough for you?" I knew what the answer to that question should *not* be, so I told him that I thought my wife and I were pretty good representatives of our country, and that perhaps America could use more people with foreign experience abroad, and so on. He understood that. It would have been very difficult, if not impossible, to explain the real reason, which is that we had come to feel that one gets more living, more enjoyment, out of every twenty-four hours here. You don't have to put out so much effort to do what you want to do with your day. For example, if you want to play golf, there are two beautiful courses, each less than two miles from here, the center of town. In fifteen minutes, I can be on either course, have a caddy, and be ready to tee off. I could go out now, play nine holes, come back, and have another hour in the office before we close. What it adds up to is this: we probably spend as much here on living as we would at home, but we get a great deal more for our money."

Whatever their background, the retired Ameropeans, like retired people generally, tend to settle in the warmer climates. There are exceptions, such as Dr. Theodore Anderson, a physician who practiced in Minneapolis until his health caused him to retire and who then moved with his wife to Gstaad, Switzerland. "I stayed at home, in Minneapolis, for a year after I retired," Dr. Anderson told me, "and I was going crazy. All of my friends were still busy, working, and it was very difficult. Finally, we decided to pack up and get out. We were charmed by the beauty of this place, and still like it better than anyplace else we've seen. Life is easier here, and your money goes further. For one thing, you don't have all the demands that you have at home for club dues, contributions to the art museum, the symphony, and all those other worthy causes. You know, if you have lived in a community for a great many years, and you have a certain income, most of your friends have a comparable income. Then suddenly your income goes down. Well, it's very hard to change your way of living in that community, but if you move to a new place, as we did, you can live on a different scale without difficulty. It's just a matter of starting over again, and that can be a very invigorating experience."

> "I don't think of myself as retired at all. I think of myself as launched on a new life, with plenty of exciting new things to do."

Philip Carter, a slender, fit-looking, sandy-haired man in his middle fifties, who wears a neatly trimmed mustache and expertly tailored clothes, entered the publishing business in New York, his birthplace, after graduating from Princeton. "I was originally an editor, I am happy to say," Mr. Carter has recalled, "but then I was lured into the advertising business, where the pay was at least half as much more than the publishing job. In that way, I fell from grace, and regretted it ever afterward." After the fall, his professional progress was swift and lucrative. Following the customary pattern, he moved from one agency to another, founded his own with two associates, built that up, sold out his interest, and then signed on in a senior capacity with one of the largest agencies in New York. "It didn't take long to discover that I wasn't quite that philistine—very close, perhaps, but not that much," Mr. Carter has said. "That job became increasingly irksome and unnerving and, ultimately, absolutely intolerable. Finally, I said, 'The hell with it,' and I quit. I said to my wife, 'Let's go to Europe and live.' She said, 'Fine,' and so we did." That was in 1962. Since then, Mr. Carter and his wife, a very animated and good-looking blond woman who was born in America of Danish parents, have made their residence in various places in Europe, returning to the United States for annual visits during the Christmas holidays. I met them on one of those visits, after I had returned from Europe, at the home of a mutual friend in New York, and made a date to see them together a couple of days later at their hotel. Recalling part of the conversation at our first meeting, I asked if there had been major problems in making the abrupt change from Madison Avenue to retirement abroad.

CARTER: From the outside, the change probably looks more abrupt than it actually was. We had been going to Europe for years and years, staying for five or six weeks at a time, so when I concluded that I'd had it on Madison Avenue, we just decided to go over and stay longer. We thought we might stay the major part of the year or perhaps all of the year, depending on what we found and how we liked it.

First, we went to the Canary Islands—friends who had been there told us we'd love it—and rented a little house, but after a few weeks, we decided the Canaries were not for us. Too isolated. From there we went to Italy, traveled up one coast and down the other, and spent quite a while in Rome. All the time we were looking for a place to live. Then we went up into France and took a house in Annecy for several weeks. Really not very attractive, and six hundred dollars a month. We learned for ourselves what everyone had told us—that France is fearfully expensive. We moved on to Switzerland, and spent a summer in Gstaad. The chalet we had there was charming but unpretentious, and the rent was eight hundred dollars a month. The chalet was for sale, for a hundred and ten thousand dollars. That seemed a bit much.

MRS. CARTER: Then we went to England, and took a house in Sussex. We loved that little house, just about an hour south of London by train. We had the happiest time in the world there, but we didn't want to go through the winter, and we were talking with one of the friends we'd made there about where we might go. Pamela—our friend—said, "Well, I have a little villa"—Philip says the English call anything with an inside john a villa—"in Portugal. I'm not going to get down there until January. Why don't you go down and use it until then?" So off we went—it was then late November—to Portugal. We had never been there, and certainly had never thought of living there. It was the last outpost of civilization, I thought. Well, when we got there, we fell in love with it instantly. Just instantly.

CARTER: As so many people do. Pamela's place is in the Algarve, the most southerly province in Portugal. It has a lovely situation, about seventy yards back from one of those secluded and utterly unspoiled horseshoe beaches that scallop the southern edge of Portugal. Beautiful. And everywhere there are blossoming almond trees and orange trees and figs and flowers. The climate, we think, is as good as anywhere in Europe. For the most part, I would say it's excellent. It's rainy in January and February and a little bit into March. It doesn't rain every day, of course. I should think that on the average, the number of days of rainfall in January and February would range from eight to twelve. Even on the worst days, the temperature almost never fails to be in the sixties.

MRS. CARTER: During that season, it's often chilly indoors, because the houses are built mainly for summer residence, and so you live pretty much by the fireplace. An electric blanket is probably essential, or at least highly desirable. In that season, there is a damp that gets into everything—mold on your shoes, you know—but that's only in January and February. When the sun shines, which is not at all infrequent, the temperature gets into the seventies. Even in January and February, we usually have our lunch and breakfast outdoors. In July and August, it may get very hot, but it's a dry climate, and if you stay out of the sun, you're always comfortable.

CARTER: We were so instantaneously pleased by the whole prospect that as soon as we'd settled in Pamela's house we started looking for a place of our own. We had the great good luck to find one right next door, and we've been living in it ever since. This is a charming house, which was built by a couple of English boys. Their success story is quite marvelous. They came seven or eight years ago into this lovely little fishing village—just a cove in the beach—and bought an abandoned sardine canning factory. It was really just a shell. Even the roof was gone. Inside this compound they built three little houses with immense charm—they had a great flair for decor, as those boys often do—and they also made the most magnificent garden you've ever seen. They paid forty-two hundred dollars for the abandoned factory, and they invested another three thousand or so in rejuvenating it and adding their little touches. They sold it last year for a hundred and forty thousand dollars.

MRS. CARTER: We've bought some land ourselves. It's about half a mile from the place we've been renting, and we're going to start building a house next spring. Like everywhere else, the price of land in Portugal has been going up and up. We paid fifteen thousand dollars for ours, which I thought was an awful lot of money for property in such an isolated area.

CARTER: Of course, it's becoming less isolated practically by the day. Furthermore, the price at which I bought my land is about half of what one would pay for land that is no more beautiful, and possibly even less desirable, fifteen miles east of us, which is where most of the foreign population in the Algarve now live. Our property, which is in an area that is almost all farmland, is about seventeen miles from Cape St. Vincent, the southwest tip of Europe. We have a little less than three acres. It's about seven hundred yards back from the water, on a gradually ascending hill—they call it a mountain there—with a magnificent sweep of the sea, and there is a wonderful variety of trees. Really beautiful.

What kind of house are you planning to build?

MRS. CARTER: A kind of Portuguese country house, all on one level and rather long and low. It will be whitewashed and have a beige tile roof. All the houses down there are like that, and I think they're very attractive. As is so frequently the case, the original peasant architecture has a charming simplicity, and the proportions are lovely. To the west of the main house the land slopes down into a little vale, which is full of almond and fig trees, and Philip is building a separate little structure there that he will use for a study. He wants a place where he can be by himself. You see, the English, who make up most of the foreign population in that area, for the most part have nothing to do, so they drop in whenever it suits their fancy.

CARTER: The final plans for the house and the study—the English, by the way, call a separate little structure like that a folly—have been drawn by an English architect, and are now in the process of being approved. First, they have to pass the local town council, and then be sent to Lisbon for approval there. If your builder is adept at pushing things through, you may have your plans approved in two months.

Richard Condon, an American writer, told me he had planned to build in Portugal, but decided against it after discovering that whereas the building regulations were very strict as far as his house was concerned, they didn't seem to be equally severe for the natives. They were putting up shacks within sight of the place where he had planned to build a rather expensive house.

CARTER: I have a strong suspicion that the natives do get away with things that foreigners cannot. Down the road from us there is a horrible little motel owned by Portuguese. There must be twelve or fifteen ugly little huts that look as if they were made of tin. A big German company in Hamburg takes over the whole thing, and sends their employees down there for vacations. Of course, it was against all the regulations to put those huts up, but the fine for contravening the regulations, when imposed on the natives, is such a small sum that they gladly pay it, and go on their way. We've been assured by the authorities that this setup is temporary and nothing else like it will be built. I think we can probably believe them, considering how expensive land has become. People who can't afford to put up anything but a shanty can't pay those prices for property.

In any event, we're going ahead. We've engaged the best builder in the area, an English engineer who's had architectural training. The foreman and the laborers will all be Portuguese, of course. Because wages are so low, the estimate for our house—two hundred square meters, which is quite a considerable house—comes to about fourteen thousand dollars.

MRS. CARTER: This is the way these things always start out. If we get away for under twenty-five thousand dollars for that house, I'll buy you a case of Scotch.

CARTER: Make it champagne, because we will. Certainly not more than fifteen thousand.

Once the house is finished, we expect to live in it from six to eight months of the year, and rent it during the high season, which is June, July, August, and September. There shouldn't be any difficulty in doing that. A friend of ours who has a house down there runs one ad in the London *Sunday Times* in February, and gets so many responses she could rent it to scores of people. Based on what we know about rentals there, we think we can get about three hundred and fifty dollars a month for our house. While it's rented, we'll follow the pattern of the last couple of years, which is to travel in Europe, driving up through Spain, France, and Italy into the Austrian Tyrol, where we'll stay for a while, and then come back to the United States to see family and friends. That makes for a very pleasant change.

Aside from housing, how do other prices in Portugal compare with those in the United States? For example, food and help.

MRS. CARTER: Our maid, for six days a week—out of the goodness of our hearts we give the girl Sundays off from nine to five, you know, spoiling the natives—for six days a week, we pay twenty-one dollars a month. And she is a gem. She looks like a little Wellesley girl. I suppose it's the spectacles that make her look so intelligent.

CARTER: Don't let Martha's twenty-one dollars a month deceive you. In Portugal, you do many things for your maids besides paying them wages. For one thing, if they get appendicitis, you take them to the hospital, and you pay all the bills. And you also pay to take care of any of their brood when they are ill. Doctors' bills are very steep in Portugal, and medicine is very expensive, because almost all of it is imported. The duty on practically all imports is tremendous. That's the way the government derives a great deal of its income.

MRS. CARTER: Food is cheaper, because you live on fish and chicken, vegetables and fruit. The beef is very tough. You don't even bother with it. While local food is usually not expensive, anything imported is hideously expensive—50 to 100 per cent more than in the United States. For example, a small jar of peanut butter that sells for twenty cents here costs eighty cents in Portugal.

CARTER: The really inexpensive product are the local wines, which are quite good. Also, an Englishman down there sells some kind of gin—I don't know where he gets it—for seven dollars a gallon, and it's all right. Nobody's gone blind yet. There is also a local brandy that is very good and cheap. People who come to visit would never dream of asking for Scotch, which sells there for about nine dollars a fifth.

As for the over-all expenses, we lived comfortably in that charming house we rented for about three hundred and twenty-five dollars a month. That's for everything, including maids, upkeep of a car, and gasoline at eighty cents a gallon.

When you're in Portugal, how do you spend your time?

MRS. CARTER: Philip is never at a loss—reading, writing, doing a dozen things. We have a kind of circulating library down there. We and the neighbors subscribe to a number of magazines and periodicals —the *Observer*, the *Guardian*, the London *Times*, and many others —and these are passed around. So we are all reasonably *au courant*. For Philip, there aren't enough hours in the day, but I, unfortunately, seem to spend most of my time entertaining the English, who have mastered the art of enjoying themselves by doing nothing. They drop in at twelve o'clock, and you have to start serving drinks.

CARTER: Martha is the community's interpreter. Besides the Scandinavian languages, she spoke French and Italian before we went to Portugal. Then she bought a little book called *Teach Yourself Portuguese in Three Months*, which she did. Now she spends too much of her time interpreting the English to their maids and the maids to their mistresses. And when the mistresses or masters happen to be in London and write letters to their maids, they come rushing over to Martha to ask for a translation. She translates. Then the maid, overcome with emotion, insists on writing a reply, so Martha has to translate the reply.

MRS. CARTER: Then, too, when some new person comes down to rent one of the houses in the community, the maid comes over and says, "I don't understand a word, *senhora.* Will you please come over?" And though I don't want to meet the people—I don't want to meet one other soul in the Algarve—I have perforce to become acquainted. Then you have to say, "Do drop in for a drink." Or, "If you need anything, let me know." And, of course, they do. In the evening, we like to read and be quiet, but people just drop in. That is one of the reasons we're building a house—to get away from that tight little group.

CARTER: Another reason is that I think it's a damned good investment. I don't see how you can possibly lose. Certainly that kind of property is as good an investment as the best of bonds. In addition, the property is appreciating. I will get a yield on it from the rental, and when I'm occupying it, I will save by not paying rent.

In the event that you may some time want to sell it, could you get your money out of Portugal without difficulty?

CARTER: I asked our Embassy about that, and I must say that all the letters I had from them were models of circumspection. Almost every statement was qualified in some cautious way. Nevertheless, I got enough assurance to satisfy me that it would be all right to go ahead. Furthermore, if you should sell, you would most likely sell to an English or a Swiss or some other foreigner, and the payment would be made in pounds or Swiss francs or some other foreign currency. I don't feel any genuine concern on that score.

The area where you're building sounds as if it would be very pleasant for adults. How would it be for people with children?

CARTER: It would just be out. There's nothing there for children. Also, I think that younger people, up to their late thirties and early forties, would find it rather dull, because there's really very little to do.

MRS. CARTER: What often happens to the people down there who have nothing to do is that they start drinking the local wines and brandy. They get in the habit of beginning at eleven o'clock in the morning. This is a problem that besets people who don't have enough interests to keep them going. Because there's nothing to do there. And I mean nothing.

You do have the water, of course. Do people sail? Do you swim?

CARTER: Some people sail. The English swim the year around. From April to October, the swimming is good, although it's the Atlantic, and the water tends to be cold. It's rather like around Long Island.

In saying that there's nothing to do, I think Martha meant that there are none of the things that retired people generally look for—golf, movies, shops, and other ready-made entertainments. Of course, I hate that word "retirement." I don't think of myself as retired at all. I think of myself as launched on a new life, with plenty of exciting new things to do. I'm writing a book, a preposterous little book that is a kind of specialized shopping guide to be sold at newsstands, and I've got enough other projects going to keep me as busy as I was on Madison Avenue, and a hell of a hot happier.

I should think that just getting away from Madison Avenue would, in itself, have made Europe seem attractive to you. It had a kind of built-in appeal. But what did you actually find there that made you want to keep going back and eventually to settle there?

CARTER: When I was talking earlier in the day with Martha, I said, "Well, why *do* you want to live in Europe?" And Martha gave quite a good succinct, maybe sententious, answer. She said, "Because you can live so much better for so much less."

MRS. CARTER: It's a much more civilized life, I think. When you quit living very high on the hog in New York as an advertising executive and that very fine salary is gone, it makes no sense to stay there and continue to live in the same stratum. If you want to retire and leave the city, where do you go? Florida is out for us. We hate that sort of life. Vermont we thought of, but the winters are so cold. And we did love Europe. It's exciting. It's such a challenge, with the different languages and foods and customs and people. And you meet so many people who are interesting. The life we found is so much more invigorating than if we had just pulled out of New York, left all of our friends, and settled down in some little village somewhere.

CARTER: I think what Martha said about meeting new people is important. As one moves along, it is desirable, and to some degree probably inevitable, to make new friends, not depending exclusively on old ones. Abroad, we have found that very easy to do. In fact, one of the pleasant things we hadn't anticipated when we moved to the other side is the unexpectedly firm friendships one stumbles into. In our case, I suppose this is due mostly to the fact that the Algarve is a year-around escape into warmth and sunshine for people in the north. Very largely English and Scotch, but a peppering of Swiss, Scandinavians, and French. Quite a bit of this floating-permanent population qualifies as special, and that makes for interesting friendships and merry companions. Ours are now scattered from Austria to Britain and from Italy to Sweden. They include lords and knights, scientists, journalists, and writers as well as a sprinkling of philosophers, scholars, and dons. It wouldn't be easy to put together such a range of fellow mortals, in, say, New York without serious dedication to the job. From among this group of people, Martha and I have made a half dozen new friends who are awfully close to us, of whom we are tremendously fond. Very interesting, intelligent, enjoyable people. They all happen to be Europeans, mostly English.

MRS. CARTER: I find the Europeans, by and large—this is a terrible thing to say—more interesting to talk to, really, than the average American. They have much wider interests. We seem, by comparison, relatively immature. When I come back and see old friends, there's hardly anything to say after a while, because it's just hashing the same topics over and over again. The people we have met in Europe are much more widely read and politically more on the ball. You can meet absolute strangers, and spend hours talking, whereas here, I think, television has sort of numbed the mind.

Another thing—entertaining over there is so much simpler, because we all live so primitively, relatively speaking. When you have guests for dinner, there's not the problem of getting out the silver and polishing it, et cetera, because the way we live, it's all a kind of a picnic. You have a maid, so you can say to anyone, "Do stay." It's *so easy*. And shopping is easier, too. As somebody has said about Portugal, "It isn't that it's so cheap. It's just that there's nothing to buy." It makes life simpler. When I came back here, I thought, "Oh, I can't wait to get into one of those supermarkets again." I got into one, and I had to push the cart four miles to find what I wanted. And when I was through, I longed for the little shop in Portugal, where I say, "Do you have the rice?" And he says, "No, I'll have it tomorrow." So we forget it.

CARTER: Next month, when you're back in the little shop, you're going to be longing for those supermarkets in New York.

MRS. CARTER: It's surprising how many things you learn you can do without, and have no sense of missing. You just don't require the little frills that we feel are absolutely essential here. Take clothing, for example. In Portugal, you go around in a pair of slacks all winter long, and it's only when you travel to a big city that you have to look around to see if you have anything to wear. Life has reduced itself to the basic essentials, and that's fun. I have learned that I don't want to spend my life bothering with little extraneous details. You can live very comfortably and very happily on very little.

CARTER: And in a very important sense, you live very well. There is no television, but good God, what television is there here? Radio is practically non-existent. Nobody has a telephone. You find that you don't need these things. It's a very pleasant and liberating discovery.

Do you worry at all what would happen if you got sick there?

MRS. CARTER: Oh yes. Then you get on a plane and get back here as fast as you can. The airport is at Faro, which is about fifty miles from us. The roads are excellent. Yes, you would have to leave immediately, and you'd be lucky if you didn't need an oxygen tent or something of the kind.

When you're in Portugal, are you aware of living under a dictatorship? Does it affect your life at all?

CARTER: Very rarely. Almost never. We were visited for the first time last spring by a rotund little chap, who said he was just making a routine check. All he did was to ask to see our passports. He was the essence of civility. When he left, he said, "Anything I can do for you, just let me know." On the other hand, I have received mail in Portugal that I am certain, absolutely positive, has been opened. For what reason, God knows.

What effect Salazar—or Aunt Sally, as he is usually referred to there in conversation—has had on the Portuguese is another matter, which I am not competent to assess. Life in Portugal is not morose. It certainly isn't solemn. But there is throughout a kind of unresponsiveness. The people are torpid. In the life generally, there's a sense of torpor. I don't know whether this is innate or whether it's a result of living in that suffocating society. It may be both. Down in the Algarve, we're really remote, and not closely aware of what goes on politically in Lisbon. We seldom go there. It's a beautiful city, with a lovely situation, but it is curiously inert, subdued, lifeless. It's as if there were a sort of pall over the whole place. In the Algarve, we are about equidistant from Lisbon and Seville, so whenever we think of going to a big town, we cross the border to Seville and live a little.

MRS. CARTER: Speaking of the Salazar regime, I don't think you're really conscious of it at all. The people are very sweet. They are completely unspoiled and very honest. You can leave all your doors open. Nothing is ever taken. There are some transitory vexations, such as not getting things done on time, but there have been no real drawbacks to living over there. The life is very easy and much more gracious. You can have help galore. Whenever we have guests, we have an extra maid, and that costs us seventy cents a day. I never have to wash a dish. I never have to cook a meal. You would have to have an awful lot of money to live like that in America.

CARTER: I would recommend Portugal to anyone who is self-sufficient, who can keep himself occupied. For that kind of person, I think there are many advantages and hardly any disadvantages. Also, anyone planning to live in Portugal would have to be rather adaptable. He couldn't complain because it's a little chilly in the house at night. We have friends who come over and say, "How do you stand living in this godforsaken end of the world? Where do you buy Kleenex around here? I tried to get Dristan. Now, don't tell me they don't sell Dristan." People like that couldn't live in Portugal. They couldn't live in the Ritz in Paris.

MRS. CARTER: They don't live, no matter where they are.

> "The Italian idea is that tomorrow is going to be a good day, too, so why ruin tomorrow today."

Fentress Kuhn, a native of San Francisco and a graduate of Yale, is a tall, handsome, gracious man, who spent much of his life in Idaho, where he had extensive business interests that included ranching, farming, radio stations, ski resorts, dairy farms, and a variety of other enterprises. He was also very active in politics on both the state and national levels. "Finally, in the winter of 1956–57, we felt that we had some time coming, so we decided to take an extended trip abroad with our children," he told me. "We toured around a good bit, and wound up in Rome, which we liked so much that we took an apartment there for a year. We kept it for about three years, and later on, after my wife's death, I bought an apartment in an old Roman house, built in about 1520, in the oldest section of the city. I fixed it up in a very comfortable way, and that has become my home." He now divides his time between his residence in Rome, a chalet that he rents in Gstaad, and visits to the United States, where he spends, all told, about three months of the year. When I called on Mr. Kuhn, in Gstaad, he explained why he originally selected Rome as a place to live.

KUHN: One factor that appealed to us in the first place was climate. Another was that both Paris and London, which we had come to know quite well from previous visits, were enormously big cities that didn't permit easy egress. We wanted a place where we could live a fairly quiet, peaceful life, and get quickly to the country, which we both loved. Rome, even though it's a city of about two million, is awfully easy to get out of. By car, you can get to the sea, the mountains, almost anywhere very easily. In fact, you don't even need a car. During our first year, my wife, the children, and I all acquired bicycles, and we did a lot of bicycling around Rome, taking trips in every direction.

You weren't bothered by the wild traffic?

KUHN: Well, we became accustomed to it. Roman traffic is the most dangerous in the world, because there is only one rule, which is: who gets there first. The police aren't much involved. Incidentally, I remember my introduction to the police effort in Rome. We hadn't been there more than twenty-four hours, and on a balmy afternoon I was walking along one of the principal streets, when I saw two of these magnificent *caribiniere*, all dressed up in striped pants and sabers rattling. They were quite a bit ahead of me, on the opposite side of the street. I saw them stop before a poster on the wall. One of them took something from his pocket, and stepped up to the poster. The other one stood back, watching. When I got up even with them, the first one had just finished drawing a mustache on Sophia Loren. Then they strolled on.

I am often amused watching one of the traffic police, out in the middle of the street, waving his white-gloved hand and using a repertoire of elaborate gestures to stop the traffic. Then somebody drives right on through. All the policeman does is shrug his shoulders. It represents a different point of view from ours in America, and I think it's wonderful.

Both my wife and I were very much interested in antiquity and in historical things, and Rome, of course, is an absolutely never-ending treasure house for people with that sort of interest. Then, within an hour or two, there are the wonderful towns surrounding the city, each with its own historical background and so different from the others that it is hard to compare them. You can go so easily to a place like

Todi, up on the edge of Umbria, or down south toward the Amalfi Peninsula, or up to L'Aquila, in the Abruzzi, or on over to Porto Santo Stefano, that glorious country on the edge of the Mediterranean. If you go up that way, you can have a marvelous time prowling around the ancient Etruscan tombs in Tarquinia, looking at things that were old long before Christ.

And then, as one stays a little while in Italy, particularly if one takes the trouble to learn the language, which isn't terribly difficult, the Italians become an ever-more appealing race of people. They're awfully kind and very sunny in temperament and very loyal friends, extraordinarily loyal. Contrary to the opinion of many American tourists who think that all Italians are out to pick your pocket, I have found over a period of years that for the most part they are intensely honest. In little petty things they do take advantage of you, but with a smile. I remember, we had a Volkswagen autobus, which we used to park outside the first apartment we lived in, right on the river. It was a place where the ladies of the evening circulated, and still do. One night, by accident, I left the door to the autobus unlocked. In the morning, when I opened the door, I saw that the bus was littered with cigarette butts and debris, and there was a note pinned onto the steering wheel. It was written in lipstick, and said, in Italian, "Many, many thanks, dear sir, for your kindness in giving us the use of your car." The ladies had sat in it all night, I guess, rather than be cold outside. They are a cheery race, and while I don't think they're as argumentative in the intellectual sense as the French, they're very alert and very alive to life. They are brought up to believe that the secret of making a life for oneself lies in seizing every possible chance to get the most out of every small enjoyment that comes along. It's astounding to me to see how much an Italian with virtually no income can get out of life.

The other thing that impressed us in Italy, from the point of view of raising our children, was the intense loyalty and the immense affection that exists between children and their parents. I think this absolute familial devotion—the love of the father and the mother for their children and the reciprocation of this love—is greater than in any other country I have visited. An Italian child is brought up to understand that his father is the head of the house and that his mother is sort of co-head, and the child never forgets. The parents never let them forget. I think that's a wonderful thing. We Americans spend an awful lot of time teaching independence to our children, and by the time they reach their early teens, they are apt to get rather hard to handle. I think parents do children an immense amount of harm by failing to hang onto that control, which is desperately needed by the adolescent.

As far as initial impressions are concerned, I suppose one of the most surprising was the discovery that nine-tenths of the Italians who vote the Socialist or Communist ticket are Catholics. I happen to be an American convert Catholic, and I remember well my first observation of the way Catholicism is practiced in Italy. One spring morning, when we were in Lucca, a lovely city near Florence, we went to the cathedral to High Mass, and I was dumbfounded to see that over half of the men, women, and children in the church were wearing the hammer-and-sickle insignia and carrying red flags. But they were all devoutly following the order of the Mass. I didn't know enough Italian at the time to tell, if, in the fiery sermon that the priest gave, he was talking against communism, but he probably was. They wouldn't mind that at all. The moment the Mass was over, they all charged out into the public square, and commenced to parade, singing the "Internationale." Although this seems very strange at first, you later come to understand that the Italians look at the Church as a place to go and enjoy and be normal and natural in. They don't treat it as a house of discipline. They treat it as a place they love.

At the time you were in the cathedral in Lucca, as you said, you didn't understand Italian very well. How did you learn the language?

KUHN: I very soon decided that if I were going to enjoy living in Italy at all and learn anything about the country, I would have to start studying, so I took a handful of lessons to begin with, and then just started to talk as best I could, and floundered along until it came easier and easier. I made it a practice early on to stay as much as possible with Italian people, because I think if you have any facility for the language, regardless of your age, by forcing yourself to be exposed to the language, you can pick it up. If you don't overcome your normal shyness and your normal distaste for saying something wrong, you never learn. The Italians, or even the French, admire you for attempting to speak in their language, and will help you along. I now speak Italian fairly constantly. Recently, I spent a four-day holiday visiting friends who have an ancient Saracen tower down on the Amalfi coastline. While several of the other guests were perfectly capable of speaking English, a few were not, so we spoke only Italian throughout the weekend.

Here in Gstaad, I suppose your main interest is skiing.

KUHN: Well, no. Having spent a good share of my life in the mountain world, as had my wife and children, we found that we missed it, despite the attractions of Rome, and started looking for something of the kind. It worked out that we were able to combine having a son in school here in Gstaad, in Le Rosey, with finding a mountain setting that we thought was perfectly lovely, with a quiet, congenial atmosphere. However, I use Gstaad a little differently than many others do. I take this little chalet of mine by the year, and usually rent it out in the popular seasons. I like to come here in the off-season, work at my desk on business affairs, read a great deal, and do a little writing. I have been working up some material about life in the West during the many, many years that I lived there. Whether it will ever lead to the publication of a book, I don't know. Since I've been in Europe, I have written, for my own amusement mainly, about three hundred and fifty columns that were sold to weeklies and dailies in the West, particularly in the Rocky Mountains. That has been a lot of fun. Gstaad is a wonderfully quiet place to come to from time to time to refuel and gather one's thoughts and get some work done. It's a small community but filled with very interesting people. I have friends here who are artists and writers and musicians. Ken Galbraith, the lively economist from Harvard, wrote two of his most successful books sitting on a hillside right here in Gstaad. Bill Buckley comes over every winter with his wife and son to ski. He and I are both Republicans, about nine thousand miles apart in viewpoint, but he's a very genial fellow.

As far as you can see into the future, this is the life that you will be following?

KUHN: Well, it agrees with me very well. I have some modest business interests that I can follow from Rome as well as from anyplace else. It's a convenient spot for my children to come to. They all happen now to have returned to their studies and their work and the raising of families in America, but we're able to keep in extremely close contact, coming back and forth. I have also found that many of my best friends seem to have found their way either to Gstaad or to Rome. In fact, there are so many that it becomes impossible to do as much for each of them as one would like to. I do find that I get a great deal of pleasure out of seeing friends here. I think when we all get up and go to work and carry on our social lives in a set pattern throughout the year in a set location that we tend to get a little bit stale with one another. We see the same people at dinner. We talk about the same things, and we exhaust the subjects at issue. We become awfully set in our provinciality. But when we've been apart from one another for a matter of months or years, epsecially after exposure to a civilization so ancient and so fascinatingly different and so ramified in its historical implications, the exchange of ideas becomes much more real and rewarding. In fact—and I'm sure the feeling is mutual—the people whom I had thought, erroneously, for years were awfully dull folk turn out to be very interesting and lots of fun when you see them in another world.

When one lives for some time in another world, as you have, he generally develops a more objective view of his own country. When you go back to the United States, what things, good and bad, come into focus most sharply?

KUHN: I tend to get constantly more fond of my own country on each successive trip. I see beauties and attractions and marvels that I had seen many times before but had never really observed, never digested. They look twice as attractive when you come back to them with your eyes open. For example, I used to work for the government, and lived a long time in Washington, D.C. I looked at it then with rather a jaundiced and bilious eye. In fact, I used to spend a good share of my time, away from work, trying to figure out how to get away from the place. One of my daughters now lives there, and so I have occasion to go back. All of a sudden, I am discovering what a fantastically lovely, charming city it is, with so much of the Old World in the Georgetown section, so much beauty in the residential districts, the good taste and the attractive gardens, the lovely scenes and vistas. Of course, those things were always there. I just never noticed them.

You also learn more about yourself and your countrymen when you have a chance to observe others. For example, I think the Italians are fascinated by our benevolent do-goodism. They admire it, I think, greatly, but fail entirely to understand what's behind it—a natural desire to be kind and helpful to people in need, to play God a little bit, perhaps. After all, don't we have something like 47 per cent of the wealth of the world, and aren't we only about 8 per cent of the people? In any case, it seems that every housewife in America wants to be on a committee to raise money to help somebody somewhere. This concept is absolutely alien to the Italians. To try to raise money here for a charity would give the Italians a good laugh. For a lottery—that's all right. For a charity—that is unheard of. And so you begin to have a greater appreciation of the American willingness to help others, which is one of the most attractive aspects of the American character. I think one of the best things our country is doing today is the Peace Corps, which is being carried on with such apparent skill and ability and with such an unselfish point of view.

Looking at another aspect of the American character, if I may digress for a moment, it has always seemed to me that the greatest fault we have as a people is the tremendous effort to stamp everybody with the same mold. I think the great strength of the European point of view lies in the intense respect for the individuality of a single human being and of his right—indeed, his *duty* to lead his own life and develop it the way he wishes. To me, that is a great thing. Individuality is something to be cherished, and to my way of thinking, it can be nurtured more satisfactorily in the European setting than it can at home. Perhaps it is because of the sense of history that is born and bred in everybody over here. The European has in his mind the feeling of antiquity, the feeling of centuries behind him. I remember one day going down from here on the train with an old friend of mine, an eminent banker from New York, who was making his first visit over here. "Isn't it astonishing," he said, "how many of these local people have been around here for two, three, or four generations? My gosh, they just stay in one place." Sitting next to us was a Swiss I'd known for many years, a ski guide named Willi Perrin. I turned to him and said, "Willi, I'd like to ask you something. How many years have your family lived in this community?" He said, "Well, Fentress, I can't tell you exactly, but the records in the church registry show that the family have been here since 1140. Actually, though, I think we've been here since about 900."

Along with the attractions of European life, I suppose you have also found some things that are irritating or that you have to get used to. For example, many Americans, as you know, complain about the slowness in getting things done.

KUHN: You have to learn to shrug your shoulders and agree to put off until tomorrow what you think you ought to get done today, and you find you probably do it better tomorrow, anyhow. After all, why is it necessary to speed life up to that intense, burning tempo as we do at home? The European manages to build an adequate, even a very full, life on values other than those based solely on material things. We get awfully excited in the United States about the importance of having every conceivable modern facility, such as putting telephones on separate lines in the rooms of our twelve-year-old children and trying to turn them into eighteen-year-olds. We keep trying to accelerate the pace of individual, personal development at, I think, a shocking and dangerous rate, beyond the ability of the mind and body to cope with it. I think that this characteristic in contemporary American life—trying to shove life into high gear and keep it there—burns us up and is at the root of the tremendous psychic and psychiatric disturbances that we're plagued with. The Italians, living at a slower pace, keep the psychiatrists—the few that there are—more or less on the verge of starvation.

In this connection, I must say that I have been fascinated by the absence of alcoholism, by and large, in Italy and in Switzerland. I don't know so much about the Swiss in this regard, but the Italian alcoholic, or the alcoholic of Italian origin, is something almost unknown. I have been far and wide in every kind of town and city and community in Italy, and I've seen only three or four drunks among the native population. The Italians drink a lot of wine, and sometimes they get to feeling pretty good, but they seem to have a built-in mechanism that tells them when to quit. The Italian idea is that tomorrow is going to be a good day, too, so why ruin tomorrow today.

"The jump from Madison Avenue to *Avenida Mañana* is a great one. I'm still trying to get adjusted."

Victor O. Schwab, a pioneer in the advertising business, started out, in 1917, as secretary to the copy chief of the Ruthrauff and Ryan agency, in New York. "The chief used to dictate his copy while walking around his office," Mr. Schwab has recalled. "He dictated very fast, and I couldn't get it all, so I filled in the gaps with my own words. One day he was reading some copy he'd dictated, and he said, 'Say, this is all right. These aren't my words, but I like 'em.' I said, 'Well, maybe I'll get the next cub job in the copy department. And I did.' From then on, his rise was steady, culminating in the formation of Schwab and Beatty, Inc. (now Schwab, Beatty and Porter, Inc.), a very successful agency, of which Mr. Schwab was president for thirty-four years. In 1962, at age sixty-four, he relinquished that post and retired with his wife to Spain. They settled in Torremolinos, a onetime fishing village that has undergone an early-Florida-boom kind of expansion. Their house, "Villa Victor," where I called on Mr. Schwab one overcast morning in January, is a large, comfortable, completely modern structure that commands a splendid view of the Mediterranean through the picture window in the living room. Mr. Schwab, a rather small, gracious, witty man, explained how he happened to come to Spain.

SCHWAB: I spent forty-five years on Madison Avenue or its equivalent, either writing copy or fighting to get it out of copy men, and finally, after all those years, it really got to me. My nerves began to go, and I had trouble with my eyes. I was starting to take my ration of Tums at ten-thirty. That's when I said, "Well, I better get out of here.

Forty-five years of this turmoil is enough." So, I did, and here I am. The jump from Madison Avenue to *Avenida Mañana* is a great one. I'm still trying to get adjusted.

We decided to settle here, because for years we had been taking the American Export Line's cruise called "Mediterranean Ferry-Go-Round," and we used to get off at Barcelona, hire a car, and drive around Spain. We came through this area a couple of times, and the second time, my wife said, "This is it." The climate and everything seemed right. Despite the weather today, this is probably the best year-round climate in Europe. July and August get pretty hot. There may be two or three days when the temperature gets up to a hundred and five or so, but we don't mind too much. When people here say it's very cold, they mean it's gotten down to about forty-five. It almost never goes below that. And they've hardly ever seen snow here—just a flurry years ago.

After selecting this general area, I found an American real estate fellow here, and asked him to keep on the lookout for a house for us. He kept sending me pictures and particulars of property, and we finally bought a house up the road, so we had that to move into when we came here on a permanent basis. That house cost eighty-six hundred dollars, and I have it up for sale now for thirty-six thousand. We put a lot of money into improvements, and we also built another small house on the property, and installed a tile swimming pool. so we'll probably not get back much more than we've invested, if that. Both that house and this one are in an area that I think is as pleasant as anything near Torremolinos. You're away from the night life and all that, but you're also near enough so you can raise hell, if you want to. I suppose you could go to a new bar around here every night for practically a year.

That leads me to ask how you do spend your time here?

SCHWAB: Well, I do some writing. I do a lot of reading. But to tell you the truth, I'm trying to find enough to do. I think the matter of retirement is different for every individual. You can't generalize and say everybody should retire at a certain age. I think quite a few factors govern the decision. One, if you're happy in your work, it's a bad time to retire. Two, if you're in good health, it's not a good idea to retire. I wouldn't have. Three, if you have some hobby that's compulsive or some great, deep interest that you know is going to continue, then it's safe to retire, because you know you will be fully occupied. If a man is very happy in his work, and is in fine health, and has no avocation or hobby that intrigues him, he had better keep working.

In my own case, I was busy enough here in the beginning, making improvements on the first house and then building this one. It's a terrific job to build a house like this one in this part of the world—what problems!—so I was sufficiently occupied during the first year or so. After that, having time on my hands, I began going through that period of adjustment from Madison Avenue that I mentioned, and I got very depressed. You know, not living in one's own country is a great problem. I mean, we're Anglo-Saxons living with Latins, and the tempo is different. Much slower. The temperament is different. The language is different. For a person like a copywriter, who must be fluent in his language, suddenly to be confronted with a language that he doesn't speak except in its so-called kitchen version is very frustrating. Of course, there are plenty of people in this area who speak English, but most of them are retired or in the town, so it's not easy to find people to talk with, except about how many martinis did you have last night.

Apparently, though, you're willing to cope with the language problem in order to enjoy the advantages of living here, such as the climate. I wonder if you have found others.

SCHWAB: Oh, certainly. I couldn't have retired and lived in the United States as well as I can here. The cost of living used to be so cheap here that it was almost silly from an American standpoint, and it's still less than in most places in Europe, and much less than anywhere in America.

As far as the financial aspect of retiring is concerned, I think a couple of things have to be considered. First, I don't think you should do it if you're going to be constantly worrying about spending a little money. By the time you retire, you're supposed to have achieved serenity and tranquillity, and if you've got to be forever concerned about inflation, if that's likely to be a bugbear, then you've defeated your purpose. Second, I think a person can retire too young. In order to retire, you obviously have to save money, and that is almost impossible in America now. So, the younger you retire, the less resources you're going to have and the thriftier you're going to have to be, and that can create a situation where it kills you to spend a dime. You've retired young, but—no fun. The other pitfall is obvious. You can retire too late, when you no longer have enough pep or interest to do anything but sit. In other words, you've missed the boat.

When thinking about retirement—you can see *I've* been thinking about it a good deal—you also have to consider whether you like your family well enough. I mean, you may love them but not like them. You have to face the question: do you like your wife well enough to spend twenty-four hours a day with her instead of four hours in the evening? In my case, that's not a problem. This is my second marriage. I have a daughter, who is married, and my wife has two married daughters, one of whom lives in Casablanca. She has been here several times, and my wife's sister has also visited us. You get plenty of visitors. In fact, so many that you have to be a little circumspect. We've been visited by friends of friends, who have been beauties. Last year, some friends of friends looked us up, and we gave a cocktail party for them. In the middle of it, when so many of our friends here were milling around the house that it looked like Grand Central Station in the rush hour, this friend of a friend came up to my wife and said, "How can you *stand* living here without any friends?"

You were speaking earlier about the slower tempo, which, as you know, many Americans over here consider the most attractive aspect of living abroad.

SCHWAB: That's very true—when you get used to it. One is not an emotional faucet that can be turned on and off at will. You have to change so many of your habits. For one thing, you must learn never to get anywhere on time. At first, if you make a date for three o'clock, you're there at ten of three, and then you wait until four-thirty or five for the other person to show. After a while, you reach the point where you say, "The hell with it. I'm one individual. Why try to win out over thirty million Spaniards? I'll meander around and do it their way."

What I try to do is to have some activity scheduled for each day. You think you're ready for this time in your life, but you're not, unless you've studiously prepared for it. You think it's going to be great, because now you can get up whenever the hell you want to, and you can relax and flop around, and do whatever you wish. But if you're used to the American tempo—and particularly, the American advertising man's tempo—you very soon realize that you can't read all the time, and you can't do this all the time, and you can't do that all the time. You find you haven't enough activities on which to spend the energy that you formerly expended at the office. It can get quite disheartening. I remember early in this siege, it was around ten o'clock one morning, and I said to my wife, "I must get up." She meant to be kind, but it was a real shocker. She said, "Why?" All of a sudden, it hits you. Why? Why ever get up? It really pulls you up short.

Building this house did keep you very much occupied, as you said, because there were so many problems. What were some of them?

SCHWAB: How many days can you listen? We coped with more problems than Mr. Blanding ever dreamed of. When you build here, you keep hearing two remarks, and I can tell you, you get pretty damned tired of both of them. One is, "*Sí, señor*, I understand what you mean, and I can do it." Then after whatever he's done has to be re-done for the first, second, third, or fourth time, they say, "*No, señor*, it's not my fault." Depending on what's involved, they tell you it's the plumber's fault, the carpenter's fault, the electrician's fault—but never the fault of the one to whom you're speaking. We went through that with the fireplace, in spades. Apparently, there is a kind of scientific ratio of proportion that says a fireplace should never be higher than it is wide. Well, this one was. Whenever we had a wind, all the smoke came back down the chimney into the living room. After the local boys had had four tries at fixing it, with no success, we met an American engineer who solved the problem simply by installing a baffle that corrected the proportion.

Then there were the water problems. The drain pipes for carrying the excess water off the roof, instead of facing out into the patio, faced into the living room. Other things like that were endless. My shower, for instance. The water gets up to your ankles. I had the plumber in I don't know how many times to try to fix it so the water would run away. Finally, I discovered there is no drain pipe under the shower. The water just runs into the soil under the house. So, I have a long argument with the plumber in my pidgin Spanish and his pidgin English, which winds up when he says, "You go into the shower to get wet, no? So, you're wet up to your ankles. The water finally drains out, doesn't it? It's not there the next day, is it?" I say, "No, it's not there the next day." He says, "So, what's not O.K.?" After that, where are you?

We put in a swimming pool, and told the builder we wanted to use salt water, since we're right next to the sea. The builder said, "*Sí, señor*, I know what you want, and I can do it. The best way to get the water is to put a pipe quite far down into the sea." I said, "Well, that's going to be pretty cold water, so we better have it heated." He said, "Yes, that would be best. Nobody's got that here, but I can do it. You'll have to have an extra furnace." The furnace we already had for the house could run the *Queen Mary*, but he installed another one as big to heat the pool water. Finally, the pool's finished, everything's hooked up and ready to go, and we jump in. It's fresh water. We say, "Where's the salt water?" He says, "Can't get salt water. I would have had to get permission from the Marine Division, in Madrid. That would have taken anywhere from six months to six years." I said, "Well, why didn't you tell me? I wouldn't have had the second furnace put in." He said—and this is another expression you've got to get used to—"*Yo no recuerdo*"—"I forgot." Well, we don't heat the pool. I tried it once, and one heating cost twenty-two dollars.

What does your wife think of living here? Does she like it?

SCHWAB: Oh my, yes. In fact, she was the principal pusher as far as moving here was concerned. She's more Spanish than the Spanish in her liking for this country. She's getting dressed now for lunch. We're going to try a new Chinese restaurant that's just opened in Torremolinos. It's upstairs over the Don Quixote Bar. The proprietor is an American woman who used to write pornographic books for the Olympia Press. That's about par for Torremolinos.

Aside from going out to lunch, how does Mrs. Schwab spend her time here?

SCHWAB: She likes the kitchen, and despite having enough people working around the house, she does most of the cooking. We have a young fellow who is a chauffeur and handyman, two maids who live in, and a gardener who works about half-time. My wife has a great many friends. She is in the village a lot. She—I don't know. What *does* one do all the time?

One thing I do know is that "discipline" is one of the key words you have to remember here. For example, in connection with drinking, you have to be careful. In my type of business in New York, you would go to lunch with a client, and you might have a couple of martinis, but that was enough, because you knew that you had to go back to the office and try to outthink somebody. Here, you don't have to outthink anybody, so, unless you're careful, it's very easy to say, "One more. One more. One more." Then you go home horizontally.

Do you keep in touch with your colleagues back at the office? What do they think of your living over here?

SCHWAB: They think it's a most daring thing to do, which, come to think of it, it is. I correspond regularly with the office, and I've been back a few times. I went over last June with the intention of staying for three weeks. I couldn't take it. The difference in tempo was such that I went back to my Tums diet right away. There were too many people. No time for courtesy. It was hard to get a room. It was hard to get a cab. And the traffic! I would wait for three green lights before getting up the courage to cross the street. Everybody I talked to seemed to be terrified about going out at night. I canceled a dozen appointments, and left after two weeks. I couldn't wait to get back to the serenity, the wonderful serenity, that we have here.

> "I felt so gay and so amused, and I thought, 'London never lets me down.' "

A woman who becomes a widow, like people who retire, must make a new life. Mrs. Betty Laycock Clegg, who is a widow and a grandmother, fashioned her new existence in London, where she has lived since 1955. "Mind you, I am an old woman," she said at one point in our conversation. Actually, she is in her late fifties, and looks much younger. She has a patrician air, gentle blue eyes, and the kind of alabaster complexion that English women so often have. As we sat in her small, tastefully furnished apartment, in Sloane Square East, I asked how she happened to settle in England.

MRS. CLEGG: My husband died suddenly and without any illness the day after Christmas, in 1954. My daughter—our only child—had been married the previous summer. So, quite suddenly, what had been my whole life was gone. We had lived the previous five years in Detroit, where my husband was establishing a distributorship for dictating machines, but I never had formed an emotional connection with Detroit. I'm afraid it isn't the sort of city that endears itself to people unless they have been brought up there. Certainly, I had no reason for staying in Detroit, nor, for that matter, did I have a reason for going to any other place in particular. My daughter had settled down with her husband in California, and the last thing in the world I wanted to do was to take my grief and myself out there and camp on her doorstep. I didn't think that would be fair at all.

So, I thought, "I must travel. I must get away. I must learn to live as an individual with no hub to my universe." I had never had the wanderlust like some people, who can travel and travel and travel, but now that I was so frightfully free, I thought perhaps I should. Everybody told me I should go to Europe—I had never been there—and at length I decided to go ahead.

I had relatives in Malta, who had written and invited me to come for a visit, so I went there first and stayed for a while. Then I spent just a fortnight in Italy, because I wasn't keen about trailing around by myself. After that, I stopped briefly in Paris, and then came on to England. At that time, I was no more considering living here than I was considering flying to the moon. In fact, I hadn't planned to stay more than a week or so. But from the moment I landed in England, I had the overwhelming feeling that I was *at home.* That had never happened to me anywhere I had lived in America—not in New England or Ohio or California or Arizona and most certainly not in Michigan. I had felt that certain houses were home, being with certain people as being at home, but that was the first time I had ever had that feeling for a *place.* I felt at home in every respect. And it was a most wonderful feeling. So, instead of staying for a week, I stayed for three months, and even then I was reluctant to leave. I had to go back to Detroit because I had been named executor of my husband's estate, and the lawyer was working on those affairs.

I arrived back in Detroit in the middle of June, and when autumn came, I was still trying to decide what to do. I knew where I *wanted* to live, but I thought that being executor required that I keep myself sort of available, and I knew that getting all those legal things settled sometimes takes up to five years. So, in the autumn I went out to California to stay with some friends, who live in Carmel. They had written that that was heaven on earth, and suggested I settle there. Carmel is lovely, of course, but I didn't want to stay. I went on down to Los Angeles to see how my daughter was getting along, and then to Arizona, where I had some very dear friends. After that, I went back east to see my brother and my sister-in-law, who live in Connecticut. I was thinking seriously of renting a small flat in the town of New Canaan, and using that as a sort of base. However, about that time, I had to go back to Detroit for another session with the lawyer, and he said, "Betty, have you any idea where you want to live?" I said, "Jim, there isn't anything I really *want* to do except go back to England and just stay sort of indefinitely." He looked at me across his desk, and said, "Well, there isn't any reason why you shouldn't, if that's what you want." He explained that another executor could be appointed, and then I would be free to go. What welcome news that was!

In London, as I looked back, I felt that even if one's personal life is a blank—mine was then, absolutely blank, except for memories—there is always something to do, even if you have no friends, and no relatives, and no connections. You couldn't exhaust the possibilities of entertaining yourself, or through volunteer work of some kind, making yourself useful in some way.

But wouldn't that all also be true of New York?

MRS. CLEGG: Yes, I suppose it would be true of New York, but New York is a much more expensive city to live in, and a much more dangerous city for a widow to live in. Probably even worse than Detroit. In Detroit, in the few months that I lived there after my husband's death, I had been subjected to a few of the rackets that are practiced on widows, and it had quite terrified me.

For example, one afternoon, when I was getting ready to go to Dayton, Ohio, where my husband's brothers lived, to spend the weekend, I was called on the telephone, and a pleasant enough man's voice said he was Mr. So-and-So, from Stamford, Connecticut, and he'd brought greetings from Bill and Harriet, my brother and sister-in-law who live there. He said that when Harriet learned he was coming to Detroit on business, she'd asked him to look me up and take me out to dinner and see how I was getting along. He sounded a blustery sort of chap, good-natured, and so on.

I said, "I'm very sorry, but I'm planning to go to Dayton, Ohio, for the weekend, so I can't go out for dinner, but thank you for sending me their greetings."

"Well," he said, "Harriet's going to be very disappointed. When are you leaving?"

I told him that I was planning to leave the next morning, and he said, "I do wish I could take you out tonight. Harriet's going to be very upset when she finds I haven't carried out my mission, you know. When are you coming back?"

I said that I didn't really know. I might stay as long as a week. He was quite insistent. "Well," he said, "couldn't you manage to go out tonight after you've finished what you have to do? I don't want to let Harriet down on this. That Harriet—you know, she's a card."

Well, when he said that, the gooseflesh rose on me, because my sister-in-law is one of the most wonderful people on God's earth, and probably the last person who would be described as a card. So, on hearing that, I thought, "This man doesn't know Harriet." I hardly knew what to answer. I'd been warned by some other widows I knew to be on guard against people who might come around to try to get me to invest and things like that. I was stunned. I realized that I had told this man that I was going to Dayton, that I would be out of my flat for perhaps a week, and that I was alone here tonight. I was aware, too, that I was living in a ground-floor apartment. I thought as quickly as I could, and I said, "I'm sorry, because I don't want to let Harriet down either, but please give her my love, and tell her it couldn't be avoided."

"Well, let's see," he said. "If you're going to Dayton, you'll be seeing Charlie, I suppose."

One of my brothers-in-law in Dayton is named Charles—and he has never been called Charlie in his life. His nickname has been Chalkie since he was a tiny boy, and that is what he was called in school and by all his friends. I said, "So you know my brother-in-law?"

He said, "Oh yes, I know Charlie, and I knew your husband when we were all in Yale together."

I realized then that he had gotten all this information from my husband's obituary in the Yale alumni magazine. And here I had told this strange man all of these things about my plans. I was frightened, but also I was getting a bit impatient, so I told him I was sorry I couldn't make any plans to see him, and I asked him to give Harriet and Bill my love, and then I rang off. I was frightened to death that night. Later, when I checked with my sister-in-law, she told me, of course, that she had never asked any man to call me. That wasn't the only thing of that nature. I got telephone calls all the time—people wanting me to invest in this or give money to that or to buy something or other. You see, they read obituary notices in the paper, and they keep telephoning your house. Sometimes, they just want to see if there's anyone at home. And then you're likely to be looted, or heaven knows what might happen.

No, one doesn't want to live in an American city any more, even New York. And I couldn't afford to live in New York, quite frankly. I think, really and truly, that London is the only major city in the world that I could afford to live in comfortably and take advantage of the things I enjoy.

Was that the primary reason for settling here?

MRS. CLEGG: No, that was not my first consideration. I wasn't even aware of that aspect of life here until later. There were other things. For example, I had found, on the occasion of my first visit, that I could walk almost anywhere that I wanted to go in London. I love to walk, and I found also that I could walk alone without being stared at or feeling conspicuous. A woman doesn't go strolling around New York alone, certainly not after dusk, nor in Paris—and most assuredly not in Detroit. In Detroit, I wouldn't put my nose outside the door after dark if I could avoid it. When I did come home at night from friends' houses in a taxi, I was afraid to walk from the taxi through the long courtyard to the entrance of our apartment. I was afraid to make that walk alone, and I was also afraid to ask the taxi driver if he would accompany me to the door. I'm not a woman who is timid by nature. It was not an imaginary fear. Men were clubbed over the head in that district, and it was right in the center of the city, not very far from my husband's office.

I know there are sneak thieves in London. Many people, including some of my friends, have been burgled by them. But robbery with violence against the person for small amounts of money and such trinkets as I might have doesn't occur in this country as it does in America. I think that in the big cities in America, it is due a great deal to dope addiction. In Detroit, dope addicts, both Negro and white, would come right into a lighted apartment, even when people were at home in it, in a desperate attempt to get money. People in our own apartment house had been robbed that way. Although there are sneak thieves here, and a lot of them and very active they are, and a lot of high crime as well—the Great Train Robbery and such—I can walk at night from the Royal Court Theater, in Sloane Square, down here to my flat without a flicker of fear. I'll see many other people walking—decent people, nice people, and I've never had a moment's fear in all the years I've been here.

Now, I am not completely free of the concern that if I were to go away for a week or a month, I might come back to find that somebody had broken in and taken a lot of things, although quite frankly, having gotten rid of this and that, I have so little left that there is nothing much to tempt anyone. Still, that sort of thing happens, and it could happen to me. But there is not that bodily fear, you know, and to enjoy freedom from that kind of fear is really and truly wonderful.

There is also a marvelous feeling of honesty in this country. It was almost like discovering that virtue all over again. It was like in the early days, when I was a youngster, and the cities hadn't grown so big, and we expected people to be honest. As time passed, honesty seemed to go out of style, and one had to try to adjust to all the new sharp practices. Then, suddenly, I found myself here in the midst of people with this old-fashioned habit of honesty, who wouldn't let me short-change myself. There is so much of what an English friend of mine calls "petty honesty" that it seems almost fantastic to me. Imagine sitting on a bus and having the person next to you, who's getting off, give you some coins and say, "Would you kindly pay my fare? The conductor hasn't collected it, you see." Or to see the money lying out on the newspaper stands—perhaps a pound note and a great mound of coins. You make your own change. Or the many times when I have overpaid and had a clerk follow me clear to the door. "Here, madam, you gave me the wrong coin." In little ways, one is enveloped with the feeling that everybody is honest and kind. It's wonderful. It really is. Oh, I'm sure one might have one's fortune filched in this country, the same as in any other, and I'm quite willing to be alert to protecting any investments or possessions that are worth anything at all. But I don't like having to be on guard against being cheated out of pennies and nickels and dimes. That's disheartening.

And you feel you don't have to because of what your friend called "petty honesty"?

MRS. CLEGG: Yes. When I spoke about this to her, she said, "Oh, I suppose there is a considerable amount of petty honesty about." She wasn't so impressed, but I think it is a lovely quality. People here say that it's not as good as it used to be in this respect, but it seems very nice to me, and it's one of the things that makes life very pleasant for a woman alone. If you have to face making a lot of decisions and looking after a lot of things for yourself that you haven't had to look after before, it's a very comforting feeling—and it relieves somewhat the loneliness of having to manage it all yourself—to know that you're going to be treated fairly and decently. It's not everybody in England who acts that way. I have American friends who dealt with a real estate firm in London that tried to fleece them of everything they possibly could. But the general atmosphere is one of honesty. The shopkeepers, the taxi drivers, the milkman, the news dealers—they are all as fair and honest as the day is long.

There are many other nice habits and customs. I found one in the postal department. Like everyone else, I sometimes put too many pages in an air mail letter, and I had become accustomed for anything with insufficient postage to be sent right back to me. Of course, this can be quite a nuisance if it's important for the letter to get there right away. Well, one day, shortly after I had arrived, I received in the mail a very official-looking envelope saying "On Her Majesty's Service." In it was a very pleasant little note that said that one of my letters, addressed to So-and-So in the United States, had not carried sufficient postage, and, realizing that I wouldn't want any delay in the dispatch of the letter, the postal authorities had affixed the proper postage and sent the letter on, and they would be grateful if I would affix the difference in stamps to the little card that was enclosed and return it to them. Which I did. And the thoughtfulness involved made me beam. These are the little touches, of course, but they seem to me very civilized and sweet.

You mentioned earlier that it is cheaper to live here than in New York. Do you find it markedly cheaper?

MRS. CLEGG: Well, it is cheaper to live the way I live and do the things I like to do. I presume it would perhaps be more expensive if one were to live in this country as a typical American who was traveling. But the things I enjoy I find I can do in London with ease, and I would find them very inaccessible and prohibitive in cost in America. I'm very fond of the theater, for instance, and I like music, and I like horse shows—I used to ride a bit when I was younger—and tennis matches and other sporting events, and I love to go to all the flower shows. I find that in this country things like flower shows are very much less expensive than in an American city. I think you would probably pay two dollars to get into a flower show in New York City, and your transportation would not be just a few pennies, as it is here, if you use the underground, which is clean and safe, but close to a dollar if you went in a taxi any distance at all. Here, one joins the Horticultural Society for two guineas a year, which is about six dollars, and for that you can go to every flower show held in London the year around. There are fortnightly flower shows throughout the year, and then there is the Chelsea Flower Show, which is unparalleled in the world and is held just across the way, in the Royal Hospital grounds. I'm really a countrywoman at heart, I suppose, and so the privilege of doing things like these—and also buying fresh flowers for your house, which have become very costly in American cities now, means a great deal to me. And if I want to go out to Wimbledon when the tennis matches are on, I can walk over to Sloane Square, get on the Underground, and be taken there in a short time, and again for a few pennies. I may not get into the center court, but I can wander around and share the excitement and thrill of it.

So, if you want to live as I live in London, you can do so for a much smaller outlay of money than in a city in America. Another thing—you can't live in America without driving a car, can you? I mean, I don't know anyone who even tries. If you live in New York and are dependent on taxis, it is a very expensive proposition indeed. Public transportation here is not only inexpensive but quick and easy.

Are the things that you enjoy doing here interests of long standing, or have you developed some of them since living in London?

MRS. CLEGG: The only new recreational or cultural interest that I have developed here, and it is a very keen one now, is in ballet. This is owing to the fact that my granddaughter, Elizabeth, has been living with me for the past eight months. She has been taking ballet lessons most of this time, has tremendous interest in it, and has shown really exceptional talent. I just can't tell you how much it has meant to have her with me and also to see the really exceptional academic progress she's made since being in school here. It's been nothing short of astonishing.

No, aside from the ballet, my interests of that kind remain what they were—gardening, nature, the countryside. It's just that I find them so easy and pleasant to pursue here. I love the feeling of being able to have one foot in the city and one foot in the country, which is quite possible here, because all of one's friends have some little spot in the country, and you are occasionally invited to come down for a weekend. So, my interest in gardening remains very active, even though it's been fifteen years now since I've had a garden of my own. I never feel cut off from it here as I would in an American city, because, in the first place, I live right across from the Royal Hospital grounds, which have the most beautiful gardens, and I can just step over there every day. And, of course, all the squares in London are full of flowers and plants and flowering shrubs, so I never feel that I am living in a city, although, of course, I am living in the heart of one of the biggest cities in the world. When I walk over to the Royal Hospital grounds, I take a book or a sandwich or something, and sit out there by the hour, reading or writing letters. I really feel then as if I'm living in a small town.

Another thing I like—there is always a band playing somewhere in London, particularly in this section. Right around here we have, besides the Royal Hospital, which is for the Chelsea pensioners—the distinguished and retired old soldiers—we have the Duke of York's headquarters and also the Chelsea Barracks. So, there's a parade or a band or something similar around this neighborhood almost every day. I very often go to St. Paul's—I love that cathedral—at the lunch hour, and then come out and spend a while listening to the band, playing on the steps. The pageantry in London is a bonus that you don't get anywhere else in the world.

And after these many years, you still enjoy it?

MRS. CLEGG: After these many years, I *love* it. As I said before, there is always something going on in London. So one is never left on holiday occasions, when it's quite painful not to have your family, with nothing to do. If you have these waves of grief and loneliness that come to any widow, there's a way, in London, to get out of yourself immediately.

I had such a pleasant example of that once. I had lived here for two or three years, and was in complete control, I felt, of my emotions as far as being a widow was concerned. On this particular morning, when I got up, I turned on the TV, which was in the bedroom, to get the results of a general election, held the day before. It took the set about five minutes to warm up, so I went out to the kitchen to start making the tea. Suddenly, music came from the bedroom, and the tune coming out of the TV was the same one that was always played as a prelude to a program that my husband and I always listened to on the radio the first thing in the morning. When I heard that tune and found myself alone in that kitchen, I was caught unaware. When you are a widow, you see, you brace yourself for birthdays, and you brace yourself for Christmas and for these other occasions, but I was not braced for this. It was the first time I had heard that tune since being alone. I was simply engulfed. I went back into my bedroom. I kept the TV on to watch the election results, and I had my breakfast, and I was absolutely at the lowest ebb I have ever been. It just got me. I sat there, weeping and wailing and thinking, "I shall never get over this." Really, I have never felt worse. The day wore on, and I just sat there, almost unable to move. Finally, I thought, "This is ridiculous. I must get out and do something." It was a Friday. I didn't think I could do the things I ordinarily would do on a Friday—go to the bank, do the marketing, and so on. I was just not in any state. I decided to go see a film called *Northwest Frontier*, which was set in India. The husband of an English friend of mine, a retired colonel, had acted as adviser on the film, and he also had a small part in it, so I roused myself and went up to Marble Arch, where the picture was playing. I paid for my ticket with a ten-shilling note, and as I did so, I noticed that it was the last ten shillings that I had in my pocket. It being Friday, I should have gone to the bank, you see. However, the ticket was seven and six, and that left me enough to get home on the bus, so I thought that would be all right.

It was an interesting film. All through the picture they played the Eton boating song, which one hears a lot over here, and that took the other tune out of my mind. I came out feeling much better. It was October and beginning to get dark, and as I was crossing that terrible traffic at Marble Arch, I noticed one of the old Chelsea pensioners—one of the old soldiers from the Royal Hospital—in his long red coat, standing in the middle of the street, talking to a bobby. The bobby was pointing over to the bus stop. I thought, "The poor old soldier is lost," so I stepped up to the bobby, and said, "If he wants some help, I would be very glad to give it, because I live quite near Royal Hospital, and I'm on my way home." The bobby, who had his hands full, coping with all this traffic, said to the old man, "If you'll just go with this lady, she'll take care of you."

So, I took the old boy, who was wearing dark glasses, by the arm, and I noticed that he was quite unsteady. As soon as he heard my voice, he said, "You're an American! You remind me of my grandmother. My grandmother was an American." I told him that was very interesting, and ushered him through the traffic, my first idea being to get him into a taxi. Then I remembered that I had only two and six in my pocket, so instead of a taxi, we would have to take a bus.

We headed toward a bus stop, and he was really quite unsteady. As we maneuvered through more traffic, he said, "I'm afraid I don't walk so well. I've been doing a little celebrating. You know, the election and all." I realized then that I had not only a very elderly old soldier on my hands but a slightly tipsy one as well. We finally made it to a bus stop, and while waiting, he entertained everybody in the queue with his observations on the election results and a great many other matters. I finally got him on a bus—sort of pushed him up onto one. There was one vacant seat toward the rear of the bus, and I put him down there, and I took the only other vacant seat, which was across the aisle and a couple of seats toward the front. He kept up the conversation across the aisle, and before long he had everybody on the bus cheered up.

Well, we finally got out at Sloane Square, and started down the street, I still holding him by the arm. Then he began again, "Oh, you sound just like my American grandmother. My grandfather went over to America when he was young, and married an American girl, and they came back later on, and she taught me all those songs." He began to sing "The Star-Spangled Banner." I joined in and sang it with him—softly, I promise you. After that, we ran through "Maryland, My Maryland," which he said was another of his favorites, and then another chorus of "The Star-Spangled Banner." As we were coming down Sloane Street, in the gathering gloom, I began to think what my friends at home would say if they saw me with a slightly drunken old Redcoat, going down Sloane Street and singing "The Star-Spangled Banner." Well, I couldn't help laughing.

When we got down to the bottom of Sloane Street, I started to turn to take him over to Royal Hospital. He said, "Oh no, I don't want to go back there yet. It's too early." I asked him where he was planning to go. "Oh," he said, "I'm going to the pub." I inquired how he would get home from the pub. "No trouble there," he said. "The manager of the pub walks me home every night. So, I'll just say goodbye to you now, and thank you, my dear, for your kindness. And God bless you." Then, as we stood there on the corner, he leaned over and kissed me.

When I came back home, I felt so gay and so amused, and I thought, "London never lets me down." And that's been true ever since. Whatever mood I'm in, something unusual or exciting or sweet can always happen. So, personally, that's what London has meant to me. Or, I should say, part of what London has meant.

Then, too, living at the crossroads of the world has meant that I have seen more American friends and relatives in the years I have lived here than I would if I had lived in any one place in the United States. Even if my friends had come to New York, had I been living there, they might have been so busy doing other things that I would not have seen them. Here, I have the pleasure of acting as a kind of information bureau not only for my friends who come here but also for my friends' friends and my friends' children. Sometimes I go with them to Stratford or to see Coventry Cathedral or on similar trips. I am constantly surprised and delighted to have the telephone ring and learn that another friend has arrived in town. Somehow, when one is a widow—it is a sea of loneliness, mind you; you never get away from that, *ever*—you must sort of step from one island of excitement to another, and if you live in London, you can do this, because something always turns up.

Speaking of friends, I know the British have the reputation of being cool and reserved. What was your experience when it came to making friends here?

MRS. CLEGG: They do have that reputation, but I don't know how they got it. I have never made friends anywhere as easily as I have in England. Real friends. I have never been welcomed more readily or treated more kindly anywhere than I have in London. I had a few acquaintances—nebulous sort of acquaintanceships—in London before I came. For example, in Malta I had met a couple who live in London, but I had known them only a short time in Malta. However, they looked me up here, and introduced me to their family, and through them I made other friends, and so on. Of course, when I came here, I didn't expect to live the life of a deb. I was a widow. I was weary. I was tired. I just wanted to get sort of settled down. I didn't expect to be very gay and to do a lot of partying, and perhaps in a way that made it easier to make friends, because the people who sought me out and were kind to me were not the sort of people who would entertain you because you were a gay person, you see. It was real kindliness and consideration and friendship that were offered to me on every hand.

Several of my first acquaintances resulted from working on projects to finance the youth club here in Chelsea. My relatives in Malta had friends who were closely connected with this work. I got in touch with them and offered to help with the bazaar they were having that spring. In the course of this, I met a number of committee members, and very soon they invited me to come on the committee. I told them that I couldn't possibly make any contribution, since I had never done any youth club work, and furthermore, being an American, I wouldn't know the ropes. They said, "But perhaps you'll bring some fresh ideas." So, I got very interested in the Chelsea youth club as well as in the youth clubs in this country generally, which are really quite wonderful.

Then, living near Royal Hospital, I soon became acquainted with the chaplain over there and his wife. I asked him if there was ever any need for someone to come in and read to the old soldiers or anything of that kind. He mentioned two or three of them who had no relatives living near or no relatives at all, and said they would certainly welcome someone who would just come in and say hello. So, I began making regular calls there. I take some magazines or just go in and say hello or listen to some of their reminiscences. I stop in to see particular ones, such as Mr. Devereaux, who is Scottish and ninety-three now. He's a very interesting character. Then I met the man in the bed next to him and some of the others in his bay, and so I look around and speak to all of them. This year, I have taken my little granddaughter with me, and she's danced for them, and they are very enthusiastic about that. I have tried in my small way to do for the children of this country and for some of the elderly who are on my doorstep here the things I might be doing in America. I like to have the feeling that I am not just taking blessings from this country but that I'm pulling my weight somehow, particularly in the youth club work.

Is there anything about the United States that you miss?

MRS. CLEGG: Of course, I miss my daughter and her children and the few other relatives that I have there and my personal friends, but mind you, I should be missing them if I lived in America, because they are all scattered, so, of course, I would never live near all of them. When I first came here, I found preparing meals very difficult. At that time, we couldn't get Campbell's cream of mushroom soup or many of the other things that I am accustomed to using in my shortcuts to quick cooking. Now, I can get most of those products as well as a wide range of frozen foods. Fortunately, I brought with me my gigantic General Electric refrigerator with a freezer compartment on top. I think I would have been driven to drink if I had had to get along with one of those minute British iceboxes—those little two-by-four fridges, as they call them—with no room for frozen things at all. It was downright funny to me when some of my friends came to my flat with their husbands, because they would often say, "Oh, do you mind if I take Geoffrey"—or whatever the husband's name was—"out to the kitchen? I want him to see your fridge." You know, they were absolutely flabbergasted by the size of my refrigerator. Now, you can get this kind here, but they cost about three hundred and fifty pounds—more than a thousand dollars. One thing: I find the shopping quite easy here. There are many little shops nearby. I just walk around the corner or up the street, and there's a big supermarket in the King's Road, also within walking distance.

What about English men—do you find them attractive?

MRS. CLEGG: Well, let me put it this way: I think that American men of English extraction are the most attractive American men. I was married to one, and my family were that sort of men. Perhaps that is why I feel at home with men of British origin in a way that I do not with Continental men or with other foreigners. Never have I had an unpleasant experience with an English man, and I have found that I am at ease with the English bachelors and widowers and single men that I have met here. Nor have I had an unpleasant experience with any English workman I've come into contact with. I've never felt the need to be on guard, as I always was in America. Mind you, that's not entirely a question of age. I've never had to feel that any of them was fresh or to be afraid of being in the flat with them or that they would misunderstand my kindness. On a cold morning, for example, I wouldn't have the slightest compunction about saying to my milkman, "Don't you want to come in and have a cup of coffee?" Or the time when my postman was bitten by a dog just down the street. I happened to be walking nearby at the time, and I said, "Oh, do come up to my flat and let me put something on that wound right away." I brought him up there, and I bathed his leg and put an antiseptic where he had been bitten, and then he went on his way, after thanking me graciously, of course. I don't think I would have done that in any other city, unless I'd lived in the same place for a long time and had had the same postman year after year, but somehow, here, it just seemed the natural thing to do.

What do you think of the English climate?

MRS. CLEGG: Well, that is one of the things here that I like best. The British can't understand my feeling about that at all. They don't expect Americans to like them or their island or, least of all, their climate. They seem to think that we think they're old fuddy-duddies, you know, old-fashioned, non-progressive, inefficient, and, of course, with the most awful climate in the world. So, they're always puzzled by what I've found to like. And when I say, "Well, right at the outset, I must say that one of the things I like best is your climate," they're simply nonplused. They say, "How can you stand the rain? Don't you miss that glorious sun? Why, we never get any sun in this country." I say, "Well, you get quite enough to make the flowers grow and for the children to be healthy, and that's enough for me." Of course, I can understand how they would want more of it, but as far as having too much sun, I am delighted to be free of that. My one idea of hell is a heat wave. The time in my life when I hated the climate most were the two years I spent in the Arizona desert. The heat, the glare, the aridity, the lack of green, the monotony of the year-around perpetual sunshine—it all added up to sheer misery for me. Here, the sun is always welcome. It never becomes severe, a thing to dread. And I don't mind the moisture, either. I've always liked a rainy day. But I don't think I'll ever convince my British friends of my feeling about their climate.

Since everything here seems to agree with you, do you plan to stay on indefinitely?

MRS. CLEGG: No, but I don't make any definite plans, really. If my daughter, who has a rather large family, should need me in any way, I should be ready to go back at the drop of a hat. Quite frankly, I don't look into the future very much. I lead my life from day to day, and as one never knows what's going to happen in London, it is an unpredictable life, and that makes it more interesting.

How much my life in London means to me was made quite clear when I made my first trip back to America after I had lived here for almost three years. The morning of the day I took the plane, I had to go up to Sloane Square to get some little thing at a store there, and as I was about to go into a revolving door, a little tot—a toddler who couldn't have been more than two years old—was just coming out, and as I stepped back and she saw that she had almost bumped into me, she said, "So sorry." That was the last bit of conversation, so to speak, that I had before getting on the plane.

Well, I arrived in New York, and because of some freak of wind or weather, the plane I was on landed in New York an hour and a half earlier than expected. Instead of arriving around seven in the morning it landed about five-thirty. Well, that meant that I would have to wait about an hour and a half for my cousins, who were driving in from Connecticut to meet me. First, of course, we had to go through customs. Perhaps our early arrival required the customs agents to start work too early, but in any case, the one who went through my luggage was very grouchy and curt, and when I asked him where would be the best place to wait to make sure I wouldn't miss the people who were coming to meet me—the situation being different because of my arriving so early—he said, "Ask a porter." One came by, and when he asked where I wanted the bags taken, I explained that I wasn't sure yet, and asked him the question I'd asked the customs agent. "I don't know about that, lady," the porter said, and he walked away. Couldn't care less. Probably because it was so early, there were only a very few porters around, so I was left with my suitcases and the coats over my arm, and so forth, and I couldn't seem to get even the slightest suggestion of help. I almost felt like crying. I thought, "Here I am, home, after nearly three years, and what a welcome."

Finally, I managed to get my luggage to the Pan American desk, and they said all they could do was to take a message that they would give to my cousins if they came to the desk and asked about me. They did tell me what door that people coming in from the parking lot would probably use. That was the extent of their help. It was all right, you know, but they hardly put themselves out. I tell you, in the hour and a quarter I waited there, I felt very forlorn. Such rudeness. Such lack of interest. And I remembered this two-year-old, and her "So sorry" as she apologized for getting in my way in the revolving door.

Well, my cousins arrived, and after that, everything was lovely. When you're with your own in America, you're all right. You're treated with the greatest kindness in the world. But when you're not with your own, you can't expect it, can you? I don't know. But that treatment at the airport came as a shock, because I had grown accustomed to being treated kindly and looked after a bit.

And then when I arrived back here from that trip, the plane was very late. There had been engine trouble, so instead of leaving at midnight, the plane left at 5 A.M. It was a terribly long trip, and by the time we arrived, I was very tired and anxious to get home as soon as possible. The minute I walked into the terminal, I found a porter, and he went and stood with me while waiting for the luggage to come up. A great many flights were arriving at that time, and we stood there, and we stood there, and we stood there. I swear to you that my luggage was the very last to appear. I felt so guilty, because this poor porter had been standing there for fifteen or twenty minutes, and though the English money that I had in my pocket would have been sufficient in ordinary circumstances, it was somewhat less than I would have given as a tip in view of the long wait. When it came time to tip him, I gave him all the change I had, and I said, "I am *very* sorry to have kept you this long." And he looked at me, and said, "No fault of yours, madam. God bless you."

"Well," I thought, "I am back home." Not only did I give him a small tip and not have rude words said to me, but instead, "No fault of yours, madam. God bless you." I mean, really, you get spoiled by this. I miss it terribly when I'm away from it. So, while I have never considered myself a permanent resident in England, and I haven't cut my bridges behind me, still I find that I feel very out of my element when I am not here.

GALLERY NOTES

In the fall of 1967, James Reston, writing from Europe about the growing American civilian occupation of the Old World, remarked, "It would be ironic if the sons and grandsons of the old American isolationists, who sneered at the artistic American expatriates of the twenties, created a new class of American expatriates themselves. But it could happen."

Actually, as we have seen, it has already happened. And it would hardly seem risky to predict that this new class will go on proliferating at such an ever-increasing rate that within a couple of decades the Ameropean way of life will have become commonplace. With the continued breaking down of national boundaries and the advent of supersonic planes that will cross the Atlantic in two or three hours, Americans by the hundreds of thousands will be spending part of their lives in Europe. They will go as casually to the Old World then as they go to the shore or the country now. They will send their children off to school in France or Switzerland as matter-of-factly as they now send them off to boarding school or college in the United States. The growth of Ameropeanism will no doubt follow the growth of travel, which has reached proportions undreamed of twenty years ago.

Although all Ameropeans are pioneering the future way of life, those who probably most closely resemble the Ameropeans of tomorrow are the ones who already combine life in the Old World with life in the New. For example, Richard Rose, a university lecturer in government and politics, has divided his time between England and America since 1953. "People ask me which side of the water I want to live on," he said not long ago. "I tell them I want to have the best of both worlds. And I'm American enough to think it can be done." The time is not far distant when so many more of his countrymen will be thinking the same way that Ameropeans will be saying with accuracy what Abigail Adams, writing from London in 1784, said with hyperbole: "I hardly know how to think of myself out of my own country—I see so many Americans about me."

INDEX

Adams, Abigail
  Europe and America compared by, 302
  quoted on Americans abroad, 373
Adams, Henry, 17
America, 292, 301, 323, 330-331
  pace of living in, 294, 324, 329, 350
  racial situation in, 282, 296
  view of, from England, 191-192
American
  characterization of an, 300
  sense of being an, 235
American Center for Students and Artists, in Paris, 250-251
American character, 349-350
American Museum in Bath, 185-186
American School in Switzerland, 167-169
American wives of Europeans, 171-172, 302
American Women's Group, 172
Americans
  comparison of, with English, 329
  comparison of, with Europeans, 342
  displaced, 127-128
  in Florence, Italy, 62, 63
  French attitude toward, 254-255
  unskilled, in Europe, 276
Ameropeans, 7, 11, 34, 70, 93
  Americanism among, 301
  businessmen among, 4, 137-164
  career women among, 165-169
  cultural exiles among, 300-301
  interviewing, 12-13
  Negro, 276-297
  political refugees among, 298-316
  precursors of, 14
  reasons given by, for living in Europe, 34-38
  tomorrow's, 373
  varied occupations of, 137-141
  retired, 332-357
  well-known, 12
  wives of, 106
Ameropeanism, growth of, 373
Ameropean women, 165-214
Anderson, Dr. Theodore, 334
Antheil, George, 7, 31
anti-Americanism, 239
  in England, 312
  in France, 32
anti-Semitism, 157, 312
architecture
  Greece, 18
  New York, 45, 154
  Paris, 17-18
Ardrey, Robert, 38
Aronsohn, Abe, interview with, 141-148
Astor, Lady, 169

Bagier, Robin, interview with, 262-268
Baldwin, James, 10, 216-217, 223, 277-278
Bankhead, Eugenia, 36, 238
Barnett, Edward, 277
Barney, Natalie Clifford, 8
Beach, Sylvia, 8
beatniks, 246, 249-250, 289
Bechet, Sidney, 279
Beene, Wallace, interview with, 54-60

Benét, Stephen Vincent, 7
Benton, Thomas Hart, 7
Berenson, Bernard, 9, 302
Bevan, Nye, 310
Bishop, John Peale, 7
Bismarck, Countess Edward, 170
blacklisting victims, 298, 299, 303, 306, 313
Bosanquet, Esther Cleveland, 169
Bowles, Paul, 249-250
  interview with, 236-245
Bradley, Harold, interview with, 284-293
Brennan, Mrs. Gerald, 301
British character, 163-164, 367
Bromfield, Louis, 7
Brooks, Phillips, 301
Brooks, Van Wyck, 66
Brumbach, Will, interview with, 264-268
Buckley, William, 348
Burroughs, William, 238
Burton, Richard, 171
businessmen, typical Ameropean, problems of, 138-141

Cabot, Robert, interview with, 60-69
Camus, Marcel, 166-167
career women, American, in Europe, 165-169
Carter, Philip, Mr. and Mrs., 1-2
  interview with, 334-344
Cather, Willa, 13
Centro per Stranieri, Florence, Italy, 269-270
Chasen, Dave, 94, 323
Cheever, John, 10
children
  advantages of European living for, 89, 90, 167, 194-195, 209, 228, 230, 320-321, 346
  disadvantages for, in Portugal, 340
  effect on, of living abroad, 55-56, 108, 111, 152-154, 160-161
citizenship
  renouncing American, 319
  retaining U.S., 172, 181-182, 302-303
citizenship, foreign
  American attitude toward, 5, 303, 319-320
  for Americans, 316, 318-319, 320-321, 331
Clare, John, quoted, 1
Clarke, Kenny, 279
Clegg, Mrs. Betty Laycock, interview with, 357-372
Cleveland, Esther (Mrs. Bosanquet), 169
Coleman, Emily Holmes, 31
Condon, Richard, 34, 73, 337
Constantine, Eddie, 36
Copland, Aaron, 237
Copley, John Singleton, 215
Cornfeld, Bernard, 139
Cowles, Fleur. *See* Meyer, Mrs. Tom Montague
Cowley, Malcolm, 7, 8, 14
Crane, Stephen, 216
crime, lack of,
  in Ireland, 323
  in London, 360-361
  in Madrid, 58
"culture shock," 105
Cummings, Constance, 310
Cummings, E.E., 7
Cummings, Samuel, 138-139
Curry, John Steuart, 7

Dassin, Jules, 298-300, 302, 303
Davis, David M., 250-252
Dawn, Marpessa, 166-167
De Gaulle, Charles, 251, 254, 256
Deiss, Casey, 262, 267, 268
Deiss, Joseph Jay, 262
  interview with, 39-49
Dickinson, Emily, 216
dictatorship, living under a, 58, 156, 343
discrimination, racial
  lack of, in Ireland, 322
  in Rome, 288, 289-290
Dobbs, Mattwilda, 278-279
Dodson, Truman Monroe, IV, 332-333
Donleavy, J.P., 12
Dos Passos, John, 7
Douglas, Lew, 186
Dreiser, Theodore, 105
Duncan, Ben, interview with, 324-331
Durbin, Deanna, 171

Durer, Albrecht, 30-31
Dylan, Bob, 287

Eigerman, Sarah Jane, 252-256
Eisenhower, Dwight D., 77
Eliot, T.S., 7, 9
  foreign citizenship chosen by, 302
Elizabeth, Queen, 144, 159, 162
Emerson, Ralph Waldo, 216
England, 358
  climate in, 190, 330, 369-370
  food in, 205
  honesty in, 361
  a man's country, 202
  pace of life in, 205, 324, 329
  permission to live and work in, 327-329
  privacy in, 189
  racial situation in, 275
  social customs in, 196, 204
escapists, Ameropeans as, 158, 223-224, 273
Estorick, Eric, 37
Europe
  economic advantages of living in, 55, 70, 91
  Hollywood emigrants to, 104
  lure of, for Americans, 3
  pace of living in, 350
exiles
  cultural, 300
  political, 300, 302-303
  racial, 300, 302-303
expatriates, 1, 2, 5, 7, 8, 9, 10, 14, 34, 239, 373

Fairbanks, Douglas, Jr., 12
  interview with, 158-164
Faulkner, William, 7
Ferroni, Arnaldo, 49, 50
Ferroni, Mrs. Arnaldo, interview with, 49-54
Fitzgerald, F. Scott, 7, 8
Flair, 184, 188, 189
Flanner, Janet (Genet), 7, 8, 14, 280, 302
  interview with, 15-25
Fleischer, Max, 107
Fleischer, Mr. and Mrs. Richard, interview with, 106-116
Fleming, Mary Crist, 167-169
Fletcher-Cooke, Charles, 328
Florence, Italy, 60, 269-274
  Americans in, 62, 63
  living in, 52-54
  people of, 61-62, 272
  students in, 269-272
  time element in, 272, 274
Folk Studio, Rome, 287
foreigner, advantage of being a, 62, 65-66
Foreman, Carl, interview with, 303-316
Fowles, John, 2
France
  advantages for children in, 194-195
  students' social life in, 254
  teaching English in, 174, 175
Frank, Mrs. Melvin, interview with, 124-136
French attitude toward Americans, 254-255, 295
French families, living with, 253
friendship
  effect of European living on, 111-112
  as a result of living abroad, 341-342
Frost, Robert, 7, 216
Fulbright Act, 246
Fulton, Robert, 215

Galante, Pierre, 194
Galbraith, J. Kenneth, 348
Gandarias, Mrs. Pedro, 1
Gardner, Ava, 12
Garvey, Marcus, 283
Gary, Romain, 171, 294
Geneva, 71, 73-75
Gerini, Marchesa Lily, 170-171
Gershwin, George, 7
Getty, John Paul, 12
G.I. Bill of Rights, 246, 285, 325
Gilmore, Eddy, 319
Glass, George, 304
Goldstein, Bob, 107-108
golfing abroad, 72
Grace, Her Serene Highness Princess, 12, 183-184
  interview with, 177-184
Graves, Robert, 70
Gstaad, Switzerland, 344, 347-348

Hally-Smith, Dr. D., 8
Hamilton, Ray, 276
Harlech, Lord, comment by, on British character, 164
Harrod, Sir Roy, 328
Harte, Bret, 216
Haselwood, Jay, 36
Havilland, Olivia de, interview with, 194-195
Hawthorne, Nathaniel, 216
Heath, Gordon, 278, 279
Hemingway, Ernest, 7, 19
Hiler, Hilaire, 30-31
Hoffman, Leigh, 31
Holden, William, 12
  interview with, 101-103
Hollywood, 313
  emigrants from, to Europe, 104
Holmes, Nancy, 166
House Un-American Activities Committee, 299, 303, 304-305
housing situation, European, 67, 71-73
Howells, William Dean, 216, 301
Hughes, Langston, 287
Humphrey, Hubert, 235
Huston, John, 12, 303
  interview with, 316-323
Hutton, Barbara, 238

income tax laws, U.S., and Americans living abroad, 6, 91-93, 97-100
Innes, Michael, 325
International Armaments Corporation, Monte Carlo, 139
International Research Consultants, Inc., Geneva, 138
Ireland, 316-323, 330
Irving, Washington, 216
Italian people, 44, 291, 346
Italian way of life, 234
Italy, 42, 49, 60, 66, 70, 265, 346, 347, 350-351
  Americanization of, 68
  art in, 290-291
  cost of living in, 114-115

Jackson, Alan K., 138
James, Henry, 7, 70
  foreign citizenship chosen by, 302
Janzon, Bengt, 279
Jarrell, Henry T., 333-334
jazz musicians, Negro, in Europe, 279, 286
Jenkins, Providence, 277
Jenkins, Roy, 328
Jerome, Jennie (mother of Winston Churchill), 169
Johnson, Lyndon B., 254, 255
Johnson, Nunnally, Mr. and Mrs., interview with, 116-124
Jolas, Eugene, 8, 29
Jolas, Maria, 8, 302
  interview with, 29-33
Jones, James, 10
  interview with, 217-225
Josephson, Matthew, 7
junior-year-abroad programs, 246, 247

Kaner, Sam, 138
Keith, Mrs. Kenneth Alexander, interview with, 195-206
Kennedy, John F., 100, 180, 251, 283
Ketcham, Henry, 2, 71-72
Kiernan, Paul, 138
Klosters, Switzerland, 93, 95-97, 100-101
Kramer, Stanley, 304
Krasna, Norman, 104
Kreisler, Edward, 35
Kuhn, Fentress, interview with, 344-351

Langhorne, Nancy, 169
language, learning a, 114, 252, 261, 285, 295, 346, 347
language problems, 117, 172, 173-174, 175, 196, 219, 285, 306, 353
languages, children's acquisition of, 111
Lattes, Herbert, 276-277
League of Americans Residing Abroad (LARA), 6
Lee, Jennie, 310, 311
Leigh, Dorian, 165-166
Levee, John, 23-24, 216
Levy, Ben, 310
Lewis, Edna, 263
Liebling, A. J., 13

Liverpool, 275
living abroad, Americans' reasons for, 10-11, 65, 239, 332-334, 341
London, 117-124, 138, 144, 146, 219, 303, 313-314, 357-370
  American Colony in, 311
  American painters in, 215
  comparison of New York and, 161-162
  cost of living in, 129-130, 147, 362-363
  domestic help in, 121, 130
  food in, 120-121, 122
  housing problems in, 128-129, 306-307
  keeping house in, 118-122, 130
  a man's world, 125
  pace of living in, 147, 310
  people of, 118, 147
  weather in, 123, 132-133, 142, 143, 145, 259, 304, 369-370
Longfellow, Henry Wadsworth, 216
"Lost Generation," the, 7, 14, 25, 26, 29
Loughrin, Andrew, interview with, 257-262
Lubroth, Lu, interview with, 148-158

MacLeish, Archibald, 7
McAlmon, Robert, 31
McCarthyism, 300, 308
  Irish attitude toward, 322
  refugees from, 298
Madrid, Spain, 333-334
  American Colony in, 88
  climate in, 208
  living in, 54-60, 77, 79-88
Majorca, 70, 279
Malcolm X, 282
Margaret, Princess, 144
Mark Twain, 216
marriage, of Americans to Europeans, 5-6, 10, 52-53, 169-173, 177, 196, 207, 209, 238, 263, 276, 279, 298, 301
Matthews, T.S., 12, 300, 301
Mellon, Ian David, 168
Melville, Herman, 216, 275
Mercer, Mae, interview with, 293-297
Mercouri, Melina, 298
Metcalf, James, 70-71, 215-216
Meyer, Mrs. Tom Montague, interview with, 184-194
Michaux, Mrs. Phyllis, 171-173, 301-302
Monaco, 177-184
Monte Carlo, 178, 183
Morocco, 240-244
  beatniks in, 249-250
Morse, Samuel F.B., 215
Moses, Robert, 138
Murchie, Guy, 72-73
Murphy, Gerald, 8
Murphy, Mrs. Gerald, 8

Naples, University of, 48
nationality laws, United States, 172
Negroes, American, in Europe, 276-280
New York City, 24, 87, 118, 148, 157, 205-206, 208, 243, 251, 300, 359, 360, 370-371
  architecture in, 45, 154
  comparison of London and, 161-162
  comparison of Paris and, 220-222
  pace of life in, 192, 197-198, 218, 224
  world art capital, 215
Nicholas, Albert, 279
Nolan, James, 35, 72, 139-140

Oberg, Kalvero, "culture shock" discussed by, 105
Odetta, 287
Olmstead, Remington, 137
Onassis, Aristotle, 178
Osborn, Bayard, 77
Oxford University, 324-326

Paget, Anthony T., Jr. interview with, 79-90
painters, American, in Europe, 215
Paris, 6, 8, 15, 19, 94, 165, 175, 176, 194, 220, 236, 250-251, 284, 293
  Americanization of, 20
  American colony in, 7-8, 172
  American painters in, 215
  apartment renting in, 219, 221, 294
  cost of living in, 19, 30, 71, 222
  jazz musicians, Negro, in, 279

Paris (*continued*)
job possibilities in, 176
Parker, Suzy, 165
Parrish, Robert, 97
passports, American evaluation of, 5
Pater, Walter, 17
patriotism, of Americans living abroad, 302
Peace Corps, 269, 270, 271, 273, 349
Pepper, Beverly, 235
interview with, 225-232
Pepper, Curtis G. (Bill), 225, 228
interview with, 232-236
Perrin, Willi, 350
Perugia, Italy, 286
school for foreigners in, 285
Philip, Prince, 144, 159, 162
Poe, Edgar Allan, 216
Pogostin, Lee, 301
political refugees, 298
Portugal
building in, 74, 337-338
climate in, 336
cost of living in, 336-340
Portuguese people, 344
Positano, Italy, 227, 248, 262, 265
life in, 39-49
rents in, 264, 265
weather in, 264-265, 266, 332
Positano Art Workshop, 263
Pound, Ezra, 7, 9
Powell, Adam Clayton, III, 280-281, 283
Powell, Bud, 279
prejudice, racial
in Europe, 277, 280, 281, 287
Putnam, Beverly, interview with, 173-177

racism, in Europe, 275-276
Rainier III, Prince, 177, 178, 179
Ray, Man, 7, 302,
interview with, 25-28
Reston, James, 3, 373
retirement
Europe for, 332-357
problems of, 353-354
Reyes, Ben, 6
Rhiney, Dolores Francine (Bambi), 276
Robilant, Countess Alvise de, 170
Rogers, Will, daughter of, 238
Romanones, Countess of, interview with, 207-214
Rome, Italy, 63, 71, 113, 137, 219, 225, 270-271
climate in, 345
cost of living in, 114-115, 229, 289
Negro Ameropean in, 276-277, 284, 286
servant situation in, 114, 115
traffic in, 345
Rose, Richard, 373
Ross of *The New Yorker*, 19, 21-22
Rothschild, Baroness Philippe de, 170
Rovere, Princess Chigi della, 170
Ruspoli, Princess Marta, 238
Rutland, Duchess of, 170

Scandinavia, Americans in, 11
Schneider, Robert, 71
schools
European, 97, 110-111, 168
in Ireland, 320
in Italy, 60-61, 63, 64, 110
in London, 126
in Paris, 109-110
in Spain, 89, 152, 213
in Switzerland, 97, 102, 109, 126, 167-168, 267
Schwab, Victor O., interview with, 351-357
Schwartz, Norman, 248-249
Scott, Hazel, interview with, 280-284
Seberg, Jean, 12, 171, 294
Seeger, Pete, 287
Sefton, Countess of, 170
Sergeant, Reverend Martin, 105-106
servants, in Europe, 56, 114, 115, 240-241
Shaw, Irwin, 10, 12
interview with, 94-101
Sheppard, Martin, 92, 93, 140
Slonim, Marc, 9, 10
Smith, Margaret Chase, 179-180
Smith, William Gardner, 277, 278, 279, 280
Smith College juniors in Paris, 252-257
sojourners, 246, 247-249, 257-262
Sorbonne, 175, 254, 256
Spain, 207-214, 351-357

Spain (*continued*)
building problems in, 355-356
climate in, 208, 345, 346
cost of living in, 77, 81, 84, 156, 346
living in, 54-60, 75-79, 210-214
religious attitudes in, 156-157
Spanish character, 59-60
Spanish people, 86-87, 149
making friends with, 56-57
Spanish trains, 82-83
Stein, Gertrude, 8, 9, 26, 27, 30, 238
Stern, Irving Constant, 137
Stewart, J.I.M., 325
Stuart, Gilbert, 215
Styron, William, 9
Swiss people, 101, 104
Switzerland, 166, 334
advantages of living in, 100-101, 104
building in, 74-75
land taxes in, 74
privacy in, 102-103
as a travel base, 102

Tangier, 237, 242
American residents of, 238
availability of drugs in, 249
cost of living in, 240
cultural life in, 243-244
taxes, 91-93, 98-100, 102, 117, 222, 321
European manner of handling, 140-141
Taylor, Elizabeth, 171, 303
television, 300, 342, 343
British, 122
theater
British, 123, 134-135
Italian, 290
Thomson, Virgil, 7
Thoreau, 45, 216
Torremolinos, Spain, changes in, 75-76
tourists, 68, 87
Townsend, Katharine, interview with, 252-257
transition, 236
Trumbull, John, 215

United States
hostility in, 268
objectivity toward, 256
perspective on, 256
possibility of returning to, 89, 225, 236, 283-284, 291, 297, 300, 349
returning to, after living abroad, 89, 300

Valencia, Duke and Duchess of, 57
Vanderbilt, Consuelo, 169
Viertel, Peter, 95
Vietnam, 255, 296, 300
voting denied to Americans living abroad, 98

Webster, Noah, quoted on foreign travel, 3
Welles, Orson, 12
Wells, Colonel Lewis G., 138
Werkman, Dr. Sidney L., interview with, 268-274
West, Benjamin, 215
Westcott, Glenway, 7
Wharton, Edith, 302
Whitman, George, 137-138
Whitman, Walt, 216
quoted on travel abroad, 2
Wildman, Frederick S., Jr., interview with, 75-79
Williams, Tennessee, 10
Windsor, Duchess of, 169-170
wives, difficulty of, in adjusting to life abroad, 105-106
women, attitude toward, in Italy, 231-232
Wood, Grant, 7
work permits, 165
in England, 327
Wouk, Herman, quoted on Americanism, 301
writers American, in Europe, 98-99, 216, 217, 233-234
Wylie, Philip, 34

young American in Europe, 246-274